Situation Assessment in Aviation

Situation Assessment in Aviation focuses on new aspects of soft computing technologies for the evaluation and assessment of situations in aviation scenarios. It considers technologies emerging from multisensory data fusion (MSDF), Bayesian networks (BN), and fuzzy logic (FL) to assist pilots in their decision-making.

Studying MSDF, BN, and FL from the perspective of their applications to the problem of situation assessment, the book discusses the development of certain soft technologies that can be further used for devising more sophisticated technologies for a pilot's decision-making when performing certain tasks: airplane monitoring, pair formation, attack, and threat. It explains the concepts of situation awareness, data fusion, decision fusion, Bayesian networks, fuzzy logic type 1, and interval type 2 fuzzy logic. The book also presents a hybrid technique by using BN and FL and a unique approach to the problem of situation assessment, beyond visual range and air-to-air combat, by utilizing building blocks of artificial intelligence (AI) for the future development of more advanced automated systems, especially using commercial software.

The book is intended for aerospace R&D engineers, systems engineers, aeronautical engineers, and aviation training professionals. It will also be useful for aerospace and electrical engineering students taking courses in Air Traffic Management, Aviation Management, Aviation Operations, and Aviation Safety Systems.

Situation Assessment in Aviation

Bayesian Network and Fuzzy Logic-based Approaches

Jitendra R. Raol, Sudesh K. Kashyap, and Lakshmi Shrinivasan

CRC Press
Taylor & Francis Group
Boca Raton London New York

CRC Press is an imprint of the
Taylor & Francis Group, an **informa** business

Designed cover image: © Shutterstock

MATLAB® is a trademark of The MathWorks, Inc. and is used with permission. The MathWorks does not warrant the accuracy of the text or exercises in this book. This book's use or discussion of MATLAB® software or related products does not constitute endorsement or sponsorship by The MathWorks of a particular pedagogical approach or particular use of the MATLAB® software.

First edition published 2024
by CRC Press
2385 NW Executive Center Drive, Suite 320, Boca Raton FL 33431

and by CRC Press
4 Park Square, Milton Park, Abingdon, Oxon, OX14 4RN

CRC Press is an imprint of Taylor & Francis Group, LLC

Library of Congress Cataloging-in-Publication Data
Names: Raol, J. R. (Jitendra R.), 1947– author.
Title: Situation assessment in aviation : Bayesian network and fuzzy logic-based
approaches / Jitendra R. Raol, Sudesh K. Kashyap and Lakshmi Shrinivasan.
Description: First edition. | Boca Raton, FL : CRC Press, 2024. |
Includes bibliographical references and index.
Identifiers: LCCN 2023025902 (print) | LCCN 2023025903 (ebook) |
ISBN 9781032440934 (hbk) | ISBN 9781032440941 (pbk) | ISBN 9781003370413 (ebk)
Subjects: LCSH: Instrument flying. | Aeronautical instruments. | Airplanes–Piloting–Data processing. |
Situational awareness. | Fuzzy systems. | Bayesian statistical decision theory. |
Expert systems (Computer science) | Airplanes–Automatic control.
Classification: LCC TL711.B6 R36 2024 (print) |
LCC TL711.B6 (ebook) | DDC 629.132/5214–dc23/eng/20240112
LC record available at https://lccn.loc.gov/2023025902
LC ebook record available at https://lccn.loc.gov/2023025903

ISBN: 978-1-032-44093-4 (hbk)
ISBN: 978-1-032-44094-1 (pbk)
ISBN: 978-1-003-37041-3 (ebk)

DOI: 10.1201/9781003370413

Typeset in Times
by Newgen Publishing UK

Access the Support Material: www.routledge.com/9781032440934

Contents

Preface

The aviation is the key industry for the routine lives of the people in any country, and more so for special needs for flights; any country's technological progress can be measured by the strength of its aviation planning, management, and business. In most or almost all these operations, the amount of information required by the aviation pilots is generally very high. The pilot must make quick decisions under large uncertainty and high time pressure. Certain empirical studies indicate that the most critical component of the decision making is the situation awareness; for which the pilot must be continually aware of his/her flying and operational environment: air space, flight path corridor, changing atmosphere, and air-flight regulations. The pilot obtains a mental 'picture' of the situation by observations, often assisted by several onboard and ground/satellite based instruments and sensors, and his/her decisions are guided and made by associations to other well-recognized tactical situations: this is called situation-awareness-centered decision-making (SAWDM), and this is widely accepted representation of the human decision making in several complex situations, and several aviation scenarios are certainly most complex, and require sophisticated understanding and then follow-up actions.

Human themselves are the best representative of an expert system, like a rule-based operational system. Let us take an example of a pilot of a fighter aircraft. The various decisions/actions that pilot can make are: i) avoid any sort of collision with nearby flying objects, ii) assess the intents of enemy aircraft, and iii) communicate with other friendly aircraft, etc. The pilot's inherent capability of making such decision works fine when the number of nearby flying objects is small; but in case of very complex scenario, how quick and accurate decision a pilot can make is questionable. In such a case, we need a mathematical model of the environment and an expert system that can aid pilot in a quick and accurate decision making so that he/she can focus more on flying the aircraft safely.

Hence, it is conjectured that if these pilots are assisted, in their decision making, by soft technologies emerging from: i) multisensory data fusion (MSDF), ii) Bayesian networks (BN), and iii) fuzzy logic (FL), then not only their (pilots') work load will be reduced, but also their decisions would be much more sophisticated, timely, and very effective.

Since the early sixties, there have been many activities for fusing several sensors' data (measurements) in order to get final set that is more accurate than only single/one sensor alone could provide; and from then on, the discipline of the MSDF has identified four levels of the gross-fusion procedure: a) Object Refinement (OR), b) Situation Refinement (SR), c) Threat Refinement (TR), and d) Process Refinement (PR). Of these the situation assessment (SA) is the main aim of the present book.

Bayesian networks are a set of connected nodes (nodal/main points) that describe a particular domain of the world, i.e. the universe of the discourse, here we can say it is the air-corridor, flight-path space, etc. These nodal points signify a variable with a set of states described by a conditional probability matrix associated with the nodes that are neighbourly connected to it. The uniqueness of the BN comes from its combination of two artificial intelligence (AI) tools: artificial neural networks (ANNs) and the Bayesian reasoning; like ANNs, the BN contains information about the domain, and can carry and modify the information when propagated among the nodal points. The knowledge in BN can be stored a priori, or is learned from existing examples, the BN has a rational reasoning process in nodal points and associated links, this gives the BN a communication ability, this further assists the pilot's decision process.

Fuzzy logic is a technique that can incorporate the human knowledge in its 'If.. Then..' rule base, and it can be very helpful in our decision making, because these rules can also be learnt by using ANNs from the existing data base of a priori knowledge about the situations. The FL provides the decisions in presence of uncertainty and vagueness, and hence it is also called soft-computing technique that works despite imprecision.

In this book we study MSDF, BN, and FL from the perspective of their applications to the problem of situation assessment and develop certain soft technologies that can be further used for devising more sophisticated technologies for pilot's decision making when he/she is performing certain tasks in aviation scenarios: i) airlane monitoring, ii) pair formation/ formation flight, iii) threat assessment, and iv) attack.

Unfortunately, there not many books about situation assessment for aviation flights, most are on aircraft certification and pilot's training aspects. In the present volume we explain the concepts of data fusion, decision fusion, Bayesian networks, fuzzy logic type 1, and fuzzy logic type 2; and develop the approaches based on these disciplines as the methods for situation assessment that would help in pilot's decision making. We also present a hybrid technique by using BN and FL.

We present realistically simulated aviation scenarios and demonstrate the effectiveness of decision making using these soft-technologies by implementations in MATLAB and/or other popular tools; these codes where appropriate, for chapters 49, and for chapter 10 and/or 11, are given in the book's website; the MATLAB SW and its tool-boxes per se are not provided; only the scripts written by the authors to generate the result of the illustrative examples and of the simulation of the aviation scenarios are provided.

So, our approach to problem of situation assessment is unique in that it utilizes some building blocks of artificial intelligence, and sensor data fusion, and paves the way forward for sophisticated and semi-automated decision-making process. The end users of this integrated semi-AI soft-technology of situation assessment in aviation scenarios will be aero-systems-educational institutions, aerospace R&D laboratories, aerospace industries, flight test agencies, aviation industries, aviation training schools, and certain transportation/automotive industry.

Disclaimer: Although, enough care has been taken in working out the solutions of examples/exercises and presentation of various theories and case study results in the book, any practical applications of these should be made with proper care and caution; any such endeavours would be the readers'/users' own responsibility. Some MATLAB programs developed for the illustration of various concepts via examples in the book would be accessible to the readers from the book's URL of the CRC Press.

Acknowledgements

Jitendra R. Raol: I started work in fuzzy logic some years ago and pursued its application to pilot's situation assessment that culminated in the doctoral theses by the joint authors of this book, wherefore Dr. Sudesh used fuzzy logic type 1, and Dr. Lakshmi applied interval type 2 fuzzy logic. I am very grateful to my family members: my 98 years old mother who is a great moral support to me, my wife Mrs. Virmati who has been a wonderful companion and a great support for last 51 years, my talented children-daughter Harshakumari H. Gohil, and son Mayur; our daughter-in-law Mrs. Amina Khan Mayur; our son-in-law Mr. Hitendrasinh, K. Gohil-who provided lot of logistic support during the initial stages of writing this book. Mr. Jonathan Plant (formerly with CRC press), I am missing you; and your colleagues are very supportive to me; thanks for your legacy, that I am still enjoying and it has been very rewarding.

Sudesh K. Kashyap: I am very thankful to Dr. J. R. Raol for believing in me and encouraging to carry out scientific work in the area of multi-sensor data fusion. Under his leadership, I have successfully handled many sponsored projects from various DRDO labs. I am also grateful to him for being my PhD guide. I am also indebted to Dr. (Mrs.) Girija G. for guiding me for ME thesis work and providing consistent support to pursue research work. I am also thankful to my other colleagues Dr. Jatinder Singh, Mr. N. Shantakumar, Mr. Bassapa and Dr. VPS Naidu for continuous support, encouragement, and inputs. Finally, I am thankful to my wonderful wife Mrs. Meenakshi for her moral support and encouragement to focus on my carrier. I would also like to acknowledge my son Ma. Harshit Kumar for bringing new light in our life.

Lakshmi S.: I am very thankful to my husband, son, and daughter, as well as my all-other family members and friends for their unbounded love, affection, and support throughout my academic and research journey. I am extremely grateful to my doctoral research supervisor, Dr. Jitendra R. Raol for his motivation, encouragement and continual technical support during my research that led me to have the Ph.D. degree in a timely manner from the Jain University, Bangalore, and that with very high level of appreciation from the peers. I am also thankful to him for giving me the opportunity to write this book as a joint author. I thank my undergraduate project student Mr. Mohammed Esa for his technical support. I am also very thankful to the management of Ramaiah Institute of Technology (RIT), Bangalore, and my senior colleagues for giving me moral and technical support during my research in the area of situation assessment and fuzzy logic.

We are very grateful to Kyra Lindholm, Sonia Tam, and her colleagues for prompt responses, and interest in our research work. We are also very thankful to Mrs. Amina for her initial ideas and draft of the cover for this book.

About the Authors

 **Jitendra R. Raol** had received B. E. and M. E. degrees in electrical engineering from M. S. University (MSU) of Baroda, Vadodara, in 1971 and 1973 respectively and Ph.D. (electrical & computer engineering) from McMaster University, Hamilton, Canada, in 1986, and at both the places he was also a post graduate research and teaching assistant. He had joined the National Aeronautical Laboratory (NAL, Bangalore) in 1975. At CSIR-NAL he was involved in the activities on human pilot modeling in fix–and motion-based research flight simulators. He re-joined NAL in 1986 and retired in July 2007 as Scientist-G (and Head, flight mechanics and control division at CSIR-NAL).

He had visited Syria, Germany, The United Kingdom, Canada, China, the United States of America, and South Africa on deputation/fellowships to i) work on research problems on system identification, neural networks, parameter estimation, multi-sensor data fusion and robotics; ii) present technical papers at international conferences; and/or iii) deliver guest lectures at some of these places. He had given several guest lectures at many Indian colleges & Universities, and Honeywell (HTSL, Bangalore).

He was a Fellow of the IEE/IET (United Kingdom) and a senior member of the IEEE (United States). He is a life-fellow of the Aeronautical Society of India and a life member of the Systems Society of India. During his studies at the MSU he had received Dean and Professor Suba Rao memorial prize and M. C. Ghia charitable fellowship. In 1976, he had won K. F. Antia Memorial Prize of the Institution of Engineers (India) for his research paper on nonlinear filtering with time delay. He was awarded a certificate of merit by the Institution of Engineers (India) for his paper on parameter estimation of unstable systems. He had received the best poster paper award from the National Conference on Sensor Technology (New Delhi) for a paper on sensor data fusion. He had also received a gold medal and a certificate for a paper related to target tracking (from the Institute of Electronics and Telecommunications Engineers, India). He is also one of the (5) recipients of the CSIR (Council of Scientific and Industrial Research, India) prestigious technology shield for the year 2003 for the leadership and contributions to the development of Integrated Flight Mechanics and Control Technology for Aerospace Vehicles in the country; the shield was associated with a plaque, a certificate, and a project-grant-prize of INRs. 30,00,000 for the project work. He was one of the five recipients of the Chellaram Foundation Diabetes Research Award-2018 for the best paper (presented at the 2nd International Diabetes Summit, March 2018, Pune, India; which carried a prize of 100,000 INRs.). He has received Sir Thomas Ward memorial prize of the Institution of Engineers (India) in 2019 (jointly) for the paper on Image Centroid Tracking with Fuzzy Logic…, and it carried a gold medal and a certificate. He is featured in the list of the Stanford University (USA) as one of the top 2% scientists/researchers of the world for the year 2019 as well as 2021.

He has published nearly 160 research papers and numerous technical reports. He had Guest-edited two special issues of Sadhana (an engineering journal published by the Indian Academy of Sciences, Bangalore) on i) advances in modeling, system identification and parameter estimation (jointly with Late Prof. Dr. Naresh Kumar Sinha) and ii) multi-source, multi sensor information fusion. He had also Guest-edited two special issues of the Defense Science Journal (New Delhi, India) on i) mobile intelligent autonomous systems (jointly with Dr. Ajith K. Gopal, CSIR-SA), and ii) aerospace avionics & allied technologies (jointly with Prof. A. Ramachandran, MSRIT).

He has co-authored i) an IEE/IET (London, UK) Control Series book Modeling and Parameter Estimation of Dynamic Systems (2004), ii) CRC Press (Florida, USA) books Flight Mechanics Modeling and Analysis (2009, and the revised edition in March 2023), iii) a CRC Press book Nonlinear Filtering: Concepts and Engineering Applications (2017), and iv) a CRC Press book Control Systems: Classical, Modern, and AI based Approaches (2019). He has also authored CRC Press books i) Multisensor Data Fusion with MATLAB (2010), and ii) Data Fusion Mathematics–Theory and Practice (2015). He has edited (with Ajith K. Gopal, CSIR-SA) a CRC press book Mobile Intelligent Autonomous Systems (2012).

He has served as a member/chairman of numerous advisory-, technical project review-, and doctoral examination committees. He has also conducted sponsored research and worked on several projects from Industry as well as other R&D organizations to CSIR-NAL with substantial budget. Under his formal technical guidance, 11 doctoral and 8 master research scholars have had received their degrees successfully; he had also guided jointly/informally one dozen research students for their doctoral studies. He is a reviewer of a dozen national/international journals, and has evaluated several M. Tech./Doctoral theses (from India and overseas). He had been with; i) MSRIT (M. S. Ramaiah Institute of Technology, Bengaluru) as emeritus professor for five years; ii) the Govt. college of engineering, Kunnur (Kerala) as a senior research advisor; and iii) the dept. of aerospace engineering (IISc., Bangalore) as a consultant on modelling and parameter estimation for the Type I diabetes-patients' data for a period of three months. He was also a consultant to a private company in Bangalore that provides software and algorithmic solutions to target tracking, navigation and data fusion problems.

His main research interests have been and are data fusion, system identification, state/parameter estimation, flight mechanics-flight data analysis, H-infinity filtering, nonlinear filtering, artificial neural networks, fuzzy logic systems, genetic algorithms, and soft technologies for robotics.

On the literary front, he has also authored a few books as the collection of his 320 (free-) verses on various facets closely related to science, philosophy, evolution, and life itself. He has also contributed 80 articles/stories and 1200 'bites' (long quotes) on matrubharti.com (#1 Indian Content Community) and 7 ebooks on Amazon KDP (kindle direct publishing) covering social, philosophical, science and human life related aspects and issues. He was featured as one of the top 100 downloaded English authors of the matrubharti.com for the year 2021.

His new area of study and research is data-systems analytics (DaSyA). His new website is: www.raoljr.com through which the researchers and students can approach for consultancy and project guidance.

Dr Sudesh Kumar Kashyap is presently working as a Chief scientist & Group Head of System Identification and Data Fusion group at Flight mechanics and control division of CSIR-NAL, Bangalore. He has done his BE in Electronics, ME in Electrical and PhD in Electrical & Electronics.

He was key member of various projects sponsored by different DRDO (India) labs for the design, development and evaluation of advanced algorithms for multisensor multitarget tracking and fusion for Air defense applications such as Real Time Flight Safety Expert System (RTFLEX) and RF Seekers based tracking of homing target. His core expertise is in the area of Kalman filtering, multisensor data fusion, gating and data association and tracking of targets with evasive maneuvers. He has also contributed to development of a concept proving Fuzzy-Bayesian based expert system to assist the pilot by providing enhanced situational awareness and threat levels in beyond visual range (BVR) air-to-air combat scenarios.

His other important contribution is a consistent effort for a decade towards the development of Enhanced and Synthetic Vision System (ESVS) for the regional transport aircraft (RTA). This vision based technology provides enhanced situational awareness of external world to pilot perspective in poor or degraded visual environment such as fog during taxi, take-off and landing operations. He has developed a ground based facility "ESVS Flight Simulator" to carry out research on ESVS and evaluation of flight data. His other contributions are INS-GPS fusion for attitude estimation of UAVs, development of symbology for Head-up display for RTA, trajectory estimation of stores of fighter aircraft during pit, captive & drop test, enhancement of target height estimation accuracy using various ground based 2D/RD radars for Indian Air Force, CSIR-NAL & CSIR-CSIO's Joint development & integration of Head-up display (HUD) with civil aircraft simulator and development of algorithms for Infrared Search and Track system (IRST). He is currently working on development of Multi Sensor Data Fusion algorithms for LCA-MK2 and AMCA platforms; the projects sponsored from ADA, Bangalore.

He has a number of National and International journal/conference papers. He is recipient of the "Young Scientist of the Year Award" by CSIR-NAL. He got the CSIR-NAL **Excellence Award in the field of 'Technology'** for "LCA Stores Separation Trajectory Estimation". He was awarded CSIR, India **Software copyright** on "Data Acquisition Software for EVS Flight Experiment".

(Ms.) **Lakshmi Shrinivasan** earned her BE and MTech degrees in Electronics from Shivaji University and Visvesvaraya Technological University (VTU) during the year 1999 and 2007 respectively. During her masters she did her internship at Intel India Pvt. Ltd and secured 1st rank at the Institute level. She got her PhD degree from Jain University, Bangalore in 2018. She has published several research papers in International and National journals and conferences. She received Best Research paper award in 2015 at Research Retreat National conference organized by the Jain University. Currently she is working as Associate Professor at Ramaiah Institute of Technology in the department of Electronics and Communication engineering. She had taught several UG and PG courses. She has also worked as Hardware Development Engineer for one year at BiSS India Pvt Ltd, Bangalore, Karnataka, India during the year 2001–2002. She also worked as lecturer at Sambhram Institute of Technology, Bangalore from 2002–2005. She has guided several UG and PG projects, many of them received Best Project Awards at the Institute levels and received Karnataka Science and Technology Council (KSCST) & MSRIT Alumni Association Funds. For publishing her paper, on Interval type 2 fuzzy logic based situation assessment, in an IET/IEE (UK) journal, she received Rs. 10,000 incentive prize from MSRIT, Bangalore. She is working with Industry collaborated projects; In Samsung SRIB PRISM Glanz National level project competition, she received her mentored team first prize for project: Sensor Placement for elderly care people in 2019. She is working on a consultancy project which is focused on battery management and prediction techniques using estimation and prediction algorithms and digital dashboard for Electric Vehicles from 2021. She was a technical consultant and Mentor for a project of Rs. 6.25 Lakhs from MSME Govt of India for a project Airpaper during the year 2013–2015.

She is a reviewer for IEEE Transactions in Industrial Electronics and couple of IEEE International conferences. She had delivered a series of lecture sessions on MultiSim Simulation tools and Digital System Design courses at Ramaiah Degree program, Bangalore and Polytechnique college at Belgaum, Karnataka, India.

She is passionate to work with real life projects which are closely related to societal issues. She believes in providing technological solutions to societal issues and challenges. Her research interests are Data Fusion, Situation Assessment, Fuzzy logic, Artificial Intelligence, Embedded System Design, VLSI, and Digital Twin Solutions for Situation Assessment. Her new focus is on data analytics and prediction methods.

1 Introduction

In this chapter we briefly describe a few aviation scenarios, Situation Awareness (SAW), decision process, Bayesian networks, and fuzzy logic, with an aim to using some of these for aviation pilots' Situation Assessment (SA).

1.1 AVIATION SCENARIOS (SITUATION IN AVIATION)

A few aviation scenarios from the available literature are briefly highlighted here.

1.1.1 PIGGYBACKING PLANES

On September 29, 1940, pilots Fuller and Hewson flew two Avro Ansons aircraft belonging to No. 2 SFT (Service Flying Training School) and the RAAF (Royal Australian Air Force, Australia) [1]. As the aircraft's navigator, Fuller received assistance from Sinclair, whose tail number was N4876. Fraser assisted Hewson in his role as the aircraft's navigator (tail number: L9162). The two pilots were above Brocklesby at a thousand feet in their respective aircraft. As they banked in a curve, Fuller lost sight of Hewson's flight. Hewson's flight and Fuller's collided when Fuller gradually lowered his altitude when Hewson's flight was passing beneath his aircraft and their Ansons blocked one another.

Whereas Hewson's flight had full power, Fuller's flight suffered damage to both of its engines. With flaps and ailerons, Fuller handled the piggybacked pair. He then began looking for a location in order to land the flight, and both navigators left their planes. Following the incident, Fuller maneuvered the aircraft for five miles before coming to a quick emergency landing in some nearby fields. His squadron leader praised him and informed him that despite the runway being not prepared, he had made a fantastic job of landing the aircraft. Fuller received recognition for both avoiding Brocklesby's damage and for preserving military equipment valued at £40,000 [1].

For a mission to drop the bombs in Dusseldorf, Mr. Reid, a 21-year-old flight lieutenant, was in command. A BF110 Messerschmitt destroyed Reid's flight's Avro Lancaster windscreen on the halfway point to Dusseldorf (the goal), and it also damaged the cockpit and gun turrets. Despite suffering injuries to his hand, shoulders, and head, Reid persisted in his pursuit of the objective. After some time, an FW190 Focke Wulf [1] attacked his flight once more, resulting in the death of his navigator and serious injuries to the wireless operator. Reid's aircraft was attacked yet again, and this time the oxygen supply system was destroyed to the point that it could not be

DOI: 10.1201/9781003370413-1

utilised any more. Despite this, Reid chose to proceed in the direction of the target. Reid must now compute the target position without using his compass or a navigator. However, he succeeded in flying the damaged aircraft in a straight line in the direction of the mission. Once at the destination, he released the payload and adjusted the route to his base station. While returning, he saw the searchlights of Norfolk, a USA-AF base station. He managed a night landing even though there was no oxygen in the bottles, blood was lost from the wounds in his body, and his head wound was obstructing his vision. Due to damage to its undercarriage, the aircraft slid along the runway. The rest of the crew suffered no injuries but the navigator and the wireless operator were killed. Mr. Reid received the Victoria Cross award in recognition of his valor and courage [1].

1.1.2   THE CRASH LANDING OF PAN AM FLIGHT 6

On October 15, 1956, a Boeing 377 Stratocruiser (*Clipper Sovereign Of The Skies*) departed Honolulu for an overnight flight to the San Francisco International Airport. When the aircraft reached an altitude of 21,000 ft. the No. 1 engine began to overspeed. Though the captain cut off the oil supply to the engine, the propeller continued to windmill in the air stream. This caused excessive drag that significantly increased fuel consumption. The No. 4 engine also failed.

With insufficient fuel to either reach San Francisco or back to Honolulu, the aircraft circled near the U.S. Coast Guard's ship at the Ocean Station November until daylight. The Captain informed the USCGC Pontchartrain that he was preparing to ditch. One wing hit a swell. The plane rotated, damaging the nose section and breaking off the tail. Everyone on board survived the ditching and were rescued by the Coast Guard before the wreckage sank at 6:35 am October 16. The ditching of Pan Am Flight was the real-life basis for the 1958 film, *Crash Landing*.

A year later, another Boeing Stratocruiser (*Clipper Romance of The Skies*) left San Francisco International Airport for Honolulu but completely disappeared. You can read more about the Mysterious Disappearance of Pan Am Flight 7 .

1.1.3   FLIGHT 143 OF AIR CANADA, A GIMLI GLIDER

Following routine inspections, Flight 143, an Air Canada B767 [1] departed from Toronto airport for Edmonton on July 22, 1983. The following day, Flight 143 continued its flight to Montreal with a new crew, and it was necessary to make a stop at Ottawa on the way back to Edmonton. The crew of the aircraft encountered problems while it was 41,000 feet above Red Lake. The aircraft's alert system in the cockpit had malfunctioned, indicating an issue with the fuel pressure on the left side. A little while later, the right side engine's second fuel pressure alarm went off. After that, the crew decided to divert to Winnipeg, and shortly after, the left side engine failed. Once more, the cockpit alarm went off, alerting the pilot that none of the engines were operating. The 767 aircraft utilised an electric flying system with instruments that ran on the power generated by the aircraft's jet engines. The plane's emergency hydraulic system, the RAT-Ram Air Turbine, was the only remaining source of power.

Despite the severe challenges in controlling the plane, pilots Pearson and Quital managed to make a safe landing. In order to decrease altitude and accelerate dragging, Pearson engaged a forward slip. The plane approached the people on the ground almost silently because the engines were not operating. There were injuries among the 61 passengers, but none of them were life-threatening. Quintal received a two-week suspension and Pearson was demoted for a period of six months. The explanation for punishment is "Permitting the incident to happen." However, the first Federation Aeronautique International Diploma for Outstanding Airmanship was given to each of them in 1985 [1].

1.1.4   US AIRWAYS FLIGHT 1549-MIRACLE ON THE HUDSON

A world-wide audience watched the emergency landing on the Hudson River on January 15, 2009. After taking off from La-Guardia in New York City, the aircraft A320-214 [2] struck a flock of Canadian Geese at an altitude of 2818 feet, just three minutes later. Both engines were switched off as a result of this. Both the crew and the passengers observed flames coming from the engines and heard loud bangs. Sullenberger and Skiles, the pilots, attempted to steer the aircraft but were unable. Consequently, the aircraft fell into an unpowered ditch in the Hudson River. With the aid of boats, all 155 passengers were rescued, with only a small number suffering critical injuries. The Master's Medal for the Guild of Air Pilot and Air Navigator was then given to the entire crew in recognition of their valiant efforts and flying accomplishments. Captain Sullenberger gained popularity after his accomplishment [2]. The pilots did, of course, run onto some problems with the aviation authorities; a movie about the incident was later generated which also highlighted the importance of flight simulation in determining the tragedy's exact cause.

1.2   SITUATION AWARENESS AND ASSESSMENT FOR PILOTS

Within the given volume of space and time, perception of environmental elements, understanding the meaning of them and projecting the status of them in the near future is called SAW-Situation Awareness. In the environment of complex operations, SAW is associated with the knowledge of the person regarding specific events and the process. It is crucial to all domains and systems for the operations that are reliable. In the industry of aviation, SAW is the prime factor in providing training to the pilot for control, maintenance and flying a flight. Usually most of the airports are specifically constructed on flat terrain, but many airports are still in higher terrains. According to the statistics of Boeing, of the commercial worldwide jet fleets from the year 1999 to the year 2008, 50% of dangerous accidents occurred at the time of landing [2].

1.2.1   SITUATION AWARENESS

Several approaches are available to assess the pilot's SAW and each approach uses diverse concepts. The most popular SAW approach is Endsley's model, which has 3 levels and was introduced in the year 1995. This model is used to collect the data and used to describe the SAW as the product of 3 levels of assessment hierarchy: i)

Level-1: Elements perception in the environment–In this level, the pilot needs to perceive the aircraft status and the surrounding environment; ii) Level-2: Understanding of current situation–In this level, the pilot needs to understand the data/information collected in the Level-1 for extrapolating its meaning from the present situation; and iii) Level-3: Projecting future states–In this level, the pilots need to merge the Level-1 and Level-2 elements for projecting data/information with respect to future states of their environment.

To complete the Level-2, it is required to complete the Level-1. In Level-1, the information or the data collected are completely based on the observation of data there within the aircraft, like speed of the aircraft, elevation, and direction of the aircraft. This complete data is gathered by observing visually; thus Level-1 can be mainly accomplished by tracking the pilot's vision, i.e., tracking the spots where the pilot is looking. For accomplishing Level-2, the pilot needs to interpret or understand the meaning of many enemy aircraft that are present within close proximity to one another, and also their formation against the pilot's aircraft. This gathering of data needs further processing and analysis of the visually observed data and needs access to both pilot's cognitive load data and gaze information [2].

1.2.2 VISUAL SCAN PATTERN ACCURACY

Scan patterns of visual data are critical in finding the SAW of a pilot specifically in Level-1 without asking questions to them directly. Tracking of eyes can be used for collecting the data through the head mounted display device [3]. This device is used to make classification of different patterns of gaze correctness in the performing maneuver. In this method, the gathered data generates a set of coordinates (x, y) for each view of eye sampled up to 120Hz of frequency. This information is transformed to a three-channel head-map in a time window and transferred to VGG based CNN– Convolutional Neural Networks to generate gaze pattern score [3-4],

1.2.3 COGNITIVE LOAD

In assessing the pilot's SAW automatically, mental workload of pilot plays significance role. In the earlier work [5], the biometric information used that was collected on the basis of time series using a device which is worn on the wrist for predicting the cognitive loads. The basics for this are from Ref. [6], and Bedford systems [7]. In this technique, multiple modalities of the biometric were collected as input information. From this raw data, acceleration of wrist, temperature of the peripheral skin, electrodermal activities, photoplethysmography and other various features were created. This information is utilized for training different models like BM3TX–Biometric, Multi Modals, and Multi Tasks X-vectors architectures.

1.2.4 SAW MEASUREMENT CATEGORIES

1.2.4.1 Freeze-probe Techniques

The tasks done by the pilot within the flight-simulator are frozen randomly for measuring the SAW [4] by the method of freeze probe in the training period. A set of queries related to SAW will be given to the pilot by making all the displays blank.

The pilot has to answer these queries by using their understanding and knowledge of the current situation of the environment, i.e., "frozen points". The responses of the pilot were recorded and compared with the actual status of the environment and the score for the SAW generated. SACRI–SAW Control Room Inventory is the extension of SAGAT–Situation Awareness Global Assessment Technique and SAW en-routing air traffic control in context with SALSA are the most popularly used methods for freeze probe [4].

1.2.4.2   Real-time Probe Techniques

Queries related to the SAW are given online to the pilot while executing the task, but freezing is not done for the task. Here, SMEs–Subject Matter Experts create the queries either during the execution or before the execution of the task and will be given to the pilot at relevant time or points while the pilot, subject, or participant is performing tasks. The responses and the answers of the participant were recorded to produce the SAW score. Situation Present Assessment Method (SPAM) and SAW for the Solutions for Human Automation Partnership in European Air Traffic management (SHAPE) online, i.e., SASHA_L are the real time probe techniques that are used to assess SA of the Air Traffic Controllers (ATCs) and these were introduced by SPAM based Eurocontrol [4].

1.2.4.3   Post-trial Self-rating Techniques

After the execution of the tasks, each subject-pilot gives a subjective measure of her/his own rating for SAW. Rich literature is available on the subjective rating techniques that include SART–SAW Rating Technique, SARS–SAW Rating Scale method, CSAS–Cranfield SA Scales, CARS–Crew Awareness Rating Scales, MARS–Mission Awareness Rating Scales and QUASA–Quantitative Analysis of SAWs. Self-rating methods are fast and simple to utilize and can be post-trials, as they are not intrusive to the execution of the tasks. Lengthy processes of training, expensive simulators and SME are not needed due to the simple nature of self-rating methods. These self-rating methods reduce the cost required for deployment [4].

1.2.4.4   Observer-rating Techniques

SMEs generate the rating for each pilot or subject by observing the subject's method of executing the tasks. The SAW rating was calculated depending on the observable SAW parameters with the behaviour of the subject in completing the task. SABARS–Situation Awareness Behavioral Rating Scales is a 5-point rating-scale approach of observer rating. The major advantage of these techniques is that they are of non-intrusive type and they don't have any effect on the execution of the tasks. These techniques can be used for the activities of the real world [4].

1.2.4.5   Performance Measures

The achievements of the subject in particular or specific events are recorded while the subject is executing the task. These ratings are analysed and given ratings based on the task and other various parameters of performance to create a measure of indirect SAW. Again these measures of performance are of non-intrusive type and are produced by a task's natural flow. These approaches are usually utilized as a backup for other methods of SAW rating, as they are simple [4].

1.2.4.6 Process Indices

Process-indices consist of procedures for recording, analyzing and rating the processes that the pilot or subject has to follow for establishing SAW while performing a task; an example is the measurement of the movements of eyes while the subject is performing the task. Eye tracking equipment is employed to identify which elements of the situation the subject has fixed upon and to evaluate how the attention of the subject is allocated. But these process-indices have the limitations associated with temperamental parameters of the device in its operation, and it needs analysis of lengthy information/data, which creates a huge workload for the analyst [4].

1.3 ANALYTICAL DECISION PROCESS

The significance of learning, understanding of Aeronautical Decision-Making (ADM), and effective skills cannot be overstressed [5]. Even though the process of training approaches of the pilot are continuously advanced in-terms of aircraft systems, instruments and services of the pilots, accidents are still occurring. In spite of all modifications in technologies for enhancing the safety of flight, one parameter remains the same, i.e., the human who leads or causes errors. It is estimated that approx. 80% of accidents in aviation are due to human parameters and the majority of them occur during take-off–23.40% and during landing–24.10%. The ADM is the systematic method of managing the stress and accessing the risks. For understanding ADM, it is required to understand the how the attitudes of the individual influences the decision making and how to correct those attitudes to improve the safety of flight. It is crucial to analyse the factors and parameters that make humans take decisions, how the process of making decisions works, and how it can be enhanced [5].

1.3.1 HISTORY OF ADM

The importance of pilot decisions, or ADM, has been recognized for the past 25 years as being essential for safer flight operations and the prevention of accidents [5]. The need to reduce accidents caused by human error has affected the aviation industry, leading to the introduction of the first training programme aimed at improving ADM. The focus of Crew Resource Management (CRM) training for flight crew members is on making effective use of all available resources, including hardware, people, and data supporting ADM, to facilitate crew operations and improve decision-making skills. The flight crew wants to achieve optimal ADM, and using CRM is one way to help them make smarter decisions. The Federal Aviation Administration, or FAA [6], has started doing research to develop a pilot training programme that includes decision-making instruction in order to improve pilots' ability to handle aviation dynamics and comply with current FAA standards. In 1987, the ADM research project concluded in terms of developments/advancements and testing, and six manuals were released. These guides are multifaceted resources for lowering decision-making-related mishaps and address the requirements of decision-making for various rated pilots. Independent studies that provide such training in addition to the conventional flying curriculum for students aspiring to become pilots verified the efficacy and accuracy of these guides. Test results indicate that, in comparison to pilots who have not received ADM instruction, pilots who have received ADM training have made fewer in-flight mistakes. The range of reduced decision-making errors is from 10% to 50%. After receiving these materials throughout training, a pilot who logged roughly 400,000 hours of flight time annually demonstrated a 54% decrease in accident risk in the real world. The ADM procedure discusses the various facets of making decisions on the flight deck and offers the following guidelines for making wise decisions: i) Recognise the attitudes that pose a risk to flight safety; ii) Learn strategies for behaviour modification; iii) Acquire the ability to recognise and manage stress; iv) Develop skills for risk assessments; v) Make use of all available resources; and vi) Assess the efficacy of one's ADM skills.

1.3.2 Risk Management

The purpose of risk management is to identify potential threats to aircraft safety and to reduce the associated risks. It is an essential part of the ADM. There will be less risk in flight, sometimes none at all, when the pilot uses sound decision-making techniques. The pilot's direct or indirect experience, in addition to their education, determines their capacity for sound decision-making. Figure 1.1 [5] illustrates the decision-making and risk-management process. Let's look at an illustration of how seat belt use works in a car. Twenty years later, wearing a seat belt has become standard. People who don't use seat belts pick it up through either direct or indirect experiences. For instance, the driver gains this knowledge from firsthand experience, such as being in or seeing a car accident that results in personal injuries. When loved ones sustain injuries in a car accident as a result of not using seat belts, there is an indirect learning experience. Knowing the four fundamentals of risk management is important, and it comes from the ADM cycle: i) Turn down unwarranted risks: Although it is impossible to fly a plane without taking any risks, taking needless chances will not pay off. For instance, flying in low visibility conditions is an unnecessary risk if the pilot is piloting a new aircraft for the first time; ii) Make risk assessments at an appropriate level: The individual with the ability to create and implement risk management strategies must make decisions on risks. Never forget that if you are the pilot, you should never let the passengers or the ATC decide what constitutes a reasonable risk for you; iii) Take a chance when the rewards exceed the risks and expenses: Any flying-related activity necessitates accepting a certain amount of danger. For instance, it is far preferable to fly an unknown aircraft on a day with good weather than one with low IFR conditions; and iv) Incorporating risk management into all planning stages: Since risk is an inherent part of all flights, it is imperative for flight safety to employ an appropriate and effective risk management system, not just during the pre-flight phase.

While making a bad choice in daily life does not always result in disaster, there is extremely little margin for error in the aviation industry. As ADM enhances the

FIGURE 1.1

management of aeronautical environments, it is imperative that all pilots possess familiarity with and apply ADM [10].

1.3.3 CREW RESOURCE MANAGEMENT (CRM)

1.3.3.1 Single-Pilot Resource Management

A majority of the principles covered in the crew management system [5] also apply to single pilot operations. The system focuses on how pilots operate in a crew setting. The development of the Single Pilot Resource Management (SRM) system is the outcome of the successful application of several CRM concepts to single-pilot aircraft. In order to ensure a successful flight, the single pilot must have access to both on-board and outside resources both before and during the flight. This is known as the SRM, which is the art and science of all resources. The ideas of SA, TM (Time Management), CFIT (Controlled Flight Into Terrain awareness), ADM, and RM (Risk Management) have all been incorporated into the SRM. SRM training helps the pilot maintain SA by assisting with automation management, aircraft aided control, and navigational responsibilities. This facilitates rapid and precise decision-making by the pilot by enabling accurate risk assessment and management. In order to help pilots learn how to gather data and analyse it so they can make smart judgements, SRM was created. The use of resources like ATC-Auto-pilot and Air Traffic Control mirrors the CRM concepts, even if aircraft are managed by a single flight rather than by crew members on board.

1.3.3.2 Hazard and Risk

The two main components that characterize the ADM are hazards and risks. A pilot may experience genuine events, perceived situations, or circumstances that pose a risk. The pilot evaluates a hazard based on multiple factors as it arises. The pilot rates the possible impact of the danger on the flight, validating the pilot's assessment of the risks and hazards. So, the pilot's individual or cumulative risks can be measured when determining risk. Individual pilots, however, evaluate the risks in unique ways.

1.3.3.3 Hazardous Attitudes and Antidotes

The pilot's physical health and more recent experiences are the only factors considered when determining whether or not they are fit to operate the aircraft. Consider the relationship between attitude and decision-making quality. The motivating inclination to react with others, to circumstances or occurrences in a particular way is known as an attitude. Resignation, anti-authority, machismo, impulsivity, and invulnerability are the five attitudes that pose a risk to flight safety and impede one's capacity to make sound decisions and exercise authority. These findings are based on a review of the research.

1.3.3.4 Risk

Every flight requires the pilot to make decisions, sometimes in dangerous situations. In order to ensure a safe flight, the pilot needs to evaluate the level of risk and choose the most effective course of action to reduce it in these dangerous circumstances.

1.3.3.5 Assessment of Risk

If there is only one pilot scenario, it is almost impossible to gauge the level of risk. Thus, the pilot's job is to make decisions on his own and to oversee their quality. It has been observed that many pilots who have flown continuously for longer than sixteen hours are excessively fatigued in certain situations. Undoubtedly, the response is "no." The rationale for this is because when asked to accept "light," the majority of pilots are inclined towards "gold." Only when their personal needs take precedence over their missions can the pilots refuse to provide emergency services. Another illustration would be helicopter emergency services, where the pilots place a greater emphasis on the welfare of their patients than on any other factor. In each of these scenarios, the pilot typically assigns a "weight" to intangible elements, failing to accurately measure the real risks (such as those pertaining to weather or weariness). A solitary pilot must contend with imperceptible elements that pull him into one or two risky situations if there are no other crew members available for consultation. Consequently, a lone pilot's susceptibility is far higher than that of the entire crew.

1.3.3.6   Likelihood of an Event

To put it simply, likelihood is the process of weighing the circumstances and estimating the likelihood that something will happen. Examine a pilot's flight from point A to point B while adhering to the minimal visual flight regulations. Regarding potential Instrument Meteorological Condition (IMC), the pilot's initial response is anticipated. The likelihood of coming across IMC can be calculated by combining the forecast with the experiences of other pilots.

1.3.3.7   Severity of an Event

A crucial parameter in the risk matrix is the event's severity. It might also be described as an outcome of the pilot's choice and actions. Damage or an injury may also be connected to this. There is a higher chance of unintentional IMC circumstances if the pilot is not classified as an "instrument pilot." These are a few recommendations for the evaluation:

- Disastrous: those that cause complete loss
- Critical: resulting in significant harm and serious injury
- Diminished: producing only slight harm and losses
- Insignificant: producing fewer minor system harms or losses.

1.3.4   MITIGATING RISK

Risk assessment is one component. After the degree of risk is established, the pilot must reduce the risk. If the pilot is travelling from point A to point B (in MVFR circumstances), there are a few techniques to lower the risk: You have five options: i) postpone the trip; ii) drive; iii) cancel the trip; iv) use an instrument-rated pilot; or v) wait for the weather to clear. The most popular risk-reduction checklist is IM-SAFE, which stands for I for illness, M for medication, S for stress, A for abstaining from alcohol, F for fatigue, and E for emotionally charged circumstances [5].

1.4   INTUITIVE DECISION STRATEGIES

1.4.1   MANAGING EXTERNAL PRESSURES

One of the most important keys is to manage the external pressure. Time related pressure is externally put on the pilot, and the pilot does not realize that he/she is facing a major accident. To manage external pressure, one has to use personal Standard Operating Procedures (SOPs). The aim is to release the external pressure of flight. There are certain procedures like [5]: i) allowing the pilots to have an extra stock of fuel, ii) allowing them to make an unexpected landing because of the weather, iii) having different alternative plans for late arrivals, iv) making backup airline reservations, and v) for critical cases, planning to leave early enough so that the time and the flight to the destination is calm.

1.4.2 HUMAN FACTORS

Many human conditions play a very important role in aviation. Examples are stress, compliancy and fatigue. Many other conditions altogether are referred to as human factors. They directly cause evolution accidents. For more than 70% of aircraft accidents, these are the primary contributors.

1.4.3 HUMAN BEHAVIOUR

From a study it is determined that the tendency of individual intake and the individual's involvement at the level of taking actions based on accidents, certainly play an important role. A study regarding injury prone children was published by Elizabeth Mechem Fuller and Helen B. Baune, of the University of Minnesota [6]. This was a study regarding injury prone children. The accident-free group showed a better behaviour with greater knowledge levels. At the same time, the accident repeater group had better gymnastics skills compared to the other group. The impulsive and aggressive ones demonstrated rebellious behaviour under stress. They had lack of attention. For better decision-making skills, the pilot has to obtain a general population presentation of all types of personality traits.

1.4.4 THE DECISION-MAKING PROCESS

The basic knowledge of the decision-making process provides a pilot with the base foundation for developing the skills of aeronautical decision making and a single pilot resource management skill. Risk intervention and risk management have complex definitions: the decision-making processes that are designed systematically to identify hazards and also assist with the degree of risk and help determine the best course of action to be taken. There are a series of tasks that must be done one after the other: assessment of the risk, analysis of controls, making control decisions, using the controls and monitoring the results of all the said actions. Hence, all these steps reach to a decision-making process. There are different models that help in problem solving and decision making: 3P, 5P using the PAVE, TEAM and CARE and the DECIDE models. All these models help pilots to organize critical decisions.

1.4.5 SINGLE-PILOT RESOURCE MANAGEMENT (SRM)

SRM, is a process of gathering the information, analyzing the information and making the best decision from it. The first task is how to identify the problem. The next is how to analyse the information from it. The next is to make an informed and timely decision. It is always said that there is no right answer in ADM. Based on the experience level of the pilot, they have to analyse the situation in their best possible way. This will be based on the current physical and mental readiness that the pilot has to take his or her own decisions.

1.4.6   THE 5 PS CHECK

One of the practical applications SRM is "Five Ps" [5]: i) the plan, ii) the plane, iii) the pilot, iv) the passenger, and v) the programming. During an emergency time or during the flight, these 5Ps are used to evaluate the current situation of the pilot. The decision points are taken as hourly, or pre-flight, or pre-take-off, or at the midpoint of the flight. Sometimes these are also preferred to be made during pre-descent, or just prior to the final approach. Many pilots will complete the risk management sheet prior to take-off. This creates a catalogue of risks that can be encountered in a day. Based on the risk, each of them is assigned with a numerical value. If this value exceeds the predetermined level, then flights are altered or cancelled. The 5P concept is a simple attempt that helps to take the information that is contained in the sheets or in the form of other available models. The 5P models make the pilot rely on the adoptable schedule review on the critical variables at point of flight where decisions are normally being effective. The very first point of decision taking is made in pre-flight in the flight planning room. At this stage all the information is readily available. So, this helps in communication and with fixed base operator services to readily avail of different alternative plans. There are few pilots who have made an "emergency take off". These 5P checkpoints help the pilot to fly after their correct application. The review of 5P can be done during the midpoint of the flight. So, at this point check whether the point of the flight will be a good option for the pilot and the aircraft. If there is a long flight or a tiring flight each day, then additional fatigue and low altitude hypoxia can rob the pilot of much of his energy.

1.4.6.1   The Plan

The other terms for the plan are mission or the task. The plan consists of: weather, fuel, and cross-country planning. During the flight, the plan must be continually evaluated multiple times. If there is a delay in take-off, then it may be due to maintenance. The plan must always be updated and regularly modified based on the responses collected from remaining Ps. In real life, the 5Ps are regularly subjected to changes.

1.4.6.2   The Pilot

For a pilot, if the flight is for a business, transportation is involved, then the pilot can be exposed to many risks such as long trip that requires significant resolution and challenging weather with high altitudes. If the pilot is at risk, then it is always better to consult the checklist "IMSAFE". Pilot fatigue, late nights and the effect of sustained flights, above the attitude of 5000 feet may cause the pilot to become less discerning, less critical of information, or more complaining and less accepting.

1.4.6.3 The Passenger

The interaction of passengers with the pilot is the key difference between SRM and CRM. If the pilot is highly capable with a single engine aircraft, he/she can maintain a much more 'personal' interaction with the passengers; positioned with arms reach of them, throughout the flight.

1.4.6.4 The Programming

In recent eras, the aircrafts have been supported with advanced avionics adding an entirely a new dimension to the operational flight. Due to the use of the autopilot and GPS, the pilots' workload is reduced. This enhances the situation awareness of the pilot to a very high level. The operation and programming of these devices is simple. They have replaced the analogue instruments in the flight and captured the pilot's attention for a long period of time. To avoid certain phenomena, the pilot must plan in advance where programming for approaches, and airport/route changes information should be gathered and achieved. The pilot should be familiar with the route and equipment and with the local ATC environment.

1.4.6.5 Perceive, Process, Perform (3P) Model

This model for ADM is a straightforward and effective approach that can be applied during any stage of flight. Pilots can utilize this model by: i) Perceiving the given set of circumstances for a flight, ii) Processing/evaluating their impact on flight safety, and iii) Performing/implementing the best course of action. It is recommended to use the Perceive, Process, Perform, and Evaluate method as a continuous model for every decision made in aviation. To simplify practical risk management, the six steps of risk management can be combined into a 3P model, utilizing the PAVE, CARE, and TEAM checklists. Pilots can identify hazards by using the PAVE checklist, including the Pilot, Aircraft, Environment, and External pressures.

1.5 COGNITIVE CONTINUUM THEORY

Hammond recognised many limitations with different models in terms of systematic positivity and intuitive human approaches [7], and that the intuition or the analysis is not solely a function of cognition. He developed a cognitive continuum theory in which he postulated that a cognitive process is operated on a continuum which was anchored with the analysis at a single pole and intuition at another opposite pole. He named the areas between the poles quasi-rational decision making; a combinational analysis of intuitive process and analytical process. The thinking ability of the person decides the cognitive dimension of the task; the thinking moves from highly intuitive to highly analytical. The process of analysis is a slow conscious process which helps in averaging the queues presented in the process of the decision maker. The analytical approach is characterized by a very high degree of consistency and accuracy, but at the same time a greater potential is required for the avoidance of major errors. The intuition always involves a rapid unconscious processing of data which combines an averaging principle of low consistency, having moderate level of accuracy and limited potential for errors. The process of dynamic cognition moves along with different rates and in different forms in the continuum. The complexity of task consists of: i) the number of information queues, ii) the principles of combining information, iii) the level of ambiguities, iv) the content of presentation, and v) the redundancy of the queues. If the tasks are more ill structured, then the decision made is intuitive. If the tasks are more well-structured, then the decisions will be analytical decisions. The different levels of cognitive processes are induced based on the characteristics of the task. In some experiments, it was found that most subjects used intuitive analytical decision making.

1.5.1 KEY TERMS AND DEFINITION

The key terms in Hammond's theory are:

1.5.1.1 Analysis

Analysis is termed as a consistent, conscious, slow, and detailed process that has the following attributes: i) a high level of cognitive control, ii) the data processing rate is very slow, iii) the conscious awareness level is very high, iv) it has a very task-specific organised principle, and v) it has high confidence in the method of processing. All the above attributes were proposed by reference [8].

1.5.1.2 Coherence

This is the kind of judgement made by a person using his relative knowledge of theories and scientific concepts. These judgments can be coherent or incoherent and accurate or inaccurate. A coherent judgement can be inaccurate and at the same time, the judgement may also be accurate and incoherent.

1.5.1.3 Correspondence

Correspondence is defined to be the level of accuracy based on the person's cognitive system.

1.5.1.4 Functional Relation

This consists of the inferences that are obtained by observations of several statistical data.

1.5.1.5 Intuition

The unconscious and rapid data processing is referred to as intuition. The main attributes of intuition are: i) low level cognitive control command, ii) high rate of data processing, iii) having low consciousness about awareness, and iv) averaging different organising principles.

1.5.1.6 Modes of Inquiry

These are: i) pure analytical cognition, ii) statistical inference, iii) quasi-analytical mode, iv) computer modelling mode, v) expert judgement obtained from the database experts, and vi) having unrestricted judgement based on intuitive thoughts.

1.5.1.7 Oscillation

This is the process wherein modes of cognition change from intuition to analysis or analysis to intuition.

1.5.1.8 Pattern Recognition

Based on experience, if the pattern of information organization is recognised, then it is referred to as pattern recognition.

1.5.1.9 Quasi-rationality

The central reason for cognitive quantum and the related mode cognition is occupied by quasi-rationality. It has both elements, analysis and intuition [8].

1.6 ROLE OF BAYESIAN NETWORK

In the era of artificial intelligence, technology and techniques play a vital role in dealing with different challenges of the present business with assistance from available and advanced machine learning tools. Among the wide range of tools available for implementation in real time industrial applications with artificial intelligence, the Bayesian network is one of the most appropriate approaches for dependable action.

1.6.1 UNDERSTANDING THE BAYESIAN NETWORK

This is an innovative technique for the study of unpredictable data in the movement of data over a network arranged in a Bayesian format referred to as Bayesian networks (BN) [9]: The aim is to: i) find a relationship with the existing variables in a probabilistic model, ii) compute different possibilities for both these values, iii) interpretation of the probabilistic models in a computational way in consideration of the random variables, and iii) representation of results graphically as a Bayesian network. BN operations can be broadly classified as structured probabilities and a graph-based direct approach.

1.6.2 WHAT IS IT USED FOR?

The BN profiles are usually incorporated for the design of customized algorithms and applications such as spam filtering in emails, diagnosis applications for different medical reports, and search engines. The prime goal of the network is to realize the knowledge of the existing relationship with network nodes and their relationships. BN can be used in the process of events for the diagnosis of health condition of patients. With simple observation and examination of a person with visual symptoms and with possible interaction with the patient by a medical expert, the health disorder can be diagnosed based on the available symptoms. If the BN is deployed, the diagnosis will be strengthened by providing options to the medical expert, giving possibilities and probabilities based on the symptoms. The probabilities are connected logically (an added advantage) to make a decision about the health-scenario for more specific outcomes. The BN operating algorithm is always connected with numbers.

1.6.3 How Does It Work?

How does the BN work? i) It is operated using Bayes theorem, that investigates the likelihood or confidence in an outcome, as opposed to other approaches that establish probabilities based on historical evidence; ii) The BN is founded on the notions of dependency and independence. Independent refers to a random quantity or variable that is unaffected by other factors, and a dependent variable is a random variable with an uncertain probability that is dependent on other variables; iii) The BN is divided into casual components and actual numbers; and iv) The concept of connecting multiple random variables (it can be independently conditional).

1.6.4 What Is an Influencer Diagram in a Bayesian Network?

A BN can be implemented for the analysis of issues related to the decision making algorithms with minimal knowledge using an influence diagram construction among the given nodes and forming the arcs/paths in the network under consideration. Each node in the network denotes a unique variable which is randomly distributed and the arcs in the network denote the probabilities of variables which are conditionally random. The connected links indicate a node directly influencing another one. If they are not connected linearly, each node is kept independent among others.

1.6.5 Constraints of the Bayesian Network

These are: i) the network construction is not economical, lacks the performance and not user friendly in terms of the deciphering, failing to define and make decisions on a closely related topic; ii) there is no widely agreed method for constructing networks from data; iii) BNs are more difficult to build than other types of networks (neural networks have the benefit of being able to learn various patterns and not being limited to the originator); and iv) the BN fails to characterize cyclic interactions, such as the deflection of an airplane wing and the fluid pressure-field around it (the pressure is determined by the deflection, and this deflection in turn is determined by the pressure).

1.6.6 How Are Bayesian Networks Developed?

BNs are created based on basic requirements such as considering how random variables are distributed, the relationships between them and most importantly, the number of random variables under consideration. All these questions may be answered by an expert, who can also propose a design for the Bayesian Belief Network model. The architecture of such models is often defined by specialists, but the probability distributions must be derived from the available data. The information may be utilised to calculate probability distributions and graph structure. However, this is a time-consuming procedure. Algorithms may be used to compute the graph, for continuous random variables, for example, assume a Gaussian distribution to determine the distribution parameters. BNs are commonly used in Artificial Intelligence to cope with commercial tasks, one of which is spam screening in your email account. It's also utilized in image processing, where it aids in the conversion of photographs into other digital formats. BNs are being used in medical research, and aviation.

1.7   ROLE OF FUZZY LOGIC

Fuzzy logic is mainly intended to consider the uncertainty and provides a better approximation of reality for modelling the changes in a system [10]. An air armament system, as with any other technical system, should be characterized by high reliability so that air missions can be performed without any disruptions. The reliability of a technical system largely depends on a failure-free operation of its individual components. The occurrence of a system failure is a random variable. Increasingly, engineers are unable to accurately determine the factors causing the failure. In the operation of armament systems, human factors play a significant role, whose momentary indisposition or error can contribute to generating the malfunction. In case non-technical damage factors are involved, fuzzy logic can provide a useful tool. Fuzzy logic is used to model the uncertainty associated with human error factors. Research has indicated the possibility of using fuzzy logic to define quality standards for operations, maintenance, and production activities, which can significantly reduce errors made by say, oil refinery personnel [11]. Fuzzy logic and expert judgement have also been successfully used to determine the probability of human error among nuclear plant operators.

The statistical data considered in probabilistic models of reliability assessment indicate failure, yet they do not take into consideration the reasons for its occurrence. Failures occur for a variety of reasons and depend on a range of variables. Therefore, it is rather difficult to predict when a malfunction may occur. An alternative solution to classical reliability estimation methods is to adopt a fuzzy logic approach.

REFERENCES

[1] A Newsletter, "*5 Emergency Landings that made History*", by Aviation Oil Outlet on May May 8, 2017, by USA

[2] Crothers, N., Yash, S., Larson, E. C. *Real-Time Situation Awareness Assessment for Pilots via Machine Learning: Constructing an Automated Classification System*, MODSIM World 2022, 2022 Paper No. 14.

[3] Wilson, J., Scielzo, S., Nair, S., and Larson, E. C. (2020*), Automatic Gaze Classification for Aviators: Using Multi-Task Convolutional Networks as a Proxy for Flight Instructor Observation*, International Journal of Aviation, Aeronautics, and Aerospace, 7(3), 7.

[4] Nguyen, T., Lim, C. P., Nguyen, N. D., Gordon-Brown, L., and Nahavandi, S. *A Review of Situation Awareness Assessment Approaches in Aviation Environments*, in IEEE Systems Journal , vol. 13, no. 3, pp. 3590–3603, Sept. 2019

[5] Pilot's Handbook of Aeronautical Knowledge, FAA-H-8083-25C (Full Version), *chapter 2 Aeronautical Decision Making* by Federal Aviation Administration (FAA), United States Department of Transportation, updated on July 10, 2023

[6] Roth, Emilie, Klein, Devorah, Ernst, Katie, "Aviation Decision Making and Situation Awareness Study: Decision Making Literature Review" , technical report Defence Technical Information Center, Accession Number: AD1160556, 2021-12-15

[7] Hammond, K. R. (1996), *Human judgment and social policy: Irreducible uncertainty, inevitable error, unavoidable justice*, Oxford, England: Oxford University Press.

[8] Cader, R., Campbell, S., and Watson, D. (2005), *Cognitive continuum theory in nursing decision-making*, Journal of Advanced Nursing, 49(4), 397–405.

[9] Zhang, J., Yue, H., Wu, X., and Chen, W. "A brief review of Bayesian belief network," *2019 Chinese Control And Decision Conference (CCDC)*, Nanchang, China, 2019, pp. 3910–3914

[10] Feng, G. "A Survey on Analysis and Design of Model-Based Fuzzy Control Systems," in *IEEE Transactions on Fuzzy Systems*, vol. 14, no. 5, pp. 676–697, Oct. 2006

[11] Żyluk, A., et al. *Fuzzy Logic in Aircraft Onboard Systems Reliability Evaluation—A New Approach*, Sensors 21.23; 7913, 2021.

2 Situation Awareness

2.1 INTRODUCTION

The definition of situation awareness (SAW) can be interpreted as a perception of elements in the environment. The environment is bound by volumes of time and space; SAW is the comprehension of their meaning and the projection of their statuses in the near future. There are three different levels of situation awareness: (i) perception and event detection, (ii) current situation assessment, and (iii) near-future situation prediction.

2.2 DEFINITIONS OF SAW

The most common and popular definition of SAW is as follows. Within the given volume of space and time, SAW is the perception of environmental elements, understanding the meaning of them and projecting the status of them in the near future [1]. However, other sources say that (i) SAW should not be restricted only to working memory capacity; rather it is based in the mental capability to access the required data or information relating to evolving flight circumstances [2]; and (ii) it is rooted in performance and that SAW should be associated with high expertise and high performance [3]. The method of explaining or reviewing models instead of definitions allows readers and students to better acquaint themselves with the general concepts of SAW [4].

2.3 APPROACHES USED TO DEFINE AND EXPLAIN SITUATION AWARENESS

The four qualitative methods of describing SAW are: (i) using a model for processing information or data to define and explain SAW, (ii) using a cycle of actions/perceptions to define and explain SAW, (iii) comparison of SAW with expertise, and (iv) using SAW to describe behavioral phenomena.

2.3.1 INFORMATION PROCESSING MODELS

Short-term memory and attention are psychological constructs that have to be considered in information or data processing models. Even though these models are

DOI: 10.1201/9781003370413-2

intended to describe the processing of information or data by humans, they can be used specifically for understanding SAW. An example of this is the method given in [5], wherein similar conceptual models were used for explaining common elements of human data processing, i.e. the data processing models used involve constructs like attention, schemata, and short-term sensory storage. One such model is shown in Figure 2.1 [1]. The extracted details of this model's components illustrate how all aspects of the data processing model can be applied. An individual's SAW is constrained by the capacity of their working memory and attention. The individual's aim and expectations greatly affect SAW: How is the attention being directed? How is the information or data being perceived? How will it be understood or interpreted? The first characteristic has three hierarchical levels:

Level 1: Perception of environmental elements,
Level 2: Comprehension of the current situation, and
Level 3: Future status projection.

As an example, consider a situation where a pilot is flying amongst hazardous terrain. This terrain will become a factor of the task and is the environmental state. If the pilot has observed the terrain, then they have perceived the current situation's element, i.e., Level 1. If the pilot identifies that the terrain is hazardous, then they have comprehension of situation, i.e., Level 2. Finally, if the pilot has the capability to accurately estimate the time it would take for the plane to collide with the terrain and identify the maneuver required to avoid it, then they have achieved future status projection, i.e., Level 3 [4]. The SAW itself should be considered separately from the process of achieving SAW. The ways in which the pilot determines that the terrain is hazardous is not vital for measuring the execution of SAW, rather SAW can be measured simply by assessing whether the pilot is aware of that terrain or not.

In the above scenario, certain data from an Air Traffic Controller (ATC) was needed to correctly achieve SAW. For this it was not considered how many airports are present in that sector; rather it was felt that the controller should know the aircraft's current position. Therefore, true measurement of SAW should assess only the knowledge about variable or dynamic environmental aspects. There are two issues with using information or data processing models to describe SAW. Firstly, these models consist of several psychological constructs which are not understood particularly well such as schemata and attention, which are the subject of debate and the focus of ongoing research efforts and experiments with a variety of different paradigms. Secondly, the process of achieving SAW appears relatively finite and static in nature.

Many other methods have been suggested to enhance the dynamic nature of the model. An example of one method that enhances the dynamism in the SAW measuring process is through the use of the perception–action cycle [5].

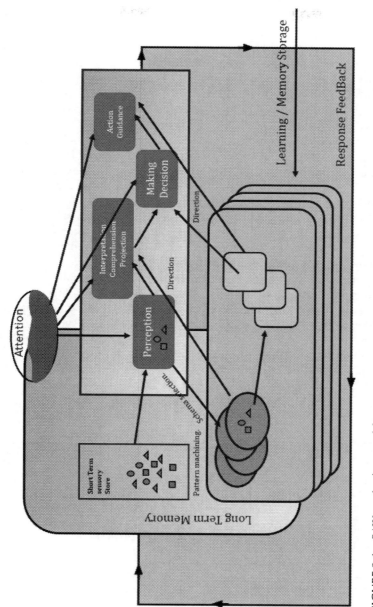

FIGURE 2.1 SAW mechanisms model

Modified from: Uhlarik, J. & Comerford, D. A. (2002), A Review of Situation Awareness Literature Relevant to Pilot Surveillance Functions, Office of Aerospace Medicine, Washington, DC, DOT/FAA/AM-02/3.

2.3.2   THE PERCEPTION–ACTION CYCLE

The perception–action cycle (PAC) is shown in Figure 2.2 [6]. It comprises three major components: (i) object (assessable information in external environments), (ii) schema (internal knowledge, which is structured theoretically in an organized way and is developed by experience or training; when it is not used, it will be stored in the long term memories), and (iii) exploration (the observer's search in the environment). The object changes the schema, which in turn activates exploration, and this results in object swamping. As an example, consider a situation where a pilot is flying a route which is familiar to them. An object, say a river, can change the present schema of the pilot and they recall that the terrain ahead of them is mountainous and potentially hazardous. The schema which has been activated can provide the pilot with directions for exploring the terrain in a northerly direction. Now, when the mountain is viewed by the pilot, i.e., when the object is sampled, the schema will either be changed correspondingly or the pilot's attention will be redirected. The schema continues to direct the attention of the pilot towards the hazardous terrain. If this does not pose a threat, then the schema will direct the attention of the pilot towards other environmental aspects, such as the cockpit display (visual sampling). The PAC represents a cyclic process of collecting data where the start and end points of the process are not important; the process of achieving SAW is quite dynamic.

It is suggested [7] that SAW must be abstracted as a combination of process and product. For emergency situations, a more elaborate model is needed to capture the behavior adequately. Emergency situations can be represented in an efficient manner by the division of the schema into implicit focus and explicit focus: implicit focus is very much SAW as the completely activated schema, and explicit focus corresponds

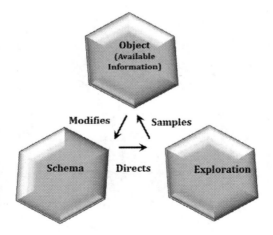

FIGURE 2.2   The perception–action cycle

Modified from: Uhlarik, J. & Comerford, D. A. (2002), *A Review of Situation Awareness Literature Relevant to Pilot Surveillance Functions*, Office of Aerospace Medicine, Washington, DC, DOT/FAA/AM-02/3.

to working memory. In another model, semantic long-term memory and episodic memory are included. Episodic memory is defined as memory that consists of complete records of schemata which are activated or created in the course of a task; semantic memory is defined as memory that contains general knowledge which is learnt for life. Some models give a method for measuring SAW. SAW can also be defined as the adaptable and externally directed consciousness: the pilot or the operator utilizes both behavior and knowledge to achieve the present situation's objectives within the constraints of the environment; 'externally directed' means that the agent's objective is in the environment rather that in their own head. Consciousness is the part of the pilot's knowledge that produces the behavior and it can be intentionally manipulated, and though competent performance is a necessary condition it is not a sufficient condition for measuring SAW [7].

2.3.3 SITUATION AWARENESS FUSED WITH MODELS OF DECISION-MAKING

SAW equates to expertise, a notion similar to competence in making quick and accurate decisions based on SAW [3, 7]. As an example, a pilot who can perform maneuvers for avoiding terrain in a quick, effortless and error-free way has SAW. It is suggested [7] that SAW may be explained as: (i) reading and understanding the situation, (ii) recognizing the problem, (iii) classifying the situation, (iv) interpreting the situation, (v) arriving at a mental model of the circumstances, and (vi) creating an image of the situation in one's mind [8]. The crossover between SAW concepts and situation assessment (SA) must be clarified: the attainment of SAW is explained as gaining an understanding of a situation or to develop a mental picture of it. There are overlapping ideas between the concepts of SAW and SA; in fact, SA does in most cases incorporate decision-making. Some use the terms 'situation assessment' (SA) and 'situation awareness' (SAW) interchangeably [9]. Some utilize SA (and the associated decision-making) for explaining SAW [8], [10].

2.3.4 SITUATION AWARENESS AS A DESCRIPTION OF AN EVENT

It has been suggested that SAW cannot be utilized to describe behavior; however it can be utilized as label of description [11]. In an experiment, the person who is conducting the experiment (the researcher) wants to compare pilot performance of terrain avoidance in two scenarios: one in which the traditional cockpit displays are used and one in which a new type of display is inserted into the cockpit. This proposition was made based on classifications of psychological concepts [12], which range from Level 1 to Level 5 according to the concepts of psychology defined by Underwood; these levels represent the pilot's mental state. Level 1 is the highest level, requiring no conceptual leaps from the data objectives and no inference is made on the behavior of the subject. Level 5 is the lowest level, as it requires many conceptual leaps from the data objectives; these concepts are rarely utilized due to the construct's group combinations.

In the example, if the operator or pilot performs a maneuver away from hazardous terrain more rapidly using the new displays than when referring to the traditional information sources, then that rapid maneuver can be attributed to SAW, but the reason for the behavior change should be seen as the introduction of a new display device and no other process or mechanism. SAW cannot be used as a means for behavior change; rather it can be utilized as the prevailing state or process, in which the new type of display makes the attainment of SAW that much quicker. In Level 3 concepts of psychology, hypothetical measurements of SAW cannot be made or even utilized as a tool for explanation without employing circular logic [12]. SAW assists the researcher in two ways: (i) it enables them to concentrate on the appropriate significant variables by making them identify both the situation of the task objectives and the operator's state of mental awareness, and (ii) the bounding of an issue enables researchers to recognize similar events that are classified into corresponding categories.

2.3.5 SUMMARY

Table 2.1 provides a summary of the four qualitative approaches discussed in Section 2.3.

TABLE 2.1
Summary of approaches used to define and explain SAW

Name of Approach	Summary	Criticisms/Potential Issues
Information models	Psychological constructs are described with respect to their effects on SAW, e.g., long-term memories, automaticity, and attention.	Several psychological constructs are not understood properly; this makes SAW a static rather than a dynamic process.
Perception–action cycle (PAC)	SAW is described as a cyclic process for data perception in the environment by using available structures of knowledge and exploration of the environment.	PAC uses many psychological constructs which are not understood properly, such as exploration and schemata; despite best efforts the measured SAW was unclear.
Models for decision-making	SAW is illustrated using expert performance levels and is equivalent to the situation assessment (SA).	SAW performance at the expert level is just a condition of necessity; however, it is not the sufficient condition. In defining performance at the expert level, few operational difficulties exist. The SA model relies on one specific psychological construct (i.e., schema) which is not understood properly.
Description of phenomena	SAW can be utilized as an instrument for classifying situations, i.e., as constructs at Level 2; however it cannot be used to demonstrate psychological constructs indicating cause and effect, i.e. Level 3 constructs.	The necessity of classifying events for SAW is questionable.

2.4 MEASURES USED TO ASSESS SITUATION AWARENESS

Understanding how SAW is defined operationally for realistic assessment assists in both in understanding the hypothetical constructs realizing the benefits.

Measurement of SAW is classified in three categories: (i) implicit, (ii) explicit, and (iii) subjective [2], [10], [13]; see Table 2.2.

At first, it is required to describe a few common measurement problems and parameters as they are applied to the psychological research [14]; . One significant problem is the validity of the dependent approaches that measure the desired factors. There are four different kinds of validity. (i) Face validity is the degree to which the measurement naturally recognizes the constructs of psychology that are in question or are due to be measured. End users and researchers often accept measurements using the face validity, but this can lead to problems if they are not actually measuring the parameters that they are intended to measure. (ii) Construct validity is the degree to which the measurement actually assesses the constructs they are intended to assess. (iii) Predictive validity is the level to which the measurement predicts behaviors in real-world tasks. (iv) Concurrent validity is the level to which the new measurement is correlated with other measures that already exist.

Along with validity, five other factors are considered significant in mental workload indices [15], [16]. These can be described as follows. (i) Sensitivity is the degree to which the measurement differentiates between the varying states or conditions. As an example, a sensitive method differentiates between degrees of SAW when the person conducting the experiments changes the data available to the pilot or participants. (ii) Selectivity is the degree to which the measurement is sensitive only to modifications of the construct of interest. As an example, SAW measurement must be sensitive only to modifications of SAW and not be affected by modifications to the mental workload. (iii) Diagnosticity is the degree to which the measurement recognizes modifications and the reasons for the modifications, i.e., diagnostic measurement helps in recognizing the reasons for modifications in the SAW. (iv) Obtrusiveness is the degree to which the measurement obstructs the primary tasks. As an example, SAW measurement cannot obstruct the duties of the pilot.

TABLE 2.2
SAW measurement: categories and subcategories

Category	Subcategories
Explicit measurements	• Retrospective measurements
	• Concurrent measurements
	• Measurements that use the freeze approach
Implicit measurements	• Global measurements
	• External Task Measurements
	• Embedded task Measurements
Subjective measurements	• Self-rating (direct)
	• Self-rating (comparative)
	• Observer rating

(v) Bandwidth and reliability are the degree to which the measurement is consistent and allows for quick and reliable assessment. As an example, if a pilot is tested twice under the same circumstances with identical understandings, reliable measurement should give the same SAW value for both cases; moreover, it is significant to note that the SAW measurement should be reliable even for dynamic or changing situations, even after the pilot has been tested many times during the flight [13].

2.4.1 Explicit Measures

Explicit measures of a study require the public to self-report data from memory [10]. They should be able to assess if the pilot is able to correctly recall the most recent altitude, location, speed, and other parameters of a flight. A measure that has high construct validity should be selected. It is argued [5, 10] that the SAW and the explicit measures are objective. In aviation, complex tasks and rapidly changing environments follow a normative model. Normally, aviation models are difficult to interpret in a laboratory environment. Explicit measures are sub-categorized into freeze, retrospective, and concurrent measurement methods. Once the tasks are completed, the retrospective measures are utilized. Based on experimental simulation of the scenario, participants are required to recall specific events and to describe the decisions made in experimental or simulated scenarios, which may reflect the participant's retrospective (linear) representation of what happened. If the questions are being asked without any rehearsal, the material accuracy in the memory for an average human will remain for about 2 seconds.

A free signal experiment was conducted during which unexpected questions were posed and treated as a retrieval cue [13]. A freezing technique that makes several assumptions about operator assessment was proposed in [17]. It consisted of a task environment that is stored in accessible memory. The predictive validity of the freeze technique was commented upon in [18], and was interpreted as a measure of utilizing the freeze method with high SAW. None of these measures can convey information about how well the participant would perform in a real-world scenario.

A well-known freeze technique is Situation Awareness Global Assessment Technique (SAWGAT). This is specifically used for air-to-air communication in tactical combat. It can be described as a computerized version of the freeze technique. The simulations are frozen at random points, and random questions are selected and posed to the pilot from a pre-defined question bank. These questions are task applicable questions. The task performance is never dependent on the duration or the frequency of the freezing time. Thus, SAWGAT is considered as neither obstructive nor affected by time-limiting working memory.

2.4.2 Implicit Measures

To compute the value of a measure, task performance is a key criterion. SAW might be assessed from the assigned headings and grid computing the derivations of current aircraft. Implicit measures have high predictive validity for the following reasons [18]: (i) they provide information about how and when the operator might react in a real-world situation where time and situation pressures are present, (ii) they account for restrictions over operator behavior resulting from training or standard procedures, and (iii) the confidence of the operator based on the reliability of information sources is taken into account.

The overall task performance is nothing but the implicit global measure of SAW. Internal tasks are used to measure the performance of sub-tasks. Some suggestions are: (i) situations where the participant can take actions that are measurable, (ii) situations in which the standard procedures mandate a particular response and support inference with relation to SAW, and (iii) in certain situations, pilots will be less confident and unable to take rapid, correct decisions based on the information sources [18].

2.4.3 SUBJECTIVE MEASURES

Based on either self-assessment or the assessment rating of an observer, the subjective measure is distinctly calculated in SAW, whereas the complete measure is based on the opinion of the observer and the participants alone. It is suggested that subjective measures can be used in both simulation and the real-world tasks [19]. The three major taxonomies are [5]: (i) comparative self-rating, (ii) direct self-rating, and (iii) observer rating. If the participants rate their own SAW, then this is classified as direct self-rating.

Direct assessment only measures trust in SAW, and it is important to note that some behaviors may depend on how people perceive themselves. For example, if the pilot does not believe that SAW is high, they can scan the instrument a second time without taking any control action [20]. The Situation Awareness Rating Technique (SAWRT) can be used for self-rating in a test for SAW [21]. This is a ten-dimensional measure encompassing familiarity, spare mental capacity, concentration, attention, viability of the situation, information quantity, complexity of suggestion, arousal of the situation, information quality, and stability. These can be grouped together in three broader dimensions, known as 3D-SAWRT: (i) demand on attention resources (consisting of complexity of the situation, variability of the situation and stability of the situation; (ii) supply of attentional resources (made up of spare mental capacity, division of attention, concentration of attention, and alertness); and (iii) understanding of the situation (a combination of information quantity, information quality, and familiarity). The level of demand has a direct influence on both the parameters of spare mental capacity and concentration of attention.

2.5 SITUATION AWARENESS AND SURVEILLANCE

SAW should encompass broad knowledge awareness in the following areas: (i) aircraft performance, (ii) environment, and (iii) the system and the crew. One of the objectives of this work is to study SAW in relation to control tasks in an environment of heavy air traffic. A surveillance task is an active interaction that pilots undertake on a regular basis to be alert to possible external obstacles and threats. These might include, but are not limited to, terrain, other aircraft, and weather conditions (leading to turbulence). The process of surveillance does not require the pilot to know all the information about the operating environment. Instead, pilots need to be acutely aware of only a few specific areas in order to perform well.

2.5.1 COMPONENTS OF SAW RELATED TO SURVEILLANCE

The main components of SAW that are needed for surveillance are (i) spatial awareness, (ii) temporal awareness, (iii) environmental awareness, and (iv) navigational awareness. The categories of knowledge that are needed for a commercial pilot to be aware of their environment include [22] windshear weather, airport conditions, other aircraft, and icing phenomena, and as regards spatial awareness, altitude, waypoints, command, navigational aids, flight path vector speed and aircraft location relative to the terrain.

2.5.2 EXAMINING THE RELEVANT COMPONENTS OF SAW

In this section we are discussing spatial awareness and navigation awareness. These are the two main concepts that define the relevant components of SAW. Situation awareness, according to one definition [10], is the perception of things in the environment. The understanding of their significance and the prediction of how they will be seen in the near future serve as the environment's physical boundaries.

2.5.3 EXAMINING SPATIAL AWARENESS

In a recent study on attention allocation [21], participants were engaged in a simulated air battle involving seven planes. One of the planes was operated by the participant using a joystick; the others were controlled by simulation tools. The identities of the aircraft (i.e., whether they were friendly, hostile, or neutral) were altered for each trial, as was the number of enemy aircraft (while keeping the overall number of aircraft constant). The identities of the aircraft were changed at random and at random time intervals. Each participant was requested to identify: (i) the geographical position of one aircraft and (ii) the identification of another aircraft, using the freeze technique. The aircraft for the test questions were picked at random; the assessment of spatial awareness was defined in terms of the Euclidian deviation of an aircraft's reported location from its actual location. It was discovered that when there were fewer neutral aircraft, the participants' spatial awareness did not increase, and it was concluded that the participants coped with increases in demand (i.e., more hostile aircraft) by sacrificing the attention paid to low-priority neutral aircraft, as opposed to sacrificing the attention paid to the higher-priority friendly aircraft. A more general conclusion was that spatial awareness was higher for aircraft that may obstruct task completion (i.e., hostile aircraft).

2.5.4 EXAMINING NAVIGATION AWARENESS

The impact of specific displays on navigation awareness was studied [22]. Participants were shown one of the following: (i) a planar inside-out display (a two-dimensional rendering of three-dimensional space with a stationary aircraft); (ii) a planar outside-in display (a two-dimensional rendering of three-dimensional space with a stationary environment), or (iii) a perspective outside-in display (a two-dimensional rendering of three-dimensional space with a stationary environment). Four different measures were used to assess navigation awareness. Two of the measures were chosen to depict tasks in which depth and distance judgments are critical: the number of predetermined waypoints participants reached and the accuracy with which participants began a course correction following a forced disorientation. The other two measures were the amount of time participants spent concurrently managing pitch and roll, and the delay between initiation and lateral control after disorientation. The results suggested that the planar outside-in displays produced the best navigation awareness when depth and distance judgment was crucial, while the perspective displays supported processing when integration was necessary.

Another study focused on the role of mental rotation and triangulation during navigation, the allocation of attentional resources during navigation, and the usefulness of different map presentations [23]. When participants were asked to refer to a map to respond to questions with a world-centered frame, rather than the forward field-of-view, reaction time increased as the aircraft's heading diverged from north. This finding implies that reference frames must be cognitively aligned in order to obtain optimal navigation awareness. Participants appeared to move from a mental rotation technique to a reversal strategy in a dual task setting (i.e., stating to oneself 'left equals right'), and the response time for course adjustments increased linearly. It was suggested that navigation and flight control compete for limited spatial processing resource; therefore, to free up some of the limited spatial processing resources, participants used an alternative strategy (in this case the reversal strategy) when available. Track-up maps resulted in shorter response times to questions regarding course changes in general. However, north-up maps resulted in the identification of more landmarks when participants were questioned on the necessary course change for a specified position that was not in their forward field-of-view. It was concluded that the designer must consider what reference frame a navigation task requires before a particular map display is chosen.

EXERCISES

1. Define situation awareness (SAW). What are the four qualitative techniques used to describe SAW?
2. How is SAW achieved through the perception–action cycle?
3. Name the three different categories for SAW measurement and the significant factors that contribute towards it.
4. What are the relevant components of SAW related to surveillance?
5. Elaborate on 3D-SAWRT for self-rating in situation awareness testing.

REFERENCES

[1] Endsley, M. R. (1995), Measurement of situation awareness in dynamic systems, *Human Factors*, 37(1), 65–84.
[2] Wickens, C. D. (1992), Workload and situation awareness: An analogy of history and implications. *Insight: The Visual Performance Technical Group Newsletter*, December, pp. 1–3.
[3] Crane, P. M. (1992), Theories of expertise as models for understanding situation awareness. In *Proceedings of the 13th Annual Symposium on Psychology in the Department of Defense*, pp. 148–152.

[4] Uhlarik, J. & Comerford, D. A. (2002), *A Review of Situation Awareness Literature Relevant to Pilot Surveillance Functions*, Office of Aerospace Medicine, Washington, DC, DOT/FAA/AM-02/3.

[5] Endsley, M. R. (1995), Toward a theory of situation awareness in dynamic systems, *Human Factors*, 37(1), 32–64.

[6] Adams, M. J., Tenney, Y. J., and Pew, R. W. (1995), Situation awareness and the cognitive management of complex systems. *Human Factors*, 37(1), 85–104.

[7] Smith, K. & Hancock, P. A. (1995), Situation awareness is adaptive, externally directed consciousness. *Human Factors*, 37(1), 137–48.

[8] Federico, P. (1995), Expert and novice recognition of similar situations. *Human Factors*, 37(1), 105–122.

[9] Wickens, C. D., Gordon, S. E., and Liu, Y. (1998), *An Introduction to Human Factors Engineering*. New York: Addison-Wesley.

[10] Fracker, M. L. (1991), *Measures of situation awareness: Review and future directions*, Armstrong Laboratory, Crew Systems Directorate, AL-TR-1991-0128.

[11] Flach, J. M. (1995), Situation awareness: Proceed with caution. *Human Factors*, 37(1), 149–157.

[12] Underwood, B. J. (1957), *Psychological Research*. Englewood Cliffs, NJ: Prentice-Hall.

[13] Sarter, N. B. & Woods, D. D. (1995), How in the world did we ever get into that mode? Mode error and awareness in supervisory control. *Human Factors*, 37(1), 5–19.

[14] Vidulich, M.A. (1992), Measuring situation awareness. In *Proceedings of the Human Factors Society 36th Annual Meeting*, Santa Monica, CA: The Human Factors and Ergonomics Society, pp. 40–41.

[15] Wickens, C. D. (1992), *Engineering Psychology and Human Performance* (2nd ed.). New York: HarperCollins.

[16] O'Donnell, R. D. & Eggemeier, F. T. (1986), Workload assessment methodology. In K. R. Boff, L. Kaufman, & J. Thomas (Eds.), *Handbook of Perception and Human Performance Vol II: Cognitive Processes and Performance* (Chapter 42). New York: Wiley & Sons, Chapter 42.

[17] Selcon, S. J. & Taylor, R. M. (1989), Evaluation of the situational awareness rating technique (SAWRT) as a tool for aircrew systems design. In *Proceedings of the AGARD AMP Symposium on Situational Awareness in Aerospace Operations*, Neuilly-sur-Seine: NATO AGARD, CP478.

[18] Pritchett Regal, D. M., Rogers, W. H., & Boucek, G. P., Jr. (1988), *Situational awareness in the commercial flight deck: Definition, measurement, and enhancement* (SAWE Technical Paper No. 881508). Warrendale, PA: Society of Automotive Engineers.

[19] Metalis, S. A. (1993), Assessment of pilot situational awareness: Measurement via simulation. In *Proceedings of the Human Factors Society 37th Annual Meeting*. Santa Monica, CA: The Human Factors and Ergonomics Society, pp. 113–117.

[20] Endsley, M. R. (1989), A methodology for the objective measurement of situation awareness. In *Situational Awareness in Aerospace Operations*, Copenhagen, Denmark: NATO–AGARD, pp. 1–9.

[21] Fracker, M. L. (1989), Attention allocation in situation awareness. In *Proceedings of the Human Factors Society 33rd Annual Meeting*, Santa Monica, CA: The Human Factors and Ergonomics Society, pp. 1396–1400.

[22] Andre, A. D., Wickens, C. D., Moorman, L., & Boschelli, M. M. (1991), Display formatting techniques for improving situation awareness in the aircraft cockpit. *The International Journal of Aviation Psychology*, 1(3), 205–218.

[23] Aretz, A. J. (1991), The design of electronic map displays. *Human Factors*, 33(1), pp. 85–101.

3 Situation Assessment

3.1 INTRODUCTION

The mental workload for all pilots, especially pilots of modern fighter aircraft used in combat, is very high. This is because the pilot has to make quick decisions under high uncertainty and high time pressure. This becomes harder when one is operating beyond visual range (BVR), in which the sensors of an aircraft must become the pilot's 'eyes and ears' [1]. Although standard sensors provide good estimates for the position and speed of an enemy aircraft, there could be a substantial loss in situation assessment. Important tactical events or situations could occur without the pilot noticing, which could change the outcome of a mission completely; this makes the introduction of an automated situation assessment system very important for future aircraft developments.

Situation assessment can be defined as the process of evaluating a situation for its suitability to support human decision-making. Experienced decision-makers and pilots would base most of their decisions and actions on situation assessment. These decision-makers select actions that previously worked well in similar situations, by extracting the most significant characteristics from the situation.

3.2 PROBLEMS WITH SITUATION ASSESSMENT

The amount of information required and to be used by pilots in modern air combat is very high. The most critical component of decision-making is situation awareness, which is gathered through continual observation of the environment. Once the pilot obtains a mental picture of the situation, their decisions are driven by associations with other recognized or perceived tactical situations. This is called situation awareness-centered (SAC) decision-making, which is a widely accepted representation of human decision-making in high tempo and important situations [1]. The sources of information/data provided to the pilot are: (i) a heads-up display, (ii) radio signals, (iii) onboard/ground-based sensors, (iv) tactical indicators, (v) flight indicators, and (vi) visual impressions (the view out of the window). The areas of immediate interest to the pilots are: (i) mission data, (ii) data link, (iii) ownership status, (iv) weapon status, and (v) maneuvering. Absorbing all of this information, analyzing the data, and making plausible and safe decisions quickly is for any pilot a formidable task.

DOI: 10.1201/9781003370413-3

Although the multisensory data fusion (MSDF) technique is well established, situation refinement (level 2 of data fusion) is generally not well understood, mainly because it is not as critical as levels 1 and 4 of data fusion. More familiarity has been established with numerical calculations than with the symbolic domain, and the increasingly complex human–environment relations are not fully understood by anyone.

3.3 UNDERSTANDING SITUATION ASSESSMENT

Situation assessment is a description of the relations between objects, or object assessments; hence to fully understand situation assessment it is important that one also understands object assessment.

3.3.1 PHILOSOPHY OF OBJECT ASSESSMENT

To interact with an event and understand what is happening, one has to associate the objects of the event with properties that should be measurable and refined in terms of identity, type, range, elevation, etc. For example, for a flying object we would need to attach properties like 'missile', velocity', and 'position' to it. In object assessment (OA), we are considering objects and their individual properties; in the object refinement (OR) process we are associating properties with the object(s) and considering the significance of the properties. OA uses rules based on geometry, kinematics, and the assumption that a certain object cannot break these rules and change its properties while remaining the same object.

3.3.2 PHILOSOPHY OF SITUATION ASSESSMENT

The concept of objects with properties alone cannot fully describe the situation. It is important to consider the relations between the properties of the objects interacting with each other; that is, instead of considering object A with the property X and object B with the property Y, it is more useful to consider the event as E: (A/X, B/Y); the world is the totality of facts, and not of things only, where facts are the application of relations to objects. This provides the ability to generally express an event or relationship between objects, without losing sight of what is happening to which object. With E: (A/X, B/Y) we can think in broad terms such as behavior and intent, instead of trying to express (only) object properties.

3.3.3 A NEUROLOGICAL EXAMPLE

As an example, one may be able to recognize that a house fly is a small object and an elephant is a big object, which is an object assessment (OA) process, but one might not be able to say whether the fly is bigger or smaller than an elephant, which would be a situation assessment (SA) process. In the latter case, one is not able to figure out in what way the words refer to the objects; the person is able to make the correct OA, but fails to make the situation assessments between the objects.

3.4   CLASSIFICATION METHODS

In order to recognize and classify various situations, a classification technique must be able to handle uncertainty and there must be an easy way of modeling the situations. Artificial neural networks (ANNs) can be used to recognize situations; these begin from a point of 'no knowledge' (or minimal a priori knowledge) and learn from training data sets which are presented to the ANN; the ANNs can thus be trained to classify the clusters. A downside is that the ANN has to be adequately trained, and a lack of (sufficient) training data is often an issue. Another approach, a forward-chaining expert system (FCES), has to be modeled by an expert and cannot update its knowledge autonomously; this system contains no more knowledge than that of its designer.

Between these two methods is the Bayesian network (BN) which can be modeled as an expert system, but also has the ability to update its beliefs. To make the system easy to use, the nodes in the BN are often discrete. An expert can easily enter estimates of the probabilities for one situation leading to another and come up with a reasonably good BN. With the use of proper training data, the performance of the BN can be enhanced. The BN also has the ability to investigate hypotheses of the future. One disadvantage of BNs is that the computational burden is heavy for large networks, and the data have to be classified first.

3.5   HYBRID TECHNIQUES

An alternative approach would be to combine different techniques, taking the most favorable properties from each technique. The Bayesian approach has many feasible features but lacks the ability to handle continuous input; if it is combined with the fuzzy logic (FL) of 'making the data members' of discrete sets, then the hybrid system should be able to handle all the demands of the situation assessor. Such a hybrid technique of using FL-based classification where input to the discrete BN network is quite promising.

3.6   PROCESS MODELS FOR SITUATION AND THREAT ASSESSMENT

Air-flight and air-defense decision-making have severe consequences for errors; they are complex operations to be accomplished by a team of highly skilled personnel and pilots. In this context, situation and threat assessment (STA) requires mental integration of data from many sources, such as MSDF; the integration requires a high level of tactical expertise, including knowledge of the types of threats, the aircraft's mission, adopted doctrines, and assessment heuristics built from previous experience [2]. This means that team members must maintain awareness of available resources, monitor audio messages, and prepare situation reports; thus such a task can be characterized as cognitively challenging under normal conditions, and possibly worse under extreme conditions.

Any such STA model is affected by human mental processing activity. In STA the main elements to be processed are [3]: (i) data from the external environment (EE),

(ii) the information provided from the MSDF process, (iii) fusion of the information from the EE and the MSDF process, (iv) explaining the presence, status and intention of the observed entity, (v) deriving a coherent and composite tactical picture of the situation, and (vi) anticipating future events in a short time horizon. A generic model derived from this would lead to high-level functional decomposition of a multilevel STA process. The main aim of this STA model is to support the human pilots to assess the situation and threat level, which is currently performed by their cognitive intelligence.

In STA, MSDF plays a very important role, and in many previous studies the human operator was regarded as an external observer, and hence was excluded from the data fusion process. The computing machine, with its phenomenal memory and processing speed, can be regarded as the most efficient means to execute the reactive tasks, whereas the human pilot with their reasoning skills is best suited for performing intentional tasks.

3.6.1   A Generic Model of STA

An STA model consists of the following modules [3]: (i) perception refinement module (PRM), (ii) threat refinement module (TRM), (iii) situation interpretation module (SIM), (iv) situation projection module (SPM), (v) monitoring module (MM), and (vi) diagnosis module (DM).

The inputs of the STA model are resource management (RM), MSDF, the human–computer interface (HCI), and external sources, which are subcategorized as: (i) organic information, which is collected, controlled, and managed by the agents under the direct control of the pilot or commanding officer (tracking information from MSDF, the data link, and the weather conditions); and (ii) non-organic information, which is collected by agents not under the direct control of the commanding officer (e.g., transient information such as intelligence reports).

The outputs of the STA model are: (i) the stabilized and ranked threat list, (ii) the results of the kill assessment process, and (iii) the feedback to the pilot concerning the tactical picture. The threat list is obtained from the threat refinement (TR) process.

Also, some a priori knowledge is required: (a) social, political, and geographical, (b) platform and weapons characteristics, (c) mission guidelines, (d) the flight path or corridor, (e) emitter characteristics, and (f) lethality.

The different functions of the modules of the STA model can be described as follows:

(a) The PRM addresses the low-level information which includes tracking data and clusters. The task is to (i) refine the data by examining the tracking data (position and velocity) received from MSDF for any incompleteness or contradictions, and establish the relationships between entities, events, and objects to form the clusters; (ii) estimate the kinematic parameters of the weapon/enemy aircraft (from RM); and (iii) perform behavior analysis on these entities to help refine the data set in order to provide the necessary cues for interpreting and understanding the tactical situation cues. The PRM consists of data refinement (position, velocity), kinematic estimation (closest point of approach, time of flight), and behavior analysis (corridor correlation, maneuver/pattern identification).

(b) The SIM obtains the second level of situation awareness. It explains the presence of the perceived entities and determines the intent of the unknown enemy trajectory paths. It has two sub-modules: (i) hypothesis generation and (ii) hypothesis validation; the resulting hypotheses are fed to the SPM.

(c) The SPM is concerned with the projection of future states, by taking outputs from the SIM and the a priori knowledge; the results go to the TRM.

(d) The MM stores hypotheses about future events and anticipates kinetic estimations, and monitors the situation to collect cues until a diagnosis is given.

(e) The DM measures the discrepancies between the expected and the perceived situations, and the diagnoses are fed back to the SIM for further interpretation and validation.

(f) The TRM assesses potential threats and produces a threat list; this consists of a threat evaluator and a threat stabilizer; more details can be found in [3].

3.6.2 A THREAT ASSESSMENT MODEL

A threat assessment model (TAM), based on some of the preceding discussions, is illustrated in Figure 3.1; it attempts to accurately incorporate the cognitive processes that are followed and practiced by experienced air-defense personnel [2]. It is presumed that the output of this TAM feeds into a decision-making process, and this model corresponds to the early stages of situation awareness involved in the perception and comprehension of situations and/or threats. The process of threat assessment proceeds as follows:

(i) *Scan and select cues.* The environment is scanned for cues, e.g., altitude and speed, that are relevant to the active template; the set of cues to be evaluated is selected from the input. The selection mechanism is inferred from the data indicating that participants were processing combinations of cues.

(ii) *Compare, adjust fit, and accommodate.* The perceived data (say, altitude 3,000 m) are compared to the expected data (say, altitude 6,000 m); if the perceived data are unexpected, then the fit of the model is reduced by the relative weight of the cue. An accommodation (an explanation or hypothesis) may be provided to reconcile the unexpected data to the template. Explanations attribute the data to another cause; hypotheses attribute the data to a plausible inferred intent of the track. Accommodations are provided in about 36% of cases where there are unexpected data.

(iii) *Compute threat rating.* The perceived data are also used to compute the current threat rating. The participants adjust the baseline threat rating up or down, depending on the degree of threat associated with the current piece of data (e.g., for an aircraft in a littoral environment, a speed of 250 knots adds 0.2 to the current threat rating; a speed of 500 knots adds 1.8 to the current threat rating). Determination of the size of the adjustment to the threat level is done with the

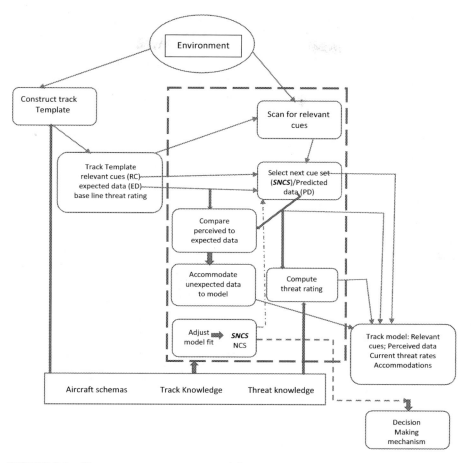

FIGURE 3.1   Threat assessment process model

Modified from: Liebhaber, M. J., and Feher, B. (2002), *Air Threat Assessment: Research,*
Model, and Display Guidelines. **Space and Naval Warfare Systems Center, San Diego, CA.**

data obtained from experienced participants. They provide information on the
degree of threat posed by specific changes to a wide range of cue values. The
threat rating is not simply the accumulation or summing of evidence; the threat
rating seems to be independent of the number of cues examined.

(iv) *Continued processing.* In keeping with empirical findings, unless unexpected
data are encountered the process/model will stop after the first six cues.
Otherwise, the model will continue reading, comparing cues, adjusting fit,
and computing the threat rating until either the fit of the model returns to
100% or there are no more cues to process. If the perceived data are within the
expected range, then the fit of the model is increased by the relative weight of
the cue; otherwise the fit is reduced, prompting assessment of further cues as
before.

(v) *Threat assessment algorithm.* A ruled-based threat assessment algorithm can be developed from the model for analyzing the relevant data and computing a threat rating for each air track. The output of the algorithm can be obtained by running the algorithm on an acquired data set. Performance of the algorithm can be compared to previous findings to determine if it rated the threat level of friendly and enemy aircraft tracks in a manner similar to the human experts.

EXERCISES

1. Why is situation assessment performed?
2. How is situation assessment carried out?
3. What are the different types of situation assessment?
4. What are the modern methods for situation analysis?
5. What is threat assessment?

REFERENCES

[1] Ivansson, J. (2002), *Situation Assessment in a Stochastic Environment Using Bayesian Networks* (Master's Thesis), Linköping University, Linköping, Sweden, LITH-ISY-EX-3267-2002.
[2] Liebhaber, M. J., & Bela, F. (2002), *Air Threat Assessment: Research, Model, and Display Guidelines* (Report), Space and Naval Warfare Systems Center, San Diego, CA.
[3] Paradis, S., Chalmers, B., Carling, R., J. Roy, J., & Bosse, E. (1997), *Towards a Generic Model for Situation and Threat Assessment* (Report DREV–R–9622), Defence Research Establishment, Valcartier, Canada.

4 Theory of Fuzzy Logic

Classically, in many decision-making processes crisp logic is used. The theory of probability is based on this logic via classical set theory. In crisp logic there are only two discrete states: Yes or No, 0 or 1, −1 or +1, and 'off' or 'on'. There is no third possibility here: a person is either in the room or is not, an event would either occur or not, a light bulb is either on or off, etc. Real-life experiences tell us that many more conditions than these two are possible: the light could be dim, the day could be bright with a certain degree of brightness, the day could be cloudy with a certain degree of darkness, and the weather could be warm, hot, too hot, cold, too cold, etc. This calls for variation in the degree of uncertainty and hence truth and falsity (1 or 0 in classical logic) are the extremes of a continuous spectrum of uncertainty. This leads to a multi-valued logic and hence to fuzzy logic (FL), a theory of sets where the characteristics/ membership function is generalized to take an infinite number of values between 0 and 1 (e.g., a triangular form) [1–4]. In fact, the theory of possibility is based on FL in a similar way as the theory of probability is based on crisp logic (via classical set theory).

FL-based methods have found good use and applications in industrial control systems, home appliances, robotics, and aerospace engineering. At the outset, the conventional control system can be regarded as a (minimally) intelligent control system, if it at least uses fuzzy logic (or some other logic) along with some learning mechanism. If, say, $y >$ some number, then use one controller or else use another one; this is a conditional logic. In fact, artificial intelligence (AI)-based systems should have strong logic capabilities and good learning/adaptive mechanisms. FL-based controllers are suited to: (i) keeping the output variable between the limits and (ii) keeping the control actuation (i.e., the control input or related variable) between the limits [2]. Thus, FL is one form of logic that can be used in the design and operation of an intelligent control. FL deals with vagueness rather than uncertainty: if a patient has a 'severe' headache, then there is a 'good chance' that they have a migraine. To avoid contradictions to the rules, some human intervention is sometimes needed at certain stages to tune various adjustable parameters in the FL system and its 'rule' base. The FL-based control is suitable when: (a) control system dynamics are slow and/or nonlinear, (b) the explicit models of the plant are not available, and (c) competent human operators who can provide expert rules are available [2].

DOI: 10.1201/9781003370413-4

Development of an FL system requires one to: (i) select fuzzy sets and their membership functions (MFs) for the fuzzification process; (ii) create a rule base, with the help of a subject expert, for input–output mapping, (iii) select fuzzy operators in fuzzy implication and aggregation processes, (iv) select a fuzzy implication method (FIM) and aggregation method, and (v) select a defuzzification method. In this chapter, we present the FL concepts, fuzzy sets and their properties, FL operators, fuzzy proposition and rule-based systems, fuzzy maps and the fuzzy inference engine, defuzzification methods, and evaluation of fuzzy implication functions [1–8].

4.1 INTERPRETATION AND UNIFICATION OF FUZZY LOGIC OPERATIONS

In this section the relationships, interconnectivities and contradistinctions between various operations/operators used in FL and fuzzy systems [2, 5, 6] are introduced using numerical simulations and examples.

4.1.1 FUZZY SETS AND MEMBERSHIP FUNCTIONS

In principle, one can say that a fuzzy set is an internal extension/expansion of a crisp set within the outer limits of the crisp set, hence the FL is richer than a crisp set/logic. A crisp set allows only full membership (1, an event occurred) or no membership at all (0, event did not occur), whereas a fuzzy set allows a partial membership of a member of a set (belonging to the set). A crisp logic/membership function is defined as:

$$\mu_A(u) = \begin{cases} 1 & if \ u \in A \\ 0 & if \ u \in A \end{cases} \tag{4.1}$$

Here, $\mu_A(u)$ is a membership function that characterizes the elements u of set A; see Figure 4.1. A fuzzy set A on a universe of discourse U with elements u is expressed as

$$A = \int \{\mu_A(u)/u\} \quad \forall \ u \in U \tag{4.2}$$

or

$$A = \sum \{\mu_A(u)/u\} \quad \forall \ u \in U \tag{4.3}$$

Here, $\mu_A(u)$ is a membership function (MF) of u on the set A and provides a mapping of universe of discourse U on the closed interval $[0,1]$. The $\mu_A(u)$ (Figure 4.2) is simply a measure of the degree to which or by which u belongs to set A, i.e., $\mu_A(u):U \to [0,1]$. The element u whose values can be considered labels of fuzzy sets is called the fuzzy variable; for example, TEMPERATURE as

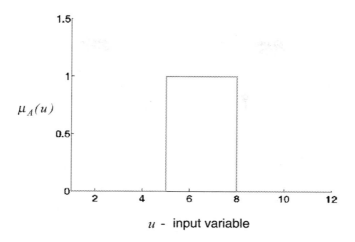

FIGURE 4.1   Membership function of a typical crisp set.

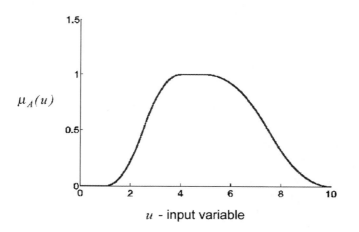

FIGURE 4.2   Membership function of a typical fuzzy set.

a fuzzy variable (or a linguistic variable) with a numerical value u can be in the range of $U = [0,100]$ °C. The fuzzy variable can take on different labels defined by linguistic values such as LOW, MEDIUM, NORMAL, and HIGH (more qualifying labels are possible, e.g., very high, etc.), with each represented by different MFs (Figure 4.3) [2].

4.1.2   EXAMPLES OF FUZZY MEMBERSHIP FUNCTIONS

There are several types of fuzzy MFs [2, 4–7], which are described below.

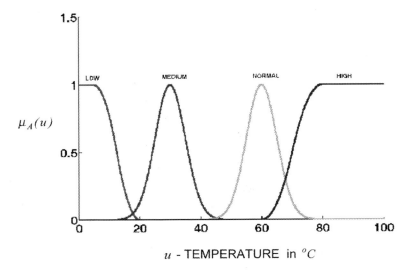

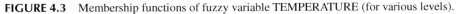

$$u \text{ - TEMPERATURE in } {}^{\circ}C$$

FIGURE 4.3   Membership functions of fuzzy variable TEMPERATURE (for various levels).

4.1.2.1   Sigmoid-shaped

Its membership function is given as

$$\mu_A(u) = \frac{1}{1 + e^{-a(u-b)}} \tag{4.4}$$

Here, u is the fuzzy variable in the universe of discourse U, and a, b are constants that shape the membership function—a sigmoid function. The sign of parameter a decides whether the sigmoid membership function will open to the right or to the left. Figure 4.4 shows the membership function for $a = 2$, $b = 4$ and $U \in [0,10]$. Interestingly, the Sigmoid nonlinearity is also used in artificial neural networks as a nonlinear activation function.

4.1.2.2   Gaussian-shaped

The corresponding membership function is given as

$$\mu_A(u) = e^{\frac{-(u-a)^2}{2b^2}} \tag{4.5}$$

Here, a,b signify the mean and standard deviation of the membership function respectively—the function is distributed about parameter a and parameter b decides the width of the function. Figure 4.5 is for $a = 5$ and $b = 2$. In FL the Gaussian curve (G-curve) is used without attaching any specific probabilistic meaning; however the shape of the function might resemble that of the Gaussian probability density function (PDF).

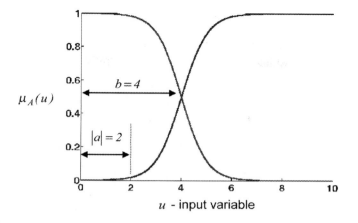

FIGURE 4.4 Sigmoid membership function (right open due to $a = 2$ and left due to a = –2).

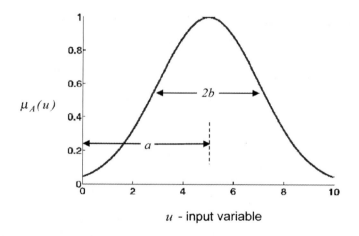

FIGURE 4.5 Gaussian membership function.

4.1.2.3 Triangular-shaped

This membership function is given as

$$\mu_A(u) = \begin{cases} 0 & for \ \ u \leq a \\ \dfrac{u-a}{b-a} & for \ \ a \leq u \leq b \\ \dfrac{c-u}{c-b} & for \ \ b \leq u \leq c \\ 0 & for \ \ u \geq c \end{cases} \tag{4.6}$$

Here, parameters a and c are the 'bases' and b signifies the 'peak' of the membership function. Figure 4.6 shows a triangular MF for $a = 3$, $b = 6$ and $c = 8$.

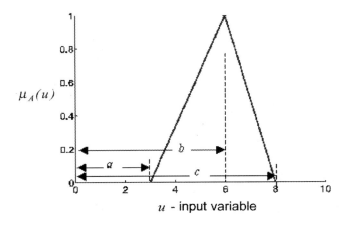

FIGURE 4.6   Triangular-shaped membership function.

4.1.2.4 Trapezoid-shaped

This function is given as

$$
\mu_A(u) = \begin{cases}
0 & for \ \ u \leq d \\
\dfrac{u-d}{e-d} & for \ \ d \leq u \leq e \\
1 & for \ \ e \leq u \leq f \\
\dfrac{g-u}{g-f} & for \ \ f \leq u \leq g \\
0 & for \ \ u \geq g
\end{cases}
\tag{4.7}
$$

Here, the parameters d and g define the 'bases' of the trapezoid and the parameters e and f define the 'shoulders'. Figure 4.7 shows a trapezoidal MF for $d = 1$, $e = 5$, $f = 7$ and $g = 8$. It is noted here that the triangular- and the trapezoid-shaped MFs are not generally differentiable in a strict sense.

4.1.2.5 S-shaped

This function is given as

$$
\mu_A(u) = S(u; a, b, c) = \begin{cases}
0 & for \ \ u \leq a \\
\dfrac{2(u-a)^2}{(c-a)^2} & for \ \ a \leq u \leq b \\
1 - \dfrac{2(u-c)^2}{(c-a)^2} & for \ \ b \leq u \leq c \\
1 & for \ \ u \geq c
\end{cases}
\tag{4.8}
$$

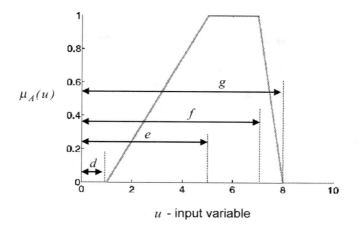

FIGURE 4.7 Trapezoidal-shaped membership function.

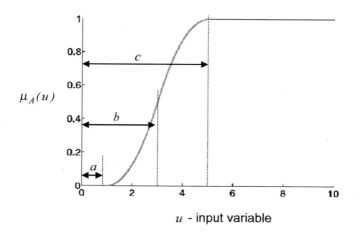

FIGURE 4.8 S-shaped membership function.

Here, the parameters a and c define the extremes of the sloped portion of the function, and b signifies the point at which $\mu_A(u) = 0.5$. Figure 4.8 shows S-shaped MF for $a = 1$, $b = 3$ and $c = 5$. This also looks like an s-curve defined in the literature using a composition of a linear function and a cosine function. In that case the z-curve is defined as a reflection of this s-curve. Interestingly the z-curve and the s-curve [5] look like the sigmoid function.

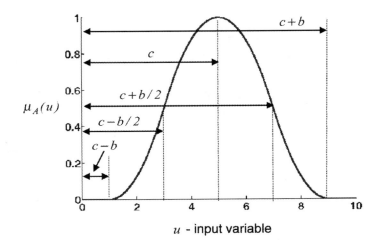

$$u \text{ - input variable}$$

FIGURE 4.9 Π-shaped membership function.

4.1.2.6 Π-shaped

This membership function is given as

$$\mu_A(u) = \begin{cases} S(u;\ c-b,\ c-b/2,\ c) & for\ u \le c \\ 1 - S(u;\ c,\ c+b/2,\ c+b) & for\ u > c \end{cases} \tag{4.9}$$

Here, the parameter c locates the 'peak', whereas parameters $c-b$ and $c+b$ locate the extremes of the curve's slopes (left and right). At $u = c - b/2$ and $u = c + b/2$ the membership grade of the function is equal to 0.5 (Figure 4.9). This curve/function can also be implemented as a combination of a z-curve and an s-curve. Although the shape looks like a bell curve/Gaussian function, normally the top part of the curve is slightly flattened out, unlike that shown in Figure 4.9.

4.1.2.7 Z-shaped

This MF is specified by

$$\mu_A(u) = \begin{cases} 1 & for\ u \le a \\ 1 - 2\dfrac{(u-a)^2}{(a-b)^2} & for\ u > a\ \&\ u \le \dfrac{a+b}{2} \\ 2\dfrac{(b-u)^2}{(a-b)^2} & for\ u > \dfrac{a+b}{2}\ \&\ u \le b \\ 0 & for\ u > b \end{cases} \tag{4.10}$$

Here, the parameters a and b define the extremes of the sloped portion of the function. Figure 4.10 is for $a = 3$ and $b = 7$.

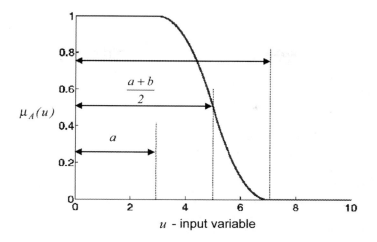

FIGURE 4.10 Z-shaped membership function.

4.1.3 Fuzzy Set Operations

The most elementary and well-known crisp set operations/operators, such as the intersection, the union, and the complement are represented by AND, OR, and NOT respectively in computer logic/Boolean logic/algebra. Let A and B be two subsets of U. The intersection of these subsets denoted by $A \cap B$ (this itself is a new resultant set) contains all the elements that are common in A and B i.e., $\mu_{A \cap B}(u) = 1$ if $u \in A$ AND $u \in B$. The union of A and B, denoted $A \cup B$, contains all elements in either A or B, i.e., $\mu_{A \cup B}(u) = 1$ if $u \in A$ **or** $u \in B$. The complement of A denoted by $\bar{A}$ contains all the elements which are not in A, i.e., $\mu_{\bar{A}}(u) = 1$ if $u \notin A$ and $\mu_{\bar{A}}(u) = 0$ if $u \in A$.

Example 4.1: Comparison of fuzzy logic operators
Like in the conventional crisp logic described above, there are FL operations defined. As an equivalent to the AND, OR, NOT operator in crisp logic, the corresponding operators in FL are the *min, max,* and *complement* [2] as given below:

$$\mu_{A \cap B}(u) = min\left[\mu_A(u), \mu_B(u)\right] \qquad \text{(intersection)} \qquad (4.11)$$

$$\mu_{A \cup B}(u) = max\left[\mu_A(u), \mu_B(u)\right] \qquad \text{(union)} \qquad (4.12)$$

$$\mu_{\bar{A}}(u) = 1 - \mu_A(u) \qquad \text{(complement)} \qquad (4.13)$$

Another way to define the AND and OR operators in FL [1] is:

$$\mu_{A \cap B}(u) = \mu_A(u)\mu_B(u) \qquad (4.14)$$

$$\mu_{A \cup B}(u) = \mu_A(u) + \mu_B(u) - \mu_A(u)\mu_B(u) \qquad (4.15)$$

Define fuzzy sets A by equation (4.5) (Gaussian MF, or GMF) and B by equation (4.7) (trapezoidal MF, or TMF). Then the fuzzy intersection (element-wise) is computed by putting $\mu_A(u)$ and $\mu_B(u)$ (values obtained with equations (4.5) and (4.7), respectively) in equation (4.11) or equation (4.14). Likewise, the fuzzy union (element-wise) is computed by using equation (4.12) or equation (4.15). Figures 4.11 and 4.12 [9] show, respectively, the results of the fuzzy intersection and union operations for both the definitions using the GMF and TMF. It is observed from Figure 4.11 that the resulting MF obtained by equation (4.14) shrinks compared to the one obtained by equation (4.11) and we see from Figure 4.12 that the resulting MF obtained by equation (4.15) expands compared to the one obtained by equation (4.12). This example illustrates the effect of using a particular definition for intersection and union, and it also indicates that any consistent definition is possible in defining basic FL operations.

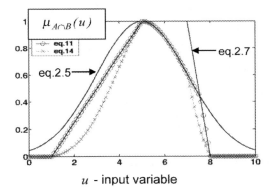

FIGURE 4.11   Fuzzy Intersection: min operations.

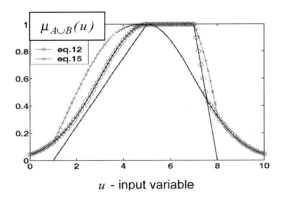

FIGURE 4.12   Fuzzy Union: max operations.

4.1.4   Fuzzy Inference System (FIS)

Define a fuzzy rule as 'IF u is A, THEN v is B'. The IF part of the rule, 'IF u is A', is called the *antecedent* or *premise*. The THEN part of the rule, 'v is B', is called the *consequent* or conclusion part. The core is a fuzzy inference engine (FIE) that, via fuzzy implication operation, defines mapping from input fuzzy sets into output fuzzy sets. It determines the degree to which the *antecedent* is satisfied for each rule. If the *antecedent* of a given rule has more than one clause (e.g., 'IF u_1 is A_1 AND u_2 is A_2, THEN v is B'), fuzzy operators (T-norm/S-norm) are applied to obtain one number that represents the result of the *antecedent* for that rule. The FIE can take different forms depending on the manner in which the inference rule is defined. It is also possible that one or more rules may fire at the same time, in which case the outputs of all rules are then *aggregated*; i.e., fuzzy sets that represent the output of each rule are combined into a single fuzzy set. An important aspect of FIE/FIS is that fuzzy rules are fired in parallel/concurrently and the order in which firing occurs does not affect the output. Figure 4.13 shows a schematic of a FIE/FIS for a multi-input/single-output system [2]. The fuzzifier/fuzzification maps input values into corresponding memberships that are essential for activating rules that are in terms of linguistic variables; i.e., the fuzzifier takes input values and determines the degree to which these numbers belong to each of the fuzzy sets via MFs. The rule base contains linguistic rules that are provided by domain/human experts. Subsequently, defuzzification converts output fuzzy sets (type-I fuzzy logic) values into crisp numbers (type-0 fuzzy logic). A comprehensive view of the FIS and the fuzzy implication process (FIP) that is studied in Section 4.2 is given in Figure 4.14 [9]. If any rule has more than one clause in the antecedent part then these clauses are combined using any one of the definitions from either the T-norm or the S-norm, and the FIP gives the fuzzified output for each fired rule. These outputs are combined using an aggregation process (by using one of the methods shown in the S-norms block).

4.1.4.1   Triangular Norm (T-norm)

In FL the corresponding operator for (Boolean logic) AND is *min* and another possibility is given by equation (4.14). The intersection of two fuzzy sets A and B is

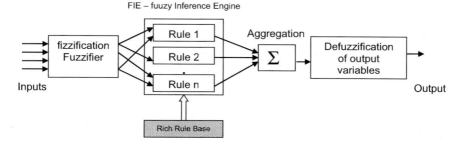

FIGURE 4.13   Overall FIS process.

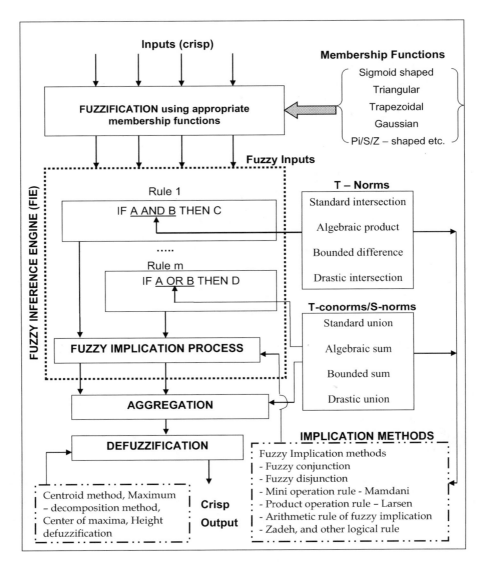

FIGURE 4.14 Comprehensive FIS and Fuzzy Implication Process.

specified by binary mapping T (T-norm) on the unit interval, i.e., a function of the form

$$T : [0,1] \times [0,1] \rightarrow [0,1]$$

or more specifically

$$\mu_{A \cap B}(u) = T(\mu_A(u), \mu_B(u)) \tag{4.17}$$

The T-norm operator is used to: (i) combine the clauses in the *antecedent* part of a given rule (e.g., 'IF u_1 is A_1 AND u_2 is A_2') and (ii) map the input fuzzy sets into output fuzzy sets. The T-norms normally used as fuzzy intersections are given by [3, 8]:

(i) Standard intersection (SI): $T_{SI}(x, y) = min(x, y)$ (4.18)

(ii) Algebraic product (AP): $T_{AP}(x, y) = x \bullet y$ (by Zadeh [1]) (4.19)

(iii) Bounded difference/product (BD): $T_{BD|BP}(x, y) = max(0, x + y - 1)$ (4.20)

(iv) Drastic intersection/product (DI): $T_{DI|DP}(x, y) = \begin{cases} x & when\ y = 1 \\ y & when\ x = 1 \\ 0 & otherwise \end{cases}$ (4.21)

Here, $x = \mu_A(u)$, $y = \mu_B(u)$ and $u \in U$. It is assumed that the fuzzy sets (A and B) are normalized and that they have membership grade values between 0 and 1. The definition of the T-norms should satisfy certain axioms [7, 8] for the entire membership grade such as x, y and z in the range [0, 1]. The fuzzy set intersections that satisfy these axiomatic skeletons are bounded by the following inequality:

$$T_{DI}(x, y) \leq T(x, y) \leq T_{SI}(x, y) \qquad (4.22)$$

The T-norm operations of (i)–(iv) and many fuzzy set operations and operators are illustrated next with some specific membership functional shapes/forms [2–8].

Example 4.2: Compute T-norms
Consider the fuzzy sets A and B defined by membership functions 'trimf' & 'trapmf' (in-built MATLAB functions), respectively, as

$$\mu_A(u) = trimf(u, [a, b, c]) \qquad (4.23)$$

$$\mu_B(u) = trapmf(u, [d, e, f, g]) \qquad (4.24)$$

In the present case, we have $a = 3$, $b = 6$, $c = 8$, $d = 1$, $e = 5$, $f = 7$ and $g = 8$. The time history of discrete input u to the fuzzy sets A and B is given as $u = 0, 1, 2, 3, 4, 5, 6, 7, 8, 9, 10$. The fuzzified values of the input u, passed through MFs $\mu_A(u) = trimf(u, [a, b, c])$ (Figure 4.15) and $\mu_B(u) = trapmf(u, [d, e, f, g])$ (Figure 4.16) are given as:

$$\begin{aligned} x = \mu_A(u) &= \{0 / 0 + 0 / 1 + 0.0 / 2 + 0.0 / 3 + 0.33 / 4 + 0.667 / 5 + 1 / 6 \\ &\quad + 0.5 / 7 + 0 / 8 + 0 / 9 + 0 / 10\} \\ y = \mu_B(u) &= \{0 / 0 + 0 / 1 + 0.25 / 2 + 0.5 / 3 + 0.75 / 4 + 1.000 / 5 + 1 / 6 \\ &\quad + 1.0 / 7 + 0 / 8 + 0 / 9 + 0 / 10\} \end{aligned}$$

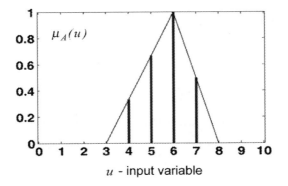

FIGURE 4.15 Triangular membership function.

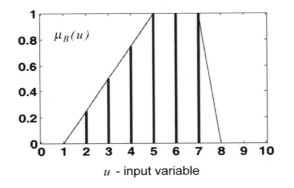

FIGURE 4.16 Trapezoidal membership function.

Compute the values of the various T-norms.

Solution 4.2
The computed values (see Figure 4.17 for a pictorial representation) for the T-norms
are as follows:

(i) Standard intersection (SI)

$T1 = T(x, y) = min(x, y)$
$= \{0 / 0 + 0 / 1 + 0 / 2 + 0 / 3 + 0.33 / 4 + 0.667 / 5$
$+ 1.0 / 6 + 0.5 / 7 + 0 / 8 + 0 / 9 + 0 / 10\}$

(ii) Algebraic product (AP)

$T2 = T(x, y) = (x \bullet y)$
$= \{0 / 0 + 0 / 1 + 0 / 2 + 0 / 3 + 0.25 / 4 + 0.667 / 5$
$+ 1.0 / 6 + 0.5 / 7 + 0 / 8 + 0 / 9 + 0 / 10\}$

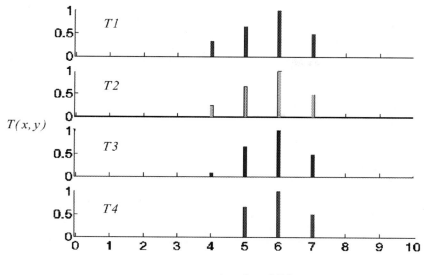

u - input variable

FIGURE 4.17   Pictorial representation of T-norms.

(iii) Bounded difference or product (BD)

$$T3 = T(x, y) = max(0, x + y - 1)$$
$$= \{0 / 0 + 0 / 1 + 0 / 2 + 0 / 3 + 0.833 / 4 + 0.667 / 5$$
$$+ 1.0 / 6 + 0.5 / 7 + 0 / 8 + 0 / 9 + 0 / 10\}$$

(iv) Drastic intersection or product (DI)

$$T(x, y) = \begin{cases} x & when \ y = 1 \\ y & when \ x = 1 \\ 0 & otherwise \end{cases}$$

$$T4 \quad = \{0 / 0 + 0 / 1 + 0 / 2 + 0 / 3 + 0 / 4 + 0.667 / 5$$
$$+ 1.0 / 6 + 0.5 / 7 + 0 / 8 + 0 / 9 + 0 / 10\}$$

The results are tabulated in Table 4.1.

4.1.4.2   Fuzzy Implication Process (FIP) Using T-norms

Before using T-norms in the fuzzy implication process (FIP) [2-4], let us understand the basics of FIP. Consider two fuzzy sets A and B that belong to the universe of discourse U and V, respectively; then the fuzzy implication is defined as

$$\text{Rule}: \text{ IF } A \text{ THEN } B = A \rightarrow B \cong AXB \quad\quad (4.25)$$

In equation (4.25), AXB is the Cartesian product (CP) of the two fuzzy sets A and B. The CP is an essential operation of all FIEs and signifies the fuzzy relationship.

TABLE 4.1
The results of four T-norms.

u	T1	T2	T3	T4
0	0	0	0	0
1	0	0	0	0
2	0	0	0	0
3	0	0	0	0
4	0.33	0.25	0.0833	0
5	0.667	0.667	0.667	0.667
6	1	1	1	1
7	0.5	0.5	0.5	0.5
8	0	0	0	0
9	0	0	0	0
10	0	0	0	0

Suppose u and v are elements in the universe of discourse of U and V, respectively, for fuzzy sets A and B, then the fuzzy relation is defined as

$$R = \{((u,v), \mu_R(u,v)) \,|\, (u,v) \in UXV\} \tag{4.26}$$

Example 4.3: Approximate equal
Assume $U = V = \{1,2,3,4,5\}$; then the fuzzy relation such that u and v are approximately equal [2, 3, 8] can be expressed as

$$\mu_R(u,v) = \begin{cases} 1 & |u-v| = 0 \\ 0.8 & |u-v| = 1 \\ 0.3 & |u-v| = 2 \\ 0 & otherwise \end{cases}$$

The convenient representation of the fuzzy relation as a sagittal diagram [2] and a relational matrix (2D membership array) are given in Figures 4.18 and 4.19, respectively. The main purpose of this example is to show that, unlike in the crisp set values, here (due to the fact that the belonging of a value to the fuzzy membership is by some degree) the approximate equals can have various grades of being equal to each other, the extreme being the exact value 1 of the MF when the values of u and v are exactly the same. As the difference between u and v increases, the value (of MF) of 'belonging to being equal' decreases. When the difference is very large this value approaches zero.

Example 4.4: Evaluation and comparison of T-norms
In order to understand FIP using different T-norm definitions, consider A and B as two discrete fuzzy sets defined as

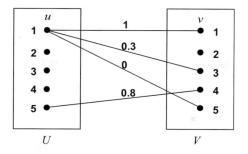

FIGURE 4.18 Sagittal diagram (with some connectivity).

$$M_R = \begin{bmatrix} 1 & 0.8 & 0.3 & 0 & 0 \\ 0.8 & 1 & 0.8 & 0.3 & 0 \\ 0.3 & 0.8 & 1 & 0.8 & 0.3 \\ 0 & 0.3 & 0.8 & 1 & 0.8 \\ 0 & 0 & 0.3 & 0.8 & 1 \end{bmatrix}$$

FIGURE 4.19 Membership matrix (all connectivity).

$$A = \{\mu_A(u) / u\} = (1 / 1 + 0.7 / 2 + 0.2 / 3 + 0.1 / 4) \qquad \forall \ u \in U \qquad (4.27)$$

$$B = \{\mu_B(v) / v\} = (0.8 / 1 + 0.6 / 2 + 0.4 / 3 + 0.2 / 4) \qquad \forall \ v \in V \qquad (4.28)$$

The CP of A and B can be obtained using fuzzy conjunction which is usually defined by triangular norms, i.e.,

$$\begin{aligned} A \rightarrow B &= AXB \\ &= \sum_{UXV} \mu_A(u) * \mu_B(u) / (u,v) \end{aligned} \qquad (4.29)$$

Here, $u \in U \ \& \ v \in V$ and * is an operator representing a triangular norm or T-norm. Compute the fuzzy conjunction using different triangular norm operators.

Solution 4.4

(i) For standard intersection (SI) we have

$$\begin{aligned} A \rightarrow B &= AXB \\ &= \sum_{UXV} (\mu_A(u) \cap \mu_B(v)) / (u,v) \\ &= \sum_{UXV} min(\mu_A(u), \mu_B(v)) / (u,v) \end{aligned} \qquad (4.30)$$

It should be noted that equation (4.30) uses the basic definition of standard intersection (equation (4.18)). Using equations (4.27) and (4.28) inequation (4.30) results in

$$A \to B = \begin{cases} min(1,0.8)/(1,1), min(1,0.6)/(1,2), min(1,0.4)/(1,3), \\ min(1,0.2)/(1,4), min(0.7,0.8)/(2,1), min(0.7,0.6)/(2,2), \\ min(0.7,0.4)/(2,3), min(0.7,0.2)/(2,4), min(0.2,0.8)/(3,1), \\ min(0.2,0.6)/(3,2), min(0.2,0.4)/(3,3), min(0.2,0,2)/(3,3), \\ min(0.1,0.8)/(4,1), min(0.1,0.6)/(4,2), min(0.1,0.4)/(4,3), \\ min(0.1,0.2)/(4,4) \end{cases}$$

$$= \begin{cases} 0.8/(1,1)+0.6/(1,2)+0.4/(1,3)+0.2/(1,4)+ \\ 0.7/(2,1)+0.6/(2,2)+0.4/(2,3)+0.2/(2,4)+ \\ 0.2/(3,1)+0.2/(3,2)+0.2/(3,3)+0.2/(3,4)+ \\ 0.1/(4,1)+0.1/(4,2)+0.1(4,3)+0.1/(4,4) \end{cases}$$

This can be conveniently represented by means of a relational matrix; Table 4.2 and Figure 4.20 [2]. It should be noted that the min-operation rule of fuzzy implication (MORFI) (Mamdani [10]) also uses the same definition as mentioned in equation (4.30).

(ii) For algebraic product (AP) we have

$$\begin{aligned} A \to B &= AXB \\ &= \sum_{UXV} (\mu_A(u) \bullet \mu_B(v))/(u,v) \end{aligned} \tag{4.31}$$

TABLE 4.2
The relational matrix R_I^T.

u / v	1	2	3	4
1	0.8	0.6	0.4	0.2
2	0.7	0.6	0.4	0.2
3	0.2	0.2	0.2	0.2
4	0.1	0.1	0.1	0.1

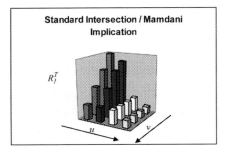

Standard Intersection / Mamdani Implication

R_I^T

FIGURE 4.20   Graphical representation of the relational matrix R_I^T.

It should be noted that equation (4.31) (for •) uses the basic definition of AP (equation (4.19)). Using equations (4.27) and (4.28) in equation (4.31) results in

$$A \to B = \begin{cases} 0.8/(1,1)+0.6/(1,2)+0.4/(1,3)+0.2/(1,4)+ \\ 0.56/(2,1)+0.42/(2,2)+0.28/(2,3)+0.14/(2,4)+ \\ 0.16/(3,1)+0.12/(3,2)+0.08/(3,3)+0.04/(3,4)+ \\ 0.08/(4,1)+0.06/(4,2)+0.04/(4,3)+0.02/(4,4) \end{cases}$$

This can be conveniently represented by means of a relational matrix; Table 4.3 and Figure 4.21 [2]. It should be noted that the product operation rule of fuzzy implication (PORFI) (Larsen [11]) also uses the same definition as mentioned in equation (4.31).

(iii) For bounded difference (BD) we have

$$A \to B = AXB$$
$$= \sum_{UXV} max(0, \mu_A(u) + \mu_B(u) - 1)/(u,v) \qquad (4.32)$$

Using equation (4.27) and equation (4.28) in equation (4.32) results in:

$$A \to B = \begin{cases} 0.8/(1,1)+0.6/(1,2)+0.4/(1,3)+0.2/(1,4)+ \\ 0.5/(2,1)+0.3/(2,2)+0.1/(2,3)+0/(2,4)+ \\ 0/(3,1)+0/(3,2)+0/(3,3)+0/(3,4)+ \\ 0/(4,1)+0/(4,2)+0/(4,3)+0/(4,4) \end{cases}$$

TABLE 4.3
The relational matrix R_2^T.

u / v	1	2	3	4
1	0.8	0.6	0.4	0.2
2	0.56	0.42	0.28	0.14
3	0.16	0.12	0.08	0.04
4	0.08	0.06	0.04	0.02

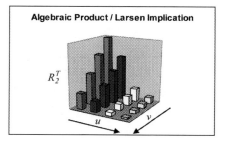

FIGURE 4.21   Graphical representation of the relational matrix R_2^T.

It should be noted that equation (4.32) uses the basic definition of BD (equation (4.20)) and can also be conveniently represented by means of a relational matrix [2]; Table 4.4 and Figure 4.22.

(iv) For drastic intersection (DI) we have

$$A \rightarrow B = AXB$$
$$= \begin{cases} \mu_A(u) / (u,v) & \text{if } \mu_B(v) = 1 \\ \mu_B(v) / (u,v) & \text{if } \mu_A(u) = 1 \\ 0 / (u,v) & \text{otherwise} \end{cases} \tag{4.33}$$

Using equations (4.27) and (4.28) in equation (4.33) results in

$$A \rightarrow B = \begin{bmatrix} 0.8 / (1,1) + 0.6 / (1,2) + 0.4 / (1,3) + 0.2 / (1,4) + \\ 0 / (2,1) + 0 / (2,2) + 0 / (2,3) + 0 / (2,4) + \\ 0 / (3,1) + 0 / (3,2) + 0 / (3,3) + 0 / (3,4) + \\ 0 / (4,1) + 0 / (4,2) + 0 / (4,3) + 0 / (4,4) \end{bmatrix}$$

TABLE 4.4
The relational matrix R_3^T.

u/v	1	2	3	4
1	0.8	0.6	0.4	0.2
2	0.5	0.3	0.1	0.0
3	0.0	0.0	0.0	0.0
4	0.0	0.0	0.0	0.0

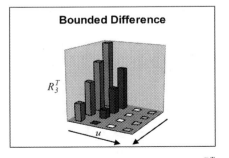

FIGURE 4.22   Graphical representation of the relational matrix R_3^T.

TABLE 4.5
The relational matrix R_4^T.

u/v	1	2	3	4
1	0.8	0.6	0.4	0.2
2	0.0	0.0	0.0	0.0
3	0.0	0.0	0.0	0.0
4	0.0	0.0	0.0	0.0

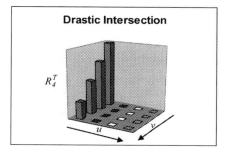

FIGURE 4.23   Graphical representation of the relational matrix R_4^T .

It should be noted that equation (4.33) uses the basic definition of DI (equation (4.21)) and can also be conveniently represented by means of a relational matrix; Table 4.5 and Figure 4.23.

4.1.4.3   Triangular Conorm (T-conorm/S-norm)

In fuzzy logic the corresponding operator for OR (of Boolean logic) is *max* (equation (4.12)). The other possible OR is defined by equation (4.15). It is called the triangular conorm (T-conorm) or S-norm and is defined as follows.

The union of two fuzzy sets A and B is specified by a binary operation on the unit interval, i.e., a function of the form

$$S : [0,1]X[0,1] \rightarrow [0,1]$$

or more specifically

$$\mu_{A \cup B}(u) = S(\mu_A(u), \mu_B(u)) \tag{4.34}$$

This fuzzy operator is used (i) to combine the clauses in the *antecedent* part of a given rule (IF u_1 is A_1 OR u_2 is A_2) (S-norm block in Figure 4.14), and (ii) in the FIP. The T-conorms used as fuzzy unions [3, 8] are:

(i)   Standard union (SU): $S_{SU}(x, y) = max(x, y)$ (4.35)

(ii) Algebraic sum (AS): $S_{AS}(x, y) = x + y - x \bullet y$ (Zadeh)   (4.36)

(iii) Bounded sum (BS): $S_{BS}(x, y) = min(1, x + y)$ (4.37)

(iv) Drastic union (DU): $S_{DU}(x, y) = \begin{cases} x & when \ y = 0 \\ y & when \ x = 0 \\ 1 & otherwise \end{cases}$ (4.38)

(v) Disjoint sum (DS): $S_{DS}(x, y) = max\left\{min(x, 1 - y), \ min(1 - x, y)\right\}$ (4.39)

Here, $x = \mu_A(u)$, $y = \mu_B(u)$, and $u \in U$. The fuzzy set unions that satisfy certain axioms are bounded by the following inequality:

$$S_{SU}(x, y) \le S(x, y) \le S_{DU}(x, y)$$ (4.40)

Example 4.5: Compute S-norms for Example 4.4

Solution 4.5
For triangular S-norms (conorms), the computed values (with pictorial representation as in Figure 4.24) are as follows:

(i) Standard union,

$S(x, y) = max(x, y)$
$S1 = \{0 / 0 + 0 / 1 + 0.25 / 2 + 0.5 / 3 + 0.75 / 4 + 1.0 / 5$
$\quad + 1.0 / 6 + 1.0 / 7 + 0 / 8 + 0 / 9 + 0 / 10\}$

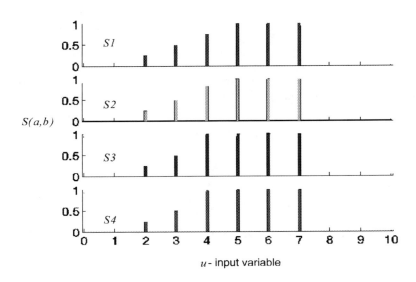

FIGURE 4.24   Pictorial representation of T-conorms or S-norm.

(ii) Algebraic sum,

$S(x, y) = x + y - x \cdot y$
$S2 = \{0 / 0 + 0 / 1 + 0.25 / 2 + 0.5 / 3 + 1.0 / 4 + 1.0 / 5$
$\quad + 1.0 / 6 + 1.0 / 7 + 0 / 8 + 0 / 9 + 0 / 10\}$

(iii) Bounded sum,

$S(x, y) = min \ (1, \ x + y)$
$S3 = \{0 / 0 + 0 / 1 + 0.25 / 2 + 0.5 / 3 + 1.0 / 4$
$\quad + 1.0 / 5 + 1.0 / 6 + 0.5 / 7 + 0 / 8 + 0 / 9 + 0 / 10\}$

(iv) Drastic union.

$$S(x, y) = \begin{cases} x & when \ y = 0 \\ y & when \ x = 0 \\ 1 & otherwise \end{cases}$$
$$S4 \quad = \{0 / 0 + 0 / 1 + 0.25 / 2 + 0.5 / 3 + 1.0 / 4 + 1.0 / 5 \\ + 1.0 / 6 + 1.0 / 7 + 0 / 8 + 0 / 9 + 0 / 10\}$$

Table 4.6 gives the results in tabular format.

4.1.4.4 Fuzzy Implication Process Using S-norm

The Cartesian product of A and B can also be obtained using fuzzy disjunction which is usually defined by a triangular conorm or S-norms:

$$A \to B = AXB$$
$$= \sum_{UXV} \mu_A(u) \dotplus \mu_B(v) / (u, v) \tag{4.41}$$

Here, $u \in U$ & $v \in V$ and $\dotplus$ is an operator representing a triangular conorm or S-norm.

TABLE 4.6
The results of four S-norms.

u	S1	S2	S3	S4
0	0	0	0	0
1	0	0	0	0
2	0.25	0.25	0.25	0.25
3	0.5	0.5	0.5	0.5
4	0.75	0.833	1	1
5	1	1	1	1
6	1	1	1	1
7	1	1	1	1
8	0	0	0	0
9	0	0	0	0
10	0	0	0	0

Example 4.6: Fuzzy disjunction
For evaluation and comparison of S-norms, consider Example 4.2 (equations (4.27)–(4.28)). Compute fuzzy disjunction using different triangular conorm operators.

Solution 4.6

(i) For **standard union** we have

$$A \rightarrow B = AXB$$
$$= \sum_{UXV} \mu_A(u) \cup \mu_B(v) / (u,v) \qquad (4.42)$$
$$= \sum_{UXV} max(\mu_A(u), \mu_B(v)) / (u,v)$$

Using equation (4.27) & equation (4.28) in equation (4.42) results in

$$A \rightarrow B = \begin{cases} max(1,0.8)/(1,1), max(1,0.6)/(1,2), max(1,0.4)/(1,3), \\ max(1,0.2)/(1,4), max(0.7,0.8)/(2,1), max(0.7,0.6)/(2,2), \\ max(0.7,0.4)/(2,3), max(0.7,0.2)/(2,4), max(0.2,0.8)/(3,1), \\ max(0.2,0.6)/(3,2), max(0.2,0.4)/(3,3), max(0.2,0.2)/(3,3), \\ max(0.1,0.8)/(4,1), max(0.1,0.6)/(4,2), max(0.1,0.4)/(4,3), \\ max(0.1,0.2)/(4,4) \end{cases}$$

$$= \begin{cases} 1/(1,1) + 1/(1,2) + 1/(1,3) + 1/(1,4) + \\ 0.8/(2,1) + 0.7/(2,2) + 0.7/(2,3) + 0.7/(2,4) + \\ 0.8/(3,1) + 0.6/(3,2) + 0.4/(3,3) + 0.2/(3,4) + \\ 0.8/(4,1) + 0.6/(4,2) + 0.4/(4,3) + 0.2/(4,4) \end{cases}$$

It should be noted that equation (4.42) uses the basic definition of standard union (equation (4.35)) and can also be conveniently represented by means of a relational matrix [2]; Table 4.7 and Figure 4.25.

ii) For **algebraic sum** we have

$$A \rightarrow B = AXB$$
$$= \sum_{UXV} (\mu_A(u) + \mu_B(v) - \mu_A(u) \bullet \mu_B(v)) / (u,v) \qquad (4.43)$$

TABLE 4.7
The relational matrix R_I^T.

u/v	1	2	3	4
1	1	1	1	1
2	0.8	0.7	0.7	0.7
3	0.8	0.6	0.4	0.2
4	0.8	0.6	0.4	0.2

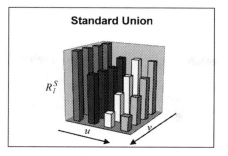

FIGURE 4.25   Graphical representation of the relational matrix R_1^S.

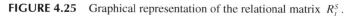

TABLE 4.8
The relational matrix R_2^S.

u / v	1	2	3	4
1	1	1	1	1
2	0.94	0.88	0.82	0.76
3	0.84	0.68	0.52	0.36
4	0.82	0.64	0.46	0.28

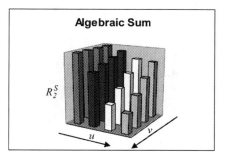

FIGURE 4.26   Graphical representation of the relational matrix R_2^S.

Using equation (4.27) and equation (4.28) in equation (4.43) results in

$$A \rightarrow B = \begin{cases} 1/(1,1)+1/(1,2)+1/(1,3)+1/(1,4)+ \\ 0.94/(2,1)+0.88/(2,2)+0.82/(2,3)+0.76/(2,4)+ \\ 0.84/(3,1)+0.68/(3,2)+0.52/(3,3)+0.36/(3,4)+ \\ 0.82/(4,1)+0.64/(4,2)+0.46/(4,3)+0.28/(4,4) \end{cases}$$

It should be noted that equation (4.43) uses the basic definition of algebraic sum (equation (4.36)) and can also be conveniently represented by means of a relational matrix; Table 4.8 and Figure 4.26.

iii) For **bounded sum** we have

$$A \rightarrow B = AXB$$
$$= \sum_{UXV} min(1, \mu_A(u) + \mu_B(v)) / (u,v) \qquad (4.44)$$

Using equation (4.27) and equation (4.28) in equation (4.44) results in

$$A \rightarrow B = \begin{cases} 1/(1,1)+1/(1,2)+1/(1,3)+1/(1,4)+ \\ 1/(2,1)+1/(2,2)+1/(2,3)+0.9/(2,4)+ \\ 1/(3,1)+0.8/(3,2)+0.6/(3,3)+0.4/(3,4)+ \\ 0.9/(4,1)+0.7/(4,2)+0.5/(4,3)+0.3/(4,4) \end{cases}$$

It should be noted that equation (4.44) uses the basic definition of bounded sum (equation (4.37)) and can also be conveniently represented by means of a relational matrix; Table 4.9 and Figure 4.27.

iv) For **drastic union** we have

$$A \rightarrow B = AXB$$
$$= \begin{cases} \mu_A(u)/(u,v) & if \ \mu_B(v) = 0 \\ \mu_B(v)/(u,v) & if \ \mu_A(u) = 0 \\ 1/(u,v) & otherwise \end{cases} \qquad (4.45)$$

TABLE 4.9
The relational matrix R_3^s.

u / v	1	2	3	4
1	1	1	1	1
2	1	1	1	0.9
3	1	0.8	0.6	0.4
4	0.9	0.7	0.5	0.3

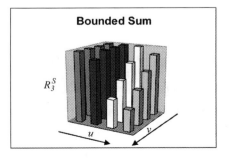

Bounded Sum

R_3^S

u v

FIGURE 4.27   Graphical representation of relational matrix R_3^s.

Using equation (4.27) and equation (4.28) in equation (4.45) results in

$$A \to B = \begin{cases} 1/(1,1)+1/(1,2)+1/(1,3)+1/(1,4)+ \\ 1/(2,1)+1/(2,2)+1/(2,3)+1/(2,4)+ \\ 1/(3,1)+1/(3,2)+1/(3,3)+1/(3,4)+ \\ 1/(4,1)+1/(4,2)+1/(4,3)+1/(4,4) \end{cases}$$

It should be noted that equation (4.45) uses the basic definition of drastic union (equation (4.38)) and can also be conveniently represented by means of a relational matrix; Table 4.10 and Figure 4.28.

(v) **Fuzzy complement.**

Consider a fuzzy set A with a membership grade of $\mu_A(u)$ for crisp input u in the universe of discourse U. The standard definition of the fuzzy complement (SFC) is given by

$$c(\mu_A(u)) = \mu_{\bar{A}}(u) = 1 - \mu_A(u) \tag{4.46}$$

TABLE 4.10
The relational matrix R_4^S.

u/v	1	2	3	4
1	1	1	1	1
2	1	1	1	1
3	1	1	1	1
4	1	1	1	1

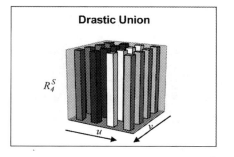

FIGURE 4.28   Graphical representation of the relational matrix R_4^S.

Like the above definition of the SFC, for any other function to be considered a fuzzy complement, it must satisfy following two axioms [3, 8]:

Axiom c1:   Boundary condition: $c(0) = 1$ & $c(1) = 0$
Axiom c2:   Monotonic nonincreasing: if $a < b$ then $c(a) \geq c(b)$

Here, $a = \mu_A(u)$ and $b = \mu_A(v)$ for some $u, v \in U$ in fuzzy set A. The above axioms are called the *axiomatic skeleton* for fuzzy complements. The other axioms, which help in creating a subclass of fuzzy complements from its general class that satisfies the above two axioms c1 and c2, are as follows:

Axiom c3: c is a continuous function
Axiom c4: c is involutive, i.e., $c(c(a)) = a$

Some possible relationships and connectivity between fuzzy logic operators and implication functions are depicted in Figure 4.29.

4.1.5   RELATIONSHIPS BETWEEN FUZZY LOGIC OPERATORS

An effort has been made to define some interconnectivity and relationships between T-norm and S-norm operators. The various relations between fuzzy logic operators (FLOR) [6] are given as follows:

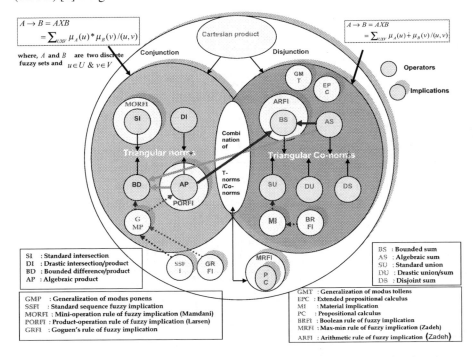

FIGURE 4.29   Depiction of interconnectivity of fuzzy operators and implication functions.

FLOR 1:

$$T_{BD}(x, y) = max(0, x + y - 1)$$

$$T_{BD}(x, y) = max(0, S_{AS}(x, y) + x \bullet y - 1) \text{, since } S_{AS}(x, y) = x + y - xy$$

$$T_{BD}(x, y) = max(0, S_{AS}(x, y) + T_{AP}(x, y) - 1), \text{ since } T_{AP}(x, y) = xy \quad (4.47)$$

FLOR 2:

$$S_{BS}(x, y) = min(1, x + y)$$

$$S_{BS}(x, y) = min(1, S_{AS}(x, y) + xy)$$

$$S_{BS}(x, y) = min(1, S_{AS}(x, y) + T_{AP}(x, y)) \quad (4.48)$$

FLOR 3:

$$T_{AP}(x, y) = x + y - S_{AS}(x, y), \text{ since } S_{AS}(x, y) = x + y - xy \quad (4.49)$$

FLOR 4:

$$T_{SI}(x, y) = x + y - S_{SU}(x, y) \quad (4.50)$$

Assume $x = 0.2$ & $y = 0.8$

$$S_{SU}(x, y) = max(x, y) = max(0.2, 0.8) = 0.8$$

$$RHS = 0.2 + 0.8 - 0.8 = 0.2$$

$$LHS = T_{SI}(x, y) = min(x, y) = min(0.2, 0.8) = 0.2$$

$$LHS = RHS$$

$$T_{SI}(x, y) = T_{AP}(x, y) + S_{AS}(x, y) - S_{SU}(x, y) \text{ (substitute FLOR 3 in FLOR 4)}$$

FLOR 5:

$$T_{BD}(x, y) = x + y - S_{BS}(x, y) \quad (4.51)$$

Figure 4.29 shows a pictorial view of these relationships and interconnectivity as well as the fuzzy operators (from Figure 4.14). The arrows originating from S-norm AS and T-norm AP and ending at T-norm BD indicate fuzzy relation FLOR 1, i.e., equation (4.47). Similarly, arrows originating from S-norm AS and T-norm AP and ending at S-norm BS indicate fuzzy relation FLOR 2, i.e., equation (4.48). It can be observed from Figure 4.29 that the fuzzy implication functions MORFI, PORFI, and ARFI (discussed in Section 4.2) utilize operators SI, AP, and BS, respectively (equations (4.18), (4.19), and (4.37)). Implication MRFI is derived from a propositional calculus (PC) implication which in turn uses operators from the T-norm and S-norm. Similarly, implication BRFI derived from material implication (MI) uses operator SU (equation (4.35)) from the S-norm. Implications SSFI and GRFI, derived from GMP, use operators BD (equation (4.20)) and AP (equation (4.19)), respectively. The foregoing observations are very important, because of the fact that normally one would expect no direct or obvious correspondence between the conjunction and disjunction definitions of a Cartesian product. Our analysis shows that these definitions are related and hence enhance the power of the inference process.

4.1.6 SUP (MAX)–STAR (T-NORM) COMPOSITION

Fuzzy operators T-norm and S-norm can also be used in rule optimization for combining two rules into one. This operation is known as the sup (max)–star (T-norm) composition. Consider fuzzy sets A, B, and C with elements u, v, and w in the universe of discourse U, V, and W respectively. Consider the following sequential fuzzy conditional rules: $R =$ IF A THEN B (rule 1); $S =$ IF B THEN C (rule 2).

Here, R and S are the fuzzy relations in UXV and VXW, respectively. It is possible to combine two rules into a single rule by absorbing the intermediate result B and finding the relationship between the antecedent and the ultimate consequent directly, i.e.,

$$RoS = \text{IF } A \text{ THEN } C \left(\text{new rule}\right)$$

The composition of R and S is a fuzzy relation denoted by RoS (where o implies *rule composition*), i.e., a fuzzy relation defined on UXW. Figure 4.30 gives a pictorial representation of fuzzy relations R and S [2]. In general, a fuzzy composition is defined as

$$RoS = \left\{\left[(u,w),\ sup_v(\mu_R(u,v)*\mu_S(v,w))\right],\ u \in U,\ v \in V,\ w \in W\right\} \quad (4.52)$$

Here, *sup* means supremum and is denoted as $\cup$ i.e., union or max (standard union), and * represents triangular norms by either (i) standard intersection, (ii) algebraic

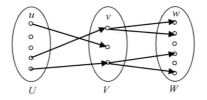

FIGURE 4.30 Sup-star composition (with some connectivity).

product, (iii) bounded difference, or (iv) drastic intersection. There are two different methods to compute the composition of fuzzy relations.

(i) **Method 1: Max–Min Composition (Mamdani)**

This is defined as:

$$\mu_{RoS}(u, w) = \max_v \min\left(\mu_R(u, v), \mu_S(v, w)\right)$$
$$= \cup_v\left(\mu_R(u, v) \cap \mu_S(v, w)\right) \qquad (4.53)$$

If fuzzy relations R and S are given by relational matrices [2] (Table 4.11, and Table 4.12) then

	0.1	0.2	0.0	1.0	(R: 1st row all columns)
	0.9	0.2	0.8	0.4	(S: 1st column all rows)
min	0.1	0.2	0.0	0.4	($\mu_R(u,v) \cap \mu_S(v,w)$)
max	0.4				($\cup_v$)

After completing the operations for all rows of R with all columns of S, RoS can be represented as in Table 4.13 (based on the relational matrices for R & S). It should be noted that in equation 4.53 (for min) the basic definition of the standard intersection (equation (4.18)) is used.

TABLE 4.11   The relational matrix R.

R	a	b	c	d
1	0.1	0.2	0.0	1.0
2	0.3	0.3	0.0	0.2
3	0.8	0.9	1.0	0.4

TABLE 4.12   The relational matrix S.

S	α	β	γ
a	0.9	0.0	0.3
b	0.2	1.0	0.8
c	0.8	0.0	0.7
d	0.4	0.2	0.3

TABLE 4.13
RoS **result (method 1).**

RoS	α	β	γ
1	0.4	0.2	0.3
2	0.3	0.3	0.3
3	0.8	0.9	0.8

TABLE 4.14
RoS **result (method 2).**

RoS	α	β	γ
1	0.4	0.2	0.3
2	0.27	0.3	0.24
3	0.8	0.9	0.72

(ii) **Method 2: Max–Product Composition (Larsen)**

This can be defined as:

$$\mu_{RoS}(u,w) = max_v \underbrace{(\mu_R(u,v) \bullet \mu_S(v,w))}_{algebric\ product} \tag{4.54}$$

Consider the same example as mentioned in Method 1. The Max–Product composition operation for the first row (all columns) of fuzzy relation R with the first column (all rows) of fuzzy relation S can be given as:

0.1	0.2	0.0	1.0	(R: 1st row all columns)
0.9	0.2	0.8	0.4	(S: 1st column all rows)
0.09	0.04	0.0	0.4	$(\mu_R(u,v) \bullet \mu_S(v,w))$
max 0.4				$(\cup_v)$

After completing the operations for all rows of R with all columns of S, *RoS* can be represented as in Table 4.14. It should be noted that in equation (4.54) (for ' $\bullet$ ') the basic definition of the algebraic product (equation (4.19)) is used.

4.1.7 INTERPRETATION OF CONNECTIVE 'AND'

Connective 'AND' is usually implemented as a fuzzy conjunction in Cartesian space.

IF (A AND B) THEN C , here the antecedent is interpreted as a fuzzy set in the product space, say, *UXV*, with the membership function given by [2]

$$\mu_{AXB}(u,v) = min\left\{\mu_A(u), \mu_B(v)\right\} \quad \text{(same as equation)} \tag{4.18}$$

or

$$\mu_{AXB}(u,v) = \mu_A(u) \bullet \mu_B(v) \quad \text{(same as equation)} \tag{4.19}$$

Here U and V are universes of discourse associated with A and B, respectively and $u \in U, v \in V$.

4.1.8 DEFUZZIFICATION

The defuzzification process is used to obtain a crisp value from/using the fuzzy outputs from the inference engine. Consider the discrete aggregated fuzzy output set B (Figure 4.31) defined as:

$$v = [0\,1\,2\,3\,4\,5\,6\,7\,8\,9\,10\,11\,12\,12.6\,13.6\,14.6\,15.6] \tag{4.55}$$

$$\mu_B(v) = [0\,0.2\,0.4\,0.4\,0.4\,0.6\,0.8\,0.8\ 0.8\,0.6\,0.6\,0.6\,0.6\,0.6\ 0.4\,0.2\,0] \tag{4.56}$$

The different ways to obtain defuzzified outputs are discussed next.

(i) **Centroid method or Center of Gravity (CoG) or Centre of Area (CoA)**

The defuzzifier determines the center of gravity (centroid) v' of fuzzy set B and uses that value as the output of the fuzzy logic system (FLS). For a continuous aggregated fuzzy set, the centroid is given by

$$v' = \frac{\int_S v\mu_B(v)dv}{\int_S \mu_B(v)dv}, \text{ where } S \text{ denotes the support of } \mu_B(v) \tag{4.57}$$

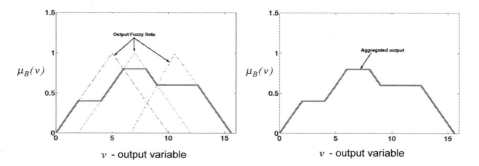

FIGURE 4.31   Output fuzzy sets (left) and aggregated (right).

In discrete fuzzy sets, the centroid can be given as

$$v' = \frac{\sum_{i=1}^{n} v(i)\mu_B(v(i))}{\sum_{i=1}^{n} \mu_B(v(i))} \tag{4.58}$$

Using the numerical values from equations (4.55) and (4.56) in equation (4.58) results in:

$$\sum_{i=1}^{n} v(i)\mu_B(v(i)) = 0*0 + 1*0.2 + 2*0.4 + 3*0.4 + 4*0.4 + 5*0.6 + 6*0.8 + 7*0.8$$
$$+ 8*0.8 + 9*0.6 + 10*0.6 + 11*0.6 + 12*0.6 + 12.6*0.6$$
$$+ 13.6*0.4 + 14.6*0.2 + 15.6*0$$
$$= 64.72$$

$$\sum_{i=1}^{n} \mu_B(v(i)) = 0 + 0.2 + 0.4 + 0.4 + 0.4 + 0.6 + 0.8 + 0.8 + 0.8 + 0.6$$
$$+ 0.6 + 0.6 + 0.6 + 0.6 + 0.4 + 0.2 + 0$$
$$= 8$$

$$v' = \frac{64.72}{8} = 8.09$$

(ii) Maximum decomposition method

In this method, the defuzzifier examines the aggregated fuzzy set and chooses the output v for which $\mu_B(v)$ is the maximum. In the example case, finding the defuzzified value for the discrete output fuzzy set B (defined by equations (4.55) and (4.56)) is not advisable due to the fact that the maximum value of $\mu_B(v) = 0.8$ (equation (4.56)) is at more than one point, i.e., at $v = 6, 7, 8$.

(iii) Center of Maxima (CoM) or Mean of Maximum (MoM)

In a multimode fuzzy region (more than one rule fires), the Center of Maxima (CoM) technique finds the highest plateau and then the next highest plateau. The midpoint between the centers of these plateaus is selected as the output of the FLS. In this case the defuzzified value for the discrete output fuzzy set B (defined by equations (4.55) and (4.56)) can be computed as follows: since the maximum value of $\mu_B(v) = 0.8$ is at $v = 6, 7, 8$, the defuzzified value computed as the Mean of Maximum (MoM) is equal to $(6+7+8)/3 = 7$.

(iv) **Smallest of Maximum (SoM)**

The Smallest of Maximum (SoM) is the smallest value of v at which the aggregated output fuzzy set has the maximum membership grade. Since the maximum value of $\mu_B(v) = 0.8$, equation (4.56), is at $v = 6, 7, 8$, the defuzzified value computed as the SoM is equal to $\min(v = 6, 7, 8) = 6$.

(v) **Largest of Maximum (LoM)**

The Largest of Maximum (LoM) is the largest value of v at which the aggregated output fuzzy set has the maximum membership grade. Since the maximum value of $\mu_B(v) = 0.8$ is at $v = 6, 7, 8$, the defuzzified value computed as the LoM is equal to $\max(v = 6, 7, 8) = 8$.

(vi) **Height defuzzification**

In this method, the defuzzifier first evaluates $\mu_{Bi}(v_i')$ at v_i' and then computes the output of the FLS given by

$$
v' = \frac{\sum_{i=1}^{m} v_i' \mu_{B_i}(v_i')}{\sum_{i=1}^{m} \mu_{B_i}(v_i')}
\tag{4.59}
$$

Here, m represents the number of output fuzzy sets B_i obtained after fuzzy implication and v_i' represents the centroid of fuzzy region i. In the example case (equations (4.55) and (4.56)), the number of output fuzzy sets is one, i.e., $m = 1$. Hence the defuzzified output after applying equation (4.59) with $m = 1$ yields same value as computed in the centroid method, i.e. equal to 8.09.

4.1.9   STEPS OF THE FUZZY INFERENCE PROCESS

Consider the ith fuzzy rule (with more than one part in the antecedent) for a multi-input/single-output system defined as

$$
R^i : \text{IF } u \text{ is } T_u^i \text{ AND } v \text{ is } T_v^i \text{ THEN } w \text{ is } T_w^i
\tag{4.60}
$$

Here u, v, and w are the fuzzy or linguistic variables, whereas T_u, T_v, and T_w are their linguistic values (LOW, HIGH, LARGE, etc.). In order to get the crisp output using the fuzzy inference system (FIS), the following steps are needed.

Step 1: Fuzzify the inputs u and v using the membership functions ($\mu^i(u)$ and $\mu^i(v)$) for the ith rule. Essentially, this means defining appropriate fuzzy MFs.

Step 2: Since the antecedent part of every rule has more than one clause, the fuzzy logic operator is used to resolve the antecedent to a single number between 0 and 1 that gives a degree of support (or firing strength) for the ith rule. The firing strength can be expressed by

$$\alpha^i = \mu^i(u) * \mu^i(v) \tag{4.61}$$

Here, * represents the triangular norm. The most popular T-norms used are SI and AP:

$$\alpha^i = min(\mu^i(u), \mu^i(v)) \ or \ a^i = \mu^i(u) \bullet \mu^i(v) \tag{4.62}$$

Step 3: Apply the implication method to shape the consequent part (the output fuzzy set) based on the antecedent. The input to the implication process is a single number (α) given by the antecedent, and the output is a fuzzy set. Commonly used methods are: (i) MORFI (Mamdani), and (ii) PORFI (Section 4.2).

$$\mu^i(w)' = min(\alpha^i, \mu^i(w)) \tag{4.63}$$

$$\mu^i(w)' = \alpha^i \bullet \mu^i(w) \tag{4.64}$$

Step 4: Since more than one rule (i.e., more than one output fuzzy set) can be fired at a time, it is essential to combine the corresponding output fuzzy sets into a single composite fuzzy set. This process of combining sets is known as *aggregation*. The inputs to the aggregation process are the outputs of the implication process and the output of the aggregation process is a single fuzzy set that represents the output variable. The order in which rules are fired does not matter to the aggregation process. The most commonly used aggregation method is the *max* (standard union) method. Suppose rule 3 and rule 4 are fired at the same time; then the composite output fuzzy set could be expressed as

$$\mu(w) = max(\mu^3(w)', \mu^4(w)') \tag{4.65}$$

It should be noted that equation (4.65) represents the final output membership curve or function.

Step 5: In order to get a crisp value of the output variable w, the defuzzification process is used. The input to this process is the output from/of the aggregation process (equation (4.65)) and the output is a single crisp number.

4.2   FUZZY IMPLICATION FUNCTIONS

Due to its approximate reasoning capability, FL can become an ideal tool for developing various applications that would require logical reasoning to model imprecisely defined events. The core of an FL-based system is an FIS in which the fuzzy 'If…Then' rules are processed using a FIM to finally obtain outputs as fuzzy sets. A FIM plays a crucial role in the successful design of the FIS/FLS. It becomes necessary to select an appropriate FIM from the existing methods. Any new implication method devised should satisfy some of the intuitive criteria of GMP/GMT (see Section 4.3) so that it can be fitted into the logical development of any system using FL.

4.2.1 Fuzzy Implication Methods (FIMs)

In any FIS, fuzzy implication provides mapping between the input and output fuzzy sets so that fuzzified inputs can be mapped to desirable output fuzzy sets. Basically, a fuzzy IF–THEN rule, provided by a domain expert, is interpreted as a fuzzy implication. Consider a simple rule such as

$$\text{IF } u \text{ is } A, \text{ THEN } v \text{ is } B \tag{4.66}$$

Here, 'IF u is A' is known as the antecedent or premise and 'THEN v is B' is a consequent part of the fuzzy rule. Crisp variable u, fuzzified by set A in universe of discourse U, is an input to the inference engine whereas crisp variable v, represented by set B in universe of discourse V, is an output from the inference engine. The fuzzified output of the inference engine, computed using sup–star composition is given by the following formula:

$$B = RoA \tag{4.67}$$

Here, 'o' is a compositional operator and 'R' is a fuzzy relation in the product space UxV. Equation (4.67) in the form of the membership function is given by

$$\mu_B(v) = \mu_R(u,v)o\mu_A(v) \tag{4.68}$$

A fuzzy implication, denoted by $\mu_{A\to B}(u,v)$, is also a type of relation that provides mapping between the input and output. Hence, equation (4.68) can be re-written as

$$\mu_B(v) = \mu_{A\to B}(u,v)o\mu_A(u) \tag{4.69}$$

There are seven standard ways/interpretations of the Fuzzy IF–THEN rule to define the fuzzy implication process [3, 8]:

(i) **Fuzzy conjunction (FC)**

$$\mu_{A\to B}(u,v) = \mu_A(u)*\mu_B(v) \tag{4.70}$$

Here, '*' represents the T-norm operator. This operator is a general symbol of the fuzzy 'AND' function or operation.

(ii) **Fuzzy disjunction (FD)**

$$\mu_{A \to B}(u,v) = \mu_A(u) \dotplus \mu_B(v) \tag{4.71}$$

Here, ' $\dotplus$ ' represents the S-norm operator. This operator is a general symbol of the fuzzy 'OR' function or operation.

(iii) **Material implication (MI)**

$$\mu_{A \to B}(u,v) = \mu_{\bar{A}}(u) \dotplus \mu_B(v) \tag{4.72}$$

Here, $\mu_{\bar{A}}(u)$ is a *Fuzzy complement* of $\mu_A(u)$. It can be observed that the S-norm operator symbol is used here.

(iv) **Propositional calculus (PC)**

$$\mu_{A \to B}(u,v) = \mu_{\bar{A}}(u) \dotplus \mu_A(u) * \mu_B(v) \tag{4.73}$$

It is noted here that PC utilizes both the operators 'AND' and 'OR', i.e., it uses the T-norm and S-norm.

(v) **Extended propositional calculus (EPC)**

$$\mu_{A \to B}(u,v) = \mu_{\bar{A}}(u) \ x \ \mu_{\bar{B}}(v) \dotplus \mu_B(v) \tag{4.74}$$

EPC utilizes the complement and S-norm.

(vi) **Generalization of modus ponens (GMP)**

$$\mu_{A \to B}(u,v) = sup\left\{c \in [0,1], \mu_A(u) * c \le \mu_B(v)\right\} \tag{4.75}$$

(vii) **Generalization of modus tollens (GMT)**

$$\mu_{A \to B}(u,v) = inf\left\{c \in [0,1], \mu_B(u) \dotplus c \le \mu_A(u)\right\} \tag{4.76}$$

By employing different combinations of T-norms and S-norms (as discussed in Section 4.1) one has access to a variety of ways to interpret the fuzzy IF–THEN rules, i.e., a number of different fuzzy implications can be derived. However, not all fuzzy implications or interpretations will necessarily satisfy fully the intuitive criteria of GMP/GMT (Section 4.3). The most commonly used specific fuzzy implications which satisfy one or more of these intuitive criteria are given below:

(i) The min-operation rule of fuzzy implication (MORFI; Mamdani) is derived by applying a standard intersection (SI) operator of T-norms in equation (4.70):

$$R_{MORFI} = \mu_{A \to B}(u,v) = \min\left(\mu_A(u), \mu_B(v)\right) \tag{4.77}$$

(ii) The product-operation rule of fuzzy implication (PORFI; Larsen) is derived by applying an algebraic product (AP) operator of T-norms in equation (4.70):

$$R_{PORFI} = \mu_{A \to B}(u,v) = \mu_A(u)\,\mu_B(v)) \tag{4.78}$$

(iii) The arithmetic rule of fuzzy implication (ARFI; Zadeh/Lukasiewicz) is derived by using a bounded sum (BS) operator of S-norms and the complement operator in equation (4.72):

$$\begin{aligned} R_{ARFI} = \mu_{A \to B}(u,v) &= \mu_{\bar{A}}(u) \dot{+} \mu_B(v) \\ &= \min\left(1, \mu_{\bar{A}}(u) + \mu_B(v)\right) \\ &= \min\left(1, 1 - \mu_A(u) + \mu_B(v)\right) \end{aligned} \tag{4.79}$$

(iv) The max-min rule of fuzzy implication (MRFI; Zadeh) is derived by using a standard intersection (SI) operator of T-norms, a standard union (SU) operator of S-norms and a fuzzy complement operator in equation (4.73):

$$\begin{aligned} R_{MRFI} = \mu_{A \to B}(u,v) &= \mu_{\bar{A}}(u) \dot{+} \mu_A(u) * \mu_B(v) \\ &= \max\left(\mu_{\bar{A}}(u), \mu_A(u) * \mu_B(v)\right) \\ &= \max\left(1 - \mu_A(u), \mu_A(u) * \mu_B(v)\right) \\ &= \max\left(1 - \mu_A(u), \min\left(\mu_A(u), \mu_B(v)\right)\right) \end{aligned} \tag{4.80}$$

(v) The standard sequence of fuzzy implication (SSFI) is derived by using a bounded difference/product (BD) operator of T-norms in equation (4.75):

$$\begin{aligned} R_{SSFI} = \mu_{A \to B}(u,v) &= \sup\left\{c \in [0,1], \mu_A(u) * c \le \mu_B(v)\right\} \\ &= \sup\left\{c \in [0,1], \max\left(0, \mu_A(u) + c - 1\right) \le \mu_B(v)\right\} \end{aligned}$$

$$= \begin{cases} 1 & \text{if } \mu_A(u) \le \mu_B(v) \\ 0 & \text{if } \mu_A(u) > \mu_B(v) \end{cases} \tag{4.81}$$

(vi) The Boolean rule of fuzzy implication (BRFI) is derived by using a standard union (SU) operator of S-norms and a fuzzy complement operator in equation (4.72):

$$R_{BRFI} = \mu_{A \to B}(u,v) = \mu_{\bar{A}}(u) \dotplus \mu_B(v)$$
$$= \max\left(\mu_{\bar{A}}(u), \mu_B(v)\right)$$
$$= \max\left(1 - \mu_A(u), \mu_B(v)\right) \qquad (4.82)$$

(vii) Goguen's rule of fuzzy implication (GRFI) is derived by using an algebraic product (AP) operator of T-norms in equation (4.75):

$$R_{GRFI} = \mu_{A \to B}(u,v) = \sup\left\{c \in [0,1], \mu_A(u)*c \le \mu_B(v)\right\}$$
$$= \sup\left\{c \in [0,1], \mu_A(u)c \le \mu_B(v)\right\}$$
$$= \begin{cases} 1 & \text{if } \mu_A(u) \le \mu_B(v) \\ \dfrac{\mu_B(v)}{\mu_A(u)} & \text{if } \mu_A(u) > \mu_B(v) \end{cases} \qquad (4.83)$$

In addition to the above-mentioned seven methods there are a few other ways to perform fuzzy implication operations that require a combination of both the T-norms and S-norms.

Example 4.7
Now consider Example 4.3 (equations (4.27) and (4.28)) to understand several methods of the fuzzy implication process.

Solution 4.7
   (4) For **ARFI** (Zadeh/Lukasiewicz implication) we have

$$A \to B = AXB$$
$$= \sum_{UXV} (1 \cap (1 - \mu_A(u) + \mu_B(v))) / (u,v) \qquad (4.84)$$
$$= \sum_{UXV} min\,(1, 1 - \mu_A(u) + \mu_B(v)) / (u,v)$$

From the equation above it is observed that equation (4.84) partially utilizes T-norm and S-norm operators. Using equation (4.27) and equation (4.28) in equation (4.84) results in:

$$A \to B = \begin{cases} 0.8 / (1,1) + 0.6 / (1,2) + 0.4 / (1,3) + 0.2 / (1,4) + \\ 1 / (2,1) + 0.9 / (2,2) + 0.7 / (2,3) + 0.5 / (2,4) + \\ 1 / (3,1) + 1 / (3,2) + 1 / (3,3) + 1 / (3,4) + \\ 1 / (4,1) + 1 / (4,2) + 1 / (4,3) + 1 / (4,4) \end{cases}$$

These results are represented as the relational matrix [2] of Table 4.15 and Figure 4.32.

TABLE 4.15
The relational matrix R_I^{TS}.

u/v	1	2	3	4
1	0.8	0.6	0.4	0.2
2	1	0.9	0.7	0.5
3	1	1	1	1
4	1	1	1	1

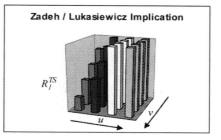

FIGURE 4.32 Graphical representation of the relational matrix R_I^{TS}.

(b) For **MRFI** (Zadeh) we have

$$A \rightarrow B = AXB$$
$$= \sum_{UXV} ((\mu_A(u) \cap \mu_B(v)) \cup (1 - \mu_A(u))) / (u,v) \tag{4.85}$$
$$= \sum_{UXV} max(min(\mu_A(u), \mu_B(v)), \mu_{\bar{A}}(u)) / (u,v)$$

Using equation (4.27) and equation (4.28) in equation (4.85) results in

$$A \rightarrow B = \begin{cases} 0.8/(1,1) + 0.6/(1,2) + 0.4/(1,3) + 0.2/(1,4) + \\ 0.7/(2,1) + 0.6/(2,2) + 0.4/(2,3) + 0.3/(2,4) + \\ 0.8/(3,1) + 0.8/(3,2) + 0.8/(3,3) + 0.8/(3,4) + \\ 0.9/(4,1) + 0.9/(4,2) + 0.9/(4,3) + 0.9/(4,4) \end{cases}$$

The relational matrix is given in Table 4.16 and depicted in Figure 4.33.

I   For **SSFI** we have

$$A \rightarrow B = AXB$$
$$= \sum_{UXV} (\mu_A(u) > \mu_B(v)) / (u,v) \tag{4.86}$$

TABLE 4.16
The relational matrix R_2^{TS}.

u/v	1	2	3	4
1	0.8	0.6	0.4	0.2
2	0.7	0.6	0.4	0.3
3	0.8	0.8	0.8	0.8
4	0.9	0.9	0.9	0.9

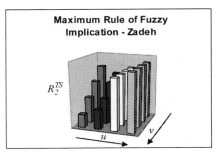

FIGURE 4.33   Graphical representation of the relational matrix R_2^{TS}.

Here,

$$\mu_A(u) > \mu_B(v) = \begin{cases} 1 & \text{if } \mu_A(u) \le \mu_B(v) \\ 0 & \text{if } \mu_A(u) > \mu_B(v) \end{cases}$$

Using equation (4.27) and equation (4.28) in equation (4.86) results in

$$A \to B = \begin{cases} 0/(1,1)+0/(1,2)+0/(1,3)+0/(1,4)+ \\ 1/(2,1)+0/(2,2)+0/(2,3)+0/(2,4)+ \\ 1/(3,1)+1/(3,2)+1/(3,3)+1/(3,4)+ \\ 1/(4,1)+1/(4,2)+1/(4,3)+1/(4,4) \end{cases}$$

This can be conveniently represented by means of a relational matrix; Table 4.17 and Figure 4.34.

(d) For **BRFI** we have

$$\begin{aligned} A \to B &= AXB \\ &= \sum\nolimits_{UXV} ((1 - \mu_A(u)) \cup \mu_B(v)) / (u,v) \\ &= \sum\nolimits_{UXV} (\mu_{\bar{A}}(u) \cup \mu_B(v)) / (u,v) \\ &= \sum\nolimits_{UXV} max(\mu_{\bar{A}}(u), \mu_B(v)) / (u,v) \end{aligned} \qquad (4.87)$$

TABLE 4.17
The relational matrix R_4^{TS}.

u/v	1	2	3	4
1	0	0	0	0
2	1	0	0	0
3	1	1	1	1
4	1	1	1	1

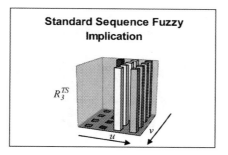

FIGURE 4.34 Graphical representation of the relational matrix R_3^{TS}.

The complement of equation (6.27) is $\mu_{\bar{A}}(u)/u = (0/1 + 0.3/2 + 0.8/3 + 0.9/4)$. Using $\mu_{\bar{A}}(u)/u$ and equation (4.28) in equation (4.87) results in the Boolean fuzzy implication as

$$A \rightarrow B = \left\{ \begin{array}{l} 0.8/(1,1) + 0.6/(1,2) + 0.4/(1,3) + 0.2/(1,4) + \\ 0.8/(2,1) + 0.6/(2,2) + 0.4/(2,3) + 0.3/(2,4) + \\ 0.8/(3,1) + 0.8/(3,2) + 0.8/(3,3) + 0.8/(3,4) + \\ 0.9/(4,1) + 0.9(4,2) + 0.9(4,3) + 0.9/(4,4) \end{array} \right\}$$

This is conveniently represented by means of a relational matrix; Table 4.18 and Figure 4.35.

(e) For **GRFI** we have

$$\begin{aligned} A \rightarrow B &= AXB \\ &= \sum_{UXV} (\mu_A(u) >> \mu_B(v))/(u,v) \end{aligned} \tag{4.88}$$

Here,

$$\mu_A(u) >> \mu_B(u) = \begin{cases} 1 & \text{if } \mu_A(u) \le \mu_B(v) \\ \dfrac{\mu_B(u)}{\mu_A(v)} & \text{if } \mu_A(u) > \mu_B(v) \end{cases}$$

TABLE 4.18
The relational matrix R_4^{TS}.

u/v	1	2	3	4
1	0.8	0.6	0.4	0.2
2	0.8	0.6	0.4	0.3
3	0.8	0.8	0.8	0.8
4	0.9	0.9	0.9	0.9

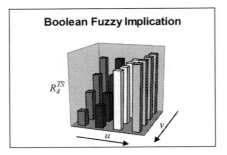

FIGURE 4.35   Graphical representation of the relational matrix R_4^{TS}.

TABLE 4.19
The relational matrix R_5^{TS}.

u/v	1	2	3	4
1	0.8	0.6	0.4	0.2
2	1	0.85	0.57	0.28
3	1	1	1	1
4	1	1	1	1

Using equation (4.27) and equation (4.28) in equation (4.88) results in

$$A \rightarrow B = \begin{cases} 0.8 / (1,1) + 0.6 / (1,2) + 0.4 / (1,3) + 0.2 / (1,4) + \\ 1 / (2,1) + 0.85 / (2,2) + 0.57 / (2,3) + 0.28 / (2,4) + \\ 1 / (3,1) + 1 / (3,2) + 1 / (3,3) + 1 / (3,4) + \\ 1 / (4,1) + 1 / (4,2) + 1 / (4,3) + 1 / (4,4) \end{cases}$$

This is represented by means of a relational matrix; Table 4.19 and Figure 4.36.

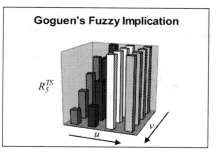

FIGURE 4.36 Graphical representation of the relational matrix R_5^{TS}.

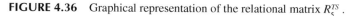

4.2.2 Evaluation Example of the Various FIMs with Numerical Data

Here, we evaluate several FIMs using some numerical data using MATLAB.

Example 4.8
Compute the norms of various fuzzy implication functions of the previous sections and compare the results.

Solution 4.8
In order to compare various fuzzy implication methods, norms of the relational matrices are computed using MATLAB. Table 4.20 shows the norm values of R_1^T, R_2^T, R_3^T, R_4^T, R_2^S, R_3^S, R_4^S, R_1^{TS}, R_2^{TS}, R_3^{TS}, R_4^{TS}, and R_5^{TS} relational matrices for the same example with equations (4.27) and (4.28). It is observed from the column under $\lVert R^T \rVert$ that the standard intersection is relatively stronger than the results of other T-norms. Similarly, drastic union (under column $\lVert R^S \rVert$) is relatively stronger than the other S-norms. It is also observed that the norms under the column $\lVert R^S \rVert$ are relatively strong as compared to the norms under column $\lVert R^T \rVert$. Most of the norms under column $\lVert R^{TS} \rVert$ fall between the norms under columns $\lVert R^T \rVert$ and $\lVert R^S \rVert$ because the implication methods under it partially utilize the T-norm and S-norm operators.

Mamdani's and Larsen's implication rules have found extensive application in practical control engineering due to their computational simplicity [2].

4.2.3 Properties and Interpretation of Fuzzy If–Then Rules

GMP and GMT (Section 4.3) are two ideal inference rules in our day-to-day reasoning or thought processes. To compute the consequences of GMT (so that they can be compared with the consequences of GMP), when the FIMs are applied in the fuzzy inference process, the following formula is used:

$$B' = RoA' \tag{4.89}$$

Here, ' o ' is known as the compositional operator represented using sup–star, with 'sup' as the supremum and 'star' as the T-norm operator. In the present case the

TABLE 4.20
Norms of several relational matrices.

Implication methods	$\|R^T\|$	Implication methods	$\|R^S\|$	Implication methods	$\|R^{TS}\|$
Standard intersection (Mamdani implication)	1.555	Standard union	2.869	Arithmetic rule of fuzzy implication (Zadeh/ Lukasiewicz implication)	3.391
Algebraic product (Larsen implication)	1.359	Algebraic sum	3.109	Maximum rule of fuzzy implication (Zadeh)	2.807
Bounded difference	1.236	Bounded sum	3.370	Standard sequence of fuzzy implication	2.877
Drastic intersection	1.095	Drastic union	4.000	Boolean rule of fuzzy implication	2.828
				Goguen's rule of fuzzy implication	3.310

Note: $\|\ \ \|$ indicates norm of relational matrix.

standard union or 'max' operator for 'sup' and the standard intersection or 'min' operator for 'star' have been used. In terms of the MF equation (4.89) is given by

$$\mu_{B'}(v) = \sup_{u \in U} \left\{ \mu_{A \to B}(u, v) * \mu_{A'}(u) \right\}$$

or

$$y = \mu_{B'}(v) = \sup_{u \in U} \left\{ \min \left[\mu_{A \to B}(u, v), \mu_{A'}(u) \right] \right\} \qquad (4.90)$$

Here, $\mu_{A \to B}(u, v)$ is the FIM and $x = \mu_{A'}(u)$ is the premise 1 of GMP (Table 4.21) containing any one of the following:

$$\mu_{A'}(u) = \mu_A(u), \ \mu_{A'}(u) = \mu^2_A(u), \ \mu_{A'}(u) = \sqrt{\mu_A(u)}, \ \mu_{A'}(u) = 1 - \mu_A(u).$$

Similarly, to compute the consequences in GMT when the FIMs are applied in the fuzzy inference process, the following formula is used:

$$A' = PoB' \qquad (4.91)$$

In terms of MF, equation (4.91) is given by

TABLE 4.21
GMP intuitive criteria: a forward-chain inference rule.

MP Criteria	u is A′ (premise 1)	v is B′ (consequence)
C1	u is A	v is B
C2-1	u is very A	v is very B
C2-2	u is very A	v is B
C3-1	u is more or less A	v is more or less B
C3-2	u is more or less A	v is B
C4-1	u is not A	v is unknown
C4-2	u is not A	v is not B

TABLE 4.22
GMT intuitive criteria: a backward-chain inference rule.

GMT Criteria	v is B′ (premise 1)	u is A′ (consequence)
C5	v is not B	u is not A
C6	v is not very B	u is not very A
C7	v is not more or less B	u is not more or less A
C8-1	v is B	u is unknown
C8-2	v is B	u is A

$$\mu_{A'}(u) = \sup_{v \in V} \left\{ \min \left[\mu_{A \to B}(u, v), \mu_{B'}(v) \right] \right\} \qquad (4.92)$$

Here, $\mu_{B'}(v)$ is the premise 1 of GMT (Table 4.22) containing any one of the following:
$\mu_{B'}(v) = 1 - \mu_B(v)$, $\mu_{B'}(v) = 1 - \mu^2_B(v)$, $\mu_{B'}(v) = 1 - \sqrt{\mu_B(v)}$, $\mu_{B'}(v) = \mu_B(v)$.

4.3 FORWARD- AND BACKWARD-CHAIN LOGIC CRITERIA

The intuitive criteria of GMP and GMT of forward and reverse logic are described in this section. These are two important rules that can be also used in FL for approximate reasoning or inference [2, 8].

(4) **Generalized Modus Ponens (GMP)**
This is a forward-driven inference rule defined by the following modus operandi [8]:

Premise 1: u is A′
Premise 2: IF u is A THEN v is B
Consequence: v is B′

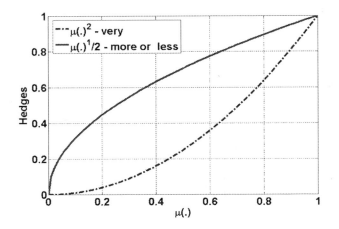

FIGURE 4.37   Variables: hedges 'very' and 'more or less'.

Here, A' and A are input fuzzy sets, B' and B are output fuzzy sets, and u and v are the variables corresponding to the input and output fuzzy sets, respectively. The fuzzy set A' of premise 1 can have the values A, *very* A, *more or less* A, and *not* A. The linguistic values 'very' and 'more or less' are hedges and are defined in terms of their membership grade as $\mu(.)^2$ and $\mu(.)^{\frac{1}{2}}$, respectively. Here (.) denotes fuzzy sets A or B. Figure 4.37 shows the profiles of these hedges. The criteria of GMP, relating premise 1 and the consequence for any given premise 2, are given in Table 4.21 [8]. There are seven criteria under GMP and each can be related to our everyday reasoning. If a fundamental relation between 'u is A' and 'v is B' is not strong in premise 2 then the satisfaction of criteria C2-2 and C3-2 is allowed.

(ii) **Generalized Modus Tollens (GMT)**

It is a backward-goal-driven inference rule is defined by following procedure [8]:

Premise 1: v is B'
Premise 2: IF u is A THEN v is B
Consequence: u is A'

The values that fuzzy set B' of premise 1 could have are: *not* B, not *very* B, not *more or less* B, and B. The linguistic values 'not very' and 'not more or less' are known as hedges and are defined in terms of their membership grade as $1 - \mu(.)^2$ and $1 - \mu(.)^{\frac{1}{2}}$, respectively. Figure 4.38 shows the profiles. The criteria of GMT, relating premise 1 and the consequence for any given premise 2, are given in Table 4.22 [8].

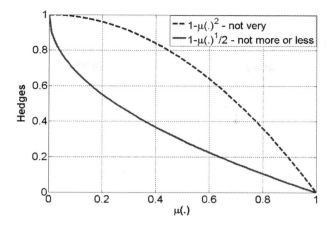

FIGURE 4.38 Variables: hedges 'not very' and 'not more or less'.

4.4 A TOOL FOR THE EVALUATION OF FUZZY IMPLICATION FUNCTIONS

A methodology to determine if any of the existing FIMs satisfies a given set of intuitive criteria of GMP and GMT is described. MATLAB® code and graphics have been used to develop a user-interactive package for evaluating the implication methods with respect to these criteria [5, 7]. Run the MATLAB codes provided in the supplemental information for this chapter on the book's website (http://routledge.com/9781032440934; .m files ForwardlogicFIMgmp and BackwardlogicFIMgmt). In this section only the main procedural steps are given and are illustrated for only one fuzzy implication method: MORFI. The details of evaluation of all seven FIMs against the criteria of GMP and GMT using this tool are given in [5, 7]. This tool helps to visualize the results analytically and numerically as well as using plots. Table 4.23 provides a summary of the menu panels for the toolbox (based on Figures 3, 4, and 5 of [5]). The first menu panel (column 1 of Table 4.23) helps the user to select a particular FIM for evaluation. The next two columns help to select premise 1 of GMP and premise 1 of the GMT criteria, respectively, to be applied to the chosen FIM. The procedural steps to establish whether or not the GMP/GMT criteria have been satisfied using MATLAB/Graphics are described next [5, 7].

(4) First generate 2D plots of the selected implication method. Let the fuzzy input set A and the output set B have the following membership grades:

$$\mu_A(u) = \begin{bmatrix} 0 & 0.05 & 0.1 & 0.15 & ,..., & 1 \end{bmatrix} \qquad (4.93)$$

$$\mu_B(v) = \begin{bmatrix} 0 & 0.05 & 0.1 & 0.15 & ,..., & 1 \end{bmatrix} \qquad (4.94)$$

TABLE 4.23
Menu panels summary for a selection of FIMs, premise 1 of GMP and premise 1 of GMT criteria.

MENU Selection of FIM	MENU Select premise 1 of GMP criteria	MENU Select premise 1 of GMT criteria
MORFI	C1: x is A	C5: y is not B
PORFI	C2-1/C2-2: x is very A	C6: y is not very B
ARFI	C3-1/C-2:x is more or less A	C7: y is not more or less B
MRFI	C4-1/C4-2: x is not A	C8-1/C8-2: y is B
BRFI	Exit	Eexit
GRFI	Exit	Exit

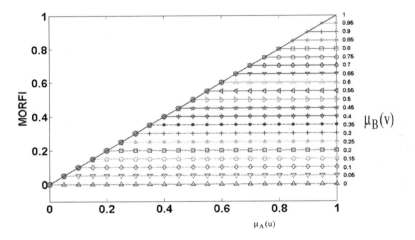

FIGURE 4.39   2D plot for MORFI.

The plots are generated by taking one value of equation (4.94) at a time for the entire $\mu_A(u)$ of equation (4.93) and applying these to the selected implication method of equations (4.77)–(4.83). In the plot's x-axis is $\mu_A(u)$ and in the y-axis is $\mu_{A \to B}(u,v)$ for each value of $\mu_B(v)$. Figure 4.39 shows the 2D plot of FIM MORFI. The coding with symbols indicates the values of the FIM method computed by varying fuzzy set μ_B between 0 and 1 (with a fixed interval of 0.05). It is important to realize that there could be infinite values possible if the interval of μ_B is reduced to a very small value. In the procedural steps 2–3 GMP and GMT criteria are applied to this FIM and the consequences are realized visually and studied analytically.

(ii) One by one, premise 1 of all GMP criteria (C1 to C4-2) are applied to the chosen FIM. This is illustrated here only for FIM MORFI.

MORFI: C1 [5, 7]. Here, $\mu_{A'}(u) = \mu_A(u)$ is applied to the right-hand side of equation (4.90) to obtain the consequence $\mu_{B'}(v)$. We start with an attempt to interpret the 'min' operation of equation (4.90) by considering Figure 4.39, the 2D view of the FIM $\mu_{A\to B}(u,v)$, and premise 1 $\mu_{A'}(u)$, Table 4.21. Figures 4.40 and 4.41 (for only one value of $\mu_B(v)$) show this particular superimposition. It can be observed that $\mu_{A'}(u)$ is always larger than or equal to $\mu_{A\to B}(u,v)$ for any value of $\mu_A(u)$. This means that the outcome of the 'min' operation is $\mu_{A\to B}(u,v)$, Figure 4.39. Also, from Figures 4.40 and 4.41, we see that $\mu_{A\to B}(u,v) = \min(\mu_A(u),\ \mu_B(v))$ converges to $\mu_B(v)$ (also the max. value of $\mu_{A\to B}(u,v)$) for $\mu_A(u) \geq \mu_B(v)$. Hence, the supremum of $\mu_{A\to B}(u,v)$ is $\mu_B(v)$, i.e., $\mu_{B'}(v) = \mu_B(v)$. *Thus, it is inferred that MORFI satisfies the intuitive criteria C1 of GmP.* This is also proved by an analytical method as follows:

$$
\begin{aligned}
\mu_{B'}(v) &= \sup_{u\in U}\left\{\min\left[\min\left\{\mu_A(u),\mu_B(v)\right\},\mu_A(u)\right]\right\}\\
&= \sup_{u\in U}\begin{Bmatrix} y1 = \min\left\{\mu_A(u),\mu_A(u)\right\};\ \text{for } \mu_A(u)\leq\mu_B(v)\\ y2 = \min\left\{\mu_B(v),\mu_A(u)\right\};\ \text{for } \mu_A(u) > \mu_B(v) \end{Bmatrix}\\
&= \sup_{u\in U}\begin{Bmatrix} y1 = \mu_A(u);\ \text{for } \mu_A(u)\leq\mu_B(v)\\ y2 = \mu_B(v);\ \text{for } \mu_A(u) > \mu_B(v) \end{Bmatrix}
\end{aligned}
\tag{4.95}
$$

The outcome of the 'min' operation between $\mu_{A\to B}(u,v)$ and $\mu_{A'}(u)$ consists of y1 and y2. The outcome starts with y1 which increases to a maximum value of $\mu_B(v)$ with an increase in $\mu_A(u)$ from zero to $\mu_B(v)$ and y2 starts from

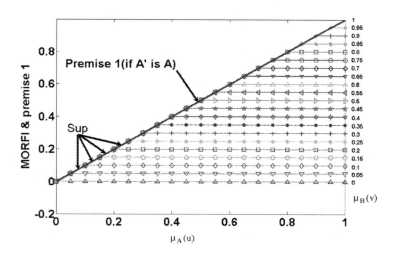

FIGURE 4.40 Superimposition of MORFI and premise 1 of C1.

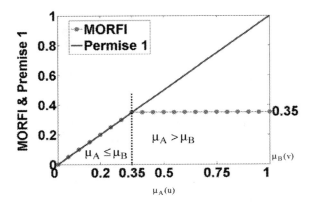

FIGURE 4.41   MORFI and premise 1 of C1 for $\mu_B = 0.35$.

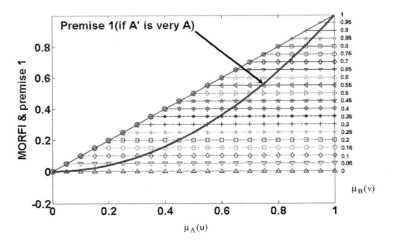

FIGURE 4.42   Superimposition of MORFI and premise 1 of C2-1/C2-2.

the maximum value of y1 and remains constant on that value in spite of any further increase in $\mu_A(u)$. Hence, it is observed that the supremum is y2 only, i.e., $\mu_{B'}(v) = \mu_B(v)$.

MORFI: C2-1/C2-2 [5, 7]. Here, $\mu_{A'}(u) = \mu^2_A(u)$ is applied to the right-hand side of equation (4.90) to obtain the consequence $\mu_{B'}(v)$. Figures 4.42 and 4.43 illustrate the superimposition of $\mu_{A \rightarrow B}(u,v)$ and $\mu_{A'}(u)$. The area below the intersection point of $\mu_{A \rightarrow B}(u,v)$ and $\mu_{A'}(u)$ corresponds to the 'min' operation of equation (4.90) and the supremum of the resultant area is those intersection points having values equal to $\mu_B(v)$. *Hence, it is inferred that*

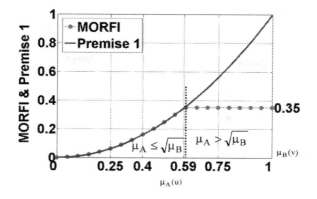

FIGURE 4.43 MORFI and premise 1 of C2-1/C2-2 for $\mu_B = 0.35$.

MORFI satisfies the intuitive criteria C2-2 (not C2-1) of GMP. The analytical process is as follows:

$$\mu_{B'}(v) = \sup_{u \in U} \left\{ \min \left[\min \{\mu_A(u), \mu_B(v)\}, \mu_A^2(u) \right] \right\}$$

$$= \sup_{u \in U} \left\{ \begin{array}{l} y1 = \min\{\mu_A(u), \mu_A^2(u)\}; \text{ for } \mu_A(u) \le \mu_B(v) \\ y2 = \min\{\mu_B(v), \mu_A^2(u)\}; \text{ for } \mu_A(u) > \mu_B(v) \end{array} \right\}$$

$$= \sup_{u \in U} \left\{ \begin{array}{l} y1 = \mu_A^2(u); \text{ since } \mu_A^2(u) \le \mu_A(u); \text{ for } \mu_A(u) \le \mu_B(v) \\ \left\{ \begin{array}{l} y21 = \mu_A^2(u); \text{ for } \mu_A(u) \le \sqrt{\mu_B(v)} \\ y22 = \mu_B(v); \text{ for } \mu_A(u) > \sqrt{\mu_B(v)} \end{array} \right\}; \text{ for } \mu_A(u) > \mu_B(v) \end{array} \right\}$$

$$(4.96)$$

The outcome of the 'min' operation between $\mu_{A \to B}(u,v)$ and $\mu_{A'}(u)$ consists of y1, y21, and y22. Since $\sqrt{\mu_B(v)} > \mu_B(v)$, y1 and y21 can be treated as one having value $\mu_A^2(u)$ for the value of $\mu_A(u) \le \sqrt{\mu_B(v)}$, and the outcome starts with y1/y21 which increases to a maximum value of $\mu_B(v)$ with an increase in $\mu_A(u)$ from zero to $\sqrt{\mu_B(v)}$. The y22 starts from the maximum value of y1/y21 and remains constant on that value irrespective of any further increase in $\mu_A(u)$. Thus, it is observed that the supremum is y22 only, i.e., $\mu_{B'}(v) = \mu_B(v)$.

(iii) Again, one by one, premise 1 of all the GMT criteria, i.e., C5 to C8-2, are applied to the FIM. The relational matrix of the FIM should be transposed; Figure 4.44. The x-axis now represents fuzzy set $\mu_B(v)$ (in the case of GMP it is $\mu_A(u)$) and the y-axis represents implication $\mu_{A \to B}(u,v)$ computed for each value of fuzzy set $\mu_A(u)$. Transposition of $_R$ is needed due to the fact that the inference rule of GMT is backward-goal driven.

MORFI: C8-1/8-2 [5, 7]. Here, $\mu_{B'}(v) = \mu_B(v)$ is applied to the right-hand side of equation (4.92) to obtain the consequence $\mu_{A'}(u)$. It can be seen from Figure

4.45 that $\mu_{B'}(v)$ is always larger than or equal to $\mu_{A \to B}(u,v)$ for any value of $\mu_B(v)$. This means that the outcome of the 'min' operation is $\mu_{A \to B}(u,v)$ itself; Figure 4.44. It is also seen that $\mu_{A \to B}(u,v) = \min(\mu_A(u), \mu_B(v))$ converges to $\mu_A(u)$ (also the max. value of $\mu_{A \to B}(u,v)$) for $\mu_B(v) \geq \mu_A(u)$. Hence, the supremum of $\mu_{A \to B}(u,v)$ is $\mu_A(u)$, i.e., $\mu_{A'}(u) = \mu_A(u)$. *Hence, MORFI satisfies the intuitive criteria C8-2 (not C8-1) of GMT.* The analytical proof is given next:

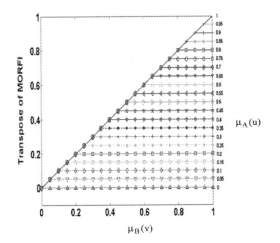

FIGURE 4.44   2D plot of MORFI-transpose.

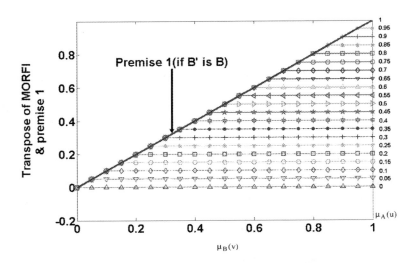

FIGURE 4.45   Superimposition of MORFI and premise 1 of C8-1/ C8-2.

$$\mu_{A'}(u) = \sup_{v \in V} \left\{ \min\left[\min\left(\mu_A(u), \mu_B(v)\right), \mu_B(v)\right]\right\}$$

$$= \sup_{v \in V} \left\{ \begin{array}{l} y1 = \min\left[\mu_B(v), \mu_B(v)\right] = \mu_B(v); \;\; \text{for } \mu_B(v) \le \mu_A(u) \\ y2 = \min\left[\mu_A(u), \mu_B(v)\right] = \mu_A(u); \;\; \text{for } \mu_B(v) > \mu_A(u) \end{array} \right\} \quad (4.97)$$

The outcome of the 'min' operation between $\mu_{A \to B}(u,v)$ and $\mu_{B'}(v)$ (for some fixed value of $\mu_A(u)$) consists of y1 having value $\mu_B(v)$ when $\mu_B(v) \le \mu_A(u)$, which increases up to a value of $\mu_A(u)$, then y2 is equal to that fixed value of $\mu_A(u)$ when $\mu_B(v) > \mu_A(u)$. It can be concluded that the supremum of y1 and y2 will be curve $\mu_A(u)$, i.e., $\mu_{A'}(u) = \mu_A(u)$.

4.5 DEVELOPMENT OF NEW IMPLICATION FUNCTIONS: ILLUSTRATIVE EXAMPLES

The various fuzzy implication functions/methods (Section 4.2) use fuzzy logic operators such as T-norms and/or S-norms. Hence, there are very possibly more such implication methods that can be obtained through various unexplored combinations of the fuzzy operators in equations (4.70)–(4.76). Based on this theory an effort was made in [7] to derive a few new fuzzy implication methods using material implication, propositional calculus, and fuzzy operators. Following the derivations, the consequences of these new FIMs were tested with those of the GMP and GMT criteria using the MATLAB/Graphics-based tool presented in Section 4.4. It is unknown whether these new FIMs will satisfy all the GMP/GMT criteria; however the approach described in Section 4.4 and here makes it feasible to arrive at a new FIM which could be useful in certain applications of FL, such as in the analysis and design of control/AI systems. The tool is flexible and hence new avenues can be explored based on the intuitive experiences of the user/designer and their particular requirements for the control design/AI processes. Note that it is only claimed here that the tool and the derivation of the new FIMs could be a good option in the search for new FIMs, and does not guarantee that any new FIM would be superior to existing ones. Hence, the results of this section should not be considered as final but as an indication of the direction in which to seek new FIM goals. Based on the existing FIM and the MATLAB/Graphics tool for the evaluation of the FIM, the new implication methods (proposed after graphical visualization and study of associated analytical derivations) are given below:

- The PCBSAP (PC-bounded sum algebraic product) rule of fuzzy implication is derived by applying the 'algebraic product' operator of T-norms and the 'bounded sum' operator of S-norms in equation (4.73):

$$\begin{aligned} R_{PCBSAP} = \mu_{A \to B}(u,v) &= \mu_{\bar{A}}(u) \dotplus \mu_A(u) * \mu_B(v) \\ &= \min(1, \mu_{\bar{A}}(u) + \mu_A(u)\mu_B(v)) \\ &= \min(1, 1 - \mu_A(u) + \mu_A(u)\mu_B(v)) \end{aligned} \quad (4.98)$$

- The PCSUAP (PC-standard union and algebraic product) rule of fuzzy implication is derived by applying the 'algebraic product' operator of T-norms and the 'standard union' operator of S-norms in equation (4.73):

$$
\begin{aligned}
R_{PCSUAP} = \mu_{A \rightarrow B}(u,v) &= \mu_{\bar{A}}(u) \dotplus \mu_A(u) * \mu_B(v) \\
&= \max(\mu_{\bar{A}}(u), \mu_A(u)\,\mu_B(v)) \\
&= \max(1 - \mu_A(u), \mu_A(u)\,\mu_B(v))
\end{aligned}
\tag{4.99}
$$

- The PCBSSI (PC-bounded sum and standard intersection) rule of fuzzy implication is derived by applying the 'standard intersection' operator of T-norms and the 'bounded sum' operator of S-norms in equation (4.73).

$$
\begin{aligned}
R_{PCBSSI} = \mu_{A \rightarrow B}(u,v) &= \mu_{\bar{A}}(u) \dotplus \mu_A(u) * \mu_B(v) \\
&= \mu_{\bar{A}}(u) \dotplus \min(\mu_A(u), \mu_B(v)) \\
&= \min(1, 1 - \mu_A(u) + \min(\mu_A(u), \mu_B(v)))
\end{aligned}
\tag{4.100}
$$

- The PCBSBP (PC-bounded sun and bounded product) rule of fuzzy implication is derived by applying the 'bounded product' operator of T-norms and the 'bounded sum' operator of S-norms in equation (4.73):

$$
\begin{aligned}
R_{PCBSBP} = \mu_{A \rightarrow B}(u,v) &= \mu_{\bar{A}}(u) \dotplus \mu_A(u) * \mu_B(v) \\
&= \min(1, \mu_{\bar{A}}(u) + \max(0, \mu_A(u) + \mu_B(v) - 1)) \\
&= \min(1, 1 - \mu_A(u) + \max(0, \mu_A(u) + \mu_B(v) - 1))
\end{aligned}
\tag{4.100a}
$$

- The PCSUBP (PC-standard union and bounded product) rule of fuzzy implication is derived by applying the 'bounded product' operator of T-norms and the 'standard union' operator of S-norms in equation (4.73):

$$
\begin{aligned}
R_{PCSUBP} = \mu_{A \rightarrow B}(u,v) &= \mu_{\bar{A}}(u) \dotplus \mu_A(u) * \mu_B(v) \\
&= \max(\mu_{\bar{A}}(u), \max(0, \mu_A(u) + \mu_B(v) - 1)) \\
&= \max(1 - \mu_A(u), \max(0, \mu_A(u) + \mu_B(v) - 1))
\end{aligned}
\tag{4.101}
$$

- The PCASBP (PC-algebraic sum and bounded product) rule of fuzzy implication is derived by applying the 'bounded product' operator of T-norms and the 'algebraic sum' operator of S-norms in equation (4.73):

$$
\begin{aligned}
R_{PCASBP} = \mu_{A \rightarrow B}(u,v) &= \mu_{\bar{A}}(u) \dotplus \mu_A(u) * \mu_B(v) \\
&= 1 - \mu_A(u) + \max(0, \mu_A(u) + \mu_B(v) - 1) \\
&\quad - (1 - \mu_A(u)) \max(0, \mu_A(u) + \mu_B(v) - 1)
\end{aligned}
\tag{4.102}
$$

- The PCASAP (PC-algebraic sum and algebraic product) rule of Fuzzy implication is derived by applying the 'algebraic product' operator of T-norms and the 'algebraic sum' operator of S-norms in equation (4.73):

$$
\begin{aligned}
R_{PCASAP} = \mu_{A \to B}(u,v) &= \mu_{\bar{A}}(u) \dotplus \mu_A(u) * \mu_B(v) \\
&= 1 - \mu_A(u) + \mu_A(u)\mu_B(v) - (1 - \mu_A(u))\mu_A(u)\mu_B(v) \\
&= 1 - \mu_A(u) + \mu_A(u)\mu_B(v) - \mu_A(u)\mu_B(v) + \mu^2{}_A(u)\mu_B(v) \\
&= 1 - \mu_A(u)(1 - \mu_A(u)\mu_B(v))
\end{aligned}
\tag{4.103}
$$

- The PCASSI (PC-algebraic sum and standard intersection) rule of fuzzy implication is derived by applying the 'standard intersection' operator of T-norms and the 'algebraic sum' operator of S-norms in equation (4.73).

$$
\begin{aligned}
R_{PCASAP} = \mu_{A \to B}(u,v) &= \mu_{\bar{A}}(u) \dotplus \mu_A(u) * \mu_B(v) \\
&= 1 - \mu_A(u) + \min(\mu_A(u), \mu_B(v)) \\
&= 1 - \mu_A(u) + \min(\mu_A(u), \mu_B(v)) - (1 - \mu_A(u))\min(\mu_A(u), \mu_B(v)) \\
&= 1 - \mu_A(u) + \min(\mu_A(u), \mu_B(v)) - \min(\mu_A(u), \mu_B(v)) + \mu_A(u)\min(\mu_A(u), \mu_B(v)) \\
&= 1 - \mu_A(u)(1 - \min(\mu_A(u), \mu_B(v)))
\end{aligned}
$$

$$\tag{4.104}$$

- The MIAS (MI-algebraic sum) rule of fuzzy implication is derived by applying the 'algebraic sum' operator of S-norms in equation (4.72):

$$
\begin{aligned}
R_{MIAS} = \mu_{A \to B}(u,v) &= \mu_{\bar{A}}(u) \dotplus \mu_B(v) \\
&= 1 - \mu_A(u) + \mu_B(v) - (1 - \mu_A(u))\mu_B(v) \\
&= 1 - \mu_A(u) + \mu_B(v) - \mu_B(v) + \mu_A(u)\mu_B(v) \\
&= 1 - \mu_A(u)(1 - \mu_B(v))
\end{aligned}
\tag{4.105}
$$

The procedural steps used to generate 2D plots of the new implication methods are the same as those discussed in Section 4.4. Some minor modifications are made to the existing MATLAB/Graphics tool by adding new cases to existing cases and writing the mathematical equations pertaining any of the new implication methods in order to realize these implication methods and perform their 'satisfaction' studies by checking them against the intuitive criteria of GMP and GMT. At this juncture it is important to mention that the various FIMs discussed in this section and in Section 4.4 might not be applicable to all types of applications and it is up to any domain expert to select the most appropriate method for a particular application. The user can cut down the effort involved by first considering those FIMs which satisfy the maximum number of intuitive criteria of GMP and GMT. For the purpose of illustration only, one new FIM (from the list above) is considered and the discussion is centered on the criteria that are satisfied by this selected FIM (not all of the new FIMs satisfy all the criteria and the discussions related to this aspect are not repeated in the present book). However, the complete details can be found in [7]. The purpose here is to illustrate how a new

FIM can be evolved and evaluated using the same MATLAB/Graphics tool as done in Section 4.4. Whether the new FIM is useful or not is a separate question. However, applications of some of the new FIMs have been validated and are presented in a later section.

4.5.1 STUDY OF THE SATISFACTION OF CRITERIA BY NEW IMPLICATION FUNCTION USING THE MATLAB/GRAPHICS TOOL

Let us begin with the implication method PCBSAP. A 2D plot of this is shown in Figure 4.46. The details of the graphical and analytical developments in respect of certain new FIMs that do not satisfy certain GMP/GMT criteria are not presented here, except the one below to show the procedure.

PCBSAP: C1. $\mu_{A'}(u) = \mu_A(u)$ is applied to the right-hand side of equation (4.90) to get the consequence $\mu_{B'}(v)$. Figures 4.47 and 4.48 illustrate the superimposed plots of $\mu_{A \to B}(u,v)$ and $\mu_{A'}(u)$. It is observed that the area below the intersection point of $\mu_{A \to B}(u,v)$ and $\mu_{A'}(u)$ corresponds to the 'min' operation of equation (4.90). It is also observed that the supremum of the resultant area is nothing but those intersection points having values equal to $\dfrac{1}{2 - \mu_B(v)}$. Therefore, it is concluded that PCBSAP does not satisfy the intuitive criteria C1 of GMP. Further analysis is given next:

$$
\begin{aligned}
\mu_{B'}(v) &= \sup_{u \in U} \left\{ \min \left[\min \left\{ 1,\ 1 - \mu_A(u) + \mu_A(u)\,\mu_B(v) \right\},\ \mu_A(u) \right] \right\} \\
&= \sup_{u \in U} \left\{ \min \left[1 - \mu_A(u) + \mu_A(u)\,\mu_B(v),\ \mu_A(u) \right] \right\} \\
&= \sup_{u \in U} \left\{ \begin{array}{l} y1 = \mu_A(u);\ \text{for } \mu_A(u) \le \mu^{\min}{}_A(u) \\ y2 = 1 - \mu_A(u) + \mu_A(u)\,\mu_B(v);\ \text{for } \mu_A(u) > \mu^{\min}{}_A(u) \end{array} \right\}
\end{aligned}
\tag{4.106}
$$

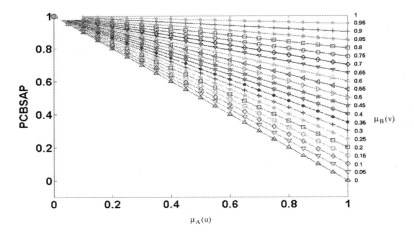

FIGURE 4.46   2D plots of PCBSAP.

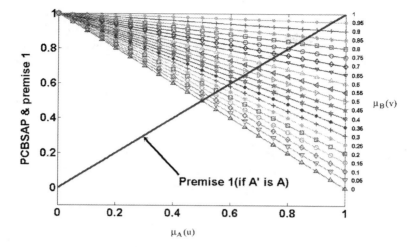

FIGURE 4.47   Superimposed plots of PCBSAP and premise 1 of C1.

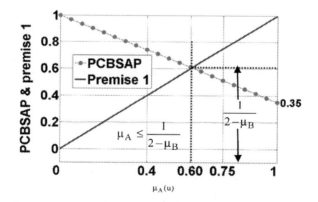

FIGURE 4.48   PCBSAP and premise 1 of C1 for $\mu_B = 0.35$.

Here, $\mu^{min}_A(u) = \dfrac{1}{2 - \mu_B(v)}$ is obtained by solving $1 - \mu_A(u) + \mu_A(u)\,\mu_B(v) = \mu_A(u)$. It is observed from equation (4.106) that the outcome of the 'min' operation between $\mu_{A \to B}(u,v)$ and $\mu_{A'}(u)$ is either $1 - \mu_A(u) + \mu_A(u)\,\mu_B(v)$ or $\mu_{A'}(u)$. Also, it is observed from the nature of the equations that $\mu_{A'}(u)$ increases with an increase in $\mu_A(u)$, whereas $1 - \mu_A(u) + \mu_A(u)\,\mu_B(v)$ decreases, and hence the supremum of the 'min' operation is the point of intersection of $y1$ and $y2$, i.e.,

$$1 - \mu_A(u) + \mu_A(u)\,\mu_B(v) = \mu_A(u) \text{ or } \mu_{B'}(v) = \frac{1}{2 - \mu_B(v)} \ .$$

PCBSAP: C4-1/C4-2. $\mu_{A'}(u)=1-\mu_A(u)$ is applied to the right-hand side of equation (4.90) to get the consequence $\mu_{B'}(v)$. It is observed from Figure 4.49 that $\mu_{A \to B}(u,v)$ is always greater than or equal to $\mu_{A'}(u)$, thus the outcome of the 'min' operation is always $\mu_{A'}(u)$, i.e., $1-\mu_A(u)$ for any value of $\mu_B(v)$. Since the supremum of $1-\mu_A(u)$ is always unity, $\mu_{B'}(v)=1$. Therefore, PCBSAP satisfies C4-1 (not C4-2) criteria of GMP. The analytical process is given below:

$$
\begin{aligned}
\mu_{B'}(v) &= \sup_{u \in U} \left\{ \min \left[\min \left\{ 1, 1-\mu_A(u)+\mu_A(u)\mu_B(v) \right\}, 1-\mu_A(u) \right] \right\} \\
&= \sup_{u \in U} \left\{ \min \left[1-\mu_A(u)+\mu_A(u)\mu_B(v), 1-\mu_A(u) \right] \right\} \qquad (4.107) \\
&= \sup_{u \in U} \left. \begin{cases} y1 = 1-\mu_A(u); \text{ for } \mu_A(u)\mu_B(v) \geq 0 \\ y2 = 1-\mu_A(u)+\mu_A(u)\mu_B(v); \text{ for } \mu_A(u)\mu_B(v) < 0 \end{cases} \right\}
\end{aligned}
$$

It is observed from equation (4.107) that y2 does not exist due to the non-valid condition $\mu_A(u)\mu_B(v)<0$; therefore consequence $\mu_{B'}(v)$ would be the supremum of y1 and will come out to be unity only.

PCBSAP: C8-1/C8-2. $\mu_{B'}(v) = \mu_B(v)$ is applied to the right-hand side of equation (4.22) to get the consequence $\mu_{A'}(u)$. Figure 4.50 illustrates the superimposed plots of $\mu_{A \to B}(u,v)$ and $\mu_{B'}(v)$. It is observed from the figure that $\mu_{B'}(v)$ is always equal to or less than implication $\mu_{A \to B}(u,v)$ for any value of $\mu_A(u)$; therefore the outcome of the 'min' operation results in $\mu_{B'}(v)$ itself. Hence, the supremum of $\mu_{B'}(v)$ comes out to be unity only (since the maximum value of $\mu_{B'}(v) = \mu_B(v)$ is unity). Therefore, it is concluded that PCBSAP satisfies the intuitive criteria C8-1 (not C8-2) of GMT. The analytical process is given below:

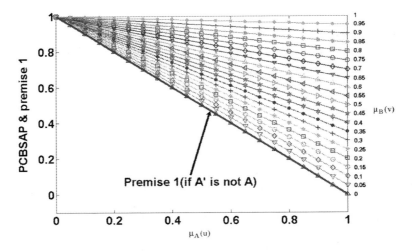

FIGURE 4.49   Superimposed plots of PCBSAP and premise 1 of C4-1/C4-2.

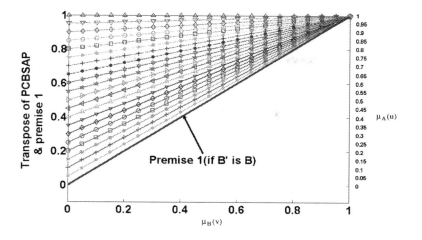

FIGURE 4.50   Superimposed plots of PCBSAP and premise 1 of C8-1/C8-2.

$$\mu_{A'}(u) = \sup_{v \in V} \left\{ \min \left[\min \left(1, \, 1 - \mu_A(u) + \mu_A(u) \, \mu_B(v) \right), \, \mu_B(v) \right] \right\}$$

$$= \sup_{v \in V} \left\{ \min \left[1 - \mu_A(u) + \mu_A(u) \, \mu_B(v), \, \mu_B(v) \right] \right\} \qquad (4.108)$$

$$= \sup_{v \in V} \left\{ \begin{array}{l} y1 = 1 - \mu_A(u) + \mu_A(u) \, \mu_B(v); \; \text{for } \mu_B(v) > 1 \\ y2 = \mu_B(v); \quad \text{for } \mu_B(v) \leq 1 \end{array} \right\}$$

It is observed that y1 is not valid as $\mu_A(u) > 1$ is not possible. Hence, the outcome of the 'min' operation between $\mu_{A \to B}(u,v)$ and $\mu_{B'}(v)$ is always $\mu_B(v)$, thus $\mu_{A'}(u) = 1$.

From the foregoing MATLAB-based experiment, we infer that implication methods such as PCBSAP, PCBSSI, PCBSBP, and MIAS satisfy exactly the same intuitive criteria of GMP and GMT with the 'satisfaction' number being two criteria. Other methods satisfy only one intuitive criterion of GMP and GMT. The logical explanation of these observations can be found in [7]. The use of some existing and some new FIMs in decision-making processes is described in a later chapter.

4.6   FUZZY LOGIC ALGORITHMS AND FINAL COMPOSITION OPERATIONS

A fuzzy logic-based system can model any continuous function or system. The quality of approximation depends on the quality of the rules that are developed by an expert. Fuzzy engineering is a function approximation with fuzzy systems, and it rests on the mathematics of function approximation (FA) and statistical learning theory (SLT). The basic unit of a fuzzy algorithm is the 'If–Then' rule: "IF the water in the washing machine is dirty, THEN add more detergent powder." Thus, a fuzzy system is a set of 'IF–THEN' rules that map input sets such as "dirty water" to output sets such

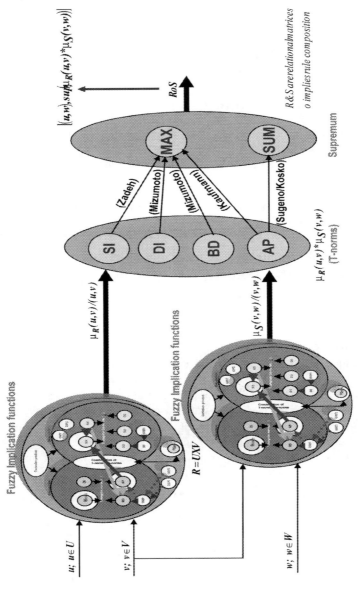

FIGURE 4.51 Fuzzy implication functions—aggregation process.

as "more detergent powder'. Overlapping rules are used to define polynomials and richer functions. A set of possible rules would be [2, 4]:

Rule 1: IF the air is cold THEN set the air conditioning motor speed to stop
Rule 2: IF the air is cool THEN set the motor speed to slow
Rule 3: IF the air is just right THEN set the motor speed to medium
Rule 4: IF the air is warm THEN set the motor speed to fast
Rule 5: IF the air is hot THEN set the motor speed to blast

This set gives the first-cut fuzzy system and more rules can be devised and added by experts or new rules can be learned adaptively from training data sets obtained from the system. Articifial neural networks (ANNs) can be used to learn the rules from the data. Fuzzy engineering mainly deals with (firstly) defining these rules, and then tuning them and adding new rules or pruning old rules. In an additive fuzzy system, each input partially fires all rules in parallel, and the system acts as an associative processor as it computes the output $F(x)$. The FL system then combines the partially fired 'then' part fuzzy sets in a sum and converts this sum to a scalar or vector output. Thus, a match-and-sum fuzzy approximation can be viewed as a generalized AI expert system or as a (neural-like) fuzzy associative memory. The additive fuzzy systems belong to the proven universal approximators for rules that use fuzzy sets of any shape and are computationally simple.

Values of the fuzzy variable can be considered labels of fuzzy sets: temperature à fuzzy variable à linguistic values such as low, medium, normal, high, very high, etc. This leads to membership values on the universe of discourse. The dependence of a linguistic variable on another variable is described by means of a fuzzy conditional statement: R: If S1 (is true), then S2 (is true) Or S1àS2; more specifically (1) IF the load is small THEN torque is very high, and (2) IF the error is negative-large, THEN output is −ve large. A composite conditional statement in an FA would be like R1: IF S1 THEN (IF S2 THEN S3) is equivalent to R1: IF S1 THEN R2 AND R2: IF S2 THEN S3. FA is formed by combining two or three fuzzy conditional statements: IF speed error is negative large THEN (IF change in speed error is NOT (negative large Or negative medium) THEN change in fuel is positive large), ... , Or, ... , Or, ... , etc.

The composite picture of the fuzzy implication functions/operators and the aggregation process is depicted in Figure 4.51. The composition operation can be realized using various combinations of T-norm and supremum operators. Composition operation using max-SI or max-AP combination is easy to implement as compared to the other possible combinations. The accuracy of the final result will mostly depend on composition operations/FIMs. Hence, there could be the possibility of having better compositional outputs by logically selecting the different fuzzy implication functions and combining them with appropriate T-norm and supremum operators. This requires further study.

EXERCISES

4.1 Why are a domain expert's knowledge and experience needed to build FL-based systems?

4.2 Why is FL particularly suitable for decision-making and in decision support systems (DSSs)?

4.3 Why is defuzzification required in an FLS?

4.4 What is the type of the inner FL system and the output fuzzy logic system?

4.5 How can the FLS be used for system identification/estimation?

4.6 Why, in Table 4.20, does the norm of the relational matrices decrease from the standard intersection to drastic intersection, while the norm increases from standard union to drastic union?

4.7 What are the most common forms of fuzzy MFs?

4.8 What are two methods of obtaining the fuzzy rules (rule base)?

4.9 What are the features of these two methods (Exercise 4.8)?

REFERENCES

[1] Zadeh, L. A. (1965), Fuzzy sets, *Information and Control Journal*, 8, 338–353.

[2] King, R. E. (1999), *Computational Intelligence in Control Engineering*, New York, USA: Marcel Dekker, Inc.

[3] Passino, K. M. and Yurkovich, S. (1998), *Fuzzy Control*, Menlo Park, CA: Addison-Wesley Longman.

[4] Kosko, B. (1997), *Fuzzy Engineering*, Upper Saddle River, NJ: Prentice Hall.

[5] Kashyap, S. K, Raol, J. R., and Patel, A. V. (2008), Evaluation of fuzzy implications and intuitive criteria of GMP and GMT. In *Foundations of Generic Optimization Volume 2: Applications of Fuzzy Control, Genetic Algorithms and Neural Networks* (Mathematical Modelling: Theory and Applications), R. Lowen and A. Verschoren (Eds.), New York: Springer, pp. 313–385.

[6] Kashyap, S. K. and Raol, J. R. (2007), Interpretation and Unification of Fuzzy Set Operations and Implications, *Journal of System Society of India*, 16(1), pp. 26–33.

[7] Kashyap, S. K. (2008), *Decision Fusion Using Fuzzy Logic*. Doctoral Thesis, University of Mysore, Mysore, India.

[8] Li-Xin, W. (1994), *Adaptive Fuzzy Systems and Control, Design and Stability Analysis*, Englewood Cliffs, NJ: Prentice-Hall.

[9] Raol, J. R. and Singh, J. (2009), *Flight Mechanics Modeling and Analysis*, Boca Raton, FL: CRC Press.

[10] Mamdani, E. H. and Assilian, S. (1975), An experiment in linguistic synthesis with a fuzzy logic controller, *International Journal of Man-Machine Studies*, 7(1), pp. 1–13.

[11] Larsen, P. M. (1980), Industrial applications of fuzzy logic control, *International Journal of Man-Machine Studies*, 12(1), pp. 3–10.

5 Fuzzy Logic-based Decision Fusion and Fuzzy Filtering

5.1 INTRODUCTION

The objective of decision fusion is to take a final course of decision/action in the entire surveillance volume at any instant of time using outputs from different levels, e.g. Level 1-object refinement and Level 2-situation refinement, of an MSDF system. The accuracy of outputs from decision fusion depends not only on the architectures/ algorithms involved in it but also on the different fusion levels. Hence, it becomes a necessity to explore the MSDF system first and then follow by decision fusion philosophy. MSDF is the process of combining measured information originating from different sources, e.g. active or passive sensors, to produce the most specific and comprehensive unified data or model about an entity or event of interest. This technique achieves improved prediction-accuracy and more specific inferences than could be achieved by the use of a single sensor alone. Various applications of MSDF are i) target tracking, ii) automated target recognition, iii) guidance for autonomous vehicles, iv) remote sensing, v) battlefield surveillance and vi) automatic threat recognition systems, etc. The techniques employed in MSDF are drawn from diverse disciplines: digital signal processing, statistical estimation and control theory and classical numerical methods. In principle, the fusion of data from multiple sources provides significant advantages over single source data. In addition to the statistical advantage gained by combining same-source data, the use of multiple types of sensors may increase the accuracy with which a quantity can be observed and characterized. The benefits of fusion are: i) Robust operational performance, ii) Extended spatial coverage, iii) Extended Temporal coverage, iv) Increased confidence, v) Reduced ambiguity, vi) Improved detection, and vii) Enhanced spatial resolution.

For example, if an aircraft is observed by pulsed radar and an infrared imaging sensor, the radar provides the ability to accurately determine the aircraft's range, but has a limited ability to determine the angular direction of the aircraft. The infrared imaging sensor can accurately determine the aircraft's angular direction, but is unable to measure range. If these two observations are correctly associated, then the fusion of the two sensors' data provides an improved determination of range and direction that which could be obtained by either of the two independent sensors. Also, based on the observation of an object's attributes, the identity of the object may be determined.

MSDF primarily involves: a) hierarchical transformation between observed parameters to estimate the location, characteristics and identity of an entity. For instance, in a target tracking application, observations of angular direction, range and range-rate may be converted to estimate the target's position and velocity. This could be achieved by using sequential estimation techniques like the Kalman filter (KF) for linear models, the Extended Kalman filter (EKF) and the Derivative Free Kalman Filter (DFKF) for non-linear models; and b) Interpretation of the observed entity in the context of a surrounding environment and relationships to other entities. For instance, the observations of target's attributes, such as radar cross-sections, infrared spectra and visual images may be used to classify the target and assign a label for its identity. Pattern recognition techniques based on clustering algorithms and neural networks, etc. are used for this purpose. Finally, understanding the motion of the target may help one in determining the intent of the target, which requires automated reasoning using implicit and explicit information, via knowledge-based methods.

Raw data from the sensors may be directly combined if the sensors are measuring the same physical phenomenon such as target range or target direction. In the case of dissimilar sensors, e.g. infra-red and acoustic, feature/state vector fusion may be employed to combine data which are non-commensurate. While attempting to build an MSDF system, certain aspects pertaining to the actual application are of fundamental importance: i) optimal techniques or algorithms, ii) architectures, iii) accuracy that can be realistically achieved by a data fusion process, iv) optimization of the fusion process in a dynamic sense, v) the data collection environment, and v) conditions under which data fusion provides improved performance

5.2   MULTISENSORY DATA FUSION LEVELS

There are various ways to model the levels of data fusion for the development of an efficient MSDF system. The most popular and established data fusion model is of the Joint Directors of Laboratories (JDL) Data Fusion working group. The JDL process model [1] is a functionally oriented model of data fusion and is intended to be very general and useful across multiple application areas. The output of the Data Fusion Process (DFP) is a minimally ambiguous identification and characterization of individual entities, as well as higher-level interpretation of those entities in the context of the application environment. The JDL-DFP model is a conceptual model that identifies the processes, functions, categories of techniques and specific techniques applicable to data fusion. This model is a two-level hierarchy, i.e. top level as shown in Figure 5.1 and detailed in Figure 5.2. DFP is conceptualized by sources of information, human computer interaction, source preprocessing, data fusion levels (Levels 1 to 4) and finally a data management system.

a) Sources of Information: The sources of information include: i) local sensors associated with the data fusion system, ii) distributed sensors linked electrically/radio linked to a fusion system, and iii) reference information, geographical information, etc.; **b) Human Computer Interaction (HCI):** HCI allows human inputs such as commands, information requests, human assessments of inferences and reports from human operators, etc. HCI is the mechanism by which a fusion system communicates results via alerts, displays, dynamic overlays of positional and identity information on

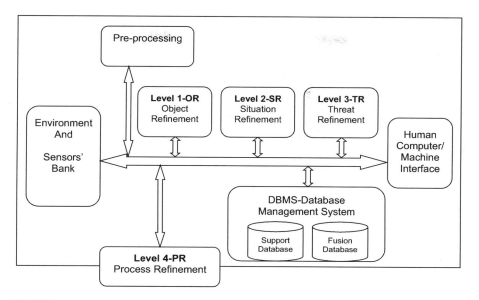

FIGURE 5.1 Top Level JDL Data Fusion Process Model (Modified from: Hall, D. L. *Mathematical Techniques in Multi-Sensor Data Fusion.* Artech House, Norwood, Massachusetts, 1992, in public domain.)

geographical displays; and **c) Source Pre-processing:** This reduces the fusion system load by allocating data to an appropriate process and also performs data pre-screening.

5.2.1 LEVEL 1: OBJECT REFINEMENT

Level 1 fusion in the JDL-DFP model is also popularly known as an Object Refinement (OR) and consists of numerical procedures such as estimation, target tracking and pattern recognition. OR forms object assessments by combining locational, parametric and identity information to achieve refined representations of individual objects like emitters, platforms and weapons in the form of their type, identity, position, velocity and acceleration, etc. Level 1 performs four key functions: i) it transforms sensor data into a consistent set of units and coordinates, ii) it refines and extends in time estimates of an object's position, kinematics, or attributes, iii) it assigns data to objects to allow the application of statistical estimation techniques, and iv) it refines the estimation of an object's identity or classification. Level 1 fusion can be categorically divided into two parts: i) Kinematic fusion–involves fusion of local information to determine the position, velocity etc. of moving objects such as missiles, aircraft, ships, etc.; and ii) Identity fusion–involves fusion of parametric data to determine the identity of an observed object e.g. to decide if the moving object is a missile or an aircraft. The identity estimation can be augmented by expert systems, wherein various types of factual or procedural information can be exploited to aid identity estimation.

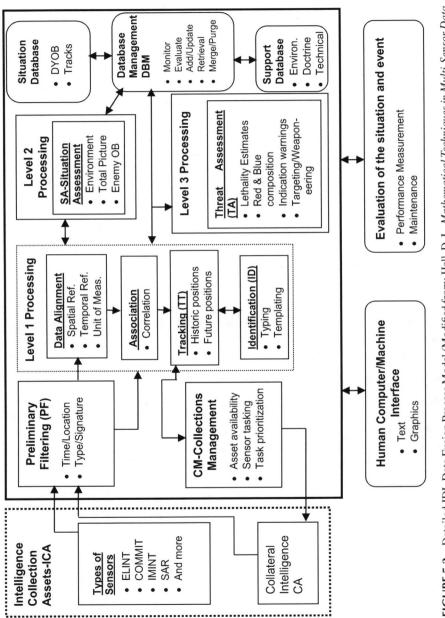

FIGURE 5.2 Detailed JDL Data Fusion Process Model (Modified from: Hall, D. L. *Mathematical Techniques in Multi-Sensor Data Fusion.* Artech House, Norwood, Massachusetts, 1992, in public domain.) 1]

a) **Kinematic Fusion:** The three broad ways to perform fusion at Kinematic level are:
  • fusion of the raw observational data – centralized fusion
  • fusion of (estimated) state vectors – distributed fusion/global fusion
  • hybrid approach which allows fusion of raw data and/or state vector as desired – hybrid fusion
b) **Centralized Fusion:** Centralized fusion architecture, Figure 5.3, mainly used in the case of similar sensors, involves time-synchronization and bias correction of sensor data, transformation of the sensor data from sensor-based units and coordinates to convenient coordinates and units for central processing, e.g. polar to ECEF (Earth Centered Earth Fixed), gating and association in the case of multiple targetss and measurement fusion.

Gating is used to screen out spurious signals such as clutter whereas association algorithms are used for automatic track initiation, measurement to track correlation and track to track correlation. In measurement to track association, the sensors' data are associated with existing numbers of tracks to determine which sensor's data or observation belongs (this is perhaps a beginning of the decision level fusion) to which target. Once a determination has been made that there is more than one observation for a particular target then these observations are combined at raw level using measurement fusion which is typically a sequential estimation technique such as a Kalman Filter. The steps needed to implement the measurement fusion algorithm are described below. In general, the target motion is modeled as

$$x(k+1)=Fx(k)+G\ w(k) \tag{5.1}$$

Here,
  x : true state vector consisting of target position, velocity, acceleration etc.
  F : state transition matrix
  G : transition matrix associated with process noise
  w : white Gaussian process noise with $E[w(k)]=0$ and $cov[w(k)]=Q$
  k : scan number

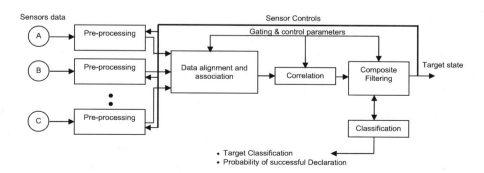

FIGURE 5.3   Centralized Fusion Architecture

The sensor model can be expressed by

$$z(k)=H\,x(k)+v(k) \tag{5.2}$$

Here,

z is observations-data vector; H is observation matrix; v is white Gaussian measurement noise with $E[v(k)]=0$ and $cov[v(k)]=R$.

c) Kalman Filter with Measurement Fusion

State and Covariance Propagation:

$$\tilde{x}(k+1)=F\hat{x}(k) \tag{5.3}$$

$$\tilde{P}(k+1)=F\hat{P}(k)F^{T}+GQG^{T} \tag{5.4}$$

State and Covariance Update:

$$K(k+1)=\tilde{P}(k+1)H^{T}\left[\underbrace{H\tilde{P}(k+1)H^{T}+R}_{S}\right]^{-1} \tag{5.5}$$

$$\hat{x}(k+1)=\tilde{x}(k+1)+K(k+1)\left[\underbrace{z(k+1)-H\,\tilde{X}(k+1)}_{e}\right] \tag{5.6}$$

$$\hat{P}(k+1)=\left[I-K(k+1)\,H\right]\tilde{P}(k+1) \tag{5.7}$$

Here,

$\tilde{x}$:   predicted target state vector
Q :   process noise covariance matrix
$\tilde{P}$:   covariance matrix of predicted target state error
S :   covariance matrix of innovations
e :   innovation sequence vector
$\hat{x}$:   estimated target state vector
$\hat{P}$:   estimated target state error covariance matrix
K :   Kalman filter gain matrix
R :   measurement noise covariance matrix
I :   identity matrix

Suppose there are 2 sensors used in centralized fusion [2]. Assume that each sensor is capable of observing only the position of a moving target, and Kalman filter having only two states i.e. $\hat{x}=[x \quad \dot{x}]$, then Z, H and R will look like:

$$Z=\begin{bmatrix} Z_1 & Z_2 \end{bmatrix} \qquad (5.8)$$

$$H=\begin{bmatrix} 1 & 0 \\ 1 & 0 \end{bmatrix} \qquad (5.9)$$

$$R=\begin{bmatrix} R_1 & 0 \\ 0 & R_2 \end{bmatrix} \qquad (5.10)$$

where, Z_1, Z_2 are the observations from sensor 1 and sensor 2 respectively and R_1, R_2 are their respective measurement noise covariance matrices.

d) Distributed Fusion: This architecture is mainly used for dissimilar sensors i.e. sensors with a different observation frame, for example infrared, radar, etc., Figure 5.4. In this architecture, observation data from each sensor are processed by an individual KF or an Extended KF. The EKF is used in the case of non-linear state or/and sensor models. The local track consisting of an estimated state vector and its covariance from each filter is input to the state vector fusion process and the output is the fused state vector and its covariance.

Now consider the same example as in a centralized fusion architecture. The basic equations for each KF used in distributed fusion are the same as eqns. (5.3)-(5.7). In addition to that Z , H and R will look like:

$$Z=Z_i \qquad (5.11)$$

$$H=\begin{bmatrix} 1 & 0 \end{bmatrix} \qquad (5.12)$$

$$R=R_i \qquad (5.13)$$

where, i =1,2 is the sensor number. Suppose the local track from both Kalman filters at the kth are represented as: $\hat{x}_1(k)$, and $\hat{P}_1(k)$ from KF 1 (for sensor 1), and $\hat{x}_2(k)$,

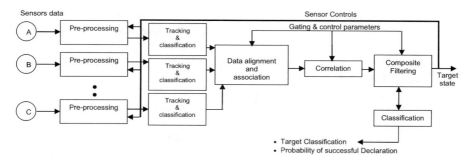

FIGURE 5.4 Distributed Fusion Architecture

and $\hat{P}_2(k)$ from KF 2 (for sensor 2), then fused data using state vector fusion can obtained using the following equations:

$$\hat{x}(k)=\hat{x}_1(k)+\hat{P}_1(k)\left(\hat{P}_1(k)+\hat{P}_2(k)\right)^{-1}\left(\hat{x}_2(k)-\hat{x}_1(k)\right) \tag{5.14}$$

$$\hat{P}(k)=\hat{P}_1(k)-\hat{P}_1(k)\left(\hat{P}_1(k)+\hat{P}_2(k)\right)^{-1}\hat{P}_1^T(k) \tag{5.15}$$

It is important to note that state vector fusion using eqns. (5.14)-(5.15) is labeled as simple fusion [3]. This is based on the assumption that the local tracks are uncorrelated. Application of this method produces an accurate estimate of the target state but still treated a suboptimal because the tracks are correlated through common process noise. In such a case, eqns. (5.14)-(5.15) are modified to account for the correlation between the local tracks of the same target. The modified state vector fusion, labeled as weighted covariance fusion (WCF), is represented using the following equations:

$$\hat{X}(k)=\hat{X}_1(k)+\left(\hat{P}_1(k)-P^C(k)\right)\left(P^E(k)\right)^{-1}\left(\hat{X}_2(k)-\hat{X}_1(k)\right) \tag{5.16}$$

$$\hat{P}(k)=\hat{P}_1(k)-\left(\hat{P}_1(k)-P^C(k)\right)\left(P^E(k)\right)^{-1}\left(\hat{P}_1(k)-P^C(k)\right)^T \tag{5.17}$$

$$P^C(k)=\left(I-K_1(k)H\right)FP^C(k-1)F^T\left(I-K_2(k)H\right)^T \\ +\left(I-K_1(k)H\right)GQG^T\left(I-K_2(k)H\right)^T \tag{5.18}$$

$$P^E(k)=\hat{P}_1(k)+\hat{P}_2(k)-P^C(k)-(P^C(k))^T \tag{5.19}$$

Where, P^C is a cross covariance matrix and its inclusion in WCF is beneficial only if this matrix is positive definite, i.e. $\|P^C\|\geq 0$

    e) Hybrid Fusion: Hybrid fusion architecture (Figure 5.5) involves both centralized and distributed fusion schemes. During the ordinary operation, distributed fusion is used to reduce the computational workload and communication demands. Under specific circumstances, when more accuracy is desirable or if there is a dense tracking environment, centralized fusion is used. Alternatively, based on available sensors, a combination of both schemes may be used to get a fused state of a particular target of interest.

    The Kalman filter is suitable only for non-maneuvering targets. In the case of a maneuvering target, an IMMKF (Interacting Multiple Models Kalman Filter) is used for state estimation. In the case of non-linear models, an EKF or IMMEKF is used. However, in practice, it has been observed that EKF has major two drawbacks: i) in most applications, the derivations of the Jacobian matrices (in the case of linearization

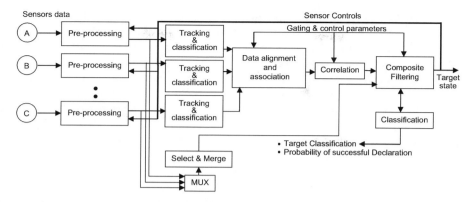

FIGURE 5.5 Hybrid Fusion Architecture [17]

of a sensor model) are nontrivial and that can lead to an implementation problem; and ii) linearization can lead to a highly unstable filter (even divergence) if the assumption that the system is almost linear (local linearity) on the time scale of the updates (i.e. sampling interval) is violated. To alleviate the problems with EKF, one can use a Derivative Free Kalman Filter (DFKF, also is popularly known as an unscented Kalman Filter, UKF) [4]. This filter yields a performance similar to EKF when the assumption of local linearity is not violated. It does not require any linearization and uses a deterministic sampling approach to capture the mean and covariance estimates with a minimal set of sample or sigma points.

5.2.2 LEVEL 2: SITUATION REFINEMENT

Level 2 fusion is also known as situation refinement, and forms situation assessments by relating the objects to existing situation assessments, or by relating object assessments to each other. Situation refinement helps in developing a description of the current relationship among objects and events in the context of environment or assessing the meaning of a Level 1 estimated state or/and identity results in the context of some background or supporting data. Situation assessment derived from word situation awareness, can be hierarchically split into different stages such as: i) Perception and event-detection, ii) Current situation assessment, and iii) Near future situation prediction. Perception and event-detection reduce the workload of the overall situation assessment process by detecting a change in the existing situation assessment i.e. if a situation already is assessed and nothing changes, the situation does not need any more evaluation until new events occur. If a new event occurs then the current situation is assessed along with a prediction to find out what could possibly happen in the near future. It is important to note that the various levels of situation assessment are modeled based on abstraction and reasoning. The intensity of abstraction increases with a climb in the levels of an MSDF system.

Situation assessment aids in decision making. One such example is the pilot of a fighter aircraft. The various decisions/actions that the pilot can make are: i) avoid any sort of collision with nearby flying objects, ii) access the intents of enemy aircraft, and iii) communicate with other friendly aircraft, etc. The pilot's inherent capability for making various decisions/actions works fine when numbers of nearby flying objects are few; but in case of a very complex scenario, how quick and accurate are the decisions that a pilot can make, is questionable. In such a case, a mathematical model of a situation refinement algorithm is required that can aid the pilot in quick and accurate decision making so that the pilot can concentrate more on flying the aircraft safely.

In order to decode the process of situation refinement into a mathematical model, it is essential to understand the basics of it. But before that let's summarize object refinement as numerical procedure that enable us to assign properties to the objects of interest. One such example is a missile with properties such as acceleration, velocity, and position etc. Object refinement also uses rules based on geometry, kinematics and the presumption that a certain object cannot change its properties by breaking these rules, while remaining the same object.

a) **Methods available to perform Situation Assessments:** For the sake of an accurate recognition and classification, most commonly used techniques in situation assessment systems are high-level classification methods. The basic requirement from these methods is that they must be able to handle uncertainty with an easy way of modeling the situations. The most common methods for assessing situations are: i) a neural network, ii) a forward-chain expert system, iii) a Bayesian Network (BN) or a so-called belief network, causal net or inference net, iv) Fuzzy logic, and v) a Hybrid method ←Fuzzy logic + a Bayesian Network [5].

a) **A comparison between a Bayesian network and Fuzzy logic:** Using FL logic, numerical data can be classified into fuzzy sets of discrete variables, whereas BN does not exhibit this feature, for example, classification of numerical data that measure the temperature of a certain quantity. In normal practice it is classified by assigning some grade to the membership function i.e. *very cold*, *quite hot* etc. The real problem comes in assigning grades to temperatures such as 19 and 21 degrees Celsius. It is observed that the difference between temperatures is not very big, but when classified using hard boundaries, 19 degrees is treated as *cold* and 21 degrees as *hot*. This is an example of false classification. In other words, trying to model a system using hard boundaries could often result in erroneous outputs. The classification can be more precise by using Fuzzy boundaries. For the same example mentioned above, 19 degrees could be classified as *cold* with membership-value 0.6 and *hot* with membership-value 0.4. In the same way 21 degrees can be classified. The importance of fuzzy classification becomes more significant while dealing with noisy signals.

b) **Situation Assessment using Fuzzy logic:** It is well known that FL is best for representing uncertainties. The level of uncertainties increases and requires an exact reasoning with a climb in the data fusion levels. It means that just by using numerical procedures it is very hard to model the uncertainties so that a situation can be assessed as accurately as possible. In such a case, an application of FL at the higher levels of data fusion could be the best choice for precise decision making. For example, one of the outputs of situation assessment is 'Aircraft is non-friendly and targeting a tank'. This can be interpreted as if a situation assessor takes the decision "Aircraft is non-friendly and targeting tank". The term fusion comes into picture when there is more than one such decision for the same object of interest seen by multiple sensors of different types and accuracies. Due to a different accuracy level of each sensor, it is possible that the confidence level while taking decisions could be of different magnitudes. Hence, in order to have an accurate decision, it is essential to fuse the decisions (outputs from a situation assessor) using a FL approach.

Let us consider a scenario consisting of an unknown aircraft, seen by two sensors of different types. Assume that the first sensor provides an identity and the second sensor measures the direction of the moving aircraft. Now the goal of a FL-based situation assessment system is to take the decision as to whether the behavior of an unknown aircraft is hostile or friendly [5]. There are two inputs (direction & identity) and single output (behavior) to a FIS, i.e. the situation assessor. The inputs are fuzzified by using their corresponding FMFs. The inputs, direction & identity have two MFs each with linguistic labels {*departing, approaching*} and {*friend, foe*} respectively; the output has MFs with linguistic labels {*friendly, hostile*}.

Then, the inputs are combined using the following inference rules:

Rule 1:   IF aircraft is *departing* OR identity is *friend* THEN behavior is *friendly*
Rule 2:   IF aircraft is *approaching* OR identity is *foe* THEN behavior is *hostile*

In the present example, the FL operator AND is represented with min(A, B) and OR represented with max(A, B), where A and B are two fuzzy sets representing inputs direction and identity respectively. There could be a possibility that both the rules fired simultaneously. In such a case there will be an output fuzzy set for each rule. These outputs sets are combined using an *aggregation* (the present case uses max(C1, C2), where C1 and C2 are fuzzy output sets) process. The crisp output is produced by applying a *defuzzification* (in the present case, Centre of Area (COA) has been used) process to obtain the resultant output fuzzy set. Let us assume that for a given crisp input, the corresponding membership value for each membership function is given as

Input 1   : direction; Membership grade: {0.2,0.8};
Input 2   : identity; Membership grade: {0.3,0.7}

Assume that both the rules are fired concurrently. In the first rule, inference is OR, which gives combined membership value of max(0.2, 0.3) = 0.3. Then, the MF of that behavior is *friendly* is cut at membership value 0.3. For the second rule, the MF of that behavior is *hostile* is cut at membership value min(0.8, 0.7) = 0.7. In the last step, the truncated output fuzzy sets are combined, and COA is calculated to determine the total hostility of an aircraft. Figure 5.6 illustrates the graphical view of situation assessment using fuzzy logic.

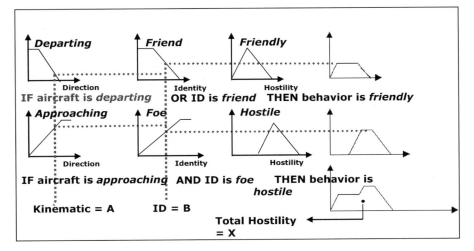

FIGURE 5.6 FL-based Situation Assessment to Find Total Hostility Shown by an Unknown Aircraft, (source: Ivansson, J. Situation Assessment in a Stochastic Environment using Bayesian Networks, *Master Thesis*. LITH-ISY-EX-3267-2002, LITH-ISY-EX-3267-2002, Institutionen för Systemteknik, 581 83 LINKÖPING, Linköping University, Linköping, March 2002)

5.2.3 LEVEL 3: THREAT REFINEMENT

Level 3 fusion projects the current situation into the future to draw inferences about enemy threats, friendly as well as enemy vulnerabilities and opportunities for operations. This requires Level 1 and Level 2 information so that quantitative estimates of an object's behavior can be computed and expected courses of action are assessed. The threat assessments are identifications of possible capabilities, intent of hostile objects and the expected outcome.

5.2.4 LEVEL 4: PROCESS REFINEMENT

Process refinement is considered as a meta process, i.e., a process concerned about other process. Level 4 processing performs four key functions: i) monitors the data fusion process performance to provide information about real-time control and long-term performance, ii) identifies what information is needed to improve the multilevel fusion product, iii) determines the source specific requirements to collect relevant information, and iv) allocates and directs the sources to achieve mission goals. The latter function may be outside the domain of specific data fusion functions.

5.3 AN APPROACH TO FL-BASED DECISION FUSION SYSTEM (DFS)

An architecture and implementation aspects of DFS are proposed [6], [3]. The details of parameters required for scenario/measurements generation are covered in a latter section.

a) **Architecture of DFS:** Figure 5.7 shows the block diagram of the proposed system. A typical scenario is obtained by defining the number of targets, target types, allocation of an identity number to each target, a flight plan of each target through kinematic simulation, number of sensors and specification of each sensor in terms of field of view, probability of detection, sampling interval, measurement frame and its accuracies, etc. The measurements for a particular scenario are generated using various sensors, for example RWR (Radar Warning Receiver), RADAR (Radio Detection and Ranging), IRST (Infrared Search and Track), FLIR (Forward Looking Infrared Receiver) and IFF (Identification Friend or Foe). The modeling aspect of each sensor is covered in the next section. It can be observed from Figure 5.7 that there is a separate block called "OA & SA" for each sensor. The purpose of an OA (Object Assessment) & SA (Situation Assessment) block is to assess the current situation, e.g. of a battlefield by processing the measurements from each sensor at the local level. The outputs from "OA & SA" blocks are fused using the FL approach to take a final course of decision for various purposes e.g., it could be to say that "*a particular fighter aircraft is a threat to us so destroy the aircraft*" or it could be "*although it is an enemy aircraft it is departing from us so wait for some time*".

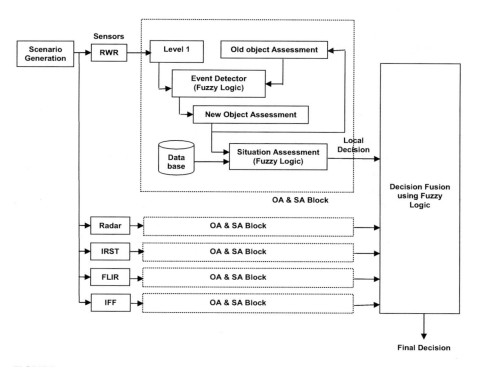

FIGURE 5.7 Architecture of proposed DFS

b) **Implementation Aspects:**
   i) **Software:** All the algorithms are developed in MATLAB ® on a Windows XP platform (by the second author).
   ii) **Sensors Modeling:** The measurement data is obtained by modeling each sensors as realistically as possible by taking all the available information such as field of view, tracking accuracy, probability of detection, false alarm density etc.
   - **Algorithms for Level 1 Fusion:** Algorithms use gating, data association, KF, Interacting Multiple Model (IMM), State Vector Fusion (SVF, simple fusion or WCF) and MLF (Measurement Level Fusion). The output of Level 1 forms an OA consisting of information such as: a) track number, b) track class–friend (.), neutral (.), Foe (.), c) track type–fighter (.), bomber (.), transport (.), AWAC (.), commercial (.), and d) track kinematics–position, speed, covariance matrix. Here, (.) indicates the assigned membership grade value.

     Object classification: The classification of an object helps in easing decision making. For example, consider the object to be an aircraft and classified as *friend*, then the system does not need to know what type of target it is. On the other hand if it is classified as *foe*, it is essential to know the type of an aircraft. The reason is simple like "a foe fighter is more harmful than a friend fighter".

   iii) **Event Detector:** The main purpose of an event detector is to compare the current output (say at the kth scan) from Level 1 fusion with stored Level 1 output from the previous one (say at the k-1th scan). If an event detector finds significant changes in outputs, then it assumes that a new event has occurred. For example, an object changes its speed and bearing or a new object with different identity/class enters the surveillance volume. Also, an event detector reduces the workload of the situation assessor of DFS by detecting a change in an existing situation assessment i.e. if a situation is already assessed and nothing changes, the situation does not need any more evaluation until new events occur. In the present work, an event detector is realized using an FL approach. The outputs of Level 1 fusion (containing object attributes) at two successive scans get fuzzified through appropriate MFs, and are represented with graded membership values. The possible way to conclude if an event has occurred within the attributes is by checking the statistical significance with some confidence that the data has changed.

   iv) **Database:** In the present context, a database could contain corridors (path or place) of friendly objects and information about terrains etc. The database and output from current object assessments are used in assessing the current situation, e.g. a battlefield. It could also be used to store information about some situations that could be used to improve the solution to a specific problem or subsets of a problem associated with the situation assessment. This is like making a database intelligent by using past experience so that it can be used in making an accurate decision based on a particular situation that has occurred.

v) **Situation Assessment and Decision Fusion:** Situation assessment helps in evaluating a situation of e.g. a battlefield, by comparing the information stored in a database and current object assessment. It is observed that experienced decision makers rely for most of their decisions on situation assessments. The decision-makers mostly use experience for their decisions–that is, they select actions that previously have worked well in similar situations. Due to the presence or lack of certain essential characteristics, they relate to similar situations and what actions that have worked well in past cases. Shortly, situation assessment is to create relevant relations between objects in the environment. At this point, it is essential to understand what is an outcome of a situation assessor or ontology for relations? The most common relations put into practice in the situation assessor are:

- **Pair**: Two or more objects flying in a specific pattern, e.g. formation flight of fighter aircraft; Fuzzy rules:
  - IF two aircraft have the same *bearing*, *elevation* and *speed,* THEN they have the same kinematics.
  - IF two aircraft have the same *kinematics*, *identity*, *class* and are at a short *distance* from each other, THEN they form a relation **Pair.**

- **Along**: An object flying along a static object, e.g. civilian aircraft flying along the air lane; Fuzzy rules:
  - IF an aircraft has the same *bearing* as an air lane and IF it is *close* to the air lane THEN the aircraft is flying **Along** the air lane.
  - IF an aircraft *class* is a civilian one THEN there is a higher possibility that the aircraft is flying **Along** the air lane.

- **Attacking**: An object attacking another dynamic or static object, e.g. a fighter aircraft attacking another fighter aircraft or a bomber is attacking a place; Fuzzy rules:
  - IF an aircraft has high *speed*, has a close *distance* to another aircraft and has a *bearing* towards it THEN the aircraft is trying to *close* in on the other aircraft.
  - IF an aircraft is *closing* in on another, and has a different *identity* and is a fighter aircraft THEN the aircraft is attacking the other.

These rules are created by a group of highly qualified and experienced individuals working in a relevant technical domain. In the present work, the output from the "OA & SA" block for each sensor assists in local decision making with a certain degree of accuracy. A unified decision with higher accuracy and robustness is obtained by fusing the local decisions using an FL approach. The next few examples illustrate the application of FL in the development of Decision Support Systems (DSS) that could be used as an aid to the pilot of a fighter aircraft for decision making in an air combat scenario (e.g. air-to-air, air-to-ground, ground-to-air, etc). FL can be applied to decision fusion, a methodology that helps in taking certain decisions based on processing a certain scenario. For example, the pilot of a combat aircraft needs to take various tactical decisions based on what he or she observes from the sensors and surroundings. The decisions made by a pilot are based on his past experiences and intuitions related to sets of realistic scenarios. However, the response from the pilot depends upon his/her amount of dynamic mental memory left (like RAM in a computer). Naturally, if there is the likelihood of complex scenarios then the response from the pilot may slow down, which in turn will be reflected in his decision making ability. Therefore, due to the limited memory factor, it is necessary to have a replica (in terms of the mathematical model that is DSS) of the pilot mental model for inference or decision.

5.4   EXAMPLES OF FUZZY LOGIC-BASED DECISION SYSTEMS

The MATLAB based soution codes are given in the book's website for examples 5.1 to 5.4 (for this chapter).

Example 5.1: Air combat scenario: This example demonstrates the use of the FL based decision system (FLDS), onboard a ship, to decide whether two enemy fighter aircraft are in a formation flight or not during the course of air combat scenario. In order to prove the concept, first kinematic data (using a point mass model) generation is carried out in which two aircarft of the same class and identity in the pitch plane (it is assumed that there is no motion in the yaw i.e. x-y plane) are mathematically simulated using MATLAB®. The parameters use in simulation are: i) initial state of aircraft 1: $X_1 = \begin{bmatrix} x & \dot{x} & z & \dot{z} \end{bmatrix} = [0\,m\ 166\,m/s\ 1000\,m\ 0\,m/s]$; ii) initial state of aircraft 2: $X_2 = \begin{bmatrix} x & \dot{x} & z & \dot{z} \end{bmatrix} = [0\,m\ 166\,m/s\ 990\,m\ 0\,m/s]$; iii) sensor update rate is 1 Hz; iv) simulation time is 30 sec.; v) aircraft motion is with constant velocity; vi) Kinematic model: $X_i(k+1) = FX_i(k) + Gw_i(k)$, where, k (= 1,2, …, v, 30) is scan number, i (= 1, 2) is the aircraft number, F is the state transition matrix, G is the process noise gain matrix, and w is white Gaussian process noise with covariance Q:

$$F = \begin{bmatrix} 1 & T & 0 & 0 \\ 0 & 1 & 0 & 0 \\ 0 & 0 & 1 & T \\ 0 & 0 & 0 & 1 \end{bmatrix} \text{ and } G = \begin{bmatrix} \dfrac{T^2}{2} & 0 & 0 & 0 \\ 0 & T & 0 & 0 \\ 0 & 0 & \dfrac{T^2}{2} & 0 \\ 0 & 0 & 0 & T \end{bmatrix}, \tag{5.20}$$

and vi) process noise covariance is $0.1 \times \text{eye}(4,4)$.

During the simulation, both the aircraft maintain a formation flight from t = 0 to 5 sec. and then split (depart) at t = 5 sec. and remain in that mode for up to t = 10 sec. From the 10th second to the 15th second they fly with constant seperation and start approaching to each other from 15th sec. Again they form a pair from the 20th sec. and stay in formation flight for another 10 sec. Figure 5.8 shows the trajectories in the pitch plane and Figure 5.9 illustrates elevation angles of two aircraft as seen from the ship.

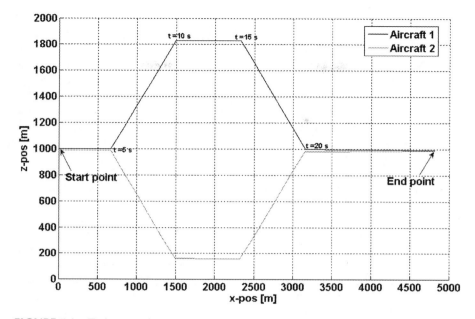

FIGURE 5.8   Trajectory of two aircraft in pitch plane-Example 5.1

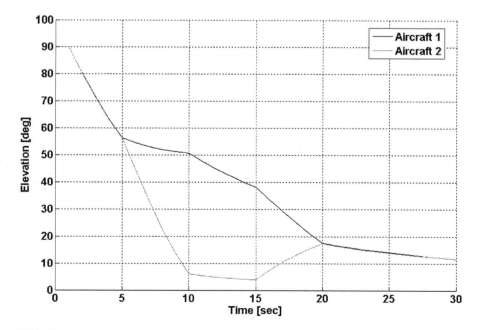

FIGURE 5.9   Elevation angle of two aircraft-Example 5.1

The performance of FLDS depends upon proper selection of the MFs of I/O Fuzzy sets, Fuzzy rules, FIMs, aggregation methods, and de-fuzzification techniques:

i) **MFs:** Inputs to FLDS are the numerical difference (absolute value) of an aircraft's bearing, elevation, distance (separation) along the z-axis, speed, identity and class. For each input and output (named pair) there is an MF which fuzzifies the data between 0 and 1. For this example, a trapezoidal shaped MF is preferred. Figure 5.10 shows the MFs for inputs and output of FLDS.

It is essential to note that the limits, such as **d, e, f,** and **g** of various MFs are provided only based on author/s intuition for the sake of concept proving, however, in practice such limits should be provided by an expert of the relevant domain.

ii) **Fuzzy rules:** Fuzzy rules provide the user a natural way (symbolic interpretation-this was humans prehistoric communication means) to map the inputs to output. These rules are processed using FIMs in FIE. The performance of FLDS depends upon the creation of rules which are often made available by either individual's experiences or an expert in a corresponding field. For this example, the following rules are used to decide whether two aircraft form a pair or not: Rule 1: IF two aircraft have the same bearing, elevation and speed THEN they have same kinematics; Rule 2: IF two aircraft have the same kinematics, identity, class and are at a short distance from each other THEN they form a pair.

iii) **Fuzzy implication method:** The fuzzy rules are processed by FIM in FIE. In the present case the Product Operation Rule of Fuzzy Implication (PORFI), also known as the Larsen implication, is used for the chosen rules.

iv) **Aggregation method:** The aggregation method is used to combine output fuzzy sets (each set is due to some rule that is triggered) to get a single fuzzy set. For this example, a Bounded Sum (BS) operator of T-conorm/S-norm is used in the aggregation process.

v) **Defuzzification method:** An aggregated output fuzzy set is de-fuzzified using the Center Of Area (COA) method.

vi) **FLDS realization:** FLDS is realized in the MATLAB/SIMULINK environment using the Fuzzy logic toolbox. Figure 5.11 shows a schematic of the system. Figure 5.12 shows the inside view (sub-block of Figure 5.11) of FIE for Rule 1 and Rule 2. The sub-block for de-fuzzification is shown in Figure 5.13.

After execution of the SIMULINK block shown in Figure 5.11, the results at various stages (e.g. fuzzified inputs such as elevation, distance, final output, etc.) of FLDS are stored. Figures 5.14, and 5.15 illustrate fuzzified values of inputs of distance and elevation respectively, from which it is observed that during the formation flight (0–5 sec. and 20–30 sec.) the membership grades of both inputs are fairly high and during the non-formation flight (5–20 sec.) the membership grade is nearly zero. Along with these inputs there are other inputs such as speed, bearing, aircraft identity and class, to decide

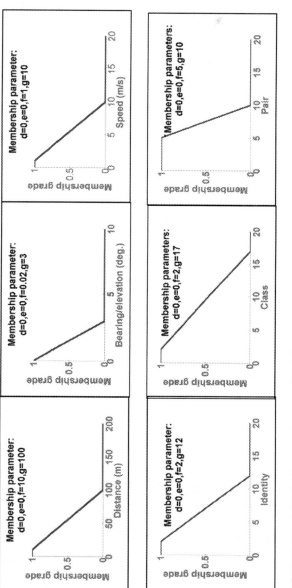

FIGURE 5.10 MHs for inputs and output of FLDS-Example 5.1

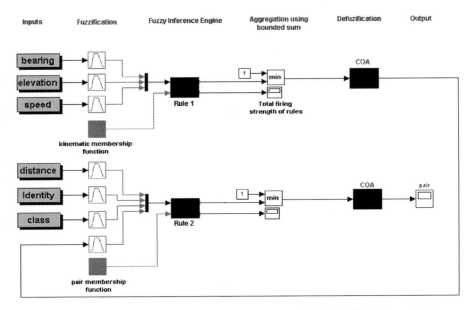

FIGURE 5.11   Schematic of FLDS realized using MATLAB/SIMULINK-Example 5.1

FIGURE 5.12   Schematic of FIF sub-block for Rule 1 & Rule 2-Example 5.1

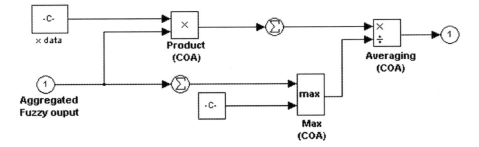

FIGURE 5.13   De-fuzzification sub-block-Example 5.1

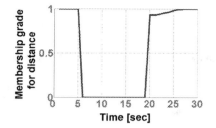

FIGURE 5.14   Fuzzified distance-Example 5.1

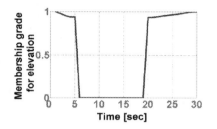

FIGURE 5.15   Fuzzified elevation-Example 5.1

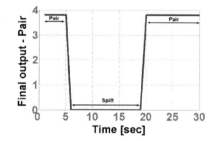

FIGURE 5.16   Final output of FLDS-Example 5.1

about whether both the aircraft forms a pair or not. Figure 5.16 shows the de-fuzzified output (pair) of FLDS, from which it is clear that the system is able to correctly detect the aircraft pair and split periods. It is also observed that system assigns a large weight during the pair region and zero weight during the split region.

Example 5.2: Flying along the air lane

This example covers the steps required to develop FLDS to decide whether a particular aircraft is flying along the air lane or not. In addition to that, a sensitivity study is carried out to check the performance of FLDS with respect to the fuzzy aggregation operator. The simulation for scenario generation is carried out using parameters: i) initial state of aircraft: $X = \begin{bmatrix} x & \dot{x} & y & \dot{y} \end{bmatrix} = [2990\,\text{m} \ 0\,\text{m/s} \ 0\,\text{m} \ 332\,\text{m/}$

s]; ii) air lane located along the y axis at x = 3000 m; iii) sensor update rate is 1 Hz; iv) simulation time is 30 sec.; v) aircraft motion is of constant velocity; vi) Kinematic model: X(k+1)=FX(k)+Gw(k) , where, k (= 1,2, ... ,30) is the scan number, F is the state transition matrix (the same as in Example 5.1), G is the process noise gain matrix (as in Example 5.1), and w is white Gaussian process noise with covariance Q, process noise covariance: 1.0x eye(4,4) . Figure 5.17 shows the aircraft and air lane location in the yaw plane and Figure 5.18 illustrates the bearings of the aircraft and air lane at various data points as seen from origin (0, 0).

i)   **MFs:** The inputs to FLDS are fuzzified values of absolute distance (separation between aircraft and air lane along the y axis), absolute value of bearing difference between them, and class of aircraft; it is assumed that the aircaft is a civilian one. The MFs to fuzzify the inputs and output (along) are of trapezoidal shape and shown in Figure 5.19.

ii) **Fuzzy rules:** For this example, the rules to decide that a particular aircraft flies along the air lane or not are: Rule 1: IF the aircraft has the same bearing as the air lane AND IF it is close to the air lane THEN the aircraft is flying along the air lane; and Rule 2: IF the aircraft is civil THEN there is high possibility that the aircraft is flying along the air lane.

iii) **FIM:** Product Operation Rule of Fuzzy Implication is used.

iv) **Aggregation method:** Bounded sum (BS)/Algebraic sum (AS)/Standard union (SU) operators of T-conorm/S-norm are used one by one in the aggregation process.

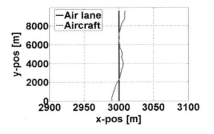

FIGURE 5.17   Aircraft and air lane Location-Example 5.2

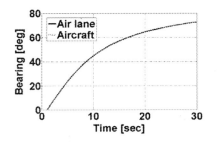

FIGURE 5.18   Aircraft and air lane Bearings-Example 5.2

v) **Defuzzification method:** An aggregated output fuzzy set is de-fuzzified using the Center Of Area (COA) method.

vi) **FLDS realization:** FLDS for this example is realized using the MATLAB/SIMULINK environment. Figure 5.20 shows the schematic of the system.

Most of sub-blocks of Figure 5.20 are already shown in Example 5.1 and an additional sub-block is "Aggregation using BS/AS/SU" only. Inside this sub-block, the user can select different aggregation methods. After execution of this SIMULINK block for each of aggregation methods mentioned in this example, results at various

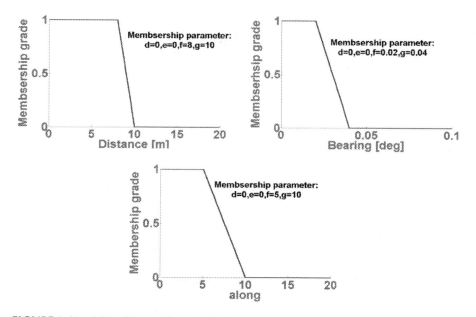

FIGURE 5.19 MFs of inputs distance, bearing, and output along-Example 5.2

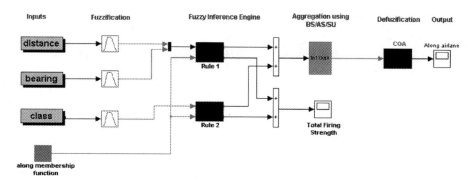

FIGURE 5.20 Schematic of FLDS realized using MATLAB/SIMULINK-Example 5.2

stages (e.g. fuzzified inputs such as bearing and distance, final output, etc.) of FLDS are stored. Figures 5.21 and 5.22 illustrate fuzzified values of input distance and bearing respectively. Figure 5.23 shows the comparison of final outputs obtained for different aggregation methods.

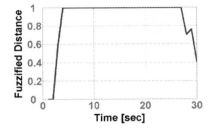

FIGURE 5.21   Fuzzified distance-Example 5.2

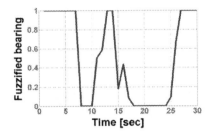

FIGURE 5.22   Fuzzified bearing-Example 5.2

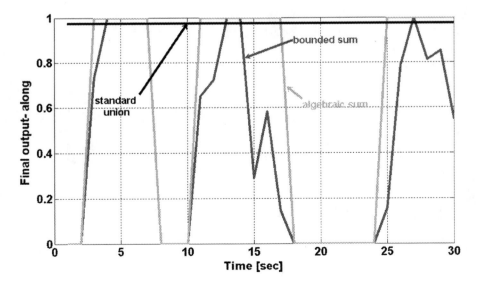

FIGURE 5.23   Final output along-Example 5.2

The following observations are made from Figure 5.23: a) In case of the SU operator used for aggregation, a constant output is observed irrespective of whether the aircraft is along the air lane or not; b) For the AS operator, the smooth transition observed is between 0 and 1 and it means that a hard decision is made by FLDS about whether the aircraft is along the air lane or not; c) For the BS operator, a non-smooth transition is observed between 0 and 1 which seems to be intuitively correct and that gives a confidence level while taking the decision about an aircraft i.e. whether it is flying along the air lane or not. In other words, the larger the final output the more the confidence; and d) For this example, use of BS in the aggregation process provides better results than other methods such as SU and AS.

5.5 EVALUATION OF NEW FUZZY IMPLICATION FUNCTIONS

The use of existing FIF PORFI has been demonstrated in Examples 5.1 and 5.2. In this section, the same examples are re-visited but instead of PORFI, one of the new FIFs, PCBSAP is used in processing the fuzzy rules, and the output of FDLS due to this new FIF is compared with output obtained in section 5.4. In order to compare the performance of SIMULINK based FLDS applied to different FIFs, some changes have been made in the block of Figure 5.12 (one of the sub-blocks of SIMULINK-Example 5.1). Figure 5.24 illustrates the modified sub-block for Example 5.1. Similar change has been made in the SIMULINK sub-block (i.e. FIE) for Example 5.2. The component 'Embedded MATLAB based FIF' of Figure 5.24 is used to define the various FIFs (existing and new ones). These FIFs are selected using fa ront end menu developed using MATLAB/graphics ('selection flag' in Figure 5.24) [7]. Figure 5.25 shows the comparison of final outputs of FLDS obtained for FIFs such as PORFI (existing) and PCBSAP (new). It is observed from the figure that outputs are comparable for up to 20 seconds of total simulation time. During this period two aircraft form a pair and then spilt. However, after the 20th second, some mismatch between outputs

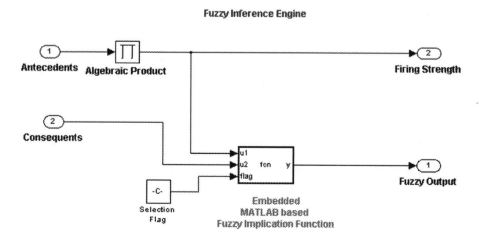

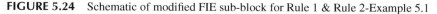

FIGURE 5.24   Schematic of modified FIE sub-block for Rule 1 & Rule 2-Example 5.1

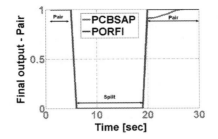

FIGURE 5.25   Comparison of final outputs of FLDS applied to different FIFs-Example 5.1

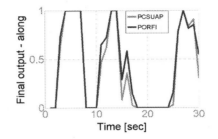

FIGURE 5.26   Comparison of final outputs of FLDS applied to different FIFs-Example 5.2

is observed. It is seen from the figure that the FLDS output obtained for PORFI quickly converges to a max value of unity, whereas, the FLDS output for PCBSAP takes more time before converging to a unity value. The output for PCBSAP is closer to realistic because it matches with the way the data simulation was carried out, see Figure 5.9, for the 20th sec. onwards, both the aircraft took some time in coming back to pair form. The FLDS for Example 5.1 is tested with various existing and new FIFs and it was found that the results obtained were almost identical and acceptable with minor disparity noticed during the last few seconds (20th second onwards) of total simulation time.

The new FIFs have also been tested by applying them to the FLDS of Example 5.2 developed for identifying whether a particular aircraft is flying along the air lane or not. In Example 5.2, it was concluded that the results obtained using the aggregation operator 'bounded sum' were matched perfectly with the way data simulation was carried out. Based on this fact, new FIFs are applied with the combination of 'bounded sum' operator only and the results obtained are compared with those obtained when the existing implication function PORFI is used. The concept proving result shown in Figure 5.26 only compares the final outputs (along) for another new Fuzzy implication function named PCSUAP and an existing PORFI. It is observed from Figure 5.26 that outputs of FLDS for these two FIFs are fairly comparable except for slight lag/ lead observed in the output of FLDS for PCSUAP as compared to output obtained for PORFI. However, the peaks of the outputs still match perfectly. In similar fashion the remaining new FIFs are studied and it is found that outputs obtained are almost identical and comparable to output obtained using the PORFI function.

5.6 SYMBOL-DECISION LEVEL FUSION

The objective of the decision fusion is to take one final decision/action in an entire surveillance volume at any instant of time using outputs from different levels, e.g. Level 1-OR and Level 2-SR, of any MSDF system, especially in a defense system. However, the procedure is applicable to other civilian data fusion systems also. Symbol level fusion (which is synonymously used for decision fusion) represents the high-level (higher than both the kinematic level and image level fusion processes) information wherein the symbol represents a decision. A symbol can represent an input in the form of a decision where the fusion describes both a logical and a statistical inference. In the case of symbolic data/information, the inference methods from AI can be used as computational mechanisms (like fuzzy logic), since the fusion of symbolic information would require reasoning and inference in the presence of uncertainty. We have in general three domains of objects which can provide information [8], [3]: i) the concrete domain of physical objects with physical characteristics, physical states, activities and tangible entities, e.g. an aircraft or a robot; ii) the abstract domain–'mind-thought' process covers the domain of the mind of all living beings and all intangible entities; and iii) in the symbol domain the characteristics of concrete and abstract entities are transformed into the representations of common systems of symbols (for communication and possible dynamic interactions). Interestingly all three domains can be found in the multiple-interacting systems, e.g. a group of mobile robots, which as such complicate the decision making, in terms of coordination and team autonomy. The sensing/data processing part of the robotic system builds the world model (the robot's 'mind', in fact the 'mind' constructs an internal model of the outside world!) of the robot's environment which contains the physical objects and symbols (e.g. sign boards, traffic signs, etc.). The decision process consists of: a) decoding of information, interpretation, and association with previous experience, and b) perception of interpreted and associated sensory impressions that would lead to some meaning (this is also called new information!). The sensing process precedes the decision process which is followed by the behavioral process. The sensing and decision processes together can be called an information process cycle with appropriate feedback where applicable. According to one theory of intelligence [9], [3] the unknowable external world ('noumena') is distinguished from the perceptual stimuli resulting from that world (phenomena). The noumena, not directly knowable (e.g. fire or a river), are the sources of the perceptual stimuli. Many worldly phenomena represent a partial projection (a small cross-section, features etc.) of the noumena. Humans organize their perceived phenomena into schemata (a systematic procedure, or some regularity, or pattern in these phenomena) which represent individual phenomena as well as abstractions. As, for example, the properties measured by the sensors are the phenomena, and the vector of these properties is a form of schemata. The schemata, also used in the theory of genetic algorithms, can include temporal sequences and images also. The reasoning process about the world requires an abstraction from the phenomena: i) categories of objects, ii) relations between objects, iii) actions, and iv) events, many of which can be represented by labels, i.e. symbols. Thus, a symbol is a sign that represents something.

The symbol states-of-information (SOI) consist of [10]: i) the set of symbol representations like text and sounds in a language and pictures, and ii) information products/outcomes like documents, and speeches. This symbol level information can be used for encoding and decoding our thought processes. The symbols like signs, letters, sound in/of languages, pictures, maps, and objects representing something can form the information products/outcomes: data, messages, facts, reports, books, intelligent information, speeches, models, simulation outputs, computer programs, media products, financial products (e.g. coins, currency notes), ethnical and religious symbols, national and political symbols (e.g. emblems, flags, election/party/union symbols or logos). In effect, the information process refinement starts from signs to data to symbols, facts, idea to knowledge and to wisdom. The symbol represents an input in the form of a decision where the fusion describes a logical and a statistical inference. The significant advantage of the symbol-level fusion is an increase in the truth value. This type of fusion can also be considered as decision fusion. The main decision level fusion approaches are [1]-[3]: identity–and knowledge-based methods. In the identity-based approach the MAP (Maximum a Posteriori), ML (Maximum Likelihood), and D-S (Dempster-Shafer) methods are used. In the knowledge-based approach the methods used are: logic templates, the syntax rule, ANNs, and FL-based methods. Many of these approaches are also applicable to feature level (for image level, or even extracting the patterns/features from speech signals) fusion. In feature level fusion the object is the characters' space. The object in decision fusion is the decision action space. The decision fusion mainly depends upon external knowledge, and hence, more on inference from the external knowledge. Interestingly, the results obtained/fused from the decision fusion can be used to classify images, detect changes, and detect & recognize targets.

There are certain principles of symbolic fusion [11]: a) primitives in the world model should be expressed as a set of properties, the schema is such a representation-the properties are the symbolic labels or numerical measures; b) the observation model should be expressed in a common coordinate system, i.e. the information should be properly associated, it could be on the basis of spatial or temporal coordinates, or on the basis of some relation between properties; c) observation and model should be expressed in a common vocabulary, it being 'context', which is a collection of symbols and relations-these are used to describe a situation, the knowledge of the 'context' provides a set of symbols, relations and leads to a process of prediction and verification; d) the properties should incorporate an explicit representation of uncertainty, this being precision and confidence; and e) the primitives should be accompanied by a confidence factor determined by, say probabilistic technique or FL in the framework of possibility theory.

In the symbolic form of fusion prediction, a match and update cycle like the ones for kinematic fusion (using KF) can be defined for a symbolic description composed of schema. In the prediction stage, a priori information of 'context' to predict the evolution of schemes in the model as well as the existence and location of the new schema, is applied [11]. The prediction stage thus selects the perceptual actions that detect the expected phenomenon. The match stage associates a new perceptual phenomenon with the predictions from the internal model, with the primary method being the spatial location and it could be an association based on similar properties. Then the update stage combines the prediction and observation stages to construct the internal model that can be thought of as a 'short term memory' which has a certain quantity of information in it. We regard the use of FL as helping a decision process either in KF or situation assessment.

5.7 SOFT DECISION IN KALMAN FILTERING

A Kalman filter has been used as one of the most promising algorithms for recursive estimation of states of linear as well as non-linear systems. The accuracy of the filter is based on: i) how accurately the mathematical model of the actual dynamic system and measurement device are known (because of the random uncertainties), and ii) its tuning parameters Q (process noise covariance matrix) and R (measurement noise covariance matrix). In some applications, we may encounter a problem of modeling error i.e. when the true models are not accurately known or they are difficult to realize/implement, and we have to use approximate representations. The modeling error is often compensated by process noise-tuning parameters/elements (of Q) which are selected on a trial-and-error basis (this is nowadays known as the sensitivity study) and the final solutions obtained through this approach may not provide optimal filter performance. Although, there are a few adaptive filters that can be used for such purposes, these are computationally very demanding. The (time varying, especially in the case of the EKF) gain of a KF decides how much weighting should be given to the present measurement (in fact to the residuals): i) if the measurement data are highly contaminated with noise, then automatically less weight is assigned to these data and filter depends on the model of the target (i.e. state propagation), and ii) if measurement data are less noisy, then more weight is given to these and the estimated state is the combination of state predicted (through target model) and measurements. Thus, the KF has an inherent decision-making capability that helps in soft-switching between process model and measurement model (via appropriate weight assignments via Kalman gain and P, Q, R). This decision of soft-switching is based on Kalman gain which depends on the relative values of tuning parameters/ matrices Q and R. Measurement noise variance reflects the noise level in measurement data, higher R (in terms of the norm of the matrix) means data are very noisy. In the case of very high R, the filter takes the decision to have much less faith on measurement data by assigning low weight, through Kalman gain to the correction part of the state update. This can also be interpreted by saying that the filter relies highly on the process model. Similarly, for very low R, the filter highly relies on the measurement model. Table 5.1 summarizes the soft-decisions in a Kalman filter.

5.8

FL assists in modeling the conditions that are inherently imprecisely defined and FL based methods in the form of approximate reasoning provide decision support and expert systems with reasonably good reasoning capabilities-this being called an

TABLE 5.1
Soft-decision making in KF

Tuning of Q and R Parameters/matrices	Kalman gain	Soft-decisions
High R or low Q	low	Less faith on measurements/more faith on the predicted states
Low R or high Q	High	Enough/more faith on measurements/less faith on the predictions
Moderate R or Q	Moderate	Moderate faith on measurements
High initial P	High	Less faith in initial states
Low initial P	Low	High/enough initial faith on states
Moderate initial P	Moderate	Moderate initial faith on states

FL-type 1 system. FL can also be used for tuning Kalman filters. The algorithms can be developed by considering the combination of FL and KF [12]. The proper combination of FL and KF based approaches can be used to obtain improved accuracy and performance in target tracking as well as in MSDF systems. In such systems, the FL can be considered as aiding soft decision-making in the filtering process because of the use of fuzzy 'IF... THEN' rules in making some judgment on the use of, say residuals, in navigating the prediction/filtering in the direction of achieving accurate results in either tracking process, feature selection/detection/matching or MSDF.

In this section two schemes based on KF, and a Fuzzy Kalman Filter (FKF) are studied for target tracking applications and their performances evaluated. The concept of FL is extended to State Vector level data Fusion (SVF) for similar sensors. The performances of FL-based fusion methods are compared with the conventional fusion method (state vector fusion, SVF) to track a maneuvering target. FL concept is combined with KF filter at measurement update level. The equations for the FKF are the same as those of KF except the following equation [8]:

$$\hat{X}(k+1/k+1) = \tilde{X}(k+1/k) + KB(k+1) \tag{5.21}$$

Here, B(k+1) is regarded as an output of the FL-based process variable (FLPV) and is, in general, a nonlinear function of the innovations, 'e' of the KF. It is assumed that position (in the x-y axes) measurements of the target are available. The FLPV vector consists of the modified innovation sequence for the x and y axes:

$$B(k+1) = \begin{bmatrix} b_x(k+1) & b_y(k+1) \end{bmatrix} \tag{5.22}$$

To determine the FLPV vector the innovation vector e is first separated into its x and y components, e_x and e_y. The target motion in each axis is assumed to be independent. The FLPV vector for the x direction can be developed and then it is generalized to include the y direction. This vector consists of two inputs, e_x and $\dot{e}_x$, and single output $b_x(k+1)$, where $\dot{e}_x$ is computed by

$$\dot{e}_x = \frac{\{e_x(k+1) - e_x(k)\}}{T} \qquad (5.23)$$

Here, T is the sampling interval in seconds, and the expression of equation (5.23) can be extended to the y-direction, and even the z-direction if required.

5.7.1 FUZZY LOGIC-BASED PROCESS (FLP) AND DESIGN

FLP is obtained via a FIS. In order to develop the FLP the antecedent membership functions that define the fuzzy values for inputs e_x and $\dot{e}_x$, and the membership function for the output b_x are shown in Figure 5.27 [12]. The linguistic variables/labels to define FMFs are LN–large negative, MN–medium negative, SN–small negative, ZE–zero error, SP–small positive, MP–medium positive, and LP–large positive. The rules for the inference in FIS, in general are created based on the experience and intuition of the domain expert, one such rule being [8]:

$$\text{IF } e_x \text{ is LP AND } \dot{e}_x \text{ is LP THEN } b_x \text{ is LP} \qquad (5.24)$$

This signifies the fact that having e_x and $\dot{e}_x$ with large positive values indicates an increase in the innovation sequence at a faster rate. Then, the future value of e_x (and hence $\dot{e}_x$) can be reduced by increasing the present value of b_x ($\approx Z - H\tilde{X}$) with a large magnitude. This will generate 49 rules to implement FLP. The output b_x at any instant of time can be computed using: i) the inputs e_x and $\dot{e}_x$, ii) input membership functions, iii) 49 rules [9, 18 iv) FIS, v) aggregator, and iv) defuzzification. The properties/features of the fuzzy operators/FIMs used are given in Table 7.2.

5.7.2 COMPARISON OF KF AND FKF

The simulated data for the x-axis position are generated using CAM (Constant Acceleration Model) with process noise increment and with T = 0.1 sec., total number of scans being N = 100. The simulation uses the parameter values and related information as: a) initial states of target ($x, \dot{x}, \ddot{x}$) are (0 m, 100 m/s, 0 m/s²) respectively, and b) process noise variance Q = 0.0001 [12]. The CAM model is given as:

$$F = \begin{bmatrix} 1 & T & T^2/2 \\ 0 & 1 & T \\ 0 & 0 & 1 \end{bmatrix} \qquad (5.25)$$

$$G = \begin{bmatrix} T^3/6 & T^2/2 & T \end{bmatrix} \qquad (5.26)$$

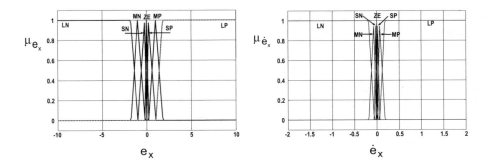

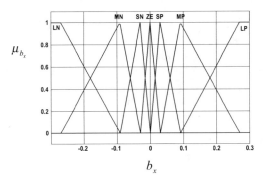

FIGURE 5.27 Fuzzy membership functions for error-input and its finite difference and for the output FLP variable

---

TABLE 5.2
Features of FIS for FKF

FIM	Mamdani
AND operator	min
OR operator	max
Fuzzy implication	min
Aggregation	max
Defuzzification	centroid

The target state equation is given as

$$X(k+1)=FX(k)+Gw(k) \qquad (5.27)$$

Here, k is the scan number and w is white Gaussian process noise with zero mean and covariance matrix Q. The measurement equation is given as

$$Z_m(k)=HX(k)+v(k) \qquad (5.28)$$

$$H=\begin{bmatrix} 1 & 0 & 0 \end{bmatrix} \tag{5.29}$$

Here, v is white Gaussian measurement noise with usual meaning ($R=\sigma^2$, σ is the standard deviation of noise with a value of 10 meters). The initial conditions, F , G , H , Q , and R for both the filters, KF and FKF, are the same. The initial state vector $\hat{X}(0/0)$ is close to true initial states. The KF and FKF algorithms were coded in MATLAB. The results for both the filters are compared in terms of true and estimated states, and state errors with bounds at every scan number. It was observed that FKF performs much better compared to KF [7]. The consistency checks on these filters were performed using the normalized cost function (CF) computed using the formula:

$$CF = \frac{1}{N} \sum_{k=1}^{N} e(k) S(k)^{-1} e(k)^T \tag{5.30}$$

Here, e is the innovation sequence vector, and S is the innovation covariance matrix. The filter performance is deemed consistent if its normalized CF, equation (5.30) is equal to the dimension of the vector of the observables. The CF for KF (= 2.94) was found to be very close to the theoretical value of 3, whereas for FKF, its CF value 2.85 was slightly different from the theoretical value 3; however, it is still comparable with the KF value and is not much different from the theoretical number. Hence, the FKF can be treated as an approximately consistent filter. The performance of both the filters in terms of states errors was also evaluated and the FKF showed better performance than KF. This validated the application of the FKF for target tracking and it is comparable to or gives better performance than the KF. Further applications of both the filters are evaluated and some results are given next.

Example 5.3 Maneuvering target-tracking
In order to use FKF for tracking a maneuvering target a re-design of the FLPV to capture the various possible maneuver modes of the target is required. This involves [12]: i) proper selection of FMFs I/O, ii) tuning of these FMFs, iii) selection of fuzzy operators (e.g. T-norm & S-norm), and iv) selection of FIFs/FIMs, aggregation and defuzzification techniques. We here use MATLAB® based functions such as 'genfis1()' to create the initial FLP vector and 'anfis()' to tune it. The required training and check data are obtained from true and measured target positions.

Figure 5.28 depicts the procedure to get a tuned FLP vector [12].

a) **Training Set and Check Set Data:** The target states are simulated using a 3 DOF kinematic model with process noise acceleration increments and additional accelerations. Measurement data is obtained with a sampling interval of 1 sec. and total of 150 scans are generated. The data simulation is done with: i) initial states ($x, \dot{x}, \ddot{x}, y, \dot{y}, \ddot{y}$) of target as (100, 30, 0, 100, 20, 0); ii) process noise variance $Q = 0.1$; with $Q_{xx} = Q_{yy} = Q$; and iii) the measurement noise variance $R = 25$; $R_{xx} = R_{yy} = R$. The target has an additional acceleration of

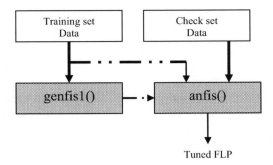

FIGURE 5.28   Procedure for tuning–FLP

(x_{acc}, y_{acc}) at scans 25 and 100 and an acceleration of ($-x_{acc}$, $-y_{acc}$) at scans 50 and 75. Data simulation is carried out with process noise vector w (2×1 vector) modified to include these additional accelerations at the specified scan points in order to induce a specific maneuver [3], [12]:

$$\left.\begin{aligned} w(1) &= \text{guass}()*\sqrt{Q_{xx}} + x_{acc} \\ w(2) &= \text{guass}()*\sqrt{Q_{yy}} + y_{acc} \end{aligned}\right\} \tag{5.31}$$

$$\left.\begin{aligned} w(1) &= \text{guass}()*\sqrt{Q_{xx}} - x_{acc} \\ w(2) &= \text{guass}()*\sqrt{Q_{yy}} - y_{acc} \end{aligned}\right\} \tag{5.32}$$

At the other scan points the vector w is simply defined without these additional acceleration terms. Accelerations $x_{acc} = -9*9.8\,\text{m/s}^2$ and $y_{acc} = 9*9.8\,\text{m/s}^2$ are used in these equations and the function guass() is used to generate Gaussian random numbers with mean 0 and variance 1. First the initial FLPV is created for the x-axis and tuned using inputs u_x^1, u_x^2 and output o_x obtained using:

$$u_x^1(k) = z_x(k) - x(k) \tag{5.33}$$

$$u_x^2(k) = \frac{u_x^1(k) - u_x^1(k-1)}{T} \tag{5.34}$$

$$output_x(k) = m\, u_x^1(k) \tag{5.35}$$

Here, x and z_x are a true and measured target x-position respectively, and m is the unknown parameter, and $m = 2$ for the present case. The first half of the total simulated data are taken for training and the remaining half as the check-set data. The same procedure is followed to get tuned FLPV for the y-axis, then the trained FLP vector is plugged in to FKF and its performance is compared with the KF for the two cases discussed in the next section.

b) **Mild and evasive maneuver data:** The mild maneuver data (MM) are generated with minor modifications in the acceleration injection points, and a total of 17 scans are generated. Accelerations are injected at scans 8 ($x_{acc} = 6\,\text{m/s}^2$ and $y_{acc} = -6\,\text{m/s}^2$) and 15 ($x_{acc} = -6\,\text{m/s}^2$ and $y_{acc} = 6\,\text{m/s}^2$) only [12]. The evasive maneuver data (EM) are generated with the same points for acceleration injection but with a maneuver magnitude of $40*9.8\,\text{m/s}^2$ (instead of $9*9.8\,\text{m/s}^2$). The results are obtained for 100 Monte-Carlo simulation runs with the initial state vectors of KF and FKF kept the same and close to the initial true states. Initial state error covariance matrices for both the filters are unity values. In Figure 5.29 the measured, true and estimated x-y target positions for MM data are shown [3], [12]. The estimated trajectories using KF and FKF compare reasonably well with the true ones. Some discrepancies are in the maneuvering phase of the flight where FKF exhibits better performance than KF. Similar observations are made for the case of EM data (the detailed results are not shown here). However, Figure 5.30 shows the comparison of RSSPE, RSSVE, and RSSAE (root of sum of squares position-, velocity-, and acceleration–errors, as performance metrics) for both the filters and these errors for the KF are found to be somewhat large compared to those for FKF [12].

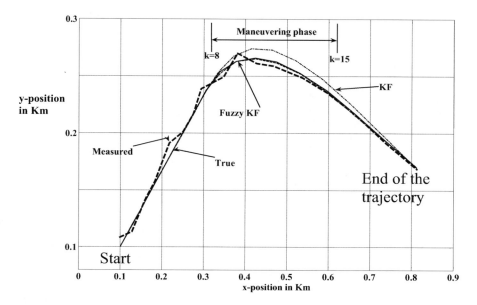

FIGURE 5.29   True, measured and estimated x-y positions of the target for Mild maneuver

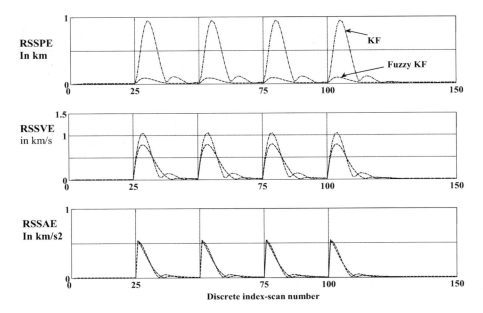

FIGURE 5.30   RSSPE, RSSVE, and RSSAE plots for KF, FKF for EM data

5.7.3   Fuzzy Logic-based Sensor Data Fusion

State vector fusion (SVF) is generally used for integration of the estimated states weighted with predicted state error covariance matrices as:

$$\hat{X}_f^{SV}(k) = \hat{X}_1^{KF}(k) + \hat{P}_1^{KF}(k)\left(\hat{P}_1^{KF}(k) + \hat{P}_2^{KF}(k)\right)^{-1}\left(\hat{X}_2^{KF}(k) - \hat{X}_1^{KF}(k)\right) \qquad (5.36)$$

$$\hat{P}_f^{SV}(k) = \hat{P}_1^{KF}(k) - \hat{P}_1^{KF}(k)\left(\hat{P}_1^{KF}(k) + \hat{P}_2^{KF}(k)\right)^{-1}\hat{P}_1^{KF}(k) \qquad (5.37)$$

Where, $\hat{X}_1^{KF}$, $\hat{X}_2^{KF}$ are the estimated states obtained using the basic KF for sensor 1 and sensor 2 respectively and $\hat{P}_1^{KF}$, $\hat{P}_2^{KF}$ are the associated state error covariance matrices. Next, we study different ways of fusion using FL-based KF schemes.

5.7.3.1   Kalman Filter Fuzzification–KFF

Here, the original data from each sensor are processed by a respective KF to estimate the states of a target (position, velocity, and acceleration). The error signal for each channel is generated by taking the difference of the measured and estimated positions of the target for that particular channel. The average estimation error is computed by:

$$\overline{e}_{idn}^{KF}(k) = \frac{e_{x_{idn}}^{KF}(k) + e_{y_{idn}}^{KF}(k) + e_{z_{idn}}^{KF}(k)}{M} \qquad (5.38)$$

We have $M=3$ the total number of measurement channels, $idn = 1,2$ as the sensor identity number, and the error signals are generated by:

$$
\left.
\begin{aligned}
e_{x_{idn}}^{KF}(k) &= x_{m_{idn}}(k) - \hat{x}_{idn}^{KF}(k) \\
e_{y_{idn}}^{KF}(k) &= y_{m_{idn}}(k) - \hat{y}_{idn}^{KF}(k) \\
e_{z_{idn}}^{KF}(k) &= z_{m_{idn}}(k) - \hat{z}_{idn}^{KF}(k)
\end{aligned}
\right\}
\tag{5.39}
$$

Where $x_{m_{idn}}, y_{m_{idn}}, z_{m_{idn}}$ are the target position measurements in the x-, y-, z–axes, and $\hat{x}_{idn}^{KF}, \hat{y}_{idn}^{KF}, \hat{z}_{idn}^{KF}$ are the corresponding estimated positions from the KF. The fused states are given by:

$$
\hat{X}_{f}^{KFF}(k) = w_{1}(k)\hat{X}_{1}^{KF}(k) + w_{2}(k)\hat{X}_{2}^{KF}(k)
\tag{5.40}
$$

Where $\{w_1, w_2\}$ are the weights generated by the FIS for sensor 1 and sensor 2, and the normalized values of the error signals $\bar{e}_1$ and $\bar{e}_2$ are the inputs to the FIS (associated with each sensor). The weights w_1 and w_2 are obtained as follows:

i)   Fuzzification: These normalized error signals are fuzzified to values in the interval of [0, 1] using corresponding FMFs labeled by linguistic variables. The FMFs for both the error signals are kept the same and the variables have the attributes: ZE–zero error, SP–small positive, MP–medium positive, LP– large positive and VLP–very large positive. Figure 5.31 shows the membership functions for error signals $\bar{e}_{idn}$ and weights w_{idn} [12].

ii) Rule generation/FIS process: The rules are created based on the magnitude of error signals reflecting the uncertainty in sensor measurements. Some rules for sensor 1 and sensor 2 are given as [12]:

Sensor 1:   IF $\bar{e}_1$ is LP AND $\bar{e}_2$ is VLP THEN w_1 is MP
            IF $\bar{e}_1$ is ZE AND $\bar{e}_2$ is MP THEN w_1 is LP
Sensor 2:   IF $\bar{e}_1$ is ZE AND $\bar{e}_2$ is VLP THEN w_2 is ZE
            IF $\bar{e}_1$ is ZE AND $\bar{e}_2$ is ZE THEN w_2 is MP

Table 5.3 gives the fuzzy rule base for the outputs w_1 and w_2, for sensor 1 and 2 respectively.

iii) Defuzzification: The crisp values of w_1 and w_2, obtained by defuzzifying (using the method of COA) the aggregated output fuzzy sets are used in fusion specified by equation (7.20).

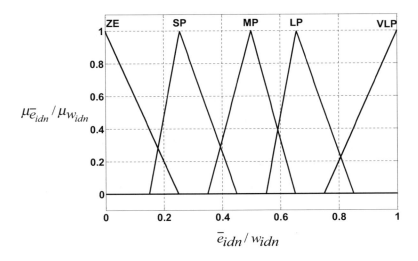

FIGURE 5.31   Error signals–weights w_1 membership functions for KFF/FKFF

TABLE 5.3
Fuzzy Rule base of 25 rules for Sensors 1 and 2

$\overline{e}_1$	$\overline{e}_2$ For sensor 1					$\overline{e}_2$ For sensor 2				
	ZE	SP	MP	LP	VLP	ZE	SP	MP	LP	VLP
ZE	MP	MP	LP	LP	VLP	MP	MP	SP	SP	ZE
SP	MP	MP	MP	LP	LP	MP	MP	MP	SP	SP
MP	SP	MP	MP	MP	LP	LP	MP	MP	MP	SP
LP	ZE	SP	SP	MP	MP	VLP	LP	LP	MP	MP
VLP	ZE	ZE	SP	MP	MP	VLP	VLP	LP	MP	MP

5.7.3.2   Fuzzy Kalman Filter Fuzzification–FKFF

An alternative architecture is shown in Figure 5.32 [12]. The basic steps to compute weights are the same as for KFF, but with the following changes: a) in equations (5.38), and (5.39) superscript 'KF' is replaced by 'FKF' meaning thereby that the state estimation is performed using FKF instead of KF, and b) the fused states are obtained by:

$$\hat{X}_f^{FKFF}(k) = \hat{X}_1^{FKF}(k) + w_1(k)\left(w_1(k) + w_2(k)\right)^{-1}\left(\hat{X}_2^{FKF}(k) - \hat{X}_1^{FKF}(k)\right) \quad (5.41)$$

Here, the values of the weights might be different from the previous ones. This new SVF equation is obtained from equation (5.36) by replacing $\hat{P}_1^{KF}$, $\hat{P}_2^{KF}$ with w_1 and w_2 respectively.

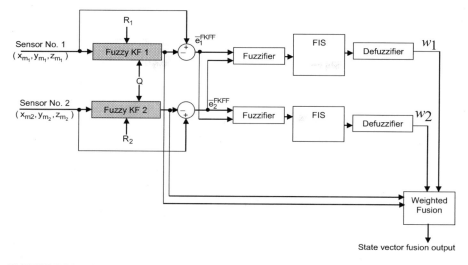

FIGURE 5.32   An alternative scheme for fusion using fuzzy logic w_2

Example 5.4 Numerical comparison of SVF, KFF, and FKF

The trained FLP vector is obtained as earlier (as used in FKF). To compare the performance of the fusion algorithms: SVF, KFF, and FKFF, another set of data is generated by
modifying the acceleration injection points used to generate the training set and check
set data and a total of 25 scans are generated. The accelerations are injected at scan 8
as $x_{acc} = 6\,\text{m/s}^2$ and $y_{acc} = -6\,\text{m/s}^2$) and at scan 15 as $x_{acc} = -6\,\text{m/s}^2$ and $y_{acc} = 6\,\text{m/s}^2$
only, and the measurements for two sensors are generated with SNR = 10 for sensor
1 and SNR = 20 for sensor 2. The data for each sensor are processed by KF and FKF
for 100 Monte-Carlo simulation runs, and their initial states (80% of true initial state)
and error covariance matrices are kept the same. The performance of these filters is
compared in terms of RSSPE, RSSVE, and RSSAE, however Figure 5.33 illustrates
only the velocity error comparisons for the three schemes. From these and related
plots (not shown here, [12]) the following observations are made: i) FKFF performs
better than SVF and KFF, and ii) during the maneuver the FKFF has less state errors
compared to other fusion methods. The two weights sum to approximately one (as
expected) for KFF and FKFF methods.

5.8   FUZZY LOGIC IN DECISION FUSION

As we have seen earlier that fusion can greatly help in situation refinement (SR). It
forms a Situation Assessment (SA) by relating the objects to the existing situation
assessment or by relating object assessments (OA) mutually. SR helps in developing
a description of current relationships among objects and events in the context of the
environment. It can also assesses the meaning of Level 1 estimated state and/or identity results in the context of some background or supporting data. SA can be divided
into stages: i) perception and event-detection (PED), ii) current SA, and iii) near

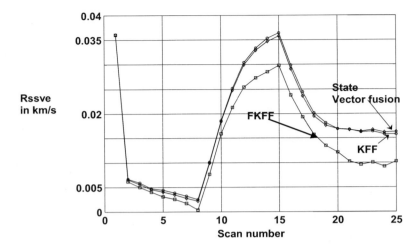

FIGURE 5.33   RSS velocity errors for three fusion approaches SVF, KFF, FKFF

future situation prediction. The PED reduces the workload of the overall SA process by detecting a change in existing SA, i.e. if a situation is already assessed and nothing changes, the situation does not need any more evaluation until new events occur. If a new event occurs then the current situation is assessed along with a prediction to find out what could possibly happen in the near future. The various levels of SA are modeled based on abstraction and reasoning. The intensity of abstraction increases as the steps in the MSDF ladder are climbed. SA aids in decision making, as for example, for a pilot of a fighter aircraft. The various decisions/actions that a pilot can/ should make are: a) avoid any collision with any nearby flying object, b) access the intentions of the enemy (if suspected to be an enemy) aircraft, and c) communicate with other nearby friendly (if found to be so) aircraft. The pilot's inherent capability for making various decisions/actions works well when the number of nearby flying objects is small. In a very complex scenario how quick and accurate a decision that a pilot can make is difficult to decide. Here, a mathematical model of the SR-algorithm is required that can aid the pilot in quick/accurate decision making allowing the pilot to concentrate more on flying his/her aircraft.

Let us consider the object refinement (OR) as a numerical procedure that enables us to assign properties to the objects of interest, as for example, a missile with certain (properties) such as acceleration, velocity, and position. The OR also uses rules based on geometry, kinematics and presumes that a certain object cannot change its properties by breaking these rules, while remaining the same object, which means that if the properties are changed then it might be a different object. A missile has the property of targeting an aircraft, whereas an aircraft has the property of being targeted by a missile. With these properties one can conclude only the relation between objects but cannot really make out whether that missile is going to target an aircraft or not. It could be possible that the missile is not interested in targeting an aircraft at the present instant of time and may target at some other/later time. One view is that we can

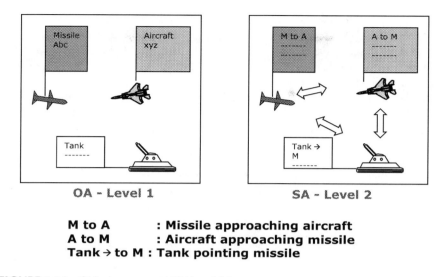

M to A : **Missile approaching aircraft**
A to M : **Aircraft approaching missile**
Tank → to M : Tank pointing missile

FIGURE 5.34   Object assessment (OA) and SA

assume the world is the totality of certain observed facts and these are the application of relations to objects. Figure 5.34 illustrates object and situation assessments for a typical battlefield scenario [13]. It is observed that objects are missile, fighter aircraft and tank. The properties of these objects are positions, velocities, directions and identities computed through numerical procedures of Level 1 fusion. Using situation assessment, it is then (to be) concluded that the missile is approaching an aircraft and the tank pointing towards the missile at any given instant of time.

5.8.1 Methods Available to Perform Situation Assessments

The most commonly used techniques in SA systems are high-level classification methods, the basic requirement being they should be able to handle uncertainty with an ease of modeling the situations. The common methods for assessing situations are: i) ANNs–basically an ANN would have been trained on some situations, then it would be given the data of the actual/current situation that might have just occurred and the ANN predicts the situation, and if there is a close match, then a further decision is taken, etc., ii) forward-chain expert system (classical–FCES), iii) Bayesian network (BN) or also referred to as a belief network (more appropriate for D-S networks/theory, causal net or inference net), iv) fuzzy logic–FL/FMF/FIS, and v) hybrid methods–fuzzy logic and BNW, ANN and FL, etc.

The FCES requires modeling by an expert and cannot update its knowledge automatically–it cannot adapt itself from the data–the system containing only the knowledge of its designer. BN can be modeled as an expert system and can also have the ability of updating the beliefs (probabilities for BN and 'masses' for the DS methods). It has the ability to investigate a hypothesis of the future. In order to make the system convenient, the nodes in the BN are often discrete and an expert can easily enter estimates of the probabilities for one situation leading to another. This will lead to a 'quite good' NW. The system is difficult to use in real time. Also, BN needs continuous input data, i.e. the data has to be classified first. The FL-expert system (FLES) can represent human knowledge/experience in the form of fuzzy rules. These rules can be tuned adaptively or new rules can be created dynamically using sets of input/output data and ANN. The learning method generates the optimal fuzzy inference (FI-engine/knowledge base) rapidly as required for time-critical missions and with good accuracy. The DF systems produced through partially processed sensory information and intelligence would have uncertain, incomplete, and inaccurate information due to limited sensor capabilities. The FL can handle this for tasks like i) SA and decision making through modeling the entity, and ii) models and the associated fuzzy sets (and possibility theory). Hybrid methods utilize an FL approach to classify the continuous input which goes as discrete input to BN and makes the net continuous.

5.8.2 A Comparison between Bayesian Network and Fuzzy Logic

Using FL, the numerical data can be classified into fuzzy sets of discrete variables, say for the temperature of a certain quantity. A normal practice is by assigning some grade to the FMF, i.e. very cold, quite hot, etc. The problem comes in assigning a grade to temperatures such as 19 and 21 degrees Celsius. It is observed that the difference between temperatures is not very big, but when classified using hard boundaries, 19 degrees is treated as cold and 21 degrees as hot. Trying to model a system using hard boundaries can often result in erroneous outputs. The classification can be more precise by using fuzzy boundaries; 19 degrees could be classified as cold with membership-value 0.6 and hot with membership-value 0.4. The same way 21 degrees can be classified. The importance of fuzzy classification becomes more important while dealing with noisy signals.

5.8.3 Situation Assessment Using Fuzzy Logic

When the level of uncertainties increases it requires an exact reasoning with an upward climb in the data fusion levels. Just by using numerical procedures it is very hard to model the uncertainties so that a situation can be assessed as accurately as possible. An application of FL at the higher levels of DF could be a good choice for precise decision making. If one of the outputs of SA is 'Aircraft is non-friendly and targeting tank' then it can be interpreted as if the situation assessor takes the decision that 'Aircraft is non-friendly and targeting tank'. The fusion comes into the picture when there is more than one such decision for the same object of interest seen by multiple sensors of different types and accuracies. Different accuracy levels of each sensor dictate different confidence levels while taking a decision. In order to have an accurate decision it is essential to fuse the decisions (outputs from the situation assessor) using fuzzy logic approach. This is a decision fusion paradigm as against data fusion (DF).

Consider a scenario consisting of an unknown aircraft seen by two sensors of different types. The first sensor provides 'identity' information and the second sensor measures the direction of the moving aircraft. The goal of FLSA is to take a decision as to whether the behavior of the unknown aircraft is hostile or friendly [13]. The two inputs are direction and identity and the single output is 'behavior' in FIS, i.e. now the situation assessor. The inputs are fuzzified by using corresponding FMFs. The inputs direction and identity have two MFs, each with linguistic labels {departing, approaching} and {friend, foe} respectively and the output has FMFs with linguistic labels {friendly, hostile}. Inputs are aggregated using following inference rules [14]-[15]:

Rule 1:   IF aircraft is departing OR identity is friend THEN behavior is friendly
Rule 2:   IF aircraft is approaching OR identity is foe THEN behavior is hostile

The FL 'AND' is min(A, B) and OR is max(A, B), with A and B as two fuzzy sets representing inputs direction and identity respectively. There is a possibility of both the rules being fired simultaneously then there will be an output fuzzy set for each rule. These outputs are combined using an aggregation process (the present case uses max (C1, C2), where C1 and C2 are fuzzy output sets). The final crisp output is produced by applying defuzzification process (e.g. COA has been used) to obtain the resultant output fuzzy set. For a given crisp input, the corresponding membership value for each membership function is given as Input 1 (direction) with Membership grade: example {0.2, 0.8}, and Input 2 (identity) with Membership grade: {0.3, 0.7}, for example. Both the rules are fired concurrently. In first rule the inference is OR giving the combined membership value of max(0.2, 0.3) = 0.3. The FMF of that behavior is friendly, and is cut at membership value 0.3. For the second rule the FMF of that behavior is hostile, and is cut at membership value min(0.8, 0.7) = 0.7. Then the truncated output fuzzy sets are combined and COA is calculated to determine the total hostility of an aircraft as shown Figure 5.35.

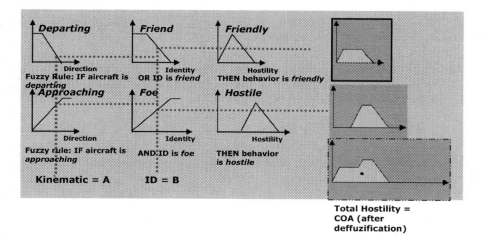

Total Hostility = COA (after deffuzification)

FIGURE 5.35   FL-Based SA to determine total hostility

5.8.4 LEVEL 3 THREAT AND LEVEL 4 PROCESS REFINEMENTS

In Level 3 the fusion projects the current situation into the future to draw inferences about enemy threats (friendly as well as enemy vulnerabilities and opportunities) for operations. This requires information from Level 1 and Level 2 so that the quantitative estimates of an object's behavior can be determined and the expected course of action cane be assessed. The Threat Refinement (TR) aspects are identification of possible capabilities, intent of hostile objects and the expected outcome. The Process Refinement (PR) is a metaprocess; a process concerned about other processes. Level 4 performs four key functions: i) monitors the DF process performance to provide information about real-time control and long-term performance, ii) identifies what information is needed to improve the multilevel fusion product, iii) determines the source specific requirements to collect relevant information, and iv) allocates and directs the sources to achieve mission goals. The latter function may be outside the domain of specific data fusion functions.

5.9 FUZZY LOGIC-BAYESIAN NETWORK FOR SITUATION ASSESSMENT

The decision-making in an air-combat (AC) is a complex task. Threat and situation assessment are the main components in this process. The AC operators of military airborne platforms depend on observed data from multiple sensors and sources to achieve their mission. The operators combine these data manually to produce a coherent air surveillance picture that portrays tracks of airborne targets and their classification. In many cases this air surveillance picture is analyzed manually (mentally) to determine the behavior of each target with respect to the owner's ship and other targets in the region and assess the intent and/or threat (threat assessment/TA) posed or any impact these might have on the planned mission [13]-[15]. As the number of targets grows or the situation escalates there is a potential for the volume of available data to overload and overwork the operators, and hence it is desirable to assist the operators by automating some of the SA/TA process.

The main problem in such decision making in any AC task is that of uncertainty. This can be handled via FL, belief functions, or ANNs. The probabilistic approach is based on rigorous theory, but it requires a vast amount of storage and computational manipulation making this method computationally burdensome. An alternative is the BN (Sections 2.3 and 2.5) since the Bayesian approach has many feasible features [16]-[17]. If the BN is integrated with FL which makes the data members of discrete sets then this hybrid approach would be able to handle many requirements of SA. The design and implementation of an expert system named the intelligent system for SA in Air combat (ISAC) as an aid to pilots engaged in SA tasks are discussed in the next.

5.9.1 DESCRIPTION OF THE ISAC

The ISAC is a Pilot-In-the-Loop (PIL) real time simulator which consists of: i) Integration of (airborne) Sensor Models (ISM), ii) an interactive GUI-Exercise

Controller (EC) for AC scenario generation/platform models, iii) pilot mental models/
concurrent BNWs, iv) data processing algorithms, and v) graphical display [14]. The
schematic of the ISAC is shown in Figure 5.36.

a) **Exercise controller-EC:** It is a C++ module as the platform with models
of a fighter, a bomber, a missile, a rotorcraft, and a transport aircraft. EC is
used to create any typical Air-to-Air Combat (AAC) scenario which can have
maximum 6 targets (excluding the owner's ship) and has a simple user interface (consisting of a display-, status-, and menu-area). The status area has
important parameters such as speed, course, bearing, coordinates, and radar
status. The targets are represented by pre-specified shapes and colors to distinguish which platform types they represent. The class and ID of all targets
should be specified for the simulation. Each target is controlled either by pre-
defined trajectories or by user interaction in real-time.

b) **Integrated Sensor Model (ISM):** This MATLAB-SIMULINK-based module
has functional models of different sensors: a) Doppler radar, b) IRST, c) Radar
Warning Receiver (RWR), and d) EOTS.

c) **Data Processor:** This module consists of i) MSDF, ii) Relative Kinematics/
Data (RKD), and iii) Fuzzy Event Detector (FED), and it combines/classifies
the data received from the multiple sensors. EKF is used to estimate the states
of the targets using fused measurements from the multiple sensors. FED
classifies the RKD data into qualitative form/events: speed is 'low', 'medium'
or 'high'. The MATLAB FL toolbox is used to design appropriate FMFs for
data classification.

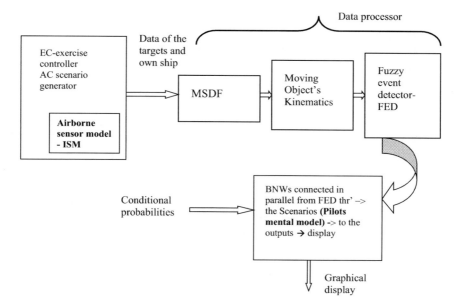

FIGURE 5.36   The ISAC Simulator schematic with Fuzzy logic-Bayesian NWs

d) **Pilot Mental Model:** The PMM emulates the pilot's information processing, SA, and decision-making functions based on information received from the DP. Agents based on BNW technology are used to assess the occurrence of different situations in AC scenarios. The **HUGIN C++ API** software tool [18] is used. Finally, the **Graphical Display** provides the updated probabilities of all the agents.

e) **Bayesian Mental Model:** A mental model of the SA requires: i) the capability to quantitatively represent the key SA concepts such as situations, events, and the pilot's mental model, ii) a mechanism to reflect both diagnostic and inferential reasoning, and iii) an ability to deal with various levels and types of uncertainties [3], [5]. BNs are ideal tools for meeting such requirements. BNs are directed acyclic graphs in which nodes represent a probabilistic variable whose probability distribution is denoted as a belief value (more so for the D-S belief NWs) and the links represent informal or causal dependencies among the variables. The weights in the BNs are the conditional probabilities that are attached to each cluster of parent-child nodes in the network [17]. The three agents based on BN are used to assess the occurrence of different situations in an AC task with their tasks as [3], [6]: a) pair agent–two or more targets are in formation e.g. a pair of aircraft, b) along agent–aircraft flying along an air lane, and c) attack agent–one target attacking another target, e.g. fighter attacking the owner's ship. The process consists of: i) a BN to represent the pilot mental model, and ii) a belief update algorithm to reflect the propagation.

f) **Pair Agent BN (PAN):** Figure 5.37 depicts these three BN-models [12]-[13]. The PAN computes the updated probabilities when the speed, elevation, and

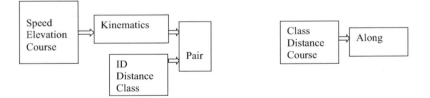

a) Pair agent BNW model   b) Along BNW model

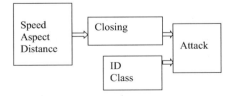

c) Attack BNW model

FIGURE 5.37   BNWs-models for SA

course, and the ID, distance, and class are the independent or information nodes. The inputs 'distance', 'course', 'elevation' and 'speed' have three states: Small, Medium and Large. The 'ID' has three states: Friend, Unknown and Foe. The 'class' has four states: Fighter, Bomber, Transport and Missile. The node 'kinematics' has two states: Same and Different. The Pair node is the Hypothesis node and has two states: Yes and No. The rules of the Pair agent are given as: i) if two aircraft have the same course, elevation and speed, then they have the same kinematics, and ii) if two aircraft have the same kinematics, the same ID, the same class, and are at a short distance from each other, then they form a pair.

g) **Along Agent BNW (AAN):** The AAN model computes the relationship between the air lane and the aircraft. The 'distance' and 'course' have three states: Small, Medium and Large. The 'class' has four states: Fighter, Bomber, Transport and Missile. The AAN node is the Hypothesis node and has two states: Yes and No. The rules are: i) if an aircraft has the same course as an air lane, and if it is close to the air lane, then the aircraft is flying along the air lane, and ii) if an aircraft is transport there is a higher possibility that the aircraft is flying along the air lane.

h) **Attack Agent BNW (AtAN):** The AtAN model computes the attacking probabilities. The states of 'ID', 'class', 'distance', and 'speed' are the same as in Pair agent. The 'Aspect' node has three states: Small, Medium and High. The closing node has two states: Yes and No. The Attack node is the Hypothesis node and has two states: Yes and No. The rules are: i) if an aircraft has high speed, has a close distance to another aircraft and has a heading towards (high aspect) it is trying to close in on the other, and ii) if an aircraft is closing in on another, and has a different ID and is a fighter aircraft, then the aircraft is attacking the other.

The scenario consists of six targets (five aircraft and one missile) with the scenario data in Table 5.4. Figure 5.38 shows AtAN probabilities–it detected 4 active relations between own ship and the targets 1(foe), 2(foe), 4(unknown) & 5(foe)–with target 5 having the highest probability as expected because it is a missile and closing in from behind [13]. Targets 3 and 6 have the lowest probability since both are friends. The PAN detected a pair between targets 1 and 2 which lasted for 20 sec (results not shown).

TABLE 5.4
Data on scenario

Taget No.	Class	ID
1	Fighter	Foe
2	Fighter	Foe
3	Fighter	Friend
4	Fighter	Unknown
5	Missile	Foe
6	Transport	friend

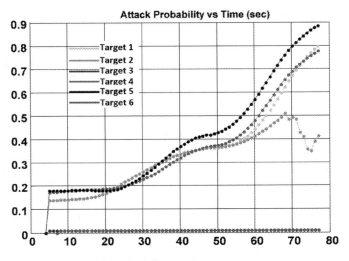

FIGURE 5.38 AtAN probabilities for AC scenario

It did not detect a pair between targets 3 and 4 because their IDs are different, Table 5.4. AAN found the relationship between target 6 and the air lane. The air lane is a virtual object and was inserted in a database before the simulation.

Thus, it is observed that the Fuzzy logic-BNs combination using several agents is able to accomplish the job assigned with a fairly good amount of precision.

EXERCISES

5.1 What are the various types of logic in a decision making process?

5.2 What are the features, and operators/rules used in these types of logic?

5.3 What is a feedback fuzzy system (FFS)?

5.4 What is the use of this FFS?

5.5 In what way can the FFS can be adjusted for the modeling?

5.6 What is the meaning of pruning the Fuzzy rules and why it might be necessary?

5.7 Why is it that the 'min' and 'max' operators in FL/S have more than one 'internal' meaning/interpretation/definition unlike the crisp logic AND, OR, etc. where the results are always unique?

5.8 What is the relation of decision fusion to data fusion?

5.9 How do the decision fusion methods of voting, Bayesian and Dempster-Shafer compare?

5.10 Is the data/decision fusion process the process of 'reduction'? How and why?

5.11 Can fuzzy set theory be considered as a method of decision fusion?

5.12 Why in general does the fuzzy logic-based KF (FLKF) not meet the filter-consistency check as accurately as the standard KF?

5.13 Why is decision making in KF called soft decision making?

5.14 What is the type of decision making in FLKF?

5.15 What kind of fusion processes can be used for the data that are not homogeneous quantities?

REFERENCES

1. Hall, D. L. *Mathematical Techniques in Multi-Sensor Data Fusion*. Artech House, Norwood, Massachusetts, 1992.

2. Abidi, M. A., and Gonzalez, R. C. (Eds.). *Data Fusion in Robotics and Machine Intelligence*. Academic Press, USA, 1992.

3. Raol, J. R. *Multisensor Data Fusion with MATLAB*. CRC Press, Florida, US. 2009.

4. Raol, J. R., and J. Singh. *Flight Mechanics Modelling and Analysis, Revised Edition*, CRC Press, Florida, US. 2023.

5. Ivansson, J. Situation assessment in a stochastic environment using Bayesian Networks. Master's thesis, Division of Automatic Control, Department of Electrical Engineering, Linkoping University, Sweden, 2002.

6. Kashyap, S. K. Decision Fusion using Fuzzy Logic. Doctoral Thesis, University of Mysore, Mysore, India, 2008.

7. Kashyap, S. K, Raol, J. R., and Patel, A. V. Evaluation of fuzzy implications and intuitive criteria of GMP and GMT. In *Foundations of Generic Optimization* Volume 2: Applications of Fuzzy Control, Genetic Algorithms and Neural Networks (The series Mathematical Modelling: Theory and Applications), Lowen, R. and Verschoren A. (Eds.), pp. 313–385, Springer, New York, USA, 2008.

8. Klein L. A. *Sensor and Data Fusion, A Tool for Information Assessment and Decision Making*, SPIE Press, Washington, USA, 2004.

9. Kant, E. Critique of Pure Reason, Translated by N. Kemp Smith, New York Random House, (original work published in 1781), New York, USA 1958.

10. Wik, M. W. A three processes effects model based on the meaning of information. 11th ICCRTS Coalition Command and Control in the Networked Era, Sept. 26–28, 2006. www.dodccrp.org/events/11th_ICCRTS/html/presentations/018.pdf.

11. Crowley, J. L., and Demazeu, Y. Principles and techniques of sensor data fusion. LIFIA (IMAG), France. www-prima.imag.fr/Prima/Homepages/jlc/papers/SigProc-Fusion.pdf, 1993.

12. Kashyap, S.K., and Raol, J. R. Fuzzy logic applications for filtering and fusion for target tracking. Defense Science Jl., 58, 120–135, January 2008.

13/14. Rao, N. P., Kashyap, G., Sudesh, K., Girija, G. Situation assessment in air–combat: A fuzzy-Bayesian hybrid approach, Proceedings of the International Conference on Aerospace Science and Technology, NAL, 26–28 June 2008, Bangalore,

15. Endsley, M. R. A Survey of Situation Awareness Requirements in Air-to-Air Combat Fighters, *International Journal of Aviation Psychology, 1993, 3 (2)*, 157–168.

16. Neapolitan, R. E. *Probabilistic Reasoning in Expert Systems*, John Wiley & Sons, New York, 1990.

17. Pearl, J. *Probabilistic Reasoning In Intelligent Systems: Networks Of Plausible Inference*. Morgan Kaufmann Publishers, Inc. San Francisco, California, 1988.

18. HUGIN Expert, *www.HUGIN.dk*.

6 Performance Evaluation of Fuzzy Logic-based Decision System

A systematic approach should be followed to find out whether any existing implication methods discussed in previous chapters (4 and 5) satisfies a given set of intuitive criteria of GMP and GMT (GMP is a method of affirming and GMT is a method of denying in Latin). MATLAB with graphics is used to develop a user interactive package to evaluate the implication methods with respect to these criteria [1], [2]. It is found that a graphical method of investigation is much quicker and requires less effort from the user as compared to an analytical method. Also, the analytical method seeks diagnosis of various curves (i.e. the nature of curves with respect to variation of fuzzy sets $\mu_A(u)$ and $\mu_B(v)$) involved in finding consequences when intuitive criteria of GMP and GMT are applied to various implication methods.

6.1 EVALUATION OF EXISTING FUZZY IMPLICATION FUNCTIONS

Tables 6.1 and 6.2 summarize the results (which are similar as in [3]) of various implication methods tested against the intuitive criteria of GMP and GMT using the new tool discussed in Chapter 5. It is observed that the FIMs such as MORFI and PORFI satisfy exactly the same intuitive criteria of GMP and GMT with the total number of satisfactions being 4. Similar observations have been made for implication methods such as ARFI, BRFI and GRFI. These methods satisfy only 2 intuitive criteria of GMP and GMT. It is also observed that MRFI has the minimum number (equals to one) of satisfactions with these criteria. The logical explanation of these observations is that the corresponding curve profiles (as far as their shapes of envelope are concerned) of implication methods such as MORFI and PORFI would be similar with both starting from the s and ending with membership grade $\mu_B(v)$. Similarly for implication methods ARFI, BRFI, and GRFI respectively, it is observed that these methods also have similar curve profiles with each of them starting with unity and finally converging to $\mu_B(v)$. The implication method MRFI has a unique curve profile that does not match with any of other methods and this makes MRFI a separate member among the existing implication methods. Finally, it can be concluded that probably due to similarity in the curve profiles of these methods (MORFI and PORFI in one group/ARFI, BRFI, and GRFI in another group) lead to equal numbers of satisfactions of intuitive criteria of GMP and GMT.

DOI: 10.1201/9781003370413-6

TABLE 6.1
Comparison of true and computed consequences of GMP

IM Criteria	T	MORFI Computed	SF	PORFI Computed	SF	ARFI Computed	SF	MRFI Computed	SF	BRFI Computed	SF	GRFI Computed	SF
C1	μ_B	μ_B	Y	μ_B	Y	$\dfrac{1+\mu_B}{2}$	N	$0.5 \cup \mu_B$	N	$0.5 \cup \mu_B$	N	$\sqrt{\mu_B}$	N
C2-1	μ_B^2	μ_B	N		N		N		N		N		N
C2-2	μ_B	μ_B	Y	μ_B	Y	$\dfrac{3+2\mu_B-\sqrt{5+4\mu_B}}{2}$	N	$\dfrac{3-\sqrt{5}}{2} \cup \mu_B$	N	$\dfrac{3-\sqrt{5}}{2} \cup \mu_B$	N	$\left(\mu_B\right)^{2/3}$	N
C3-1	$\sqrt{\mu_B}$	μ_B	N		N		N		N		N		N
C3-2	μ_B	μ_B	Y	μ_B	Y	$\dfrac{\sqrt{5+4\mu_B}-1}{2}$	N	$\dfrac{\sqrt{5}-1}{2} \cup \mu_B$	N	$\dfrac{\sqrt{5}-1}{2} \cup \mu_B$	N	$\left(\mu_B\right)^{1/3}$	N
C4-1	1	$0.5 \cap \mu_B$	N	$\dfrac{\mu_B}{1+\mu_B}$	N	1	Y	1	Y	1	Y	1	Y
C4-2	$\mu_{\bar{B}}$		N		N		N		N		N		N

T= true consequence of GMP; SF = satisfaction flag;
'Y' if computed consequence matches with true one
'N' if computed consequence not matches with true one

TABLE 6.2
Comparison of true and computed consequences of GMT

IM \ Criteria T	T	MORFI Computed	MORFI SF	PORFI Computed	PORFI SF	ARFI Computed	ARFI SF	MRFI Computed	MRFI SF	BRFI Computed	BRFI SF	GRFI Computed	GRFI SF
C5	$\mu_{\overline{A}}$	$0.5 \cap \mu_A$	N	$\dfrac{\mu_A}{1+\mu_A}$	N	$1-\dfrac{\mu_A}{2}$	N	$0.5 \cup 1-\mu_A$	N	$0.5 \cup 1-\mu_A$	N	$\dfrac{1}{1+\mu_A}$	N
C6	$1-\mu_A^2$	$\dfrac{\sqrt{5}-1}{2} \cap \mu_A$	N	$\dfrac{\mu_A\sqrt{\mu_A^2+4}-\mu_A^2}{2}$	N	$\dfrac{1-2\mu_A+\sqrt{1+4\mu_A}}{2}$	N	$\dfrac{\sqrt{5}-1}{2} \cup 1-\mu_A$	N	$\dfrac{\sqrt{5}-1}{2} \cup 1-\mu_A$	N	$\dfrac{\sqrt{1+4\mu_A^2}-1}{2\mu_A^2}$	N
C7	$1-\sqrt{\mu_A}$	$\dfrac{3-\sqrt{5}}{2} \cap \mu_A$	N	$\dfrac{2\mu_A+1-\sqrt{4\mu_A+1}}{2}$	N	$\dfrac{3-\sqrt{1+4\mu_A}}{2}$	N	$\dfrac{3-\sqrt{5}}{2} \cup 1-\mu_A$	N	$\dfrac{3-\sqrt{5}}{2} \cup 1-\mu_A$	N	$\dfrac{2+\mu_A-\sqrt{\mu_A^2+4\mu_A}}{2}$	N
C8-1	1	μ_A	N	μ_A	N	1	N	$\mu_A \cup 1-\mu_A$	N	1	Y	1	Y
C8-2	μ_A		Y		Y		Y		N		N		N

The relevant MATLAB based codes for generating various results for the examples of this chapter are provided in book's website.

6.2 DECISION FUSION SYSTEM 1: EXAMPLE 6.1 FORMATION FLIGHT

In this section fuzzy logic-based decision software/system (FLDS) residing in the user's own ship (platform) to decide whether two enemy fighter aircraft have a formation flight or not during the course of an AC scenario is demonstrated. The kinematic data using point mass models are generated for two aircraft of the same class and identity in the pitch plane (with no motion in x-y plane) using MATLAB® with parameters: 1) initial state of aircraft 1: $X_1 = \begin{bmatrix} x & \dot{x} & z & \dot{z} \end{bmatrix} = [0\,\text{m} \ 166\,\text{m/s} \ 1000\,\text{m} \ 0\,\text{m/s}]$; 2) initial state of aircraft 2: $X_2 = \begin{bmatrix} x & \dot{x} & z & \dot{z} \end{bmatrix} = [0\,\text{m} \ 166\,\text{m/s} \ 990\,\text{m} \ 0\,\text{m/s}]$; 3) sensor update rate is 1 Hz, 4) total simulation time is 30 s.; 5) aircraft motion is with constant velocity; and 6) kinematic model is $X_i(k+1) = FX_i(k) + Gw_i(k)$ with k (=1,2, … , 30) as scan/index number, i (= 1,2) as the aircraft number, F as the state transition matrix, G as the process noise gain matrix, and w as white Gaussian process noise with covariance

$$
\text{matrix } Q = 0.1 * \text{eye}(4,4), \ F = \begin{bmatrix} 1 & T & 0 & 0 \\ 0 & 1 & 0 & 0 \\ 0 & 0 & 1 & T \\ 0 & 0 & 0 & 1 \end{bmatrix} \text{ and } G = \begin{bmatrix} \dfrac{T^2}{2} & 0 & 0 & 0 \\ 0 & T & 0 & 0 \\ 0 & 0 & \dfrac{T^2}{2} & 0 \\ 0 & 0 & 0 & T \end{bmatrix}.
$$

The aircraft maintain a formation flight from t = 0 to 5 s. and then split apart at t = 5 s. and remain in that mode for up to t = 10 s. From the 10th s. to the 15th s. they fly with constant separation and start approaching each other from the 15th s. Again they form a pair from the 20th s. and stay in formation flight for another 10 s. Figure 6.1 shows the trajectories in the pitch plane and elevation angles of the two aircraft as seen from the user's own ship. The performance of FLDS depends upon proper selection of membership functions of fuzzy sets, fuzzy rules, fuzzy implication methods (FIMs), aggregation methods, and de-fuzzification techniques which are described next.

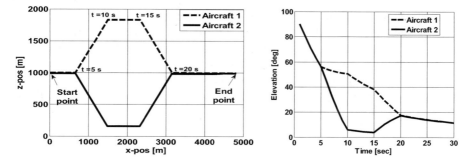

FIGURE 6.1   Trajectory and elevation angles of two aircraft

6.2.1 Membership Functions

The inputs to FLDS are numerical differences (absolute values) of aircraft's bearings, elevations, separation distances along the z-axis, speeds, identities and classes. For each input/output there is a membership function which fuzzifies the data between 0 and 1. The trapezoidal shaped membership functions are chosen as shown in Figure 6.2. It should be noted that the limits (**d, e, f,** and **g**) of these functions are provided only based on (designers'/authors') intuition for the sake of concept proving. In practice these limits should be provided by an expert in the relevant domain.

6.2.2 Fuzzy Rules and FIM

The fuzzy rules provide the way to map the inputs to output and are processed using FIM in a Fuzzy Inference Engine (FIE). The rules used to decide that two aircraft form a pair or not are: 1) Rule 1: IF two aircraft have the same bearing, elevation and speed THEN they have same kinematics, and 2) Rule 2: IF two aircraft have the same kinematics, identity, class and are at a short distance from each other THEN they form a pair. The fuzzy rules are processed by FIM and the Product Operation Rule of Fuzzy Implication (PORFI/Larsen implication) is used.

6.2.3 Aggregation and Defuzzification Method

An aggregation method is used to combine output fuzzy sets (each set is due to some rule triggered) to get a single fuzzy set. Here, a Bounded Sum (BS) operator of T-conorm/S-norm is used in the aggregation process. The aggregated output fuzzy set is de-fuzzified using the Center of Area (COA) method.

6.2.4 FLDS Realization

The FLDS is implemented in a MATLAB/SIMULINK environment using the MATLAB-fuzzy logic toolbox. Figures 6.3 to 6.5 show the schematic of the FLSD system, the sub-block of FIE/S for Rule 1 and Rule 2, and the sub-block for de-fuzzification. After the run of the FLDS the results at various stages (fuzzified inputs elevation, distance, final output, etc.) of FLDS are stored. Figure 6.6 illustrates fuzzified values of inputs distance and elevation respectively, and it is observed that during the formation flight (0–5 s. and 20–30 s.) membership grades of both the inputs are fairly high and during the non-formation flight (5–20 s.) the membership grade is nearly zero. There are other inputs such as speed, bearing, aircraft identity and class, to decide about whether both the aircraft form a pair or not. Figure 6.6 also shows the de-fuzzified output (pair) of FLDS and we see that FLDS is able to correctly detect the aircraft pair and split periods and it assigns large weight during the pair region and zero weight during the split region.

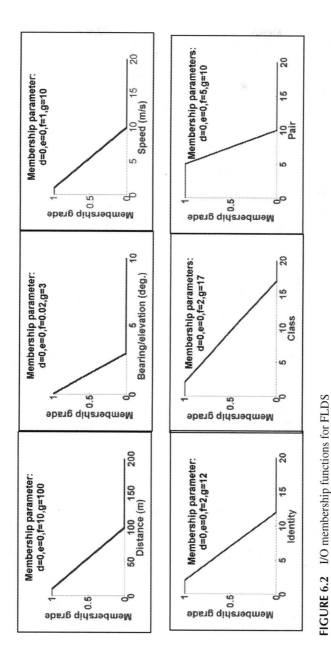

FIGURE 6.2 I/O membership functions for FLDS

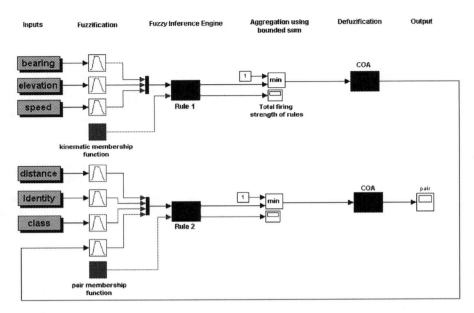

FIGURE 6.3   FLDS in MATLAB/SIMULINK

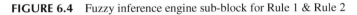

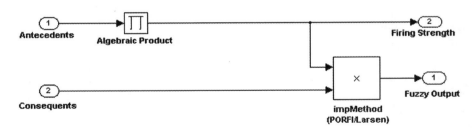

FIGURE 6.4   Fuzzy inference engine sub-block for Rule 1 & Rule 2

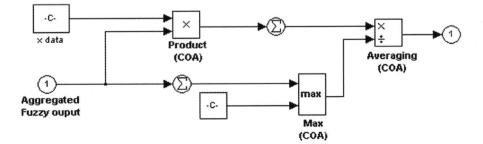

FIGURE 6.5   De-fuzzification sub-block

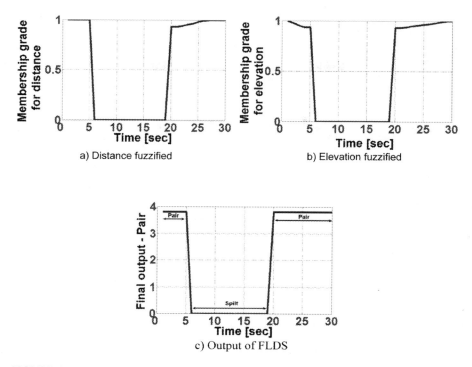

a) Distance fuzzified

b) Elevation fuzzified

c) Output of FLDS

FIGURE 6.6   I/O of the FLDS

6.3   DECISION FUSION SYSTEM 2: EXAMPLE 6.2 AIR LANE FLIGHT

Here, we describe the steps required to develop FLDS to decide whether a particular aircraft is flying along the air-lane or not. A sensitivity study is carried out to check the performance of FLDS with respect to a fuzzy aggregation operator. The simulated data for scenario generation are obtained with parameters: 1) initial state of air-craft: $X=\begin{bmatrix} x & \dot{x} & y & \dot{y} \end{bmatrix}=[2990\,\text{m} \ 0\,\text{m/s} \ 0\,\text{m} \ 332\,\text{m/s}]$; 2) air-lane located along the y axis at x = 3000 m; 3) sensor update rate is 1 Hz; 4) simulation time is 30 s.; 5) aircraft motion is with constant velocity; and 6) kinematic model is $X(k+1)=FX(k)+Gw(k)$, with k (= 1, 2, ..., 30) as the scan number, F as the state transition matrix (as in Section 6.2), G as the process noise gain matrix (as in Section 6.2), and w as white Gaussian process noise with process covariance Q: $1.0\,\text{eye}(4,4)$. Figure 6.7 depicts the aircraft and air lane location in the yaw plane and the bearings of the aircraft and air lane at various data points as seen from the origin (0, 0). Other aspects related to FIS are discussed next.

6.3.1   MEMBERSHIP FUNCTIONS

The inputs are fuzzified values of distance (absolute separation between aircraft and air lane along the y axis), the absolute value of the bearing difference between them,

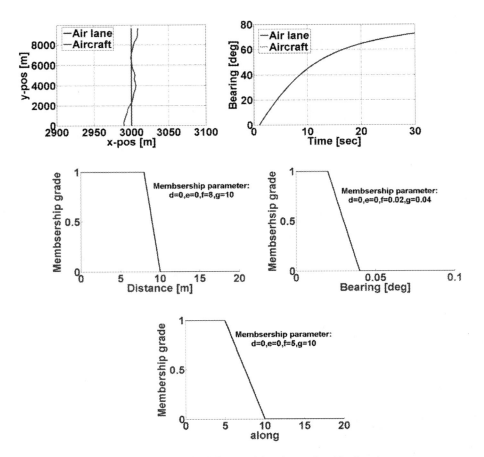

FIGURE 6.7 Inputs (distance, bearing) /output (along) membership functions

and the class of aircraft. It is assumed that the aircraft is a civilian one. The membership functions to fuzzify the inputs and output (along) are of trapezoidal shape as shown in Figure 6.7.

6.3.2 Fuzzy Rules and Other Methods

The rules used to decide that a particular aircraft flies along an air lane or not are: i) Rule 1: IF the aircraft has the same bearing as the air lane AND IF it is close to the air lane THEN the aircraft is flying along the air lane, and ii) Rule 2: IF the aircraft is civil THEN there is a high possibility that the aircraft is flying along the air lane. The product operation Rule of fuzzy implication is used for this example. The Bounded Sum (BS)/Algebraic Sum (AS)/Standard Union (SU) operators of T-conorm/S-norm are used one by one in the aggregation process. The aggregated output fuzzy set is de-fuzzified using the Center of Area (COA) method.

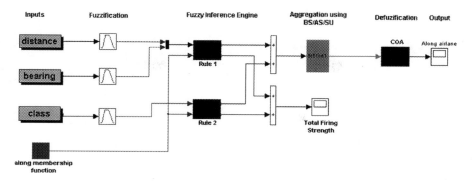

FIGURE 6.8   FLDS for air lane example using MATLAB/SIMULINK

6.3.3   FLDS REALIZATION

The FLDS is realized using MATLAB/SIMULINK as shown in Figure 6.8. Some important sub-blocks are already given in Section 6.2, and an additional sub-block is 'Aggregation using BS/AS/SU' only. Inside this sub-block are different aggregation methods that the user can select. After the execution of this FLDS for each of aggregation method the results at each stage (fuzzified inputs such as bearing and distance, final output) are stored. Figure 6.9 illustrates fuzzified inputs distance and bearing and the comparison of final outputs obtained for different aggregation methods. We observe that: i) in the case of an SU operator used for aggregation, constant output is observed irrespective of whether the aircraft is along the air lane or not; ii) for an AS operator, smooth transition takes place between 0 and 1 and it means a hard decision made by FLDS about an aircraft whether it is along lane or not; iii) whereas for a BS operator, a non-smooth transition is observed between 0 and 1 which seems to be intuitively correct and which gives a confidence level while taking the decision about an aircraft, i.e., whether it is flying along the air lane or not (the larger the final output the more the confidence); and iv) the use of BS in aggregation process provides better results than other methods such as SU and AS.

6.4   EVALUATION OF SOME NEW FUZZY IMPLICATION FUNCTIONS

The existing and new fuzzy implication functions and their derivations and performance/satisfaction checking with respect to intuitive criteria of GMP and GMT were discussed in Chapter 5. The use of the existing fuzzy implication function, named PORFI was demonstrated in Sections 6.2 and 6.3. In this section the same case studies are re-visited, but one of the new implication functions, named PCBSAP is used in processing the fuzzy rules. To compare the performance of SIMULINK-based FLDS applied to different fuzzy implication functions some changes have been made and Figure 6.10 depicts the modified sub-block. A similar change has been made in SIMULINK sub-block (FIE/S) for the case study of Section 6.3 also.

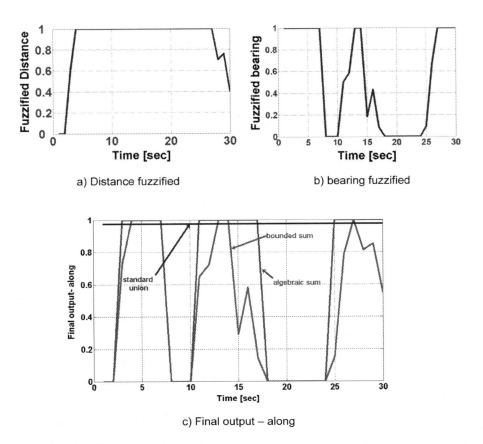

a) Distance fuzzified   b) bearing fuzzified

c) Final output – along

FIGURE 6.9   FLDS for the air lane decision

The 'Embedded MATLAB based Fuzzy Implication Function' (EMFIM) of Figure 6.10 is used to define various FIMs (existing and new ones). These FIMs are selected using a front end menu developed using MATLAB/graphics, via a 'selection flag' in the figure. Figure 6.11 shows the comparison of the final outputs of FLDS obtained for implication functions PORFI (existing FIM) and PCBSAP (a new FIM). It is observed that the outputs are comparable for up to 20 s. of total simulation time. During this period the two aircraft form a pair and then spilt. After the 20th second some mismatch between outputs is observed. It can be seen from the Figure 6.11 that the FLDS output obtained for PORFI quickly converges to a max value of unity, whereas, the FLDS output for PCBSAP takes more time before converging to a unity value. The output for PCBSAP is closer to realistic because it matches the way the data simulation that was carried out. The new FIM is also tested by applying it to FLDS for identifying whether a particular aircraft is flying along the air lane or not. Earlier (in Section 6.3) it was concluded that the results obtained using the aggregation operator 'bounded sum' were matched perfectly with the way the data simulation was carried out. Based on this fact, a new implication function is applied with the

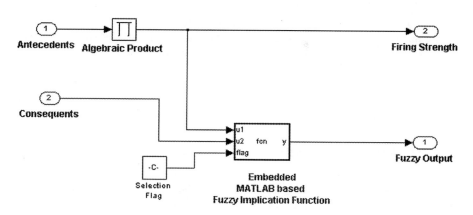

Fuzzy Inference Engine

FIGURE 6.10   Modified sub block of FLDS for Rule 1 and Rule 2 to study new FIM

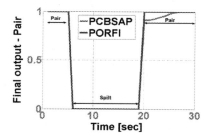

FIGURE 6.11   The outputs of FLDS using different FIMs–one existing and one new for formation flight

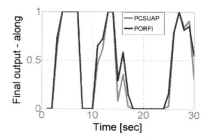

FIGURE 6.12   Performance of FLDS for two FIMs–one old and one new for air lane case

combination of the 'bounded sum' operator only and results obtained are compared with those obtained when the existing implication function PORFI is used. Figure 6.12 only compares the final outputs (along) for another new FIM, named PCSUAP and the existing one, PORFI. It is observed from Figure 6.12 that the outputs of FLDS for these two implication functions are fairly comparable except for a slight lag/lead observed in the output of FLDS for PCSUAP as compared to the output obtained for PORFI. The peaks of the outputs still match perfectly.

The above examples establish that some newly developed FIMs could be used for decision making. They give almost identical or somewhat better performance (than some of the existing FIMs). However some more rigorous study is required to evaluate all the newly developed FIMs and their applicability in general control systems as well as in DF systems, as the studies, analyses and investigations of the new FIMs reported in the present volume are not claimed to be exhaustive.

6.5   ILLUSTRATIVE EXAMPLES

These examples would serve to strengthen the base in the application of FL to decision fusion and related DF processes. These are mainly centered on some topics in Chapter 4 and 5. Using the results of these examples one can build other decision level fusion processes.

Example 6.3 Using equation (4.7, Chapter 4) and with $u = -15 : 0.1 : 15$,
  a) simulate three trapezoidal functions (corresponding to a rule fired) having the following parameters:

  Rule 1: $d = -11$, $e = -9$, $f = -2$ and $g = 1$
  Rule 2: $d = -6$, $e = -4$, $f = 1$ and $g = 4$
  Rule 3: $d = 1$, $e = 2$, $f = 7$ and $g = 8$

  b) combine/aggregate/fuse the fuzzified outputs using the following equation

$$y_o = max\left(0.5y_2, max\left(0.8y_1, 0.05y_3\right)\right)$$

  Here, y_1, y_2, y_3 are the outputs for rule 1, rule 2 and rule 3 respectively,
  c) defuzzify the aggregated output (y_o) using the following methods and compare them: 1) centroid, 2) bisector, 3) middle of maximum, 4) smallest of maximum, and 5) largest of maximum.

Solution 6.3 The trapezoidal membership function is defined in equation (4.7, Chapter 4).

  a) Using the equation of the membership function, the fuzzy membership function for each rule is simulated using the MATLAB code, named **ch6_ ex1.m,** see Figure 6.13. As we know, any fuzzy rule can be defined as: IF x1 is A AND x2 is B THEN y1 is C, where, the part before THEN is known as antecedent and the part after known as consequent. The antecedent parts in the above rule are combined using the fuzzy logic AND operator (T-norm).
  b) The outputs of the antecedent part of Rule 1, Rule 2 and Rule 3 are 0.8, 0.5 and 0.05, respectively (dotted horizontal lines in Figure 6.13). The fuzzy

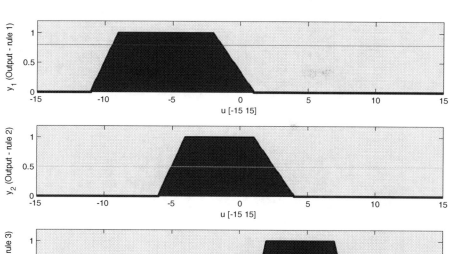

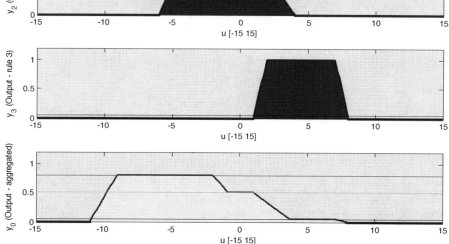

FIGURE 6.13   Membership functions for Example 6.1

output of each rule is obtained using a fuzzy implication function known as the Larsen (Algebraic product), e.g. for Rule 1: $0.8*y_1$. In order to get a single fuzzy output, the outputs of the three rules are combined using the equation, $max\left(0.5y_2, max\left(0.8y_1, 0.05y_3\right)\right)$ (bottom plot of Figure 6.13).

c) In order to get crisp output, output obtained after the aggregation operation is defuzzified, Figure 6.14 shows (with symbol 'dot') the defuzzified outputs corresponding to these methods.

Example 6.4

An aircraft can go unstable during any flight if there is a loss of control surface effectiveness due to damaged or blown control surfaces. In order to make aircraft robust to loss of control surface effectiveness, there should be some mechanism to estimate the parameters representing how much the loss of control surface effectiveness is. An EKF can be used to estimate the parameters of control distribution matrix (B) as augmented states of the system. In this method, the true parameters, estimated

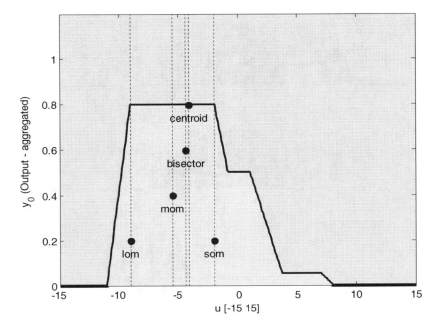

FIGURE 6.14   De-fuzzified outputs (dots) for Example 6.2

parameters and feedback gain (computed using the Linear Quadratic Regulator (LQR) algorithm–under healthy condition) are then used to compute feedback gain using the pseudo-inverse technique to reconfigure the impaired aircraft [4], [5]. The limitation of this approach is that the model of the system should be known accurately, which is not always the case, for example, sometimes models are very complex to be mathematically formulated and may be highly non-linear and time varying. In such a situation an ANFIS (Adaptive-Neuro Fuzzy Inference System) [6] wherein FL is used to predict or estimate the system states used in control law to achieve the desired system response can be employed. In this scheme sensor data at the present instant are smoothened by averaging the previous samples over a selected window length using the sliding window technique. ANFIS is trained offline using inputs as errors between the nominal states of an aircraft and its faulty states and it is then used to estimate a factor of effectiveness and hence the elements of a control distribution matrix under a faulty condition. The reconfiguration is then carried out by computing new feedback gain using the pseudo-inverse technique.

Simulate the longitudinal dynamics of a Delta-4 aircraft [7], (Tables 6.3 and 6.4) using the following state space matrices/equations:

$$
A = \begin{bmatrix} -0.033 & 0.0001 & 0.0 & -9.81 \\ 0.168 & -0.367 & 260 & 0.0 \\ 0.005 & -0.0064 & -0.55 & 0.0 \\ 0.0 & 0.0 & 1.0 & 0.0 \end{bmatrix} ; \quad B = \begin{bmatrix} 0.45 \\ -5.18 \\ -0.91 \\ 0.00 \end{bmatrix}
$$

TABLE 6.3
Delta aircraft data for simulation (*)

Geometrical data		Approach	Other FCs
Wing area =576 m²			
Aspect ratio =7.75			
Chord $\bar{c}$ =9.17 m			
Total related thrust =730 kN	Weight Kg	264,000	300,000
	I_{xx} Kg m²	2.6×10⁷	3.77×10⁷
c.g. = 0.3 $\bar{c}$	I_{yy}	4.25×10⁷	4.31×10⁷
Pilot's location (relative to c.g.)	I_{zz}	6.37×10⁷	7.62×10⁷
l_{x_p} = 25 m l_{z_p} = +2.5 m	I_{xz}	3.4×10⁶	3.35×10⁶

Various flight conditions (FC)	FC1	FC2	FC3	FC4
Altitude in m	Sea Level	6100	6100	12200
Mach no.	0.22	0.6	0.8	0.875
U_0 m s⁻¹ (trim forward speed)	75	190	253	260
$\bar{q}$ in Nm² (dynamic pressure)	3460	11730	20900	10100
α_0 in deg. (trim angle of attack)	+ 2.7	+2.2	+0.1	+4.9
γ_0 in deg. (trim flight path angle)	0	0	0	0

TABLE 6.4

Longitudinal stability derivatives (*) { $X_{\delta_{th}}$, $Z_{\delta_{th}}$, $M_{\delta_{th}}$ = 0.0 (approximately)}

FCs	FC1	FC2	FC3	FC4
X_u	-0.02	-0.003	-0.02	-0.033
X_w	0.1	0.04	0.02	0.0
X_{δ_E}	0.14	0.26	0.0	0.45
Z_u	-0.23	-0.08	-0.01	-0.17
Z_w	-0.634	-0.618	-0.925	-0.387
Z_{δ_w}	-2.9	-6.83	-9.51	-5.18
M_u	0	0.000033	0.00142	0.00548
M_w	-0.005	-0.007	-0.0011	-0.006
$M_{\dot{w}}$	-0.003	-0.001	-0.001	-0.0005
M_q	-0.61	-0.77	-1.02	-0.55
M_{δ_E}	-0.64	-1.25	-1.51	-0.91

(*Data adapted from: McLean, D., *Automatic Flight Control Systems*, Prentice Hall International (UK), 1990)

$$\dot{x} = Ax + Bu_c = Ax + B(-Kx) = (A - BK)x$$

Here, the state vector is given by $x = [u, w, q, \theta]^T$ and $K = \begin{bmatrix} 0.0887 & 0.0046 & -0.8968 & -2.106 \end{bmatrix}$ is the feedback gain computed using the LQR method. Introduce the control surface fault and develop the solutions using EKF and ANFIS methods (using MATLAB).

Solution 6.4

The control surface fault is introduced by multiplying the 'B' vector with factor 0.8 i.e. 20% loss of the control surface effectiveness. Run the **ch6_ex2** (.m program from the directory **Chapter 6.5, the MATLAB SW provided**). Figure 6.15 shows the actual and estimated control matrix elements by EKF and ANFIS schemes using noisy measured data. For offline training in the ANFIS scheme, the state error is computed using filtered measured data (of impaired aircraft) and nominal states. The filtering is carried out using the sliding window technique with a window length of 20. It is seen that the estimated parameters are close to the true values for both the schemes. The delay in estimation is noticed in both the schemes but the estimated values settle to the true values somewhat earlier in ANFIS scheme. Figure 6.16 shows the error (true state–estimated state) for the cases with and without reconfiguration. It can be interpreted that reconfigured aircraft states converge to the true states as desired and the error is less compared to the error under no reconfiguration.

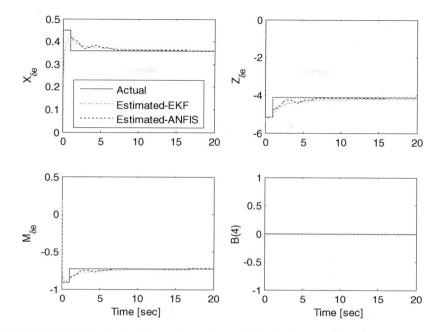

FIGURE 6.15 Estimated and true values of control distribution matrix

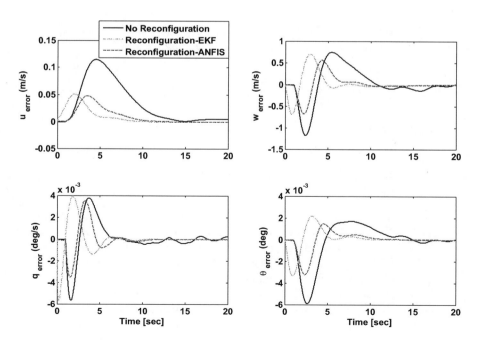

FIGURE 6.16 Comparison of state errors

Example 6.5
Apply the concept of fuzzy Kalman filter of Section 5.3 for measurement fusion and compare the results with KFF, FKFF and SVF using the same numerical simulation.

Solution 6.5
The concept of the Fuzzy logic Kalman Filter (FKF) is extended to measurement fusion and the algorithm is referred to as FKMF–Fuzzy Kalman Filter Measurement Fusion. The basic equations of FKMF are the same as those of FKF with following additional changes:

- Measurement noise covariance matrix, $R = \begin{bmatrix} R_1 & 0 & 0 & 0 \\ 0 & R_2 & 0 & 0 \\ 0 & 0 & . & 0 \\ 0 & 0 & 0 & R_m \end{bmatrix}$, where, R_m is

  the measurement noise covariance matrix of the mth sensor. In the present case, no of sensors, m = 2.

- For m = 2, the observation matrix, $H = \begin{bmatrix} H_1 \\ H_2 \end{bmatrix}$ and concatenated sensor

  measurements $Z_m = \begin{bmatrix} Z_{m_1} \\ Z_{m_2} \end{bmatrix}$

The FLP equation (5.21, Chapter 5) is computed sequentially and separately for sensor 1 and sensor 2 and then concatenated as the final/fused FLP:

$$B^m(k+1) = \begin{bmatrix} b^m_x(k+1) & b^m_y(k+1) \end{bmatrix}, m = 1 \text{ to } 2$$

The final FLP is given by

$$B(k+1) = \begin{bmatrix} b^1_x(k+1) & b^1_y(k+1) & b^2_x(k+1) & b^2_y(k+1) \end{bmatrix}^T$$

Run the **ch6_ex3** (.m program from the directory **Chapter 6.5, the MATLAB SW provided).** Figure 6.17 shows the comparison of the true, measured (sensor 1 and sensor 2) and the estimated x-y trajectory of the target using fusion algorithms– SVF, KFF, FKFF and FKMF. Figures 6.18 to 6.20 show the comparison of the root sum square position/velocity/acceleration errors for these algorithms. It is clear that overall errors are less for FKMF as compared to other fusion algorithms. Since only position measurements are used in these algorithms the merit of FKMF over other algorithms is not clearly visible for the case of errors in target accelerations.

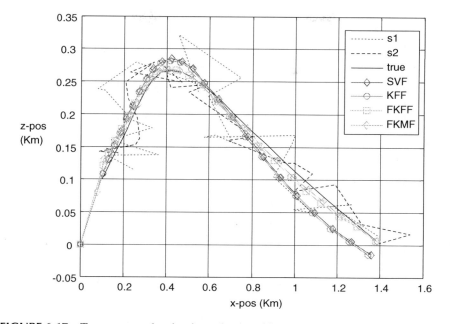

FIGURE 6.17   True, measured and estimated x-y positions

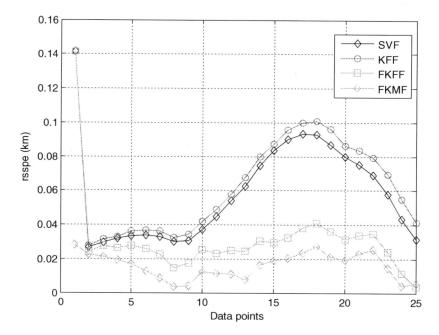

FIGURE 6.18   RSS position errors for four fusion approaches SVF, KFF, FKFF, FKMF

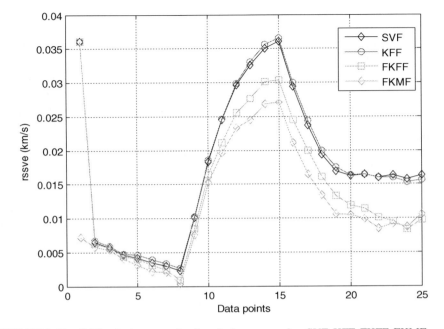

FIGURE 6.19   RSS velocity errors for four fusion approaches SVF, KFF, FKFF, FKMF

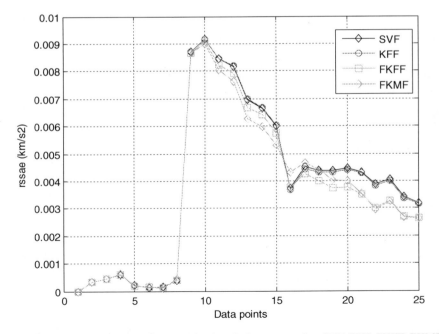

FIGURE 6.20   RSS acceleration errors for four fusion approaches SVF, KFF, FKFF, FKMF

EXERCISES

6.1 What is the major difference between the forward–and backward–chaining inference rules?

6.2 Is it possible in some sense to combine fuzzy logic and the Bayesian method for data fusion/decision fusion?

6.3 Can you visualize a decision fusion strategy?

6.4 Is it possible to combine fuzzy logic, genetic algorithm and ANN to form a decision fusion system?

6.5 What are the strong and weak aspects of fuzzy logic for fusion?

6.6 In what possible ways could the combination of fuzzy logic, ANN and KF can be used in the tracking of a maneuvering target?

6.7 Is there any mapping involved in FL/FIS for the design of a fusion system based on fuzzy logic? Is this mapping linear or non-linear?

6.8 What does fuzzy logic as such represent in the case of noisy sensors used for tracking/data fusion, since the noise is already represented by say a Gaussian probability density function (pdf) with (often) zero-mean and a given standard deviation?

6.9 How can Fuzzy logic be used for data classification?

REFERENCES

1. Kashyap, S. K. Decision Fusion using Fuzzy Logic. Doctoral Thesis, University of Mysore, Mysore, India, 2008.

2. Kashyap, S. K., Raol, J. R., and Patel, A. V. Evaluation of fuzzy implications and intuitive criteria of GMP and GMT. In *Foundations of Generic Optimization* Volume 2: Applications of Fuzzy Control, Genetic Algorithms and Neural Networks (The series Mathematical Modelling: Theory and Applications), Lowen, R. and Verschoren A. (Eds.), pp. 313–385, Springer, New York, USA, 2008.

3. Li-Xin, W. Adaptive Fuzzy Systems and Control, Design and Stability Analysis. Prentice-Hall, Englewood Cliffs, NJ, USA, 1994.

4. Hajiyev, C. M., Caliskan, F. Integrated sensor/actuator FDI and reconfigurable control for fault tolerant flight control system design, The Aeronautical Journal, Sept 2001.

5. Hajiyev, C., and Caliskan, F. *Fault Diagnosis and Reconfiguration in Flight Control Systems*, Kluwer Academic Publishers Boston/Dordrecht/London, 2003.

6. Shobha, R.S., Sudesh, K.K., and Raol, J. R. Adaptive Neuro-Fuzzy based Control surface fault Detection and Reconfiguration, Proceedings of International Conference on Aerospace Science and Technology, 26–28 June 2008, Bangalore, India.

7. McLean, D. *Automatic Flight Control Systems*, Prentice Hall International, London, (UK),1990.

7 Situation Assessment Models and Use of Fuzzy Logic

With the advent of powerful long-range radar and Beyond Visual Range (BVR) missiles, pilots are increasingly reliant on the sensors on board the aircraft to make tactical decisions. Real time decisions require the pilot to assimilate and process large amounts of data from multiple sources in a short span of time. This problem is further compounded when there are multiple unknown targets or, in the case of an extremely complex air scenario, involving multiple friendly and enemy aircraft. Hence, there is a need for an automated system, which is robust and comprehensive to aid in the decision-making activity. In a decision fusion, FL is used in making definite real time crucial decisions based on inferences derived from a certain scenario to assist the fighter aircraft pilot in making various tactical decisions based on data obtained from the on and off-board sensors. In this chapter perception models used for situation assessment models, and their use with fuzzy logic are discussed.

7.1 DECISION FUSION IN SITUATION ASSESSMENT USING TYPE 1 FUZZY LOGIC (T1FL)

A decision fusion system for situation assessment is developed using T1FL for four aviation scenarios. The main aim is to replicate a pilot's mental thought process and implement the same in the form of an automated system and also to test the performance of the system in the presence of noise.

Four aviation situations are simulated with multiple variations of the standard aviation scenarios, and are described first and then their performance evaluated.

7.1.1 PAIR FORMATION

The model used is shown in Figure 7.1 for the assessment of pair formation of the two aircraft. The inputs: 'speed', 'elevation' and 'bearing', are initially computed and processed to determine if the two aircraft have the same kinematics. The data are obtained (or calculated) from sensors such as the speed, the elevation and the bearing; and are treated to identify 'if the kinematics of the two aircraft are the same', and other inputs (ID (identity), speed and distance) are used to decide 'the pair formation aspect of the two aircraft; i.e. if they fly in formation or not.' Each I/O data set is fuzzified by using trapezoidal MFs between 0 and 1 [1], [2]. The author's/

    DOI: 10.1201/9781003370413-7

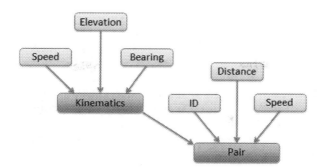

FIGURE 7.1 Original Model of Pair Formation

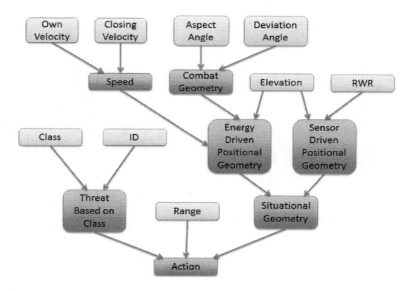

FIGURE 7.2 Threat Assessment Model

designers' knowledge-based intuition has been utilized in setting the data range limit for all these MF functions which have been used to prove the concepts. In real time situations, a domain expert provides these limits.

7.1.2 THREAT ASSESSMENT

The model for threat assessment is shown in Figure 7.2, and combines conventional inputs such as velocity, aspect angle, deviation angle (angle off), elevation, RWR sensor reading, class, ID and range in a systematic manner to compute various intermediary parameters like Combat Geometry, energy driven positional geometry, sensor driven positional geometry and Situational Geometry to determine the action of the unknown aircraft [3]. The inputs, Own Velocity and Closing Velocity have three membership functions: Low, Medium and High. Speed has four membership functions: High Adv., Medium Adv., Low Adv. and Disadvantage. Aspect Angle and Deviation Angle, each with the membership functions: Low, Medium and High, are combined in order to assess the Combat Geometry of the two aircraft. Elevation represents the elevation of the other aircraft with respect to own-ship and has three membership functions: Negative Low, Positive Low and Positive Medium. The input RWR has two membership functions: Illuminating and Non-Illuminating. Speed, Combat Geometry and Elevation are used to compute the Energy Driven Positional Geometry (EDPG). EDPG is a measure of the advantage possessed by an aircraft from a kinetic and potential energy point of view [3], [4]. Sensor Driven Positional Geometry (SDPG) is a measure of the sensor advantage that the aircraft's elevation and RWR would provide. Situational Geometry represents the overall situation, based on EDPG and SDPG. An aircraft at a higher elevation might be at an energy advantage but at a sensor disadvantage. Situational Geometry is a parameter that takes both into consideration. Combat Geometry, EDPG, SDPG and Situational Geometry have five membership functions: High Advantage, Advantage, Disadvantage, Mutual Disadvantage and Neutral. Class represents the type of aircraft and has four membership functions: Fighter, Bomber, Missile and Transport. ID and has three membership functions: Friend, Foe or Unknown. Class and ID of the unknown aircraft are taken into consideration to compute Threat based on Class. It has four membership functions: High Threat, Medium Threat, Low Threat and Benign. Range represents the distance between own-ship and the other aircraft and has three membership functions: Short, Medium and Long. Threat based on Class, Range and Situational Geometry are used to predict the unknown aircraft's actions. Output, Action, has four membership functions: Offensive, Evasive, Defensive and Passive.

7.1.3 FLYING ALONG THE AIR LANE

A sensitivity study is carried out to check the performance of a system in the presence of noise and without noise. The model for this system is as shown in Figure 7.3, where noise has been added to each of the inputs. The inputs to the system are distance (which is the absolute separation between the aircraft and the air lane along the y-axis), the absolute value of bearing difference between them, and the class of the aircraft. Trapezoidal MFs are used to fuzzify the inputs and outputs.

The rules used to decide whether a particular aircraft flies along an air lane or not are as follows:

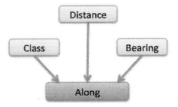

FIGURE 7.3   Model for Flying Along the Air Lane

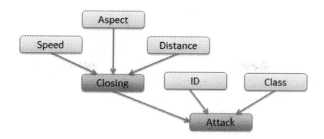

FIGURE 7.4 Model of an Attack Prediction Aviation Scenario System

Rule 1: IF the aircraft has the same bearing as the air lane and IF it is close to the air lane THEN the aircraft is flying along the air lane.

Rule 2: IF the aircraft is civil THEN there is a high possibility that the aircraft is flying along the air lane.

PORFI is used as the implication method for this example. The Bounded Sum (BS) operator of the T-conorm/S-norm is used in the aggregation process. The aggregated output fuzzy set is defuzzified using the Centre of Area (COA) method.

7.1.4 ATTACK

The proposed model to determine the possibility of an attack from another aircraft [2,6] is shown in Figure 7.4. First, the speed of the aircraft, aspect with respect to own-ship and distance from own-ship are checked to see if the aircraft is closing in on own-ship. Then, the identity of the aircraft and its class are used to predict whether the closing aircraft is planning to attack own-ship. The inputs, Speed and Distance have three membership functions: Small, Medium and Large. Aspect (angle) has three membership functions: Small, Medium and High. The intermediate output Closing has two membership functions: Yes, and No. The input ID represents the status of the IFF (Identification Friend or Foe) and has three membership functions: Friend, Foe or Unknown, and the input Class has four membership functions: Fighter, Bomber, Transport and Missile. Finally, the output Attack has two membership functions: Yes, and No.

7.2 STUDY OF VARIOUS MODIFIED SITUATION ASSESSMENT MODELS

In this section the effect of some modified SA models is studied in order to see the performance improvement in certain scenarios.

7.2.1 THREAT ASSESSMENT MODEL

A promising aviation scenario is simulated (with model in Figure 7.2), in MATLAB for a 20 second duration to realize the correct functioning of the system, the typical initial condition of an opponent bomber airship is considered at a great distance from own-ship, with a little elevation, speed and aspect angle. The deviance angle is

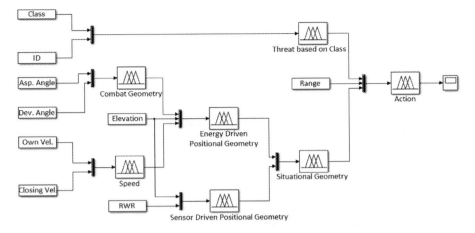

FIGURE 7.5   Fuzzy Logic-based Decision Fusion System in Simulink for Threat Assessment

medium at this time-stamp. The flights are approaching towards very close vicinity to each other for the next 10 seconds and then moving with a very great speed. This results in a large aspect angle and very small deviance angle. During the entire simulation time period the velocity of own-ship is a fixed value and small, also the RWR is continuously lightened. Appropriate rules are defined in each FIS, taking all possible scenarios into consideration. The FIM used is PORFI and Bounded Sum (BS) is used for aggregation. The Center of Area (COA) method is used to defuzzify the output.

The system's implementation in MATLAB/Simulink environment, using FL Toolbox to model the inference system is shown in Figure 7.5. To verify the proper working of the system, a possible situation is simulated for 20 seconds. In this scenario, an enemy bomber is considered. Initially, the bomber is at a large distance from own-ship, with a low elevation, speed and aspect angle. During this time, the deviation angle is medium. After ten seconds, the aircraft has moved closer and is now travelling with a high speed. It has moved higher up and turned such that it has a high aspect angle and a low deviation angle (facing own-ship head-on). The velocity of own-ship is a constant low for the entire simulation period and the RWR is always illuminated. Figure 7.6 shows the decision given by the system for this scenario. The system is able to correctly identify the threat posed by the enemy aircraft.

7.2.2   COMPARISON OF DECISION OUTPUT WITH ORIGINAL AND MODIFIED MODELS

The comparison of different models with decision-performance is described in this section.

7.2.2.1   Modified Pair Formation Model

As shown in Figure 7.7 new inputs 'altitudes' for both the aircraft are added along with the 'aspect' (angle) between them being considered. The aspect angle is expressed in degrees off the tail of a reference aircraft to the heading aircraft [5]. This

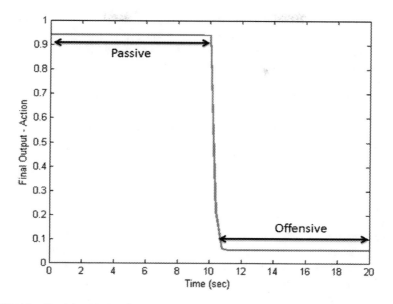

FIGURE 7.6 Decision Fusion System Output for Threat Assessment

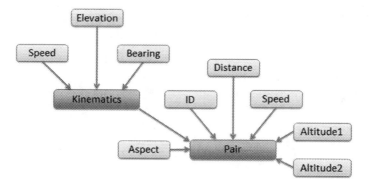

FIGURE 7.7 Modified Pair Formation Model

in conjunction with the distance input helps in providing an accurate view of the sideways movement between the two aircraft and enhances the accuracy in the decision about the two aircraft as to whether they form a pair or not. Also further sensor input data, i.e. flight level or altitude was used. For both the flights this level was checked and if it was above the minimum altitude level, then it adds to the correctness of the pair formation decision, else they are not in pair formation. New altitude level information makes for a more accurate and robust decision result. Kinematic data for the simulation are generated for the two aircraft using MATLAB. The total simulation time is 50 seconds. In the first five seconds, the distance between the two aircraft is small and at the end of these five seconds, their flight paths begin to diverge. In the subsequent five seconds the two aircraft travel with a constant parallel separation. From the 15th second to the 20th second, their flight paths converge and then they fly at a constant altitude for the next five seconds. From the 25th second, both aircraft begin descending until they reach 200 m at the 30th second, remain at that altitude for five seconds and then start their ascent to 1000 m, after which they fly at constant altitude. Figures 7.8 and 7.9 depict this entire scenario in terms of the trajectories and elevation angles of the aircraft. As we can see from these, the altitudes of the two aircraft fall below 460 m (1500 ft), which is the minimum altitude that the aircraft should possess for formation flight, at the 29th second, and also at the 9th second in the case of the second aircraft. Further, the aspect angle between the two aircraft goes below the required range (30 deg.) at the 44th second. Two important assumptions are made during the course of this simulation–the aircraft are friendly to each other and are always within the vicinity of the sensor. Also, the two aircraft in the simulation are assumed to be enemy fighter aircraft. The inputs to the system are the numerical differences of the aircraft' bearing, elevation, separation distance along the z-axis, speed, identity, and class. The new input, aspect is the aspect angle between the two aircraft. The altitudes of the two aircraft are input separately. Trapezoidal MFs are used to fuzzify each input and output data between 0 and 1 [2], [4]. The system is implemented in MATLAB's Simulink as shown in Fig. 7.12. The outputs of the original model and the new model are compared in Fig. 7.13. We can see that the system is able to correctly detect the aircraft' pair and split periods.

Table 7.1 illustrates the comparison of the final outputs from the two models, original and new, to determine pair formation. It is observed that there is a minor change in the value of the final defuzzified output representing the decision 'Yes'. However,

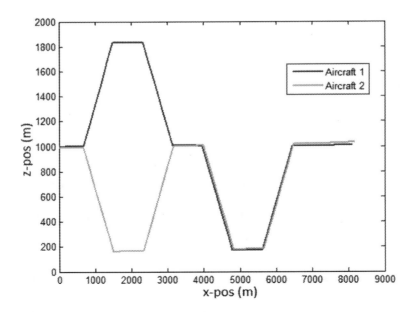

FIGURE 7.8   Trajectories of the Two Aircraft

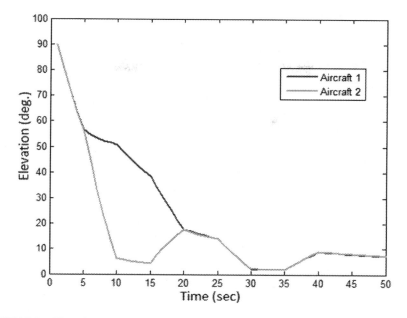

FIGURE 7.9   Elevation Angles of the Two Aircraft

both systems are able to correctly identify the pair and split periods of a given situation with good accuracy, assigning a large weight during the pair period and zero weight during the split period. We observe that the output of the new model is different from that of the original at the 29th and 44th second as a result of the two new inputs, altitude and aspect angle, causing the third rule to be satisfied at those times.

7.2.3   FLYING ALONG THE AIR LANE MODEL

Here, we describe a system that is used to decide if a particular aircraft is flying along the air lane. A sensitivity study is carried out to check the performance of system in the presence of noise. The model for this system is as shown in Figure 7.3, where noise has been added to each of the inputs. The Simulink model to determine if an aircraft is following the air lane uses the FL Toolbox for the inference system and is shown in Figure 7.14. Simulated data for this scenario is generated using MATLAB for 30 seconds. Figure 7.15 depicts the aircraft and air lane locations in the yaw plane and Figure 7.16 depicts the bearings of the aircraft and air lane at various data points as seen from the origin point (0, 0). This shows that the performance of the developed decision system is satisfactory.

7.2.4   MODIFIED ATTACK PREDICTION MODEL

The modified model for attack, shown in Figure 7.17, considers the velocity of the own-ship and that of the other aircraft whose intentions are unknown. These two

TABLE 7.1
Comparison of results between the original
and the new model for formation flight

Time (sec)	Original Output	New Output
1.	3.7984	3.385
3.	3.7984	3.385
5.	3.7984	3.385
7.	0	0
9.	0	0
11.	0	0
13.	0	0
15.	0	0
17.	0	0
19.	0	0
21.	3.7984	3.385
23.	3.7984	3.385
25.	3.7984	3.385
27.	3.7984	3.385
29.	3.7984	0
31.	3.7984	0
33.	3.7984	0
35.	3.7984	0
37.	3.7984	3.385
39.	3.7984	3.385
41.	3.7984	3.385
43.	3.7984	3.385
45.	3.7984	0
47.	3.7984	3.385
49.	3.7984	3.385

velocities are compared in order to determine the speed advantage of the other air-craft over own-ship. Further, the RWR [6], [7] sensor reading is also factored in. This sensor detects the radio emissions of radar systems. Its primary purpose is to issue a warning when radar signals that might be a threat, such as that from an enemy aircraft, are detected. This, when combined with the other information available, will help in assessing the intentions of the other aircraft. In the new model, the inputs: Own Velocity and Closing Velocity have three membership functions: Low, Medium and High. Speed has four membership functions: High Advantage, Medium Advantage, Low Advantage and Disadvantage. The input RWR has two membership functions: Illuminating and Non-Illuminating. All other inputs and the output, Attack, remain the same. The system is implemented in MATLAB/Simulink using features of the FL Toolbox. To check the validity of the system, the data for simulation is

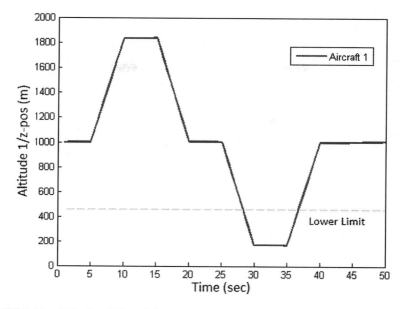

FIGURE 7.10   Altitude of Aircraft 1

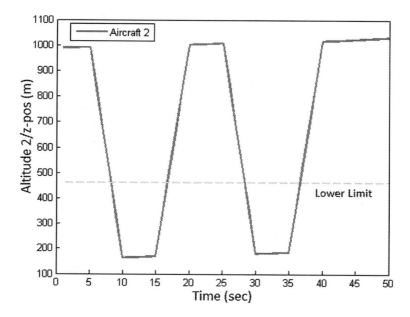

FIGURE 7.11   Altitude of Aircraft 2

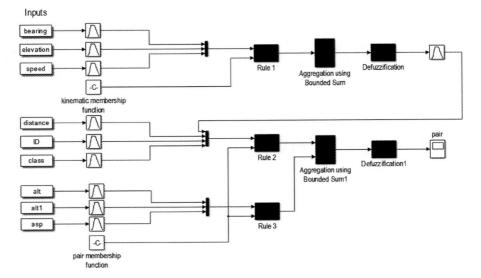

FIGURE 7.12 Fuzzy Logic-based Decision Fusion System in Simulink to Determine Pair Formation from the New Model

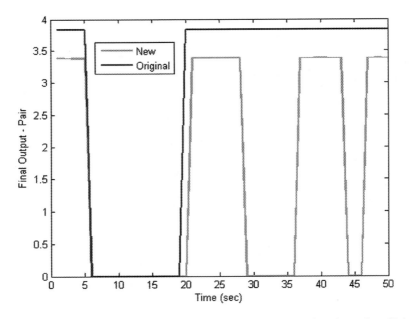

FIGURE 7.13 Outputs of the decision fusion system to determine formation flight for original model and new model

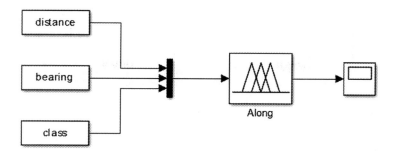

FIGURE 7.14   Fuzzy Logic-based Decision Fusion System in Simulink for Flying Along an Air Lane

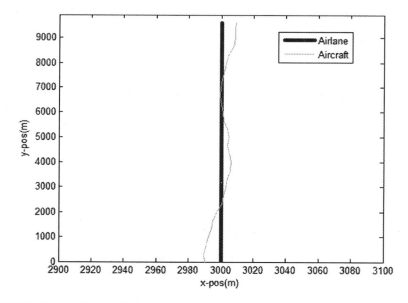

FIGURE 7.15   Position of Air Lane and Aircraft

generated in MATLAB for 20 seconds. A fighter enemy aircraft is assumed. Initially, the aircraft is at a large distance with respect to own-ship and a medium aspect angle. After ten seconds, the aircraft has moved closer and the aspect angle is now high. The velocity of own-ship is low for the entire period of the simulation whereas that of the fighter is high. The RWR sensor reading is "illuminated" for the first fifteen seconds and "non-illuminated" for the reminder of the time. As seen from Figure 7.18, the system is able to correctly detect the action of the aircraft to be attacking or non-attacking

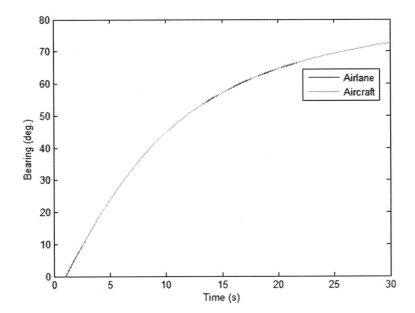

FIGURE 7.16   Bearings of Aircraft and Air Lane

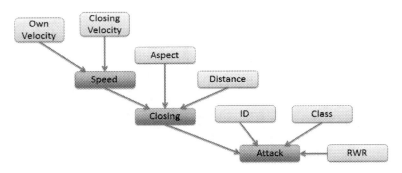

FIGURE 7.17   Modified Attack Model

7.3   STUDY WITH DIFFERENT IF ... THEN ... RULES

In the T1FL system, the mapping of input variables to output is done and fuzzy output sets are obtained, this is assisted by the linguistic rules framed by domain human experts. Rules are very important as they guide the final fuzzified output. A couple of models are illustrated with a set of defined rules

7.3.1   PAIR FORMATION MODEL

The modified pair formation model has been added with one more new rule based on domain expert. Rules are very important as they guide the final fuzzified output. This set of rules plays a major role in deciding the output accuracy of the system.

The rules used to decide whether two aircraft form a pair or not are as follows:

Rule 1: IF two aircraft have the same Bearing, Elevation and Speed THEN they have the same Kinematics.

Rule 2: IF two aircraft have the same Kinematics, the same Identity, the same Class, and are at a short Distance from each other THEN they form a pair.

Rule 3: IF the Altitude of either aircraft is below 1500 ft (460 m) [7] or Aspect lies outside of the 30–60-degree range THEN they do not form a pair.

Here, the PORFI implication method is used and the Bounded Sum (BS) operator of the T-conorm/S-norm is used in the aggregation process [2]-[4]. The aggregated output fuzzy set is defuzzified using the Center of Area (COA) method. The new addition of Rule 3 would enhance decision results in terms of 'pair formation or not' of two aircraft. The comparative results of 'pair formation or not' are as described in Section 7.2.2.1, and are shown in Figures 7.12 and 7.13 and Table 7.1.

7.3.2   Flying Along the Air Lane

The inputs to the system are distance (which is the absolute separation between the aircraft and the air lane along the *y*-axis), the absolute value of bearing difference between them, and the class of the aircraft. Trapezoidal MFs are used to fuzzify the inputs and outputs.

The aircraft whether flying along the designated path or route or air lane or not is guided by specific rules which are mentioned below.

Rule 1: IF the aircraft has the same bearing as the air lane and IF it is close to the air lane THE the aircraft is flying along the air lane.

Rule 2: IF the aircraft is civilian THEN there is a high possibility that the aircraft is flying along the air lane.

As explained in Section 7.2.2.2, these rules help to identify the typical aircraft whether it is flying along the air lane or not. The results are shown in Figures 7.15 and 7.16.

7.3.3   Attack Model

This attack model system has the FIS to determine 'speed advantage', the implication method used is PORFI and the aggregation method is Bounded Sum (BS), while MORFI and Standard Union (SU) are used as the implication and aggregation methods in Closing and Attack FISs. All three FISs use Centre of Area (COA) for defuzzification. The rules used to decide the possibility of attack by the other aircraft are:

Rule 1: IF an aircraft has a high speed advantage, has a close distance to another aircraft and is heading towards it (high aspect) THEN the aircraft is trying to close in on the other.

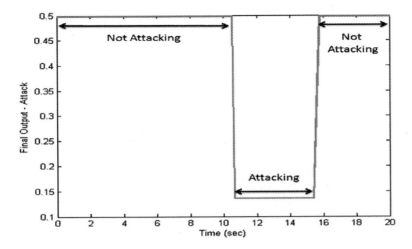

FIGURE 7.18   Output of the Decision Fusion System for Modified Attack

> **Rule 2:** IF an aircraft is closing in on another, has a different ID, is a fighter air-
> craft and RWR is illuminated THEN the aircraft is attacking the other.

With the help of these rules and new inputs, the attack system is able to correctly detect
the action of the aircraft to be attacking or non-attacking as depicted in Figure 7.18.

7.4   EFFECT OF NOISE ON SA MODELS

Most times in avionics situations, the real time sensor input data would be noisy in
nature. Hence, it is extremely important to check and validate decision fusion system
models for various parametric performance metrics in the presence of uncertainties.
To carry out the testing the inputs are considered with noises and then the reliability
and robustness of the system has been validated. A certain number of iterations with
different amounts of noise has been carried out. Then, the 'least-SNR' (meaning relatively more noise) of the noise has been identified to be added to the data inputs.
Based on this quantity level of SNR, the performance of the system is evaluated. The
study with two models, with and without the addition of noise is presented next.

7.4.1   THREAT ASSESSMENT MODEL

To prove the concept of robustness in decision output results, one sample signal
with a random signal is considered, Figure 7.19. Decision fusion result outputs comparison is carried out with and without the addition of uncertainties (noise signal) and
is depicted in Figure 7.20 With a certain number of iterations, it is identified that the
system could generate precise and accurate results for noise levels of 20 dB ('least-
SNR') and above (higher SNR) with efficient accurate tolerance levels.

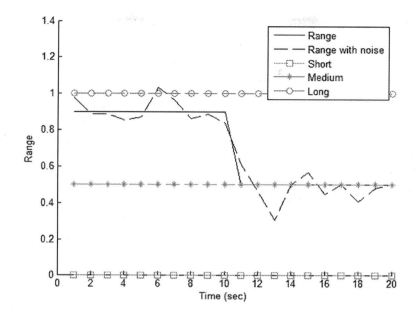

FIGURE 7.19 Range Input with Noise of Decision Fusion System for Threat Assessment

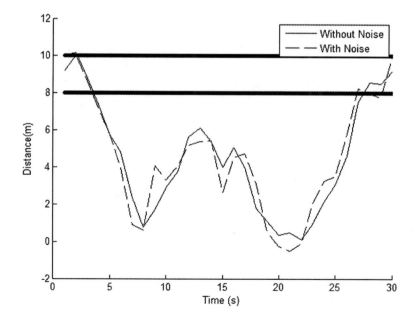

FIGURE 7.20 Distance Between the Aircraft and Air Lane with and without Noise

7.4.2 Flying along the Air Lane

In complete decision fusion system, the noisy data environment in various avionics situations, is simulated by the addition of certain levels of noise in the sensor input data. One of the situations is the identification of the two aircraft whether they are flying along the air lane or not. This decision is dependent upon the two main sensor inputs i.e. distance and bearing. Figures 7.21 and 7.22 show the noise added distance and bearing input signal plots. Noise is added to the system's inputs to simulate the presence of noise in the system from the various sensors that might be interfaced with our system. The performance and stability of the decision fusion system when noise is present is validated through this simulation. From trial and error, it was found that the system could produce accurate results for or above an SNR of 16 dB with reasonable tolerance levels. A comparison between the outputs of the system with (new) and without (original) the addition of noise is as shown in Figure 7.23.

EXERCISES

1. Which method is used in decision fusion for real time crucial decisions to be made by fighter aircraft pilots and why?
2. Name the four standard aviation scenario examples described in this chapter for situation assessment and explain how the modified pair formation model is different to the normal pair formation model.
3. What do we understand from a threat assessment model? What are the different sets of input and output obtained from the model?

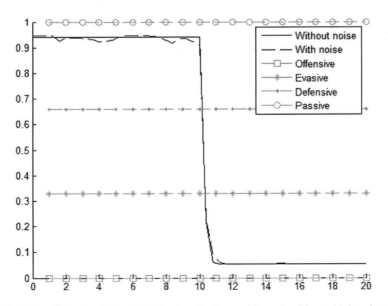

FIGURE 7.21 Output of Decision Fusion System with and without Noise for Threat Assessment

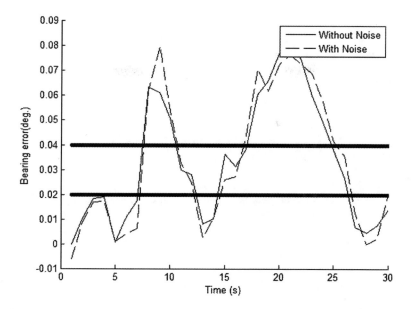

FIGURE 7.22   Bearing Difference Between Aircraft and Air Lane with and without Noise

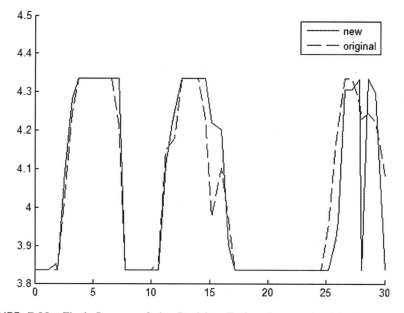

FIGURE 7.23   Final Outputs of the Decision Fusion System for Air Lane with and without Noise

4. Which model predicts whether the aircraft is attacking or non-attacking? What is the implication, aggregation and defuzzification method used in the model?
5. Real time sensor data are noisy. How this has been validated in decision fusion system models? Name two aviation scenarios which have been validated for noisy data.

REFERENCES

1. Johan, I. Situation assessment in a stochastic environment using Bayesian Networks. Master's thesis, Division of Automatic Control, Department of Electrical Engineering, Linkoping University, Sweden, March 2002.
2. Raol, J. R. *Multi-Sensor Data Fusion with MATLAB*. CRC Press, Florida, USA, 2009.
3. Narayana, R., Kashyap Sudesh, K., and Girija, G. Mandal Debanjan, Situation and Threat Assessment in BVR Combat, AIAA Guidance, Navigation, and Control Conference, Portland, Oregon, USA, 8–11 August 2011.
4. Raol, J. R., and Kashyap, S. K. Decision fusion using fuzzy logic type 1 in two aviation scenarios, Jl. of Aerospace Sciences and Technologies, Vol. 65, No. 3, pp. 273–286, Bangalore, India 2013.
5. Bonanni, P. The art of the kill, ISBN–9780928784831, Spectrum HoloByte, USA, 1st edition, 165 pages, 1993.
6. Rao, N. P., Kashyap, S. K. and Girija, G. Situation assessment in air-combat: A fuzzy-Bayesian hybrid approach, International Conference on Aerospace Science and Technology, Bangalore, INCAST 2008-094, 26-28 Jun 2008.
7. Anon. Federal Aviation Administration, Portable Electronic Devices Aviation Rulemaking Committee Report, *Aviation Rulemaking Committee Report,* September 30,2013.www.faa.gov/about/initiatives/ped/media/ped_arc_final_report.pdf(Accessed October, 2016).

APPENDIX 7A USE OF FUZZY LOGIC FOR RISK MANAGEMENT

The use of fuzzy sets to describe the risk factors and fuzzy-based decision techniques to help incorporate inherent imprecision, uncertainties and subjectivity of available data, as well as to propagate these attributes throughout the model, yield more realistic results. FL modelling techniques can also be used in risk management systems to assess risk levels in cases where the experts do not have enough reliable data to apply statistical approaches. There are even more applications to deal with risk management in fuzzy environments. Fuzzy-based techniques seem to be particularly suited to modelling data that are scarce and where the cause-effect knowledge is imprecise and observations and criteria can be expressed in linguistic terms [1].

7A.1 FUZZY LOGIC-BASED RISK MANAGEMENT METHODS

The aim of developing risk management models, as project risks are often uncertain and vague in nature, leads to the use of the fuzzy logic concept [2]. Hybrid methods are also increasingly being used. Generally, fuzzy logic-based methods can be classified into three broad groups: i) basic fuzzy, ii) extended fuzzy, and iii) hybrid fuzzy methods.

Fuzzy logic has been used in risk evaluation for a long time, as it can be used to develop models on the basis of both qualitative data and quantitative values from historical records [3] and is, therefore, a very effective management technique for achieving all the objectives of projects under uncertainties, and vagueness environment [4]. Fuzzy numbers can be handled by conventional arithmetic operations such as addition, subtraction, and multiplication, also known as fuzzy arithmetic. Dealing with circumstances involving fuzzy sets, both linear and unknown qualities, is made simple by fuzzy expert systems [5]. The results are based on expert judgment, quality assessment, causal relationships, and impact analysis. Any fuzzy expert system has three basic components: fuzzy membership function, fuzzy rules, and fuzzy inference mechanism.

7A.1.1 Fuzzy Comprehensive Evaluation and Cloud Model

The cloud model is appropriate for situations requiring discreteness and randomness, even if Comprehensive Fuzzy Estimating (CFE) can handle uncertainty and ambiguity. If project risks are vague, fuzzy and uncertain, and by nature discrete and random, and include data from domain experts, the integrated CFE and cloud model provides reliable results for assessing and prioritizing risks. Risk assessment index, pair-wise comparison of hazards using AHP (Analytic Hierarchy Process) to estimate their weight, fuzzy weighted average, and risk evaluation based on the associated risk score interval are the fundamental parts of the CFE. The fundamental flaws in this approach are that it ignores complicated linkages between hazards as well as how they affect each other within and outside of the group. Consequently, the model could not be appropriate for risk assessment if certain dangers have a structured nature (with causal links).

7A.1.2 Fuzzy Fault Tree and Fuzzy Event Tree Analysis

Multi-criteria decision-making (MCDM) issues have been resolved using the probabilistic risk assessment tools: i) fuzzy Fault Tree Analysis (FTA), and ii) fuzzy Event Tree Analysis (ETA). Although, very complicated project risk relationships are challenging to record in this fashion, FTA has the advantage of offering a good sketch of the root-causes of hazards, making it easy to depict and understand an event with imprecise information [6]. FTA is a graphical representation of a number of parallel events under a number of compound events, as well as a number of fundamental events that result in a number of unexpected occurrences known as top events [7]. To determine the higher event from the cumulative effects of lower events, a fault tree structure is first built for FTA utilising an "AND" or "OR" gate as a mediator. The next step is to qualitatively represent a minimal cut set utilising a fault's Boolean algebraic analysis (basic event). Finally, a quantitative analysis is carried out to calculate the probability of occurrence of the top event.

7A.1.3 Fuzzy Artificial Neural Network (F-ANN)

The ANN is a nonparametric model with artificial intelligence that has been applied to risk analysis. ANN has the capacity to be trained from past data and be applied to generating a future outcome [8]. A number of simulated neurons (processing elements) are united in the ANN process so that the neurons can be trained. When there is a shortage of risk information or a complex, nonlinear, or unknowable relationship between project risks, ANN is suitable since it frequently yields more accurate answers than other traditional methods (such regression analysis). Yet, because of ambiguity, vagueness, ignorance, and imprecision in understanding and evaluating the project risks, expert judgement is unclear [9]. FL is frequently utilised to fill this application gap in ANN because the classic ANN model is unable to address this uncertainty [10].

7A.1.4 Fuzzy TOPSIS

The TOPSIS (Technique for Order Performance by Similarity to Ideal Solution), a novel approach, is well suited for project selection, bid evaluation, and risk assessment by MCDA in a fuzzy environment [11]. The TOPSIS approach offers a good and simple way to compute the weights of options based on similar preferences, but it is unable to handle any ambiguity and vagueness in expert responses. As an alternative, the fuzzy technique can handle ambiguity and uncertainty, but it only offers a single risk value for the outcome, which is not always suitable for decision-making due to some information gaps. In such a scenario, this issue can be resolved by combining TOPSIS with fuzzy logic [11]. Both qualitative and quantitative data can be handled by the combined fuzzy TOPSIS technique, which can also produce a quantitative result for project risk assessment [12].

7A.1.5   Fuzzy Analytical Network Process

The Fuzzy Analytical Network Process (FANP) captures the interdependencies and impacts of various risks for risk ranking [13]. Similar to the AHP, ANP considers pairwise comparisons of the risks, but unlike AHP, it captures all the possible causal relationships and networks between the clusters (group-risks) and among the elements (sub-risks) within a cluster. However, ANP assigns a crisp value in the pairwise comparison of risks, which is a limitation to capturing vagueness and uncertainty in risk analysis. Thus, introducing fuzzy concepts in ANP provides an advanced step in overcoming this limitation. The fuzzy-ANP (FANP) first identifies all potential risks and their interdependencies and builds a network model showing their causal relationships. It then makes pairwise comparisons between the risks using a suitable fuzzy linguistic scale or fuzzy number, tests for consistency between the data sets, aggregates the judgment matrices, calculates priority weights, computes, and limits the super-matrix, and ranks the risks based on the calculated scores. As with the AHP, however, assessing project risks based on many criteria requires an enormous number of pairwise comparisons.

7A.1.6   Fuzzy Bayesian Belief Networks (F-BBN)

The BBN can handle complex and uncertain relationships in risk networks. It is graphically defined by a Directed Acyclic Graph (DAG) where nodes represent risks, and arrows represent the causative relationships between the risks. The arrows also denote the uncertainties inside the risk network, which are mutually inclusive under the concept of conditional probability. Using the BBN, large and complex risk networks can be easily constructed by the aggregation of sub-networks into hierarchy levels. In BBN analysis, very precise data is required for the prior and conditional probabilities, which is difficult to obtain from large and complex projects because of the amount of uncertainty involved. There is also a lack of sufficient data for the risk assessment of complex projects, which leads to having to rely on expert opinion for data elicitation. In addition, while expert judgment is required to develop BBNs, there is limited research on how to elicit knowledge from the experts and ensure the reliability of the model. FL helps domain experts to express the frequency and consequences of risk linguistically, which can be transformed into a range or PERT-like three-point probabilities (low, medium, and high). However, FL alone cannot express the causal relationships between the risks and is unable to conduct inverse inference [14]. Thus, a combination of FL and BBN theory [15] (i.e., FBBN) has a significant role to play in expediting project risk analysis in an uncertain environment.

7A.2   Fuzzy Logic-based Risk Management

Some important steps in the FL based risk management are: i) Finding dangers, and possible risks to system functioning at all levels is the first step; ii) Evaluation: the measure and structural systematization of the identified risks, how significant the risks are in terms of the potential effects, and the likelihood of their occurrence, defines measurement. Their impact on the environment might be described quantitatively or qualitatively; iii) Plan and control to prepare the risk management system which can include the development of response actions to these risks, and the applied decision or reasoning method; and iv) The monitoring and review stages are important if the aim is to have a system with feedback, and the risk management system is open to improvement.

As a result, the risk management process will be dynamic, ongoing, and subject to proper validation and control. New hazards may emerge during the assessment process, as well as new ways to describe concerns. Typically, the decision model, the representation of the measured risks, and the identification of the risk factors of the researched process comprise the preliminary form of the risk management system. Monitoring and review can be used to expand the system and enhance the decision-making and risk measure descriptions. Knowledge-based models are used to solve problems; these models require verbal communication for modelling, and decision-making involves both objective and subjective information (definitional, causal, statistical, and heuristic knowledge). Fuzzy set theory considers all of these circumstances and could provide a user-friendly depiction of the system structure and functioning model in addition to helping manage complexity and uncertainty [16].

REFERENCES

1. Kleiner, Y., Rajani, B., and Sadiq, R. *Failure Risk Management of Buried Infrastructure Using Fuzzy-based Techniques*, In Journal of Water Supply Research and Technology: Aqua, Vol. 55, No. 2, pp. 81–94, March 2006.
2. Tahami, H., Mirzazadeh, A., and Gholami-Qadikolaei, A. *Simultaneous control on lead time elements and ordering cost for an inflationary inventory production model with mixture of normal distributions LTD under finite capacity.* RAIRO-Operations Research, 53(4), 1357–1384.
3. Subramanyan, H., Sawant, P. H., and Bhatt V. *Construction project risk assessment: development of model based on investigation of opinion of construction project experts* from India. Journal of Construction Engineering and Management, 138(3), 409–421
4. Abdul Rahman, Z. A. A. *The use of cohesive devices in descriptive writing by Omani student-teachers.* Sage Open, 3(4), 2158244013506715, 2013.
5. Tahami, H., Mirzazadeh, A., Arshadi-khamseh, A., and Gholami-Qadikolaei, A. *A periodic review integrated inventory model for buyer's unidentified protection interval demand distribution.* Cogent Engineering, 3(1), 1206689, 2016
6. Abdelgawad, M., and Fayek, A. R. *Fuzzy reliability analyzer: quantitative assessment of risk events in the construction industry using fuzzy fault-tree analysis.* Journal of Construction Engineering and Management, 137(4), 294– 302, 2011
7. Abdollahzadeh, G., and Rastgoo, S. *Risk assessment in bridge construction projects using fault tree and event tree analysis methods based on fuzzy logic.* ASCE-ASME Journal of Risk and Uncertainty in Engineering Systems, Part B: Mechanical Engineering, 2015
8. Loizou, P., and French, N. *Risk and uncertainty in development.* Journal of Property Investment & Finance, 2012
9. Ferdous, R., Khan, F., Sadiq, R., Amyotte, P., and Veitch, B. *Fault and event tree analyses for process systems risk analysis: uncertainty handling formulations. Risk Analysis:* An International Journal, 31(1), 86–107,2011
10. Wang, Y.-M., and Elhag, T. M. S. *An adaptive neuro-fuzzy inference system for bridge risk assessment. Expert Systems with Applications*, 2011, 34(4), 3099–3106

11. Taylan, O., Kabli, M. R., Saeedpoor, M., and Vafadarnikjoo, A. Commentary on *Construction projects selection and risk assessment by Fuzzy AHP and Fuzzy TOPSIS methodologies,* [Applied Soft Computing 17 (2014): 105–116]. Applied Soft Computing, 36, 419–421

12. Ebrahimnejad, S., Mousavi, S. M., Tavakkoli-Moghaddam, R., Hashemi, H., and Vahdani, B. *A novel two-phase group decision making approach for construction project selection in a fuzzy environment.* Applied Mathematical Modelling, 2012, 36(9), 4197–4217.

13. Bu-Qammaz, A. S., Dikmen, I., and Birgonul, M. T. *Risk assessment of international construction projects using the analytic network process.* Canadian Journal of Civil Engineering, 2009, 36(7), 1170–1181.

14. Choi, H.-H., and Mahadevan, S. *Construction project risk assessment using existing database and project-specific information.* Journal of Construction Engineering and Management, 2008, 134(11), 894–903

15. Hengameh Fakhravar, research project, *Quantifying Uncertainty In Risk Assessment Using Fuzzy Theory,* Old Dominion University April 2020

16. Takacs, M. *Soft Computing-Based Risk Management–Fuzzy, Hierarchical Structured Decision-Making System,* Óbuda University Budapest Hungary, 28th July 2011, https://cdn.intechopen.com/pdfs/17361/InTech-Soft_computing_based_risk_ management. Df

8 Interval Type 2 Fuzzy Logic (IT2FL)-based Decision System

Decision making capabilities of T1FL systems are affected when uncertainties or noise are present in the input data. To overcome this issue an Interval Type-2 Fuzzy Logic–based Decision (making-cum-fusion) process/System (IT2FLDS) is proposed for air lane monitoring that is realized using an interval type-2 Mamdani model, i.e. the IT2FL [1] system at the algorithmic level is proposed and developed. Experimental results presented establish that the IT2FLDS exhibits better decision-making capabilities compared to T1FL systems considering uncertainties in input sensor data. IT2FLDS is further extended to include flight level parameters for air lane monitoring. The results presented establish that IT2FLDS works better than its T1FL counterpart when flight level examples are considered. A simulation experiment to evaluate performance of IT2FLDS and T1FL [2] in the presence of uncertainties is discussed. In Appendices 8A, and 8B we provide further exposition on type 2 and interval type 2 fuzzy logics.

8.1 IT2FL DECISION SYSTEM

This system primarily consists of three blocks: i) input processing, ii) FIE, and iii) output processing, and the proposed system for air lane monitoring is shown in Figure 8.1. The system is realized using the Mamdani model. Sensor data from an aircraft act as the crisp inputs of IT2FLDS. Input sensor data are represented as a set, I. A fuzzifier is used to map sensor inputs I into fuzzy set D using T2 trapezoidal FMF $\mu_{\tilde{F}}$. The fuzzifier is used to convert sensor input I to fuzzy values. FIE applies T2 fuzzy reasoning on fuzzy set $\ddot{D}$ to obtain fuzzy output set E [3]. T2 fuzzy reasoning in FIE is based on $If, \dots, then$ rules provided by suitable domain experts. An output processing block provides crisp outputs O based on a fuzzy output set obtained from FIE, that consists of a T2 reducer and defuzzifier. A Center of Sets (COS) type converter (from T2FL to T1FL) reducer technique is used to transform T2 fuzzy sets into T1 fuzzy sets. A centroid based defuzzifier converts the type reduced output set to precise or T0FL output values. The crisp input set I is a set of data obtained from various sensors used to monitor the location of the airplane. Sensor values are updated at regular intervals or regular rates to ascertain if the aircraft is flying within the specified air lane.

DOI: 10.1201/9781003370413-8

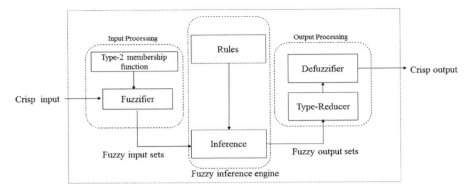

FIGURE 8.1   Schematic of proposed IT2FLDS for air lane monitoring

8.1.1 Fuzzy Logic Type 2 Input Fuzzy Set Realization

Type 2 FL (T2) fuzzy input, output sets [4], [5] are 'sets whose membership grades are themselves fuzzified to type-1 (T1) fuzzy sets'. A T2 fuzzy set is denoted by $\ddot{D}$ and defined by a T2 MF $\mu_{\ddot{D}}(i,j)$ as

$$\ddot{D} = \left((i,j),\mu_{\ddot{D}}(i,j)\right)\Big|\, \forall i \in I,\ \forall j \in G_i \subseteq [0,1] \tag{8.1}$$

where $i \in I$, $j \in G_i \subseteq [0,1]$ and $0 \le \mu_{\ddot{D}}(i,j) \le 1$. In (8.1), G_i represents the codomain at each $i \in I$ of type-2 fuzzy set $\ddot{D}$. Similar to the T1FL system for airline monitoring proposed in [6], IT2FLDS also incorporates trapezoidal FMFs. A trapezoidal T2 MF is shown in Figure 8.2, from which it is evident that the trapezoidal T2 MF consists of an upper (UMF) and a lower (LMF) T1 trapezoidal MF.

The T2 FL is a general type but an interval type-2 trapezoidal MF is a typical form where set $\ddot{D}_x$ in the universe of discourse I [7] is defined as

$$\ddot{D}_x = \left(\dot{D}_{\uparrow x}, \dot{D}_{\downarrow x}\right), \tag{8.2}$$

where $\dot{D}_{\uparrow x}$ and $\dot{D}_{\downarrow x}$ represent upper and lower T1 fuzzy sets of a trapezoidal T2 MF. The T2 fuzzy set $\ddot{D}_x$ can be elaborated as

$$\ddot{D}_x = \left(\left(d_{\uparrow x1}, d_{\uparrow x2}, d_{\uparrow x3}, d_{\uparrow x4};\, f_1\left(\dot{D}_{\uparrow x}\right), f_2\left(\dot{D}_{\uparrow x}\right)\right),\right.$$
$$\left.\left(d_{\downarrow x1}, d_{\downarrow x2}, d_{\downarrow x3}, d_{\downarrow x4};\, f_1\left(\dot{D}_{\downarrow x}\right), f_2\left(\dot{D}_{\downarrow x}\right)\right)\right) \tag{8.3}$$

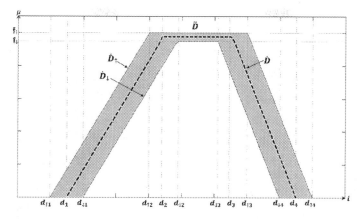

FIGURE 8.2 An interval type-2 trapezoidal fuzzy membership set $\ddot{D}$

where $d_{\uparrow x1}, d_{\uparrow x2}, d_{\uparrow x3}, d_{\uparrow x4}, d_{\downarrow x1}, d_{\downarrow x2}, d_{\downarrow x3}, d_{\downarrow x4}$ represent reference points of set $\ddot{D}_x$ shown in Figure 8.2. Considering $1 \leq y \leq 2$, then the membership value of $d_{\uparrow x(y+1)}^{th}$ element in $\dot{D}_{\uparrow x}$ is represented as $f_y\left(\dot{D}_{\uparrow x}\right)$ in (8.3). Similarly, $f_y\left(\dot{D}_{\downarrow x}\right)$ is the membership value of the $d_{\downarrow x(y+1)}^{th}$ element in $\dot{D}_{\downarrow x}$ and $1 \leq y \leq 2$. In

(8.3) $f_1\left(\dot{D}_{\uparrow x}\right) \in [0,1]$, $f_2\left(\dot{D}_{\uparrow x}\right) \in [0,1]$, $f_1\left(\dot{D}_{\downarrow x}\right) \in [0,1]$; *with* $1 \leq i \leq 2$.

a) Fuzzifier

The fuzzifier block takes crisp input i.e. sensor data $i = \left(i_1, \ldots, i_p\right)^T \in I_1 \times I_2 \times \ldots I_p \equiv I$ and maps it into fuzzy input set D_i *in I* [8]. Usually, the T2 singleton fuzzifier is used in which the input fuzzy set has only a one point on non-zero membership. The output of the fuzzifier i.e. fuzzy output set E is used for decision making in the FIE.

8.2 TYPE 2 MAMDANI FUZZY INFERENCE ENGINE (FIE)

This consists of set of rules described by the domain expert knowledge and inference mechanism.

8.2.1 FUZZY RULES

The rule representation structures of a T1 FLS and T2 FLS are similar. A (fuzzy) rule consists of an *IF,...* and *THEN,...* sections. The *IF...* section is called antecedent and *THEN...* section is called consequence. In T2 FLS the antecedent and consequence is characterized by a T2 fuzzy set E. Let us consider p number of inputs (linguistic variables) represented as $i_1 \in I_1, \ldots i_p \in I_p$ and an output $o \in O$. The lth rule can be represented as

$$R^l : IF\ i_1\ is\ \ddot{E}_1^l\ and\ i_2\ is\ \ddot{E}_2^l\ \ldots\ and\ i_p\ is\ \ddot{E}_P^l\ THEN\ o\ is\ \ddot{H}^l\ l = 1,2,3\ldots M, \quad (8.4)$$

where E and H represent appropriate fuzzy sets for each rule. The two rules which are applied here are the same as described in Chapter 7 for flying along the air lane.

8.2.2 MAMDANI IT2 FUZZY INFERENCE ENGINE

The FIE converts the T2 input fuzzy sets into T2 output fuzzy sets via fuzzy implication method (FIM). By combining the rules R, FIE derives a mapping between T2 input fuzzy sets and T2 output fuzzy sets. If there are more than one antecedent then fuzzy operators (join $\sqcup$ and meet Π) work and give a single digit that represents the effective outcome for that rule. In case that more than one rule is fired, the output is aggregated and it obtains a single output T2 fuzzy set. To ensure all T2 relations (obtained from set R), these are mapped; the computations of union $\sqcup$, intersection Π, and sup-star compositions of T2 relations are considered. If $\ddot{E}_1^l \times \ddot{E}_2^l \ldots \times \ddot{E}_P^l = \ddot{B}^l$, then the lth fuzzy rule is represented as

$$R^l : \ddot{E}_1^l \times \ddot{E}_2^l \ldots \times \ddot{E}_P^l \rightarrow \ddot{H}^l = \ddot{B}^l \rightarrow \ddot{H}^l\ l = 1,2,3,\ldots, M. \quad (8.5)$$

Here, R^l is defined by the MF $\mu_{R^l}(i,o) = \mu_{R^l}(i_1,\ldots,i_p,o)$. The MF $\mu_{R^l}(i,o)$ is defined as

$$\mu_{R^l}(i,o) = \mu_{\ddot{B}^l \rightarrow \ddot{H}^l}(i,o) \quad (8.6)$$

Using fuzzy operators MF, a $\mu_{R^l}(i,o)$ is represented as

$$\mu_{R^l}(i,o) = \mu_{\ddot{E}_1^l}(i_1)\ \Pi\ \mu_{\ddot{E}_2^l}(i_2)\ \Pi\ \mu_{\ddot{E}_3^l}(i_3)\ \Pi,\ldots, \Pi\ \mu_{\mu_{\ddot{E}_p^l}}(i_p)\Pi\mu_{\ddot{H}^l}(o). \quad (8.7)$$

Simplifying (8.7) we obtain,

$$\mu_{R^l}(i,o) = \left[\prod_{j=1}^{p}\mu_{\ddot{E}_j^l}(i_j)\right]\prod\mu_{\ddot{H}^l}(o). \quad (8.8)$$

The p inputs to the lth rule are provided through a type-2 FS $\ddot{B}^l$. The MF $\mu_{\ddot{B}}$ of $\ddot{B}^l$ is defined as

$$\mu_{\ddot{B}_i}(i) = \mu_{\ddot{i}_1}(i_1) \Pi \mu_{\ddot{i}_2}(i_2) \dots \Pi \mu_{\ddot{i}_p}(i_p); \ \mu_{\ddot{B}_i}(i) = \prod_{j=1}^{p} \mu_{\ddot{i}_j}(i_j), \quad (8.9)$$

Here, the labels of fuzzy sets are represented by $\ddot{I}_j$ $(j = 1,2,3,\dots,p)$ that describe p inputs. Each rule in set R defines a T2 fuzzy set using compositions $\ddot{C}^l = \ddot{B}_i \circ R^l$ such that

$$\mu_{\ddot{C}^l}(o) = \mu_{\ddot{B}_i \circ R^l};$$

$$\mu_{\ddot{C}^l}(o) = \bigsqcup_{i \in I} \left[\mu_{\ddot{B}_i}(i) \sqcap \mu_{R^l}(i,o) \right], \ \forall o \in O, \ \forall l = 1,2,3,\dots, M \quad (8.10)$$

In IT2FLDS we have used a T2 fuzzy set and intersection under product T-norm where the resultant of input and antecedent operation is available in a set (i.e. $\sqcap_{j=1}^{P} \mu_{\ddot{E}_{l_j}}(i'_j) \equiv E^l(\mathbf{i}')$), called the firing set. The firing set is defined as

$$E^l(\mathbf{i}') = \left[e^l_{\downarrow}(\mathbf{i}'), e^l_{\uparrow}(\mathbf{i}') \right] \equiv \left[e^l_{\downarrow}, e^l_{\uparrow} \right]. \quad (8.11)$$

If $*$ is the product operator, then $e^l_{\downarrow}(i')$ and $e^l_{\uparrow}(i')$ in (8.11) are defined as,

$$e^l_{\downarrow}(\mathbf{i}') = \mu_{\downarrow \ddot{E}^l_1}(i'_1) * \mu_{\downarrow \ddot{E}^l_2}(i'_2) * \mu_{\downarrow \ddot{E}^l_3}(i'_3) * \cdots \mu_{\downarrow \ddot{E}^l_p}(i'_p), \quad (8.12)$$

$$e^l_{\uparrow}(\mathbf{i}') = \mu_{\uparrow \ddot{E}^l_1}(i'_1) * \mu_{\uparrow \ddot{E}^l_2}(i'_2) * \mu_{\uparrow \ddot{E}^l_3}(i'_3) * \cdots \mu_{\uparrow \ddot{E}^l_p}(i'_p). \quad (8.13)$$

8.2.3 OUTPUT PROCESSING

Output processing block of IT2FLDS comprises of a fuzzy T-2 reducer along with a defuzzifier block. The output fuzzy set obtained for FIE is converted to crisp output sets O.

a) Type Reducer

The type reducer block of IT2FLDS converts the resultant set of FIE into a T1 Fuzzy set. A Center of Sets (COS) T2 reduction technique is adopted in

IT2FLDS. The COS reduction technique adopted, O_{cos} is a T1 data input range interval set and characterized by its end points represented as o_l and o_r. In other words, $O_{cos}(i) = [o_l, o_r]$ or

$$O_{cos}(i) = \int_{o^1} \in [o_1^l, o_r^1] \int_{o^2} \in [o_2^l, o_r^2] .. \int_{o^M} \in [o_l^M, o_r^M] \int_{e^1}$$
$$\in [e_\uparrow^1 . e_\uparrow^1] .. \int_{e^M} \in [e_\uparrow^M . e_\uparrow^M] \, 1 / \frac{\sum_{j=1}^{M} e^j o^j}{\sum_{j=1}^{M} e^j} . \tag{8.14}$$

The points $o_{l\,j}$ and o_r belongs to the centroid of the T2 interval resultant set $\ddot{H}^j$. The centroid of H is given as

$$C_{\ddot{H}^j} = \int_{\theta_1} \in K_{o^1} \int_{\theta_2} \in K_{o^2} .. \int_{\theta_N} \in K_{o^N} \, 1 / \frac{\sum_{j=1}^{N} \theta_j o_j}{\sum_{j=1}^{N} \theta_j} = [o_l^j, o_r^j], \tag{8.15}$$

Here θ_j belong to interval $[0,1]$ and $\ddot{H}^j$ is considered to have N discrete points. The variables o_l^j and e_l^j represent association of o_j and e_j with o_l. Similarly, o_r^j and e_r^j represent association of o_j and e_j with o_r.

Using (8.15), o_l^j and o_r^j are computed and later used to compute $O_{cos}(i)$ in IT2FLDS. The output interval of IT2FLDS i.e. o_l and o_r is defined as

$$o_l = \left(\sum_{i=1}^{M} e_l^j o_l^j / \sum_{i=1}^{M} e_l^j \right), \tag{8.16}$$

$$o_r = \left(\sum_{i=1}^{M} e_r^j o_r^j / \sum_{i=1}^{M} e_r^j \right), \tag{8.17}$$

Output of *cos* reduction technique is defuzzified to obtain crisp outputs.

b) Defuzzification

The centroid method for defuzzification is adopted in IT2FLDS. The defuzzification process of IT2FLDS is achieved using

$$o(i) = (o_l + o_r) 0.5 \tag{8.18}$$

Crisp output obtained from defuzzification enables us to determine if an aircraft under test is in the prescribed air lane or not.

8.3 EVALUATION OF AIR LANE MONITORING

Two/three sets of simulation experiments are conducted to evaluate performance of IT2FLDS for air lane monitoring. All the experiments are conducted in the .ex/ Simulink. The IT2FLDS is implemented using the T2 fuzzy toolbox [7], [9]. Performance of IT2FLDS is compared with T1FLS as described in [6].

8.3.1 EXPERIMENT 8.1: BASIC COMPARISON

The initial experiment is conducted to establish the uncertainty handling capabilities of IT2FLDS as compared to the T1FLDS of [6]. The experimental Simulink model of IT2FLDS for air lane monitoring is shown in Figure 8.3, and the simulation parameters used [6] are given in Table 8.1.

A constant velocity of aircraft is considered in the experiment whose kinetic model is defined as

$$X(k+1) = FX(k) + Gw(k) \qquad (8.19)$$

Here, F represents state transition matrix, G the process noise matrix, w is the Gaussian process noise with covariance Q, and $k = (1, 2, \cdots, 30)$ is referred to as the index or scan value. Values of Q, F and G are obtained using:

$$Q = 1 \times eye(4,4); F = \begin{bmatrix} 1 & T & 0 & 0 \\ 0 & 1 & 0 & 0 \\ 0 & 0 & 1 & T \\ 0 & 0 & 0 & 1 \end{bmatrix};$$

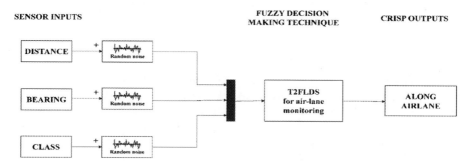

FIGURE 8.3   IT2FLDS for experiment 1 in Simulink-Experiment 8.1

TABLE 8.1
Simulation parameters for Experiment 8.1

Parameter	Simulation values
Initial aircraft state $X = [x\,\bar{x}\,y\,\bar{y}]$	$X = [2990\,m\ 0\,m\ 0\,m/s\ 332\,m/s]$
Number of sensor data considered	3
Type of sensors considered	*Speed, bearing and aircraft class*
Sensor update rate	$1\,Hz$
Air lane location along y axis	$x = 300\,m$
Simulation time	$30\,s$
Number of fuzzy rules	2

$$G = \begin{bmatrix} 0.5 \times T^2 & 0 & 0 & 0 \\ 0 & T & 0 & 0 \\ 0 & 0 & 0.5 \times T^2 & 0 \\ 0 & 0 & 0 & T \end{bmatrix} \tag{8.20}$$

In the experiment a civilian aircraft is considered. Initially, a scenario wherein no noise is included (high SNR = 100 dB) is considered. Outputs obtained from the Type-1 system [6] and IT2FLDS are recorded. Considering the yaw plane, the position of air lane (at x-pos = 3000 m) and the aircraft along the x and y axes using IT2FLDS is shown in Figure 8.4a). The trajectory results are reported in [11] proving uniformity of the simulation environment considered. The bearing results at various data points k of air craft and air lane obtained with respect to the origin (0, 0) are shown in Figure 8.5. Similar results are reported in [6] proving uniformity of simulation environment considered. The crisp output obtained from IT2FLDS is shown in Figure 8.6, which depicts the decision output of IT2FLDS: whether the aircraft is flying along the air lane or not. The decision output of IT2FLDS is true/yes if the output value is greater than or equal to 0.5 and false/no if the value is below 0.5. Decision making results obtained using IT2FLDS and T1FLDS [6] (based on standard fuzzy operator/implication functions) are shown in Table 8.2.

8.3.2 EXPERIMENT 2: EFFECT OF UNCERTAINTIES

In this experiment the additional sensor data (altitude or flight level) are used. The SNR variations induce uncertainties in sensor input data provided to fuzzy decision systems for air lane monitoring (for IT2FLDS and the Type-1 system [6]). SNR variations of 90 dB, 80 dB, 70 dB, 50 dB and 10 dB are considered to simulate different scenarios. The output decision errors observed are quantified using standard measures like Mean Square Error (MSE), Root Mean Square Error (RMSE), Peak Signal to Noise Ratio (PSNR) and Maximum Error (MAX ERROR). Considering IT2FLDS and Type-1 FLDS, the error measures are shown in Table 8.3. Comparing results obtained across all scenarios, it is seen that better performance is obtained by

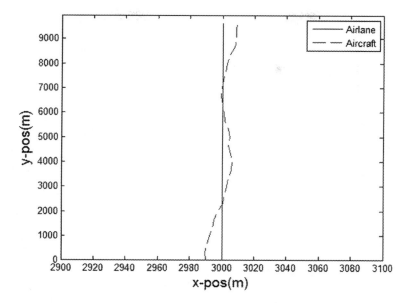

FIGURE 8.4   X and Y positions of air lane and aircraft in the yaw plane

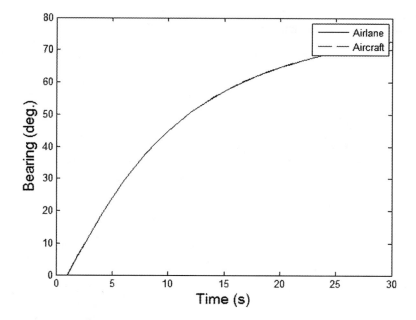

FIGURE 8.5   Bearing angle of air lane and aircraft with respect to (0, 0)

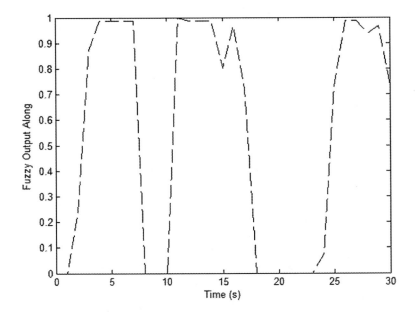

FIGURE 8.6 IT2FLDS output for air lane decision

TABLE 8.2
Decision making result comparison: Experiment 8.1

Time (s)	Defuzzified output FLDS (AS) [2]		Defuzzified output of IT2FLDS	
1	0.0000	No	0.0000	No
3	1.0000	Yes	0.8738	Yes
5	1.0000	Yes	0.9872	Yes
7	1.0000	Yes	0.9872	Yes
9	0.0000	No	0.0000	No
11	1.0000	Yes	1.0000	Yes
13	1.0000	Yes	0.9872	Yes
15	1.0000	Yes	0.8021	Yes
17	1.0000	Yes	0.7251	Yes
19	0.0000	No	0.0000	No
21	0.0000	No	0.0000	No
23	0.0000	No	0.0000	No
25	1.0000	Yes	0.7310	Yes
27	1.0000	Yes	0.9872	Yes
29	1.0000	Yes	0.9655	Yes

TABLE 8.3
Air lane decision making error observed for IT2FLDS and T1FLDS: Experiment 8.2

Scenario #	Scenario SNR in dB	MSE		RMSE		PSNR		MAX ERROR	
		IT2FLDS	T1 FLDS [2]	IT2FLDS	T1 FLDS [2]	IT2FLDS	T1 FLDS [2]	IT2FLDS	T1 FLDS [2]
1	90	2.16E-09	2.07E-08	6.57E-05	2.03E-04	1.35E+02	1.25E+02	1.99E-04	8.12E-04
2	80	3.75E-08	3.58E-07	2.74E-04	8.46E-04	1.22E+02	1.13E+02	8.31E-04	3.30E-03
3	70	4.34E-07	4.13E-06	9.32E-04	2.81E-03	1.12E+02	1.12E+02	2.80E-03	1.14E-02
4	50	1.36E-05	3.79E-04	5.20E-03	2.76E-02	9.68E+01	8.23E+01	1.98E-02	1.07E-01
5	10	1.70E-02	4.75E-02	1.84E-01	3.10E-01	6.58E+01	6.24E+01	2.70E-01	4.98E-01

IT2FLDS compared to Type-1 FLDS. Performance improvement is summarized in Table 8.4. The IT2FLDS exhibits better performance due to the robust T2 trapezoidal membership function being considered. The IT2FL based decision system exhibits better uncertainty handling capabilities as compared to T1FLS proved by the results presented in Table 8.4.

8.3.3 EXPERIMENT 8.3: CONSIDERATION OF SPEED, BEARING, CLASS, AND FLIGHT LEVEL

According to the Federal Aviation Administration (FAA), flight level [10] is a critical criterion to monitor whether an aircraft is flying along the designated air lane or not. The significance of considering the altitudes of aircraft is evident from Figure 8.7 and [11]. According to a recent report published by Boeing [11], 89% of fatal accidents and all onboard accidents occur during phases 3 to 8. Air lane discipline is a way to reduce these accidents. The altitude to be maintained (generally in feet) by an aircraft is known as flight level. An aircraft is 57% of total flight time in cruising altitude or phase 5 [11], hence it is essential to include flight level in an air lane system and to simulate an aircraft in this phase. The Simulink model considered is as shown in Figure 8.8. Table 8.5 shows the simulation parameters. The kinetic model of an aircraft considered is similar to the previous experiment. For distance, bearing and class sensor inputs, FMFs from Experiment 1 are adopted here. A trapezoidal interval type-2 MF to fuzzify the altitude error of aircraft is considered. Fuzzy rules of FIE are as follows:

Rule 1: IF an aircraft has same bearing as the air lane AND IF it close to the air lane THEN the aircraft is flying along air lane.

Rule 2: IF an aircraft class is civilian THEN possibility of the aircraft flying along the air lane is high.

Rule 3: IF the altitude of an aircraft is within permissible levels THEN the aircraft is flying along the air lane.

Trapezoidal T2 MF and a fuzzy rule for altitude data are designed in accordance to Reduced Vertical Separation Minimum (RVSM) specifications, established by the FAA and the Director General of Civil Aviation (DGCA, India) [12]. T1 trapezoidal MFs and fuzzy rules are also designed for the FLDS system proposed in [6] with altitude data along similar lines.

Considering parameters from Table 8.5, the IT2FLDS and modified T1FLDS of [2] are simulated. Post simulation, the location of aircraft and air lane in the yaw plane (Figure 8.9), pitch plane (Figure 8.10) and in $3D$ space (pitch + yaw Figure 8.11) are shown. The bearings of air lane and aircraft as seen from the origin $(0, 0)$ and at various data points [6] are shown in Figure 8.12. At various data points, the altitudes of the air lane and aircraft considered in the simulation are shown in Figure 8.13. The absolute bearing difference between air lane and aircraft is the bearing input in Figure 8.8. According to T1FLDS output as shown in Figure 8.14, the aircraft is flying along the air lane between 10–20 seconds. The air lane decision results obtained from the IT2FLDS system are shown in Figure 8.15. IT2FLDS results obtained depict that

TABLE 8.4
Air lane decision making error comparison results considering IT2FLDS and T1 FLDS [2]: Experiment 8.2

Scenario #	Scenario SNR in dB	MSE Reduction in %	RMSE Reduction in %	PSNR Improvement in %	MAX ERROR Reduction in %
1	90	89.55	67.68	7.85	75.44
2	80	89.54	67.65	8.70	74.83
3	70	89.49	66.73	9.59	75.44
4	50	96.40	81.09	17.53	81.48
5	10	64.21	40.26	7.29	45.79

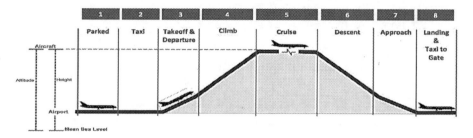

FIGURE 8.7 Phases of a flight from ARC Report: Experiment 8.3

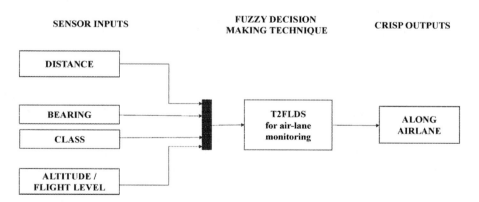

FIGURE 8.8 IT2FLDS Simulink model for air lane monitoring considering distance, bearing, aircraft class and altitude: Experiment 8.3

the aircraft is flying along the air lane between 10–20 seconds with certainty. Between 1–10 seconds and 21–30 seconds the aircraft is flying along the air lane with 62% certainty. In the IT2FLDS crisp output results greater than 0.5 are considered as true values. Results obtained from IT2FLDS are more realistic. The discretized values of the results obtained using IT2FLDS and T1FLDS are compared with ground truth

TABLE 8.5
Simulation parameters for Experiment 8.3

Parameter	Simulation values
Initial aircraft state $X = [x\,\bar{x}\,y\,\bar{y}]$	$X = [361.67\,ft\ 361.67\,ft\ 567\,knots\ 567\,knots]$
Number of sensor data considered	4
Type of sensors considered	*Speed, bearing, aircraft class and altitude*
Sensor update rate	$1\,Hz$
Flight Level of air lane location along z axis	$z = 29,000\,ft$
Simulation time	$30\,s$
Number of fuzzy rules	3

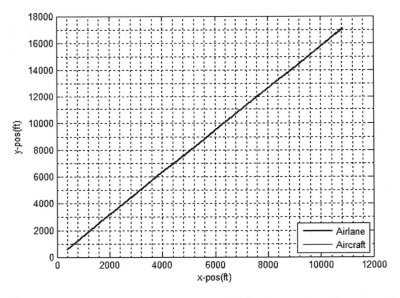

FIGURE 8.9   X and Y positions of air lane and aircraft in the yaw plane: Experiment 8.3

values in Table 8.6. Ground truth values are arrived at from expert opinion and knowledge of FAA/DGCA rules. The results presented in Table 8.6 prove that IT2FLDS outperforms the T1 FLDS system in air lane decision making.

EXERCISES

8.1 How T2 and interval type 2 fuzzy logics are useful in decision making?
8.2 Do these types of logic provide better performance than the type 1 FL?
8.3 Can we obtain the results of using IT2FL by using T1 FL mathematics?
8.4 Why is the type reducer required in the FIS of IT2FLS?
8.5 How many membership functions are in T2 FLS?

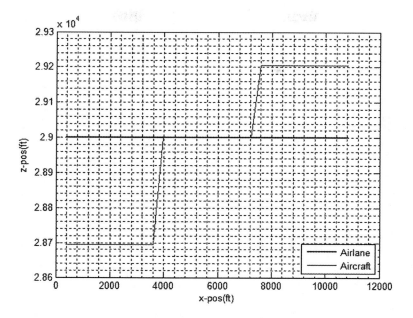

FIGURE 8.10   X and Z position of air lane and aircraft in the pitch plane: Experiment 8.3

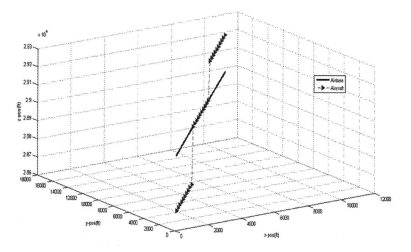

FIGURE 8.11   X, Y and Z position of air lane and aircraft considering pitch and yaw planes: Experiment 8.3

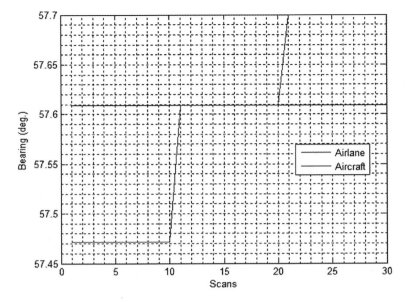

FIGURE 8.12   Bearing angle of air lane and aircraft with respect to (0, 0): Experiment 8.3

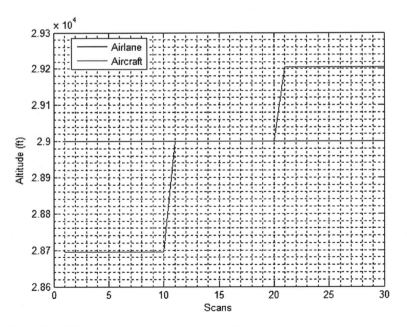

FIGURE 8.13   Altitude in feet of air lane and aircraft: Experiment 8.3

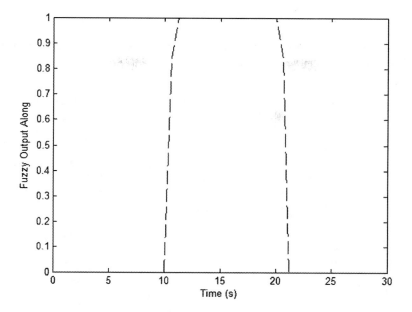

FIGURE 8.14   Modified T1FLDS [2], Experiment 8.3

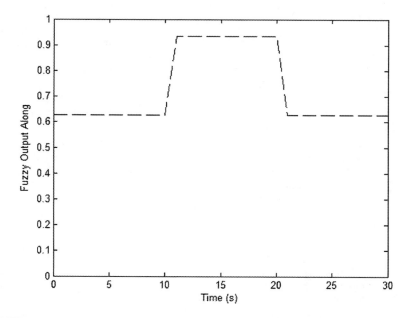

FIGURE 8.15   IT2FLDS output for air lane decision in Experiment 8.3

TABLE 8.6
Along air lane decision making result comparison between ground truth, T1 FLDS and IT2FLDS: Experiment 8.3

Time (s)	Ground Truth		Defuzzified output Type-1 FLDS [2]		Defuzzified output of IT2FLDS	
1	1.0000	Yes	0.0000	No	0.6280	Yes
3	1.0000	Yes	0.0000	No	0.6280	Yes
5	1.0000	Yes	0.0000	No	0.6280	Yes
7	1.0000	Yes	0.0000	No	0.6280	Yes
9	1.0000	Yes	0.0000	No	0.6280	Yes
11	1.0000	Yes	1.0000	Yes	0.9349	Yes
13	1.0000	Yes	1.0000	Yes	0.9349	Yes
15	1.0000	Yes	1.0000	Yes	0.9349	Yes
17	1.0000	Yes	1.0000	Yes	0.9349	Yes
19	1.0000	Yes	1.0000	Yes	0.9349	Yes
21	1.0000	Yes	0.0000	No	0.6280	Yes
23	1.0000	Yes	0.0000	No	0.6280	Yes
25	1.0000	Yes	0.0000	No	0.6280	Yes
27	1.0000	Yes	0.0000	No	0.6280	Yes
29	1.0000	Yes	0.0000	No	0.6280	Yes

REFERENCES

1. Mendel, J. M. and John, R. I. B. Type-2 fuzzy sets made simple, in IEEE Transactions on Fuzzy Systems, vol. 10, no. 2, pp. 117–127, Apr 2002.
2. Patra, S. K. and Mulgrew, B. Efficient architecture for Bayesian equalization using fuzzy filters, IEEE Trans. Circuits Syst.—II: Analog Digital Signal Processing, vol. 45, pp. 812–820, July 1998.
3. Mizumoto, M. and Tanaka, K. "Some Properties of Fuzzy Sets of Type-2," Information and Control, vol. 31, pp. 312–340, 1976,Elsevier
4. Mendel, J. M. General Type-2 Fuzzy Logic Systems Made Simple: A Tutorial, in IEEE Transactions on Fuzzy Systems, vol. 22, no. 5, pp. 1162–1182, Oct. 2014.
5. Karnik, N. N., and Mendel, J.M. An Introduction to Type-2 Fuzzy Logic Systems, Univ. of Southern Calif, Los Angeles (1998).
6. Raol, J. R., and Kashyap, S. K. Decision fusion using fuzzy logic type 1 in two aviation scenarios, Journal of Aerospace Sciences and Technologies, Vol. 65, No. 3, pp. 273–286, 2013.
7. Castro, J. R., Castillo, O., Melin, P., and Rodrguez-Daz, A. Building fuzzy inference systems with a new interval type-2 fuzzy logic toolbox, in Transactions on Computational Science I (LNCS) vol. 4750, pp. 104–114, 2008, Springer.
8. Mizumoto, M. and Tanaka, K. "Some Properties of Fuzzy Sets of Type-2," Information and Control, vol. 31, pp. 312–340, 1976,Elsevier
9. Castro, J. R., Castillo, O., and Melin, P. An Interval Type-2 Fuzzy Logic Toolbox for Control Applications, 2007 IEEE International Fuzzy Systems Conference, London, 2007, pp. 1–6.

10. Anon. Federal Aviation Administration, Portable Electronic Devices Aviation Rulemaking Committee Report, Aviation Rulemaking Committee Report, September 30, 2013. www.faa.gov/about/initiatives/ped/media/ped_arc_final_report.pdf (Accessed October, 2016).
11. Anon. Boeing Publication: Statistical Summary of commercial Jet Airplane Accidents. Worldwide Operations 1959–2015. (2015).
12. Anon. Director General of Civil Aviation, India, Requirements For Implementation Of Reduced Vertical Separation Minimum (RVSM), Civil Aviation Requirements Section 8–Aircraft Operations Series 'S', PART II ISSUE I, 17th JANUARY, 2013. Online: http://dgca.nic.in/cars/D8S-S2.pdf (Accessed October, 2016)

APPENDIX 8A   FUZZY LOGIC TYPE 2

Conventionally what is well known to us are the FL type 1 (T1FL), and fuzzy sets type 1 (T1FS). In this case the crisp logic can be regarded as FL type '0' (T0FL) for uniform notation. The type '0' can handle only the conventional uncertainty, i.e. random noise in the classical sense as described by probability models, whereas the T1FL can handle the vagueness. T1FL can also be used to incorporate the heuristic knowledge of the human expert via (fuzzy) IF ... THEN ... rules; these rules are not fuzzy in themselves. Then the output of T1FL, i.e. the defuzzified output, is like a deterministic variable, i.e. the T0FL. In a probability density function (pdf), the variance provides a measure of dispersion/uncertainty about the mean and hence captures more information in the probabilistic models. In that case a T1FL is analogous to a probabilistic system only through the first moment, the mean. Then the so called T2FL is analogous to a probabilistic system via the first and second moments. Thus, the T2FL provides an additional design Degree of Freedom (DOF) (Mamdani and TSK fuzzy logic systems). The provision of this extra DOF is useful when FL based systems are used in cases when lots of uncertainties (and that too of different types) are present. In that case the resulting T2FLS can potentially provide better performance than a T1FL. This additional design DOF would be very useful for modelling sensors/communications channels that would be affected by vagueness and impreciseness, and then provide efficient and realistic DF and decision (DeF) fusion systems.

The T2FL can handle uncertainties by modelling them and minimizing their effects on the control system's performance. When these uncertainties disappear T2FL reduces to T1FL. The T2FL consists of fuzzifier (with T2FL MFs), FIS, IF ... THEN ... rules, and FIF for operations on fuzzy sets that are characterized by MFs, the Type Reducer (TR), and finally the DeFuzzification Operation (DFO). The O/P (Output Processor) of a T2FLS has two components: a) T2FSs are transformed into T1FSs by means of TR, and then b) the T1FS is transformed into a crisp number by means of DFO, i.e. into T0FS.

The T1FL does not directly handle rule uncertainties because it uses T1FSs (that are certain to some extent). T2FL is very useful where it is difficult to determine an exact MF for a FS. Thus, the T2FL can be used to handle the uncertainties in the rules themselves (if so desired) and even measurement uncertainties. As such a T2FL provides more DOF for design than a T1FL, and this is because its T2FSs are described by more parameters than are the T1FSs (in fact the MFs for the T2FS have one extra DOF, i.e. a third dimension more than the T1FL MFs). This aspect itself opens up new possibilities for representing and modelling more or several types of uncertainties in measurements as well as in the fuzzy rule base thereby enlarging the scope of the T2FL in applications to MSDF including situational awareness (SA) and wireless sensor networks (WSN).

8A.1   Type 2 and Interval Type 2 Fuzzy Sets

As we have seen, in T1FLS the MFG (grade) for each element is a crisp value in the range [0, 1], whereas T2FL is characterized by a 3D MF and a footprint of uncertainty (FOU) [1], [2], Figure 8A.1; the MFG for each element of this set is an FS in [0, 1] itself. This T2FS is bounded from below by the Lower MF (LMF), and from above by the Upper MF (UMF). The area between the LMF and UMF is the FOU. Thus, we see that the new and third dimension of T2FS and the FOU provide additional degrees of freedom that make it possible to directly model and treat the uncertainties. This is the IT2FL that use the T2FS in either of their inputs or outputs and thus provides the potential to have a suitable framework to handle the uncertainties in real world problems. The T2FSs encompass a large number of T1FSs. We can quickly realize that in T2FLS the DOM (Degree of Membership) is in itself fuzzy (it has a range of values rather than one value), and ids represented by a secondary membership function (SMF). If the SMF is at its maximum of *1* at every point, we refer to it as an interval type 2 set (IT2FS, most people use this IT2FL and hence we continue to denote it as IT2FLS). The SMF in T1FS has only one value in its domain corresponding to the primary membership function/value (PMF/V) in which the SMF grade equals *1*. Thus, in T1FS for each value of *x*, there is no uncertainty associated with the PMV.

In IT2FLSs (still we may use the notation, T2FS) as the primary membership takes values within the interval [*a, b*], where each point in this interval has an associated SMF of *1* [1], [2]. Hence, there is maximum uncertainty associated with the SMF. However, in the general type 2 fuzzy sets (T2FS per se are not discussed further in the present book), the uncertainty represented by SMF can be modelled with any degree between T1FLSs and IT2FSs, for example by the triangular SMF, Figure 8A.1. Since, the IT2FS-MFs are fuzzy and have a FOU, they can model and handle the linguistic and numerical uncertainties associated with the I/O of the FL Control/Systems (FLS). The merit is that the use of IT2FS will result in the reduction of the rule base when compared to using T1FS. This is because the uncertainty represented in the FOU in IT2FL allows us to cover the same range as T1FS with a smaller number of labels. The additional DOFs given by the FOU enables IT2FS to produce outputs that cannot be achieved by T1FSs (with the same number of MFs). In fact, an IT2FS gives rise to an equivalent T1 MFG that is negative or larger than unity. Each I/O will be represented by a large number of T1FSs that are embedded in the T2FSs, and hence the use of a large number of T1FSs to describe the I/O variables permits a detailed description of the analytical control. This addition of the extra levels of classification made possible by using T2FS gives a much smoother control response. In addition, the IT2FL can be thought of as a collection of many different embedded T1FSs.

The T2FL is computationally intensive, however, this computation can be simplified a lot by using IT2FL which enables us to design an FLS in a lesser time and with less effort. Hence, the majority of FLSs are based on IT2FL. Traditionally the T1FL is not visualized as a 3D set. However, its conception and visualization in 3D is straightforward when we consider each of its points to be associated with the value *1* in the third dimension [1], [2]. This means that a complete confidence is attached to each achieved MFG associated with a given crisp input, see Figures 8A.1 and 8A.2 [1], [2]. In Figure 8A.1, the same input *p* is applied to the three types of fuzzy sets: T1FS, IT2FS (interval type), and T2FS, resulting in a DOM that is specific to the type of FL. The extent of uncertainty/distribution linked with the degree is a (whitish) patch in Figure 8A.1. This is explicitly depicted in Figure 8A.2. This figure shows the SMFs–the 3rd dimension of the T1FS, IT2FS, and T2FS fuzzy sets/logic as elicited by the same input *p*.

The FIS of the IT2FL control/system depicted in Figure 8A.3 consists of a fuzzifier, FIE, rule base, TR, and defuzzifier. The IT2FS rules are the same as in the T1FS system, but the antecedents and/or the consequents will be represented by IT2FL. The FIS combines the fired rules and gives a mapping from the input IT2FS to the output IT2FS sets. Then TR needs to be performed. This can be done in either of two ways: i) use the iterative Karnik-Mendel (KM) procedure/algorithm, or ii) use the Wu-Mendel (WM) uncertainty bounds method.

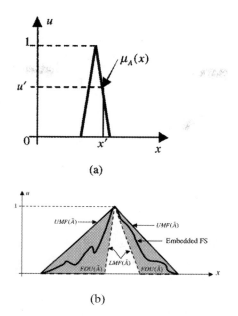

(a)

(b)

FIGURE 8A.1 Types of fuzzy logic membership functions : a) Type-1 FL/FS (T1FL), b) Interval type-2 FL/FS (IT2FL) and FOU, c) General type-2 FL/FS (T2FL) and FOU. (Adapted/modified from: Hagars, H., and Wagner, C. Introduction to interval type-2 fuzzy logic controllers–towards better uncertainty handling in real world applications. eNewsletter, IEEE SMC Society, No. 27, June 2009, with permission. www.my-smc.org/news/back/2009_06/SMC-Hagras.html, accessed Nov. 2012)

8A.2 INTERVAL TYPE 2 FUZZY LOGIC MATHEMATICS

If we blur the T1FS MF, for example, say triangular one, by shifting the points on the triangle either to the left or to the right, then we obtain the T2MF as seen in Figure 8A.1. This blurring need not necessarily be of the same amount and it could be regular, irregular, or uniform, the latter being preferred. Then, at a specific value of x, say x^j, there is no single value for the MF; instead it takes on values wherever the vertical line intersects the blur. All of these values need not be weighted the same, so we assign an amplitude distribution to all these points. As a result of this process, we obtain 3-D MF-a T2MF, this characterizes a T2FS. We emphasize here that much of the mathematics of T2FSs and IT2FSs is based on ref. [3]. {*Caution: we make the least attempt to change the format and style of representing various equations, formulae and expressions of ref. [3]; this is done in order to maintain the uniformity of such representations in the literature on FL, wherein sometimes the mathematics becomes too messy. Any attempt to make arbitrary changes in such formulations, just for the sake of making changes, would affect the flow, the regularity and the standardization of the symbols used in the ref. [3], since these formulations/equations/expressions have multiple levels of subscripts and superscripts*}.

So, we have the following definition of the T2FS [3]:

$$\tilde{A} = ((x,u), \mu_{\tilde{A}}(x,u)); \quad \forall x \in X, \forall u \in J_x \subseteq [0,1] \tag{8A.1}$$

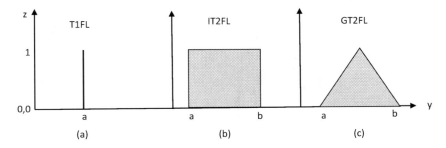

FIGURE 8A.2 SMFs (secondary membership functions, see here the z-dimension) depicting the 3rd dimension for: (a) Type-1 (T1FL), (b) Interval type-2 (IT2FL), (c) General type-2 (T2FL)

In eqn. (8A.1) we have $\tilde{A}$ as the T2FS, and it is characterized by a T2MF (Type 2 membership function), $\mu_{\tilde{A}}(x,u))$ where $x \in X$, and $u \in J_x \subseteq [0,1]\}$. Also, we have $0 \leq \mu_{\tilde{A}}(x,u) \leq 1$. T2FS can also be expressed as follows:

$$\tilde{A} = \int_{x \in X} \int_{u \in J_x} \mu_{\tilde{A}}(x,u)/(x,u) \quad J_x \subseteq [0,1] \tag{8A.2}$$

In eqn. (8A.2), the integral signs denote the union-operator over all the permissible x, and u, and for the discrete UOD (DUOD), the integral sign is replaced by the summation (sigma) sign. In and for equation (8A.1) we see two conditions: i) $\forall u \in J_x \subseteq [0,1]$ is in line with the T1FL constraint i.e. $0 \leq \mu_{\tilde{A}}(x,u) \leq 1$. This is because when the uncertainty disappears a T2FL should degenerate to T1FS, i.e. T2MF should reduce to T1MF; and ii) the condition $0 \leq \mu_{\tilde{A}}(x,u) \leq 1$ is also in line with the fact that the amplitudes of MF should be within 0 and 1, both inclusive. We have now the following definition for the IT2FS [3]:

$$\tilde{A} = \int_{x \in X} \int_{u \in J_x} 1/(x,u), \quad J_x \subseteq [0,1]\} \tag{8A.3}$$

We emphasize here, that IT2FS/IT2FL are more prevalent and usable in FLS/FL control and are easier to handle than T2FL. Next, for each value of x, say x', the 2D plane, whose axes are u and the $\mu_{\tilde{A}}(x',u)$, is called a vertical slice of the $\mu_{\tilde{A}}(x,u)$. Then, a secondary MF (SMF) is considered as a vertical slice of $\mu_{\tilde{A}}(x,u)$, it is $\mu_{\tilde{A}}(x=x',u)$ for $for\ x' \in X, \forall u \in J_{x'} \subseteq [0,1]$ and is given as follows:

$$\mu_{\tilde{A}}(x=x',u) \equiv \mu_{\tilde{A}}(x') = \int_{u \in J_{x'}} 1/u, \quad J_{x'} \subseteq [0,1] \tag{8A.4}$$

Invoking the concept of secondary sets, one can interpret IT2FS as the union of all the secondary sets. Thus, one can express $\tilde{A}$ in a vertical-slice manner as follows [3]:

$$\tilde{A} = (x, \mu_{\tilde{A}}(x)); \forall x \in X \qquad (8A.5)$$

$$\text{Or} \quad \tilde{A} = \int_{x \in X} \mu_{\tilde{A}}(x) / x = \int_{x \in X} [\int_{u \in J_x} 1/u]/x ; \quad J_x \subseteq [0,1] \qquad (8A.6)$$

Next, we define the domain of an SMF. It is called the Primary Membership (PMF) of x. Thus, J_x is the PM of x, and $J_x \subseteq [0,1]; \forall x \in X$. The amplitude of an SMF is called the SMFG (-grade), and these for an IT2FS are all equal to 1. In case X and J_x are discrete then we can express the right most part of equation (3.38) as follows [3]:

$$\tilde{A} = \sum_{x \in X} [\sum_{u \in J_x} 1/u]/x, = \sum_{i=1}^{N} [\sum_{u \in J_{x_i}} 1/u]/x_i, = [\sum_{k=1}^{M_1} 1/u_{1k}]/x_1 + ... + [\sum_{k=1}^{M_N} 1/u_{Nk}]/x_N$$

$$(8A.7)$$

In equation (8A.7), '+' sign denotes union operation, and we see that x is discretized into N values and at each of x value, u is also discretized into M_i values. The discretization along each u_{ik} is not necessarily the same, if it is the same then $M_1 = M_2 = ... = M_N = M$. The uncertainty in the PMF of an IT2FS, $\tilde{A}$, has the bounded region and is called the FOU (Foot-print of Uncertainty), and this FOU is the union of all the PMFs expressed as follows:

$$FOU(\tilde{A}) = \bigcup_{x \in X} J_x \qquad (8A.8)$$

This FOU is a vertical-slice representation of the FOU, see Figure 8A.1. This is so because each of the PMs is a vertical slice. The FOU is a complete description of an IT2FS, since the SMFGs of an IT2FS do not convey any new information. The upper and lower MFs (UMF. LMF) are next defined as follows:

$$\bar{\mu}_{\tilde{A}}(x) \equiv \overline{FOU(\tilde{A})} ; \qquad \forall x \in X$$
$$\underline{\mu}_{\tilde{A}}(x) \equiv \underline{FOU(\tilde{A})} ; \qquad \forall x \in X \qquad (8A.9)$$

Thus, we have $J_x = [\underline{\mu}_{\tilde{A}}(x), \bar{\mu}_{\tilde{A}}(x)] ; \forall x \in X$ for IT2FS. For DUODs X, and U, an embedded IT2FS has N elements. The set embedded such functions/FSs is given as follows:

$$\tilde{A}_e = \sum_{i=1}^{N} [1/u_i]/x_i, \quad u_i \in J_{x_i} \subseteq U = [0,1] \qquad (8A.10)$$

In equation (8A.10) we have $\prod_{i=1}^{N} M_i \tilde{A}_e$ embedded functions. Also, for DUODs X, and U an embedded T1FS has N elements. The set is given as follows:

$$A_e = \sum_{i=1}^{N} u_i / x_i, \quad u_i \in J_{x_i} \subseteq U = [0,1] \tag{8A.11}$$

In equation (8A.11) also, we have $\prod_{i=1}^{N} M_i A_e$ embedded functions. We have now the representation theorem [6]: for an IT2FS with discrete X, and U, we have the following expressions:

$$\tilde{A} = \sum_{j=1}^{n_A} \tilde{A}_e^j \tag{8A.12}$$

With $(j = 1,2, ..., n_A)$ and

$$\tilde{A}_e^j = \sum_{i=1}^{N} [1/u_i^j]/x_i, \quad u_i^j \in J_{x_i} \subseteq U = [0,1] \tag{8A.13}$$

with $n_A = \prod_{i=1}^{N} M_i \tag{8A.14}$

In equation (8A.14), M_i denotes the discretization levels of SMF variables. Equation (8A.12) gives a wavy slice of the set $\tilde{A}$. We make the following observations regarding equation (8A.12): i) the MF of a IT2FS is 3D wavy, ii) one can take all the possible wavy slices and take their union to reconstruct the original 3D MF, iii) then, the same points that occur in different wavy slices, only occur once in the set-theoretic union, iv) then it means collecting all of the embedded IT2FSs into a bunch of such T2FS, and v) equivalently one can collect all of the embedded T1FS into a bunch of such T1FSs. We have also the following relationship (from equation (8A.12):

$$\tilde{A} = 1 / FOU(\tilde{A}) \tag{8A.15}$$

With the following expressions for the set:

$$FOU(\tilde{A}) = \sum_{j=1}^{n_A} A_e^j = \{\underline{\mu}_{\tilde{A}}(x),...,\overline{\mu}_{\tilde{A}}(x)\} \quad ; \quad \forall x \in X_d$$
$$[\underline{\mu}_{\tilde{A}}(x),\overline{\mu}_{\tilde{A}}(x)] \quad ; \quad \forall x \in X \tag{8A.16}$$

With

$$A_e^j = \sum_{i}^{N} u_i^j / x_i, \quad u_i^j \in J_{x_i} \subseteq U = [0,1] \tag{8A.17}$$

In equation (8A.16), X_d is the DUOD, and X is the continuous UOD, and the equation gives an interval set of functions implying that it contains an uncountable number of functions that would completely fill the space between $\overline{\mu}_{\tilde{A}}(x) - \underline{\mu}_{\tilde{A}}(x)$; $\forall x \in X$.

8A.3 THE SET THEORETIC OPERATIONS FOR IT2FS

We here consider the operators of intersection, union and complement for the IT2FS/IT2FL:

i) The union of two FLSIT2 sets is given as follows:

$$\tilde{A} \bigcup \tilde{B} = 1 / [\underline{\mu}_{\tilde{A}}(x) \vee \underline{\mu}_{\tilde{B}}(x), \overline{\mu}_{\tilde{A}}(x) \vee \overline{\mu}_{\tilde{B}}(x)] \quad ; \quad \forall x \in X \qquad (8A.18)$$

ii) The intersection operation is given as:

$$\tilde{A} \bigcap \tilde{B} = 1 / [\underline{\mu}_{\tilde{A}}(x) \wedge \underline{\mu}_{\tilde{B}}(x), \overline{\mu}_{\tilde{A}}(x) \wedge \overline{\mu}_{\tilde{B}}(x)] \quad ; \quad \forall x \in X \qquad (8A.19)$$

iii) The complement operation is given as:

$$\overline{\tilde{A}} = 1 / [1 - \underline{\mu}_{\tilde{A}}(x), 1 - \overline{\mu}_{\tilde{A}}(x)] \qquad\qquad \forall x \in X \qquad (8A.20)$$

8A.4 FURTHER OPERATIONS ON IT2FS

The IT2FS-FIS is shown in Figure 8A.3. The additional block is the TR block and it reduces the T2FSs to T1FSs. In IT2FS all the antecedents and consequent FSs are T2. The structures of the rules remain exactly the same as in the case of T1FL. The rules have the following form:

$$R^l : If \ x_1 \ is \ \tilde{F}_1^l \ and... \ x_p \ is \ \tilde{F}_p^l, \ Then \ y \ is \ \tilde{G}^l \ ; \quad l = 1, 2, ..., M \qquad (8A.21)$$

We consider, initially $l = 1$, and the rule is activated by a crisp number (i.e. singleton fuzzification, SF) [3].

a) Singleton Fuzzification and One Antecedent

Let us have the single rule:

$$If \ x_1 \ is \ \tilde{F}_1, \ Then \ y \ is \ \tilde{G} \qquad (8A.22)$$

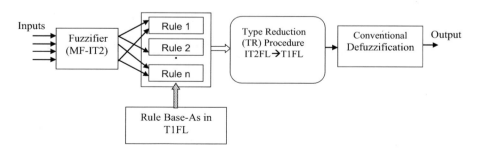

FIGURE 8A.3   IT2FL Fuzzy inference system (IT2FL/S-FIS)

in the DUOD. Now, decompose $\tilde{F}_1$ into n_{F1} embedded IT2FSs $\tilde{F}_{1e}^{j1}$ $(j_1 = 1,2,...,n_{F1})$. Similarly for G. According to the representation theorem equation (8A.12), we have the following expressions for F and G:

$$\tilde{F}_1 = \sum_{j1=1}^{n_{F1}} \tilde{F}_{1e}^{j1} = 1 / FOU(\tilde{F}_1) \tag{8A.23}$$

Where we have

$$FOU(\tilde{F}_1) = \sum_{j1=1}^{n_{F_1}} F_{1e}^{j1} = \sum_{j1=1}^{n_{F_1}} \sum_{i=1}^{N_{x_1}} u_{1i}^{j1} / x_{1i} \; ; \; u_{1i}^{j1} \in J_{x_{1i}} \subseteq U = [0,1] \tag{8A.24}$$

Similarly for the output (consequent) part we have:

$$\tilde{G} = \sum_{j=1}^{n_G} \tilde{G}_e^j = 1 / FOU(\tilde{G}) \tag{8A.25}$$

$$FOU(\tilde{G}) = \sum_{j=1}^{n_G} G_e^j = \sum_{j=1}^{n_G} \sum_{k=1}^{N_y} w_k^j / y_k \; ; \; w_k^j \in J_{yk} \subseteq U = [0,1] \tag{8A.26}$$

As a result of equations (8A.25), and (8A.26) we have $n_{F_1} \times n_G$ number of possible combinations of embedded T1 antecedent and consequent FSs. With this the totality of the fired output sets for all the possible combinations of these embedded T1 antecedent and consequent FSs will be a bunch of functions $B(y)$ with:

$$B(y) \underset{\equiv}{\Delta} \sum_{j_1=1}^{n_{F_1}} \sum_{j=1}^{n_G} \mu_B(j_1, j)(y) \; ; \quad \forall y \in Y_d \tag{8A.27}$$

In equation (8A.27) the summation operation signifies the union. The relation between the bunch of the functions B(y) and the FOU of the T2-fired output FS can be summarized as: the bunch of the functions $B(y)$ obtained using T1FS operations is the same as the FOU of the T2FS fired output obtained T2FS operations.

b) Singleton Fuzzification and Multiple Antecedents

Let us have $\tilde{F}_1, \tilde{F}_2,..., \tilde{F}_p$ as the IT2FSs in DUODs $X_{1d}, X_{2d},..., X_{pd}$ and $\tilde{G}$ as the IT2FS in the UOD Y_d. We decompose F's to obtain the IT2FSs as follows:

$$\tilde{F}_i = \sum_{j_i=1}^{n_{F_i}} \tilde{F}_{ie}^{j_i} = 1/FOU(\tilde{F}_i), \quad i = 1, 2, ..., p \tag{8A.28}$$

The Cartesian product $\tilde{F}_1 \times \tilde{F}_2 \times ... \times \tilde{F}_p$ has $\Pi_{i=1}^{p} n_{F_i}$ combinations of the embedded T1FSs $F_{ie}^{j_i}$. Let us have F_e^n as the nth combination of these embedded T1FSs as follows:

$$F_e^n = F_{1e}^{j_1} \times ... \times F_{pe}^{j_p} \; ; \; 1 \leq n \leq \prod_{i=1}^{p} n_{F_i} \; and \; 1 \leq j_i \leq n_{F_i} \tag{8A.29}$$

Equation (8A.29) requires a combinatorial mapping from $(j_1, j_2, ..., j_p) \to n$. We express equation (8A.29) as follows:

$$F_e^n = F_{1e}^{j_1(n)} \times ... \times F_{pe}^{j_p(n)}, 1 \leq n \leq \prod_{i=1}^{p} n_{F_i} \; and \; 1 \leq j_i(n) \leq n_{F_i} \tag{8A.30}$$

Then, we have

$$\mu_{F_e^n}(x) = T_{m=1}^{p} \mu_{F_{me}^{jm(n)}}(x_m), 1 \leq n \leq \prod_{i=1}^{p} n_{F_i} \; and \; 1 \leq j_m(n) \leq n_{F_m} \tag{8A.31}$$

With

$$n_F \equiv \prod_{m=1}^{p} n_{F_m} \tag{8A.32}$$

In equation (8A.31) the usual T-norm of FL is used. We obtain $n_F \times n_G$ combinations of antecedent and consequent embedded T1FSs, with n_G embedded T1FSs for the consequent. This generates a bunch of $n_F \times n_G$ fired output consequent T1FS functions as follows:

$$B(y) = \sum_{n=1}^{n_F} \sum_{j=1}^{n_G} \mu_B(n, j)(y) \; ; \; \forall y \in Y_d \tag{8A.33}$$

The results of Type-1 non-singleton fuzzification and multiple antecedents are based on the results of the case presented in b) above [3].

   c) Type-2 Non-singleton Fuzzification and Multiple Antecedents

In this case the p-dimensional input rule is given by the IT2FS $\tilde{A}_x$ with the assumption that MF is separable and $\tilde{X}_i$ denotes the labels of the IT2 FSs describing each of the p inputs. Specifically $\tilde{X}_1, \tilde{X}_2, ..., \tilde{X}_p$ are IT2FSs in the DUOD of X_d. Then, further we obtain the following decomposition [3]:

$$\tilde{X}_i = \sum_{\gamma_i}^{n_{X_i}} \tilde{X}_{ie}^{\gamma_i}; \quad i = 1, 2, ..., p. \tag{8A.34}$$

The domain of the each of the components of equation (8A.34), $\tilde{X}_{ie}^{\gamma_i}$ is the embedded T1FS, $X_{ie}^{\gamma_i}$. The Cartesian product $\tilde{X}_1 \times \tilde{X}_2 \times ... \times \tilde{X}_p$ has $\prod_{\delta=1}^{p} n_{X_\delta}$ combinations of the embedded T1FSs, i.e. $X_{ie}^{\gamma_i}$. So, if we have X_e^k as the kth combination of these embedded T1FS, then we have the following expression:

$$X_e^k = X_{1e}^{\gamma_1} \times ... \times X_{pe}^{\gamma_p}; \quad 1 \leq k \leq \prod_{\delta=1}^{p} n_{X_\delta} \text{ and } 1 \leq \lambda_\delta \leq n_{X_\delta} \tag{8A.35}$$

Equation (8A.35) requires a combinatorial mapping from $\{\lambda_1, \gamma_2, ..., \gamma_p\} \rightarrow k$; only we need to understand that it is possible to obtain such a mapping. So, we have the following expression for the mapping:

$$X_e^k = X_{1e}^{\gamma_1(k)} \times ... \times X_{pe}^{\gamma_p(k)}; \quad 1 \leq k \leq \prod_{\delta=1}^{p} n_{X_\delta} \text{ and } 1 \leq \lambda_\delta \leq n_{X_\delta} \tag{8A.36}$$

Then we have the following additional requirements:

$$\mu_{X_e^k}(x) = T_{m=1}^p \mu_{X_{me}}^{\gamma_m(k)}(x_m); 1 \leq k \leq \prod_{\delta=1}^{p} n_{X_\delta} \text{ and } 1 \leq \lambda_m(k) \leq n_{X_m} \tag{8A.37}$$

$$\text{And } n_X \equiv \prod_{\delta=1}^{p} n_{X_\delta} \tag{8A.38}$$

There are n_G embedded T1FSs for the consequent, $n_F = \prod_{m=1}^{p} n_{F_m}$ embedded T1FS for the antecedents. We also, have n_X embedded T1FSs for the inputs. Hence, we have $n_X \times n_F \times n_G$ combinations of the input, the antecedent and consequent embedded T1FSs that obtain a bunch $B(y)$ of these combinations as the fired output consequent T1FSs functions so, we have the following expression for $B(y)$:

$$B(y) = \sum_{k=1}^{n_X} \sum_{n=1}^{n_F} \sum_{j=1}^{n_G} \mu_{B(k,n,j)}(y) \tag{8A.39}$$

d) Multiple Rules

Usually we have M rules and often more than one rule fire when some input is applied to the FLS. In this case, we should incorporate l in all the expressions of IT2FSs. Then, in this case we have the following expressions [3]:

$$\tilde{B}^l = 1 / FOU(\tilde{B}^l) \tag{8A.40}$$

$$FOU(\tilde{B}^l) = [\underline{\mu}_{\tilde{B}^l}(y), \overline{\mu}_{\tilde{B}^l}(y)] \; ; \; \forall y \in Y \tag{8A.41}$$

$$\underline{\mu}_{\tilde{B}^l}(y) = \inf_{\forall k,n,j}(\mu_{B^l(k,n,j)}(y)) = [T_{m=1}^P(\sup_{x_m \in X_m} \underline{\mu}_{X_m}(x_m) * \underline{\mu}_{F_m^l}(x_m))] * \underline{\mu}_{G^l}(y) \; ; \; \forall y \in Y \tag{8A.41}$$

$$\overline{\mu}_{\tilde{B}^l}(y) = \sup_{\forall k,n,j}(\mu_{B^l(k,n,j)}(y)) = [T_{m=1}^P(\sup_{x_m \in X_m} \overline{\mu}_{X_m}(x_m) * \overline{\mu}_{F_m^l}(x_m))] * \overline{\mu}_{G^l}(y) \; ; \; \forall y \in Y \tag{8A.42}$$

Next, we assume that the l rules/sets are combined using the union operation, then we have the following relations:

$$\tilde{B} = 1 / FOU(\tilde{B}) \tag{8A.43}$$

$$FOU(\tilde{B}) = [\underline{\mu}_{\tilde{B}}(y), \overline{\mu}_{\tilde{B}}(y)] \; ; \; \forall y \in Y$$

$$\underline{\mu}_{\tilde{B}}(y) = \underline{\mu}_{\tilde{B}_1}(y) \vee \underline{\mu}_{\tilde{B}^2}(y) \vee ... \vee \underline{\mu}_{\tilde{B}^M}(y) \tag{8A.44}$$

Similarly, we can obtain the expression for the UMF values by replacing in equation (8A.44), the LMF values/grades by the UMF values/grades.

e) Output Processing

The TR (see Figure 8A.3) is the first step of output processing and it computes the centroid of an IT2FS. Next, we require that the IT2FLS must reduce to a T1FLS. We know that several T1-defuzzification methods are based on computing the centroid of a T1FS. We define the centroid of an IT2FS as the collection of the centroids of all of its embedded IT2FSs. We have the following formulae to compute the centroid [6]:

$$C_{\tilde{B}} = 1 / \{c_s, ..., c_l\} \tag{8A.45}$$

with

$$c_s = \min_{\forall \theta_i \in [\underline{\mu}_{\tilde{B}}(y_i), \overline{\mu}_{\tilde{B}}(y_i)]} \frac{\sum_{i=1}^N y_i \theta_i}{\sum_{i=1}^N \theta_i} \tag{8A.46}$$

$$c_l = \max_{\forall \theta_i \in [\underline{\mu}_{\tilde{B}}(y_i), \overline{\mu}_{\tilde{B}}(y_i)]} \frac{\sum_{i=1}^N y_i \theta_i}{\sum_{i=1}^N \theta_i} \tag{8A.47}$$

In equation (8A.45) we have the smallest and the largest elements denoted by s, and l subscripts. The general formulae for the smallest and the largest values are given as [3]:

$$c_s = \frac{\sum_{i=1}^{S} y_i \bar{\mu}_{\tilde{B}}(y_i) + \sum_{i=S+1}^{N} y_i \underline{\mu}_{\tilde{B}}(y_i)}{\sum_{i=1}^{S} \bar{\mu}_{\tilde{B}}(y_i) + \sum_{i=S+1}^{N} \underline{\mu}_{\tilde{B}}(y_i)} \tag{8A.48}$$

$$c_l = \frac{\sum_{i=1}^{L} y_i \underline{\mu}_{\tilde{B}}(y_i) + \sum_{i=L+1}^{N} y_i \bar{\mu}_{\tilde{B}}(y_i)}{\sum_{i=1}^{L} \underline{\mu}_{\tilde{B}}(y_i) + \sum_{i=L+1}^{N} \bar{\mu}_{\tilde{B}}(y_i)} \tag{8A.49}$$

In equations (8A.48) and (8A.49) S, and L are the switching points that can be determined by the K-M algorithm [3]. There are as many TR methods as there are T1FL-defuzzification techniques, because each one of the TR methods is associated with one of the latter. After the TR is performed, one uses the defuzzification as follows:

$$y(x) = 0.5\{c_s(x) + c_l(x)\} \tag{8A.50}$$

Also, one can use an ad hoc TR formula as follows [6]:

$$y(x) \cong 0.5\{\underline{\mu}_{\tilde{B}}(y) + \bar{\mu}_{\tilde{B}}(y)\} \tag{8A.51}$$

REFERENCES

1.   Hagras, H., and Wagner, C. Introduction to interval type-2 fuzzy logic controllers– towards better uncertainty handling in real world applications. eNewsletter, IEEE SMC Society, No. 27, June 2009. www.my-smc.org/news/back/2009 _06/SMC-Hagras.html, accessed Nov. 2012).
2.   Hagras, H. CE888: Type-2 fuzzy logic systems. Lecture ppts.courses.essex.ac.uk/ce/ce888/Lecture%20Notes/FuzzyLecture1.pdf. Accessed Nov. 2012.
3.   Mendel, J. M., John, R. I., and Liu, F. Interval type-2 fuzzy logic systems made simple. IEEE Trans. On Fuzzy Systems, Vol. 14, No. 6, pp. 808–821, Dec 2006.

APPENDIX 8B IT2FL MADE SIMPLE WITH T1FL

Further clarifications [1], [2] to the derivations in Appendix 8A are provided in this appendix.

8B.1 COMPARISON OF TWO TYPES OF FLS

The type-2 fuzzy sets (T2FSs) were introduced by Zadeh (1975); these provide additional design Degrees of Freedom (DOF) in Mamdani and TSK FLS. This can be very useful when such systems are used in certain real-life situations where lots of uncertainties are present. The resulting T2FLS have the potential to provide better performance than T1FL. Because of the computational complexity of using a general T2FL, most users only use *interval* T2FSs in a T2FLS, the result being an *interval* T2FLS (IT2FLS). The computations associated with interval T2FSs are very manageable making an IT2FLS quite practical.

In order to use an IT2FLS, one must become proficient about (top-down approach): i) T1FLSs, ii) General T2FSs, iii) Operations performed upon them (T2FS mathematics), iv) T2 fuzzy relations, v) T2FLSs, vi) Interval T2FSs, vii) their associated operations and relations, and viii) IT2FLSs. To obtain such a level of proficiency, one has to make a very significant investment of time and effort, which many practising engineers (and even the project scientists) do not have; and the university courses about FL also do not have enough time to do this, and hence requiring a person to use T2FS mathematics represents a barrier to the use of IT2FSs. In fact, it is not necessary to take the 'top-down' approach from general T2FS to IT2FS, rather one can used the 'bottom-up' approach, because all of the results that are needed to implement an IT2FLS can be obtained using T1FS mathematics, and this makes IT2FLSs much more accessible to all.

A major difference between a T2FS and a T1FS is that T1FS has a grade of membership that itself is crisp, even though the T1FS does make the independent variable, say the temperature of something, a range of certain values, but for each of these values the grade of membership (function) has a single crisp value; i.e. for any value of the primary variable (say temperature on the horizontal x-axis) when you project upwards (onto the membership function curve) you will intersect the Membership Function (MF) at a single point, in this case, 'the T1FS has a grade of membership that is crisp'. Whereas, T2FS has a grade of membership that itself is fuzzy (a fuzzy-fuzzy set); i.e. now the temperature does not have one value of grade membership, but has more than one value, it has a (vertical) range like the temperature itself had on the x-axis (a range on the horizontal axis). For this it is assumed that there is some uncertainty about both the left-end and right-end vertices of the T1MF, here it is assumed to be a triangular one. This is just one example, e.g. uncertainty could have also been assigned to the apex of the triangle. Here, we can assume that there are some additional triangle MFs that begin at some point in the interval of uncertainty for the left-end vertex, then pass through the apex and finally terminate at some point in the interval of uncertainty for the right-end vertex. If all of the possible triangle MFs are shown (of course, one cannot do that because there are an uncountable number of them), we would get a region that is called the Footprint of Uncertainty (FOU). When some 'temperature' has a value x_1 then projecting vertically from x_1, a continuum of triangle MF values will be intersected; however, this continuum of MF values is bounded by both lower and upper values (bounds). Each point in the interval of MF values (the primary memberships) can be weighted differently; the weights—secondary grades—come out of the page (of the 2D picture of the primary MF plotted versus the temperature, you can imagine this picture easily), and provide the MF of a general T2FS with a new third dimension.

A T2FS reduces to a T1FS, when all uncertainties disappear, this is analogous to randomness reducing to determinism when random uncertainty disappears. So, a T2FS reduces to a T1FS when the FOU collapses to a T1FS; this T1FS is called a primary MF; consequently, T2FS theory contains T1FS theory as a special case; and the T2FS has a secondary membership function (grade) which could be itself like any primary membership function, hence the dimensionality of the fuzzy logic from the modeling point of view has increased and now it has become a 3D representation, so that it can cover a larger set of uncertainties in the data. Thus, T0FL is one dimensional, and is deterministic that is obtained after defuzzification of T1FL, which in itself is 2D, and T2FL is 3D; thus the MF of a T1FS is 2D, and the MF of a T2FS is 3D. The latter is too difficult to draw, hence, the convention is to focus on the 2D domain of the 3D MF-that domain is called the footprint of uncertainty. Recall that the MF of a general T2FS is 3D, the FOU is the domain of the T2FS MF; the secondary grades sit atop the FOU.

The left-hand FOU was obtained by beginning with a triangle primary MF and assuming uncertainty only about its apex. Assume the uncertainty is given by the interval [m – a, m + a]. Now beginning at m, slide the triangle a units to the left and a units to the right. Doing this you will obtain the filled-in FOU. The middle FOU demonstrates that uncertainty does not have to be symmetrical, i.e. the FOU to the left of the apex is 'larger' (e.g., contains more area) than the FOU to the right of the apex. So, a FOU does not have to be symmetrical. The right-hand FOU demonstrates that its bounds do not have to be piecewise linear. In this case, they are both Gaussian. Observe that a FOU is described by more parameters than is the original primary MF. It is these additional parameters—degrees of freedom—that provide T2 FSs the potential to out-perform T1 FSs. Today, using general T2 FSs is computationally intractable, efficient algorithms are difficult to find. Thus, T2 FSs require more computation than do T1 FSs. In similar ways, using probability (theory and computations) is also more complicated than the deterministic ana-lysis; and yet we use it, because it provides us with a very useful model of unpredictability. Here, the T2 FSs provide us with a very useful model of linguistic uncertainty; hence, we use interval T2 FSs, i.e. these only use the FOU. In an interval T2FS (IT2FS) all secondary grades have the same value, namely 1; consequently, they convey no useful information, and can be discarded.

Then, the rationale is: there is no best choice for even the MF of a type-1 FS (which one to use: Triangle? Trapezoid? Or Gaussian?); let us uniformly weight the entire FOU→ IT2 FS. T1 FS applications seem to be very robust to the specific choice made for the shape of the MF. The shape is usually fixed and then the associated parameters of that shape are optimized (tuned). The advantage is that the formulas for computing all operations are simple-we only have to keep tabs of the two endpoints of an interval. An interval is completely defined by its left-end and right-end points. One would see that when operations are performed on IT2 FSs, the intervals get mapped into other intervals. Simple formulas for the mapped intervals are now available. First, the FOU has a shape like a combination of a trapezoidal MF and a tri-angular MF, as if the second one is lower than the first one; and hence we have the upper MF abbreviated as UMF, and lower MF abbreviated as LMF. An over-bar on the T2 MF denotes the former, and an under-bar on the T2 MF denotes the latter; the LMF and UMF play very important roles in all computations involving IT2 FSs; and these two MFs are individually like any T1 FS MF; this is the nicety of the IT2FSs and hence of the IT2FL. An IT2 FS is com-pletely described by its Footprint of Uncertainty (FOU).

An embedded set (also called an embedded T1 FS) is a function that lies within or on the FOU; the two other examples of embedded sets are the LMF and UMF. Because the third dimension of a general T2 FS is irrelevant for an IT2 FS, it is not necessary to carry along the equal unit secondary grades. The FOU says it all for an IT2 FS. For a continuous FOU (i.e., a completely filled-in FOU) there are an uncountable number of embedded sets; the latter sets are only used for theoretical derivations, and never for computation. If both the primary and secondary variable axes are discretized, then there will be a countable number of embedded sets, but there could still be an astronomical number of them; again such sets will only be used for theoretical derivations, and never for computation. Observe that an embedded set looks like a wavy slice that cuts through the FOU.

8B.2 The Representation Theorem

Known as the Mendel-John Representation Theorem (RT), it is to-date the most important theoretical result in T2 FS theory; it states that the FOU can be covered by the union of all of its embedded sets. The 1/FOU(.) is a shorthand notation, eqn. 8A.16. It means the secondary grades equal 1 at all points in the FOU. The upper line in this equation (8A.16) is for a discrete universe of discourse, for which there will be a finite number of embedded sets. The second line in this equation (8A.16) is for a continuous universe of discourse, for which there will be an infinite and uncountable number (a continuum) of embedded sets. This theorem is important because it allows us to represent the FOU (the IT2 FS) in terms of T1 FSs. Although, there are a lot of these T1 FSs, the Representation Theorem will only be used to derive formulas, and, because it only involves T1 FSs, this means derivations will only use T1 FS mathematics. One can see that the resulting formulas are very easy to compute, and do not involve an astronomical number of T1 FS computations. We need formulas for union, intersection and complement which can be derived using the Representation Theorem. Just as in T1 FS theory, where the union, intersection and complement of T1 FSs are frequently computed, these same quantities will also have to be computed for IT2 FSs.

8B.3 THE USE OF THE REPRESENTATION THEOREM

The union of two IT2 FSs is another IT2 FS, one that is completely described by its FOU. The Representation Theorem has been used for the two sets, A and B; twice, once for IT2 FS A, and once for IT2 FS B. The sigma signs represent unions of elements within each of the two IT2 FSs, whereas the union sign represents the union across the two IT2 FSs; 'a union is a union is a union'; consequently, the second part with a double 'summation signs' reorganizes all of the unions. An important observation is that the union of the two embedded sets is the union of two T1 FSs, and this can be computed using T1 FS mathematics. In this derivation, the maximum operation is used for the disjunction operation. In a more general derivation, the disjunction could be replaced by a T-conorm (i.e. S-norm) operator, of which the maximum is but one such operator. The maximum is taken at all N points in the discretized domains of the two T1 embedded sets. It is important to recall that the union of two T1 FSs is another T1 FS, i.e. it is a function (in this case it is defined at N points).

The collection of all unions will have lower and upper bounding functions; hence, the second critical step in the derivation is to find the largest and the smallest of the just calculated unions. The largest of these unions is found by determining the supremum of all of the unions. Because the UMFs are legitimate T1 embedded sets, at each sampled value of the primary variable the supremum must occur at the UMFs of both IT2 FSs. The smallest of all the unions is found by determining the infimum of all of the unions. Because the LMFs are legitimate T1 embedded sets, at each sampled value of the primary variable the infimum must occur at the LMFs of both IT2 FSs. Observe that the union of two IT2 FSs is also an IT2 FS, one whose LMF is obtained from the LMFs of the original IT2 FSs, and whose UMF is obtained from the UMFs of the original IT2 FSs. Observe, also, that although the RT was used in the first steps of the derivation, additional analyses were needed to reach the final results. These analyses led to a simple computational algorithm for the union. As promised, the RT is a means to an end, and is not used as the final computational algorithm. It is straightforward to extend the computational formulas for THE union, intersection and complement of two IT2 FSs, from two to a finite number of IT2 FSs; just repeat the process adding in one new IT2 FS at a time.

8B.4 INTERVAL TYPE 2 FUZZY LOGIC SYSTEM

A T2 FLS has almost the same structure as a T1 FLS, the main difference being in the 'output processing'. Note that T2 and IT2 will be used interchangeably from here on in; and yet all of our results are only for the latter. Crisp inputs are fuzzified by the fuzzifier. Unlike a T1 FLS, in which only two kinds of fuzzification are possible-singleton and T1; in an IT2 FLS three kinds of fuzzification are possible: i) singleton, ii) T1, and iii) IT2. The latter offers a possibility that is not available at all in a T1 FLS. When either T1 or IT2 fuzzification is used, it is common to state that non-singleton fuzzification is used. Rules do not. What does change are the models used for antecedents and consequents in the rules; and again, 'A rule is a rule is a rule'. As long as even one antecedent or consequent is modeled as T2, the entire FLS is T2. In fact, if all antecedents and consequents are modeled as T1 FSs, but at least one input is fuzzified as an IT2 FS, then the FLS is T2. The FIE/FIS maps T2 FSs into a fired-rule T2 FSs. Closed-form formulas for inferencing are available, and are derived by using the RT.

a) Output Processing Usually, the desired output of a FLS is a number. Output processing maps the fired rule IT2 FSs into a number, but it does so in two steps: a) Type-reduction (TR) maps IT2 FSs into an interval set, and b) Defuzzification maps the TR set into a number. A bottom-up approach is taken, one that begins with the simplest situation, a single rule with one antecedent and singleton fuzzification (SF). Once the details of the derivation of the fired-rule set are understood for this case, it will be very straightforward to extend the results to more general cases. The RT is used for both the antecedent and consequent IT2 FSs.

b) Inferencing Process Consider all $n_{F} \times n_{G}$ possible combinations of embedded T1 antecedent and consequent FS, all possible $n_{F} \times n_{G}$ type-1 rules. One can use a directed graph that shows (from left-to-right) the singleton input (fuzzified into A_{x}) fanning out into each of the n_{F} embedded T1 FSs of the antecedent. Each of these then fan out into each of the n_{G} embedded T1 FSs of the consequent. In total, there are $n_{F} \times n_{G}$ paths. A group of such n_{G} paths is enclosed by the red dashed rectangle, in reference [1], and the path shown with red arrows is one such path. For convenience, this derivation is done for a discrete universe of discourse so that it is possible to use directed graphs. So, the 'key idea' is to use a directed graph to show all of the $n_{F} \times n_{G}$ paths, and each path is associated with a T1 calculation. Observe the indexing of the T1 fired rule consequent set. The first index in $B(i, j)$ is associated with the superscript of the antecedent embedded T1 FS, and the second index in $B(i, j)$ is associated with the superscript of the consequent embedded T1 FS. All of the $n_{F} \times n_{G}$ T1 FSs are unioned in order to obtain the MF of the fired rule consequent set of the rule. This union has a smallest and a largest member, and these are shown with conventional under and over bars. We use the Mamdani implication (method) (a T1 Mamdani FLS); so the formula for the MF of the T1 consequent set $B(i, j)$ is very simple. The t-norm is either minimum or product. Further analysis shows that its lower (upper) bound is achieved when both the antecedent and consequent MFs are their respective LMFs (UMFs). The IT2 fired rule consequent set is equated to its FOU. The RT is now being used in reverse, i.e. the totality of T1 FSs contained within the bracketed set is the union of all MFs that describe the FOU of the IT2 fired rule consequent set. Take all of the T-norms between the antecedent and consequent MFs, and note that this collection will have a smallest and a largest function. It is common practice to label the elements of the excited antecedent MFs using the symbol 'f' to denote 'firing' (i.e. the rule is fired). The uncertainties about the antecedent as it is excited by the singleton input x = x' are carried through the computations by means of the firing interval. When the antecedent collapses to a T1 FS, then the firing interval collapses to a point value, the firing level. And, when the consequent is also a T1 FLS, then this is how an IT2 FLS reduces to a T1 FLS.

c) IT2 Singleton Fuzzification (SF) and Multiple Antecedents Next, consider a single rule with p antecedents. Each input is singleton-fuzzified and then fans out into its respective embedded T1 antecedent sets. Each of those in turn fans out into the n_{G} embedded T1 consequent sets. A block around all the embedded antecedent sets would denote the fact that all possible n_{F} combinations of them must be formed. Of course, in this case there are many more paths than in the previous case, but conceptually there is nothing new.

d) IT2 NSF (non-singleton fuzzification) and One Antecedent This time the single input is modeled as an IT2 FS. A representative FOU for the input is used, e.g. two triangles displaced but with their apexes at the same point. Now the representation is used three times, once each for the input, antecedent and consequent; of course there are many more embedded sets in the present case than in the first case. Now the formula for the IT2 fired rule consequent set has three unions, where the third one is for the input IT2 FS. The derivation makes use of the sup-star composition that is used in a T1 FLS when the input is modeled as a T1 FS, the so-called non-singleton T1 case. The final results can again be expressed as the T-norm between a firing interval and the entire IT2 consequent set, but the calculation of the firing interval is more complicated in the present case. It involves a value of x that derives from the sup-star composition calculation. Once again, all the mathematics that is needed to obtain formulas for the LMF and UMF of the IT2 fired-rule consequent set is T1 FS mathematics.

e) Interval T2 FLS Formulas: Multiple Rules The next generalization is from one rule to multiple rules (M rules). If 'l' fired rules are combined using the union operation, leading to a composite IT2 FS, B, then $B = 1/FOU(B)$. We do not necessarily advocate combining the fired rule consequent sets by the union. Union combining is used here merely as an illustration. Recall, even in a T1 FLS there can be different ways of combining the fired rule consequent sets, and many times it is done as part of defuzzification. The same is true for an IT2 FLS. Fired rule consequent sets can be combined as a part of the type-reduction process. When fired rule consequent sets are combined by the union operation there is then only one combined fired rule consequent set. Mainly the formulas for the LMF and UMF change.

f) Output Processing Recall, that if this were a T1 FLS, only defuzzification would be needed in order to map the fired rule consequent sets (or their union) into a number. In an IT2 FLS, output processing consists of two stages, type-reduction and then defuzzification. Type-reduction maps the fired rule consequent sets (or their union) into a T1 FS. Type-reduction (TR) begins with the interval T2 output of the inference engine of an IT2 FLS. Because there are many type-1 defuzzification methods, there are a comparable number of type-reduction methods. TR reduces an IT2 FS to a T1 FS, which we call the type-reduced set. Type-reduction methods are 'extended' versions of T1 defuzzification methods, and compute the centroid of the T2 output FS. The word 'extended' refers to Zadeh's Extension Principle. The earliest derivation of the type-reduced set relied on it. As a result of the RT, it is no longer necessary to use it.

At this stage we would have got the FOU of the unioned fired rule consequent sets; FOU for an interval T2 FS. We will now have the sampled primary variable and primary memberships leading to a discretized FOU, because we will perform the computations using a digital computer, and this sampling need not have to be uniform. We will have a solid curve that is one embedded type-1 set, within the FOU. Recall that the FOU is the union of all its embedded T1 FSs. Because each embedded set is a type-1 FS, its Center of Gravity (COG) can be computed using existing and well-known type-1 COG formulas. We already know that an IT2 FLS can be interpreted as a collection of a very large number of embedded T1 FLSs. We can use an interpretation for an IT2 FLS that lets one easily communicate what an IT2 FLS is to others–a collection of a very large number of embedded T1 FLSs. Of course, because the number of embedded T1 FSs for the FOU of an IT2 FS is very large, one would never think of actually computing using all of these embedded T1 FSs. Now, compute the centroid for all embedded T1 FLSs, then, fuse the centroids using union. Now one will get the defuzzified outputs of all of the embedded T1 FLSs; visualize them as points on a horizontal axis; these points will have a smallest and a largest value. This collection of points is the TR (type reduced) set. Aggregation refers to defuzzification of the type-reduced set.

You can imagine, an inserted FOU that shows the union of two IT2 fired rule consequent sets, now picture in your mind the Representation Theorem applied to this FOU. Even though there may be an astronomical number of embedded T1 FSs in the FOU, there will be embedded T1 FSs which have the smallest and largest centroid; hence, the centroid of an IT2 FS is an IT1 FS. The membership value for all points in this interval equals 1, because the secondary grades for an IT2 FS all equal 1. The smallest centroid is denoted cl and the largest centroid is denoted cr. The computation of cl is challenging because of the interval sets that appear in both its numerator and denominator. Because the same interval sets appear in numerator and denominator, standard interval arithmetic cannot be used to compute cl. The same thing applies to the computation of cr also.

Karnik and Mendel have shown the method of this computation for cl: the first summation in both the numerator and denominator uses the UMF of the combined fired rule output set, whereas the second summation in both the numerator and denominator uses the LMF of the combined fired rule output set. The key is to determine the switch point L, an index in the series: 1, ..., L, ..., N. Karnik and Mendel have also shown the method of this computation for cr: the first summation in both the numerator and denominator uses the LMF of the combined fired rule output set, whereas the second summation in both the numerator and denominator uses the UMF of the combined fired rule output set. The key is to determine the switch point R, an index in the series: 1, ..., R, ..., N; here R is not the same as L, in general.

Switch points L and R can be computed using algorithms that were developed by Karnik and Mendel. There are no closed form formulas for them. The Karnik-Mendel (KM) algorithms are iterative and each of the two algorithms can be run in parallel. It was proved that these algorithms converge to their exact answer monotonically and super-exponentially fast (really fast!). The algorithms are very easy to derive and implement, and they are very widely used by practitioners of IT2 FLSs. The KM algorithms can be used to compute the left and right end-points of the type-reduced set. Again, the type-reduced set is an IT1 FS. Intuitively, we expect the width of the type-reduced set to increase as the area of the FOU increases and to decrease as the area of the FOU decreases. In fact, if all uncertainty disappears then the FOU becomes a curve–a T1 FS–and the type-reduced set is a single number, i.e. the IT2 FLS reduces to a T1 FLS.

g)   Defuzzification We defuzzify the type-reduced set to get a crisp output from a type-2 FLS. The most natural way of doing this seems to be by finding the centroid of the type-reduced set. Once the type-reduced set has been computed, defuzzification is trivial. Just compute the average of the left and right end-points of the type-reduced set.

REFERENCES

1. Mendel, J. M. Interval Type-2 Fuzzy Logic Systems Made Simple by Using Type-1 Mathematics. University of Southern California, Los Angeles, Slides 1-90 CA, WCCI, USA 2006.
2. Mendel, J. M., Hagras, H. and John, R. I. Standard Background Material About Interval Type-Fuzzy Logic Systems that can be Used by All Authors,–http://ieee-cis. org/_files/standards.t2.win.pdf, Accessed 2012.

9 IT2 Fuzzy Logic Decision Fusion for Formation-Flying Recognition

9.1 A DUAL LAYER ARCHITECTURE

For FF recognition, a dual layer architecture is developed and validated. The IT2FL based decision support system is shown in Figure 9.1(a). This dual layer of IT2FLS consists of two systems for: i) tracking kinematics $(IT2FLS-TK)$, and ii) FF recognition ($IT2FLS-FFR$). A Mamdani model with $\alpha-$ plane concept is adopted in $IT2FLS-TK$ and $IT2FLS-FFR$. The FMFs and the corresponding (fuzzy) rules vary for each IT2FLS considered. These rules are designed using experts' opinions. IT2FLSDF consists of: i) an I/P processing block, ii) FIE, and iii) O/P processing block. Figure 9.1(b) shows a trapezoidal FMF used for fuzzification.

9.1.1 INPUT PROCESSING TO OBTAIN A FUZZY INPUT SET

In $IT2FLS-TK$, the flight speed, bearing and elevation data that are obtained from appropriate sensors are used as the input set. In layer 2 of IT2FLSDF ($IT2FLS-FFR$), kinematics that are tracked from the output of layer 1, i.e., flight identity, flight separation distance and class of aircraft, are used as the crisp input set. I/P processing blocks of $IT2FLS-TK$, and $IT2FLS-FFR$ consist of three and four trapezoidal MFs to fuzzify their respective crisp input sets. T2 trapezoidal MFs used are designed by expert opinion and account for the uncertainties present in the sensor data accumulated/observed. Type-2 fuzzy set MF is 3-D in nature, Figure 9.1(b), where the 3rd dimension is the value of the MF $\mu_{\tilde{A}}(x,u)$ at each point on its 2D domain that is called its FOU. A T2 fuzzy set $\tilde{A}$ is defined by a MF given as:

$$\tilde{A} = \left\{((x,u),),\mu_{\tilde{A}}(x,u) | \forall_x \in X, \forall\, u \in J_x \subseteq [0,1]\right\}, \tag{9.1}$$

Here, $0 \le \mu_A(x,u) \le 1$ and $u \in U$ (universe of discourse on the closed interval $[0,1]$). Here primary membership of x is $J_x \subseteq [0,1]$ and $\mu_{\tilde{A}}(x,u)$ is a type-1 fuzzy set. The $FOU(\tilde{A})$ is defined as

DOI: 10.1201/9781003370413-9

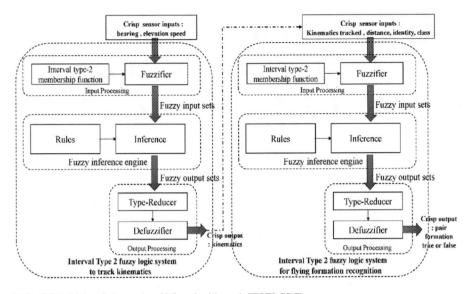

FIGURE 9.1(a)   Schematic of Mamdani based IT2FLSDF

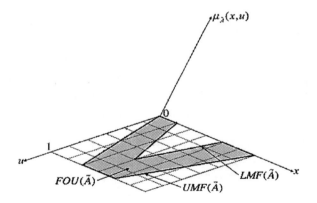

FIGURE 9.1(b)   T2 set membership function

$$FOU(\tilde{A}) = \left\{ (x,u) \in X \times [0,1] \mu_{\tilde{A}}(x,u) > 0 \right\} \qquad (9.2)$$

FOU is bounded with lower $\underline{\mu}_{\tilde{A}}$ and upper $\overline{\mu}_{\tilde{A}}$ membership functions [1]. The lower membership function (referred to as $LMF(\tilde{A})$ in Figure 9.1(b)) is represented as:

$$\underline{\mu}_{\tilde{A}} = inf \left\{ u | u \in [0,1], \underline{\mu}_{\tilde{A}}(x,u) > 0 \right\}, \qquad (9.3)$$

The upper MF $\bar{\mu}_{\tilde{A}}$ (referred to as $UMF\left(\tilde{A}\right)$ in Figure 9.1(b)) is represented as:

$$\bar{\mu}_{\tilde{A}} = sup\left\{u|u \in [0,1], \underline{\mu}_{\tilde{A}}\left(x,u\right) > 0\right\}, \tag{9.4}$$

In IT2FLSDF T2 fuzzy set $\tilde{A}$ is represented using $\alpha-cuts$ or $\alpha-planes$. The $\alpha-plane$ of $\tilde{A}$ is denoted as $\tilde{A}_{\alpha}$ and is defined as

$$\tilde{A}_{\alpha} = \left\{\left(x,u\right), \mu_{\tilde{A}}\left(x,u\right) \geq \alpha \mid \forall x \in X, \forall u \in J_{x} \subseteq [0,1]\right\}, \tag{9.5}$$

$\tilde{A}_{\alpha}$ is the union of all primary memberships of the T2 fuzzy set $\tilde{A}$ whose secondary grades are equal to or greater than $\alpha\left(0 \leq \alpha \leq 1\right)$. According to [2], $\tilde{A}_{\alpha}$ can also be expressed as

$$\tilde{A}_{\alpha} = \int_{\forall x \in X} \frac{\tilde{A}_{\alpha}\left(x\right)}{x}, \tag{9.6}$$

Here, $\tilde{A}_{\alpha}\left(x\right)$ represents the $\alpha-cut$ decomposition of the type 1 fuzzy set $\tilde{A}\left(x\right)$. In [3] a T1 fuzzy set, $\tilde{A}_{\alpha}\left(x\right)$ is defined using T1 secondary MFs $\forall x \in X$ i.e., $\left[a_{\alpha}\left(x\right), b_{\alpha}\left(x\right)\right]$. Eqn. (9.6) can therefore be represented as

$$\tilde{A}_{\alpha} = \int_{\forall x \in X} \frac{\left[a_{\alpha}\left(x\right), b_{\alpha}\left(x\right)\right]}{x}, \tag{9.7}$$

Using $\alpha-cut$ decomposition, the T2 fuzzy set $\tilde{A}$ can be represented as

$$\tilde{A} = \bigcup_{\forall \alpha[0,1]} \left[\frac{\alpha}{\left[\int_{\forall x \in X} \frac{\tilde{A}_{\alpha}\left(x\right)}{x}\right]}\right], \tag{9.8}$$

Fuzzy MF defines the degree of trueness of a fuzzy set $\tilde{A}$ member. In IT2FLSDF, we have considered a trapezoidal T2 MF. The α-cut of the trapezoidal MF used in IT2FLS – TK and IT2FLS – FFR is formulated as:

$$\tilde{A}_{\alpha}\left(x\right) = \left[a_{\alpha}\left(x\right), b_{\alpha}\left(x\right)\right], \tag{9.9}$$

Here, $a_{\alpha}\left(x\right)$ and $b_{\alpha}\left(x\right)$ represent α-cuts of T1 secondary MFs defined as:

$$a_{\alpha}\left(x\right) = \underline{\mu}_{\tilde{A}}\left(x\right) + \frac{1}{2}\omega\left[\underline{\mu}_{\tilde{A}}\left(x\right) - \bar{\mu}_{\tilde{A}}\left(x\right)\right]\alpha$$

$$b_\alpha\left(x\right)=\overline{\mu}_{\tilde{A}}\left(x\right)-\frac{1}{2}\omega\left[\overline{\mu}_{\tilde{A}}\left(x\right)-\underline{\mu}_{\tilde{A}}\left(x\right)\right]\alpha \tag{9.10}$$

T2 fuzzy input sets that are obtained from dual layer of IT2FLSDF are used for further processing, and are considered as inputs to the FIEs of IT2FLS – TK and IT2FLS – FFR .

9.1.2 FUZZY INFERENCE ENGINE

The FIE of IT2FLS – TK in IT2FLSDF is considered to establish kinematic tracking of flights in formation under test based on T2 fuzzy input sets obtained. Two fuzzy rules are designed to establish kinematic tracking in level 1 of IT2FLSDF . In level 2 of IT2FLSDF, the FIE considers a set of two fuzzy rules and T2 fuzzy sets of: i) kinematics, ii) distance, iii) identification, and iv) class inputs; for FF event recognition and decision. Outputs of each FIE are represented using T2 output fuzzy sets that need to be further processed in O/P processing block. Let us consider p number of inputs represented as $x_1 \in X_1$, $x_2 \in X_2, \ldots, x_p \in X_p$. The p inputs provide output $y \in Y$ incorporated with M rules. Human experts' knowledge is incorporated using these rules. This rule $s \in M$ is generally represented as

$$\mathcal{R}^s : \textbf{IF } x_1 is \tilde{F}_1^s \textbf{ AND / OR / NOT } x_2 is \tilde{F}_2^s \ldots \textbf{ AND / OR / NOT } x_p is \tilde{F}_p^s \textbf{ THEN } y is \tilde{G}^s,$$
$$\tag{9.11}$$

Here, $\tilde{F}$ is the input T2 fuzzy set and $\tilde{G}$ is the output T2 fuzzy set. In $\mathcal{R}^s$ '**AND / OR / NOT**' are used to represent the fuzzy relations and are also referred to as 'compounded'. The intersection, complement and union operations on input T2 fuzzy sets result in realization of AND, NOT, OR, operations in $\mathcal{R}$. Additional details of fuzzy set operations are provided in [2]. If $x_m \in X_m = x'_m$, then for each rule i.e., $\mathcal{R}^s : \forall s \in M$ a type 1 α slice of rule antecedent type two fuzzy set $\tilde{F}_m^s$ i.e., $\tilde{F}_m^s\left(x'_m\right)$ is activated. The α slice representation of $\tilde{F}_m^s\left(x'_m\right)$ is defined as

$$\tilde{F}_m^s\left(x'_m\right) = \sup_{\forall \alpha \in [0,1]} \frac{\alpha}{\left[a_{m,\alpha}^s\left(x'_m\right),b_{m,\alpha}^s\left(x'_m\right)\right]} \tag{9.12}$$

The firing interval of $\tilde{F}_m^s\left(x'\right)$ at α slice is obtained using

$$F_\alpha : \begin{cases} F_\alpha^s\left(x'\right) \equiv \left[\underline{f}_\alpha^s\left(x'\right),\overline{f}_\alpha^s\left(x'\right)\right] \\ \underline{f}_\alpha^s\left(x'\right) \equiv \left[T_{m=1}^p, a_{m,\alpha}^s\left(x^{l'}_m\right)\right] \\ \overline{f}_\alpha^s\left(x'\right) \equiv \left[T_{m=1}^p, b_{m,\alpha}^s\left(x'_m\right)\right] \end{cases} \tag{9.13}$$

Here, T represents a $T-norm$ and T is either the product or minimum. The firing interval of each rule $s \in M$ is aggregated with its consequent Type 2 fuzzy set to obtain an output Type 2 fuzzy set $\tilde{G}^s$. FIEs of IT2FLS $-$ TK and IT2FLS $-$ FFR evaluate all rules $\mathcal{R}^s s = 1,2,3,\ldots,M$ and combine the firing intervals of the consequents of all appropriate $\mathcal{R}$ into a T2 fuzzy set by aggregation.

9.1.3 OUTPUT PROCESSING TO OBTAIN THE CRISP OUTPUT

The O/P processing blocks on IT2FLS $-$ TK and IT2FLS $-$ FFR in IT2FLSDF consist of a type reducer and defuzzification function; for the latter, a centroid type reduction is adopted. The type reducer transforms the T2 output set obtained from the FIE engine to a T1 fuzzy set. Defuzzification of the T1 fuzzy set from the reducer provides crisp outputs. In IT2FLS $-$ TK crisp outputs represent tracked kinematics of aircraft under test. In the case of IT2FLS $-$ FFR crisp outputs represent the fusion decision of whether aircraft are in a formation pair or not. At α time level, the Type 2 fuzzy output set is $\tilde{G}^s$, represented as $\tilde{G}^s_\alpha$ is computed using

$$\tilde{G}^s_\alpha = \int_{\forall y \in Y} \frac{G^s_\alpha(y)}{y}, \tag{9.14}$$

Here, $G^s_\alpha(y)$ represents an α cut of the T1 fuzzy set as in equation (9.6). According to [4], T1 fuzzy set $G^s_\alpha(y)$ is represented using T1 secondary MFs as

$$\tilde{G}^s_\alpha = \int_{\forall y \in Y} \frac{\left[g^s_{L,\alpha}(y), g^s_{R,\alpha}(y) \right]}{y}. \tag{9.15}$$

The sth fired rule α cut denoted as $\tilde{B}^s_\alpha$ is obtained by combining each rule's firing interval for level α and its corresponding $\tilde{G}^s_\alpha$. In other words $\tilde{B}^s_\alpha$, represented by its FOU is obtained using

$$\tilde{B}^S_\alpha : \begin{cases} FOU\left(\tilde{B}^s_\alpha\right) = \left[\underline{\mu}_{\tilde{B}^s_\alpha}\left(\frac{y}{x'}\right), \overline{\mu}_{\tilde{B}^s_\alpha}\left(\frac{y}{x'}\right) \right] \forall y \in Y \\ \underline{\mu}_{\tilde{B}^s_\alpha}\left(\frac{y}{x'}\right) = \underline{f}^s_\alpha(x') * g^s_{L,\alpha}(y) \\ \overline{\mu}_{\tilde{B}^s_\alpha}\left(\frac{y}{x'}\right) = \overline{f}^s_\alpha(x') * g^s_{R,\alpha}(y) \end{cases} \tag{9.16}$$

Here, '$*$' is a $T-norm$, $\underline{f}^s_\alpha(x')$ and $\overline{f}^s_\alpha(x')$ are computed using equation (9.13). A union of all $\tilde{B}^S_\alpha$ for $s = 1,2,3,\ldots, M$ is computed to obtain $\tilde{B}_\alpha$ defined as

$$
\tilde{B}_{\alpha} : \begin{cases}
FOU\left(\tilde{B}_{\alpha}\right) = \left[\underline{\mu}_{\tilde{B}_{\alpha}}\left(\dfrac{y}{x'}\right), \overline{\mu}_{\tilde{B}_{\alpha}}\left(\dfrac{y}{x'}\right)\right] \forall y \in Y \\[2ex]
\underline{\mu}_{\tilde{B}_{\alpha}}\left(\dfrac{y}{x'}\right) = \underline{\mu}_{\tilde{B}_{\alpha}^1}\left(\dfrac{y}{x'}\right) \cup \dots \cup \underline{\mu}_{\tilde{B}_{\alpha}^M}\left(\dfrac{y}{x'}\right) \\[2ex]
\overline{\mu}_{\tilde{B}_{\alpha}}\left(\dfrac{y}{x'}\right) = \overline{\mu}_{\tilde{B}_{\alpha}^1}\left(\dfrac{y}{x'}\right) \cup \dots \cup \overline{\mu}_{\tilde{B}_{\alpha}^M}\left(\dfrac{y}{x'}\right)
\end{cases}
\tag{9.17}
$$

A centroid computation C on $\tilde{B}_{\alpha}$ is carried out i.e., $C_{\tilde{B}_{\alpha}}\left(x'\right)$ to obtain a T1 reduced set at level α of output Y as follows.

$$
Y_{C,\alpha}\left(x'\right) = C_{\tilde{B}_{\alpha}}\left(x'\right) = \frac{\alpha}{\left[l_{\tilde{B}_{\alpha}}\left(x'\right), r_{\tilde{B}_{\alpha}}\left(x'\right)\right]}
\tag{9.18}
$$

Here, $l_{\tilde{B}_{\alpha}}\left(x'\right), r_{\tilde{B}_{\alpha}}\left(x'\right)$ are computed using extended Karnik-Mendel algorithms on $\tilde{B}_{\alpha}$. Aggregating all slices or all levels α of $Y_{C,\alpha}\left(x'\right)$ T1 fuzzy set (output of type reducer) is obtained and is defined as

$$
Y_C = \sup_{\forall \alpha \in (0,1)} \frac{\alpha}{Y_{C,\alpha}\left(x'\right)}
\tag{9.19}
$$

Defuzzification of the type reduced-set is carried out to obtain crisp outputs by using

$$
y\left(x'\right) = (0.5) \times \left(\frac{1}{\left[l_{\tilde{B}_{\alpha}}\left(x'\right), r_{\tilde{B}_{\alpha}}\left(x'\right)\right]}\right),
\tag{9.20}
$$

Here, $y \in Y$, Y is the output crisp set of $IT2FLS-TK$ and $IT2FLS-FFR$ embodied in $IT2FLSDF$.

9.2   EXAMPLE 9.1 PERFORMANCE EVALUATION

The $IT2FLSDF$ is developed and validated using a MATLAB/Simulink platform. An IT2FL toolbox [4] is used to realize Mamdani models for $IT2FLS-TK$ and $IT2FLS-FFR$. Comparison of the proposed $IT2FLSDF$ is made with a T1 decision-fusion system developed in [5] and is referred to as $T1FLS$. IT2 trapezoidal MFs for $IT2FLS-TK$ and $IT2FLS-FFR$ are designed to minimize the effects of uncertainties on decision making and kinematic tracking. Two aircraft are considered in the simulation experimental study. Performance of IT2FLSDF and T1FLS models are compared (and are supposed to be on board the combat aircraft). The IT2FLSDF and T1FLS models are developed to understand whether enemy aircraft exhibit formation flying or not. Initial conditions of the experiment conducted are summarized in Table 9.1, from which it is evident that constant velocity is considered for both aircraft X_1, X_2 and their model representation is already discussed in Chapter 8, and repeated here for the sake of convenience:

A point mass model is used to generate kinematic data of aircraft defined as

$$X_i(k+1)=FX_i(k)+Gw_i, \qquad (9.21)$$

In (9.21), i denotes the aircraft ($i = 1, 2$), k is scan number ($k = 1, 2, 3, \ldots, 30$ in this experiment), the state transition matrix is F and G is the process gain noise matrix. White Gaussian process noise with variance $Q = 0.1 \times eye(4,4)$ is used. T is the sampling interval, and the matrices F and G are given as

$$F = \begin{bmatrix} 1 & T & 0 & 0 \\ 0 & 1 & 0 & 0 \\ 0 & 0 & 1 & T \\ 0 & 0 & 0 & 1 \end{bmatrix} \quad G = \begin{bmatrix} \dfrac{T^2}{2} & 0 & 0 & 0 \\ 0 & T & 0 & 0 \\ 0 & 0 & \dfrac{T^2}{2} & 0 \\ 0 & 0 & 0 & T \end{bmatrix}, \qquad (9.22)$$

In IT2FLS−TK three IT2 trapezoidal MFs (one each for bearing, elevation speed) and two rules are considered to track kinematics of the two aircraft. In IT2FLS−FFR four IT2 trapezoidal MFs are used for kinematics, aircraft separation distance, aircraft identity and aircraft class. Two rules are used for decision making. The IT2FLSDF

TABLE 9.1
Parameters for FF recognition in IT2FLSDF and T1FLS [2], Example 9.1

Parameter	Simulation values
Initial state of flight 1 $X_1 = \begin{bmatrix} x_1 & \overline{x_1} & y_1 & \overline{y_1} \end{bmatrix}$	$X_1 = \begin{bmatrix} 0\,m & 166\,m/s & 1000\,m & 0\,m/s \end{bmatrix}$
Initial state of flight 2 $X_2 = \begin{bmatrix} x_2 & \overline{x_2} & y_2 & \overline{y_2} \end{bmatrix}$	$X_2 = \begin{bmatrix} 0\,m & 166\,m/s & 990\,m & 0\,m/s \end{bmatrix}$
No of sensor data considered	6
Type of sensors considered	Speed, Bearing, elevation, distance, identity and aircraft class
Sensor update rate	$1\,Hz$
Simulation time	$s30$

system is designed using 7 MFs and 4 rules. In T1FLS a total of 9 MFs are used with 2 rules. In the proposed IT2FLSDF a reduction in number of MFs with additional rules for accurate tracking/fusion decision making is considered.

9.2.1 WITHOUT UNCERTAINTIES

Initially no noise is considered in sensor values (SNR is set to 100), referred to as an ideal condition. For comparison, similar scenarios are used for the dual system and T1FLS. The trajectories along the x– and z-axes and elevation-measured are shown in Figures 9.2 (a) and 9.2 (b) respectively. In this experimental scenario, the aircraft X_1, X_2 are modelled to be in FF during the initial 5 seconds. After 5 seconds aircraft X_1, X_2 split from each other moving away for the next 5 seconds. From 10 to 15 seconds aircraft maintain constant separation post splitting. From 15 to 20 seconds X_1, X_2 are considered to approach each other (merging formation). The formation pair is again observed at 20 seconds and X_1, X_2 maintain FF for remaining 10 seconds. In IT2FLS – TK the kinematics of X_1, X_2 are tracked, and the output of tracked kinematics from IT2FLS – TK is shown Figure 9.3(a). A logic symbol '1' of IT2FLS – TK denotes similar kinematics of the aircraft and logic symbol '0' is used to represent different/varying kinematics of the aircraft. The crisp output obtained from IT2FLS – FFR depicting whether FF is observed or not is shown in Figure 9.3(b). Decision fusion results of T1FLS and IT2FLSDF are compared with ground truth (obtained from expert opinion) in Table 9.2. Similar results are reported for T1FLS and IT2FLSDF which proves that the interval type 2 fuzzy logic system provides better (and certainly no worse) performance than using T1FLS.

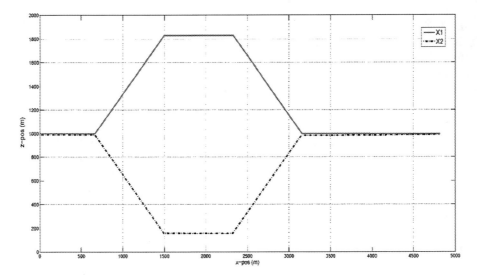

FIGURE 9.2(a) FF experiment: ideal scenario considered: Flying trajectories of aircraft X_1, X_2 in the x-z plane

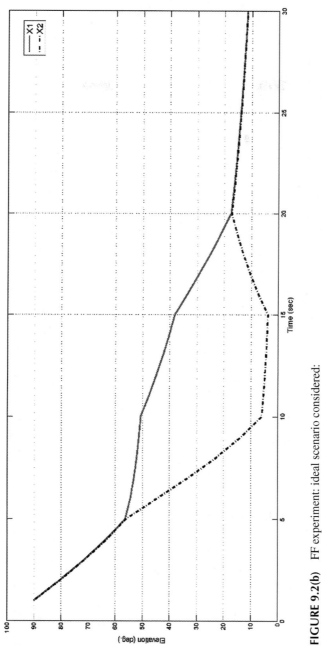

FIGURE 9.2(b)   FF experiment: ideal scenario considered:
Elevation angle observed aircraft X_1, X_2 in experiment scenario

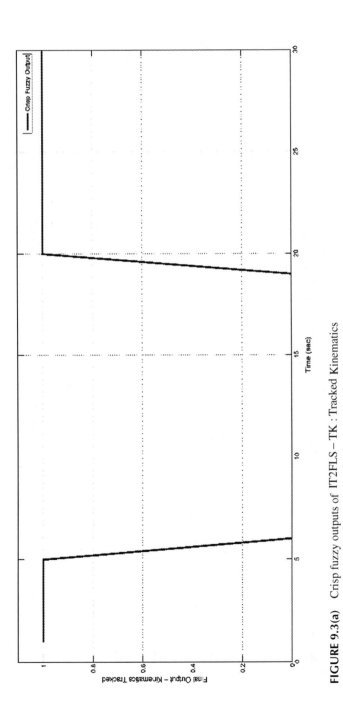

FIGURE 9.3(a)   Crisp fuzzy outputs of IT2FLS – TK : Tracked Kinematics

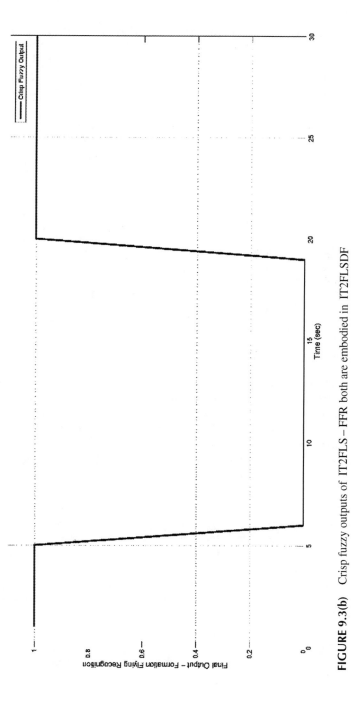

FIGURE 9.3(b) Crisp fuzzy outputs of IT2FLS – FFR both are embodied in IT2FLSDF

TABLE 9.2
FF decision results comparison of T1FLS and IT2FLSDF with ground truth

Time (s)	Ground Truth	T1FLS [2]		IT2FLSDF	
		Fuzzy Output	Decision Value	Fuzzy Output	Decision Value
1	Yes	3.7984	Yes	1.0000	Yes
3	Yes	3.7984	Yes	1.0000	Yes
5	Yes	3.7984	Yes	1.0000	Yes
7	No	0.0000	No	0.0000	No
9	No	0.0000	No	0.0000	No
11	No	0.0000	No	0.0000	No
13	No	0.0000	No	0.0000	No
15	No	0.0000	No	0.0000	No
17	No	0.0000	No	0.0000	No
19	No	0.0000	No	0.0000	No
21	Yes	3.7984	Yes	1.0000	Yes
23	Yes	3.7984	Yes	1.0000	Yes
25	Yes	3.7984	Yes	1.0000	Yes
27	Yes	3.7984	Yes	1.0000	Yes
29	Yes	3.7984	Yes	1.0000	Yes

9.2.2 With Uncertainties

To simulate uncertainties in sensor input data, random Gaussian noise is induced in input sensor data. The noise introduced is quantified in terms of SNR. Noise variations of 50, 40 and 30 dB is introduced in the simulation and correspondingly named as Scenarios 1 (less noise), 2 and 3 (more noise) for representation. With this noise variation in input sensor data, T1FLS and IT2FLSDF models are simulated, and the output of FF recognition results are noted in each case. The results obtained are compared with ground truth as shown in Table 9.3.

   i) **Scenario 1:** Performance of T1FLS is faulty beyond 27 seconds of simulation. Comparison of ground truth and results obtained from T1FLS and IT2FLSDF models for Scenario 1 are shown in Figure 9.4.
  ii) **Scenario 2:** IT2FLSDF results coincide with the ground truth until 24 seconds, beyond which recognition is not accurate. Inaccuracies of T1FLS in Scenario 2 when compared with the ground truth is large. Comparison results of T1FLS, IT2FLSDF models with the ground truth obtained in Scenario 2 are shown in Figure 9.5.
 iii) **Scenario 3:** When large uncertainties are introduced, formation flying recognition decisions of T1FLS, IT2FLSDF models are inaccurate. A marginal improvement of IT2FLSDF model is reported. Comparison results of T1FLS, and IT2FLSDF models with the ground truth obtained in Scenario 3 are shown in Figure 9.6.

TABLE 9.3
FF recognition error observed for T1FLS and IT2FLSDF

Scenario No.	Case	MSE				RMSE				PSNR(dB)				SNR (dB)		
		IT2FSDeF	T1FLS			IT2FLSDeF	T1FLS			IT2FLSDeF	T1FLS			IT2FLSDeF	T1FLS	
1	SNR 50dB	0	0.0333			0	0.183			∞	14.77			∞	12.0412	
2	SNR 40dB	0.1	0.1667			0.316	0.408			10	7.782			7.2700	5.0515	
3	SNR 30dB	0.2667	0.4333			0.5164	0.658			5.7403	3.632			3.0103	0.9018	

The variations in FF recognition results (for each non-ideal scenario considering T1FLS and IT2FLSDF) with respect to the ground truth is quantified using standard measures like Mean Square Error (MSE), Root Mean Square Error (RMSE), Peak Signal to Noise Ratio (PSNR) and Signal to Noise Ratio (SNR); quantification of decision errors is achieved using the metrics: i) $MSE = mean\left(\left(Groundtruth - Decision\_Out\right)^2\right)$;

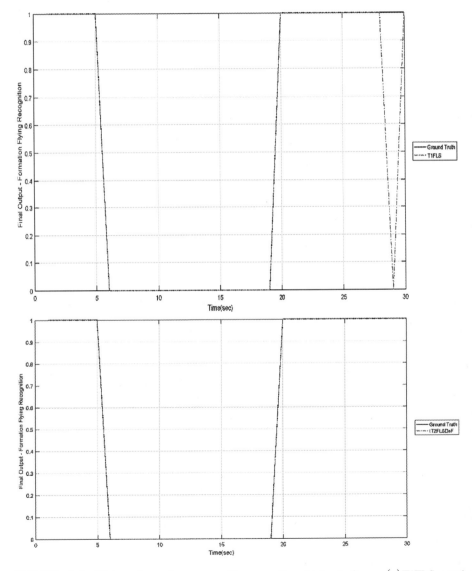

FIGURE 9.4 Flying formation recognition results obtained from (a) T1FLS and (b) IT2FLSDF with ground truth in scenario–1

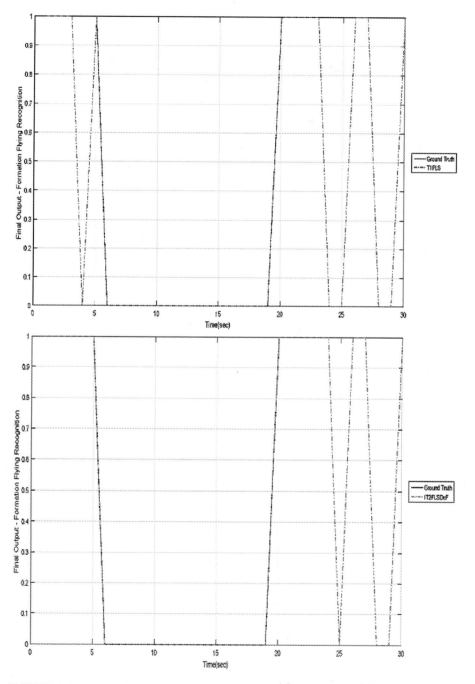

FIGURE 9.5 FF recognition results obtained from (a)T1FLS and (b)IT2FLSDF with ground truth in scenario–2

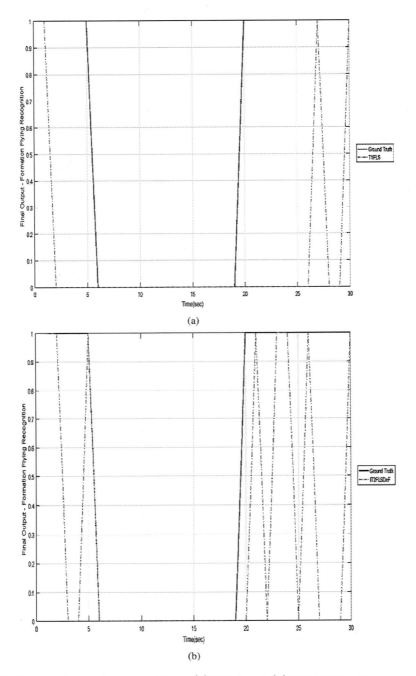

FIGURE 9.6   FFR results obtained from (a)T1FLS and (b)IT2FLSDF with ground truth in scenario-3

TABLE 9.4
Performance improvements of IT2FLSDF against T1FLS for FF recognition

Scenario No.	Case	MSE Improvement (%)	RMSE Improvement (%)	PSNR Improvement (dB)	SNR improvement (dB)
1	SNR 50 dB	100	100	∞	∞
2	SNR 40 dB	40.012	22.53797	8.3727	2.2185
3	SNR 30 dB	38.44911	21.55552	2.1085	2.1085

ii) $RMSE = \sqrt{MSE}$;   iii) $PSNR = 10\log_{10}\left(\dfrac{Maxval^2}{MSE}\right) = 10\log_{10}\left(\dfrac{1^2}{MSE}\right)$;   and

iv) $SNRd = 10\log_{10}\left(\dfrac{mean(Groundtruth)^2}{MSE}\right)$.

The results are shown in Table 9.3. Considering T1FLS alone amongst all scenarios, best performance is reported in Scenario 1 (less noise) and worst performance in Scenario 3 (more noise). Comparing results obtained across all scenarios, better performance is reported with IT2FLSDF compared to T1FLS. Performance improvement is quantified and given in Table 9.4. These results prove that the proposed IT2FLSDF exhibits better FF recognition compared to T1FLS, even in the presence of large uncertainties.

9.3   LYAPUNOV STABILITY ANALYSIS FOR SA WITH IT2FL

Here, we evaluate the stability of the IT2FL system using the Lyapunov method for which we need to combine FL with an SA controller.

9.3.1   FUZZY LOGIC COMBINED WITH PILOT'S SA CONTROLLER

The pilot's SA, aircraft (plant) dynamics and decision-making processes are considered as a composite control system that is controlled or regulated by using IT2FL. In such a case, it is of great importance to ascertain stability of the combined control system since the augmenting sub-systems are inherently nonlinear. Also, since the IT2FL does not lend itself to any mathematical model, in the conventional sense, the method of Routh-Hurwitz criterion cannot be used for stability analysis, in general. Hence, the stability of the combined control system is studied by using Lyapunov energy function. A combined FL-based control, and composite dynamic system (the latter consists of the pilot's command input based on the decision-making system which is implemented using IT2FL to lend accuracy in decision making), and the aircraft's (plant) dynamics, all as shown in Figure 9.7 are considered as a nonlinear (state-) feedback control system.

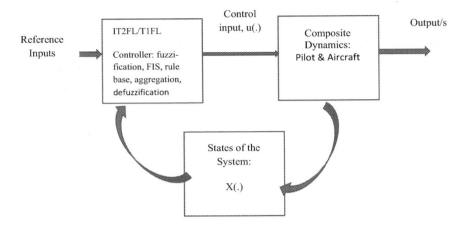

FIGURE 9.7   Combined fuzzy logic-based pilot's assessment system (FIS)

Let X be the universe of discourse. Consider a single input n^{th} order composite nonlinear system that represents the state space equations of the controlled process, including the pilot's activity and the aircraft dynamics:

$$\dot{x} = f(x) + g(x)u; \quad x(t(0)) = x_0 \tag{9.23}$$

In eqn. (9.23), the variables have the usual state space meanings with the appropriate dimensions. When FL-based control is used then one needs to specify the rule base: the ith fuzzy control rule in the rule base of the T-S (Takagi-Sugeno) FLC (fuzzy logic control) base is of the form [6]:

$$\text{Rule i: IF } x_1 \text{ is } X_{i,1} \text{ AND } x_2 \text{ is } X_{i,2} \text{ AND, ..., AND } x_n \text{ is } X_{i,n}$$

THEN $u = u_i(x), I = 1 \text{ to r, r} \in N.$ (9.24)

Thus, r is the total number of rules; the $X_{i,1}, X_{i,2}, .., X_{i,n}$ are fuzzy sets that describe the linguistics terms of the input variables $x_{k,k} = 1 \text{ to n}$; $u = u_i(x)$ is the control signal of rule i; and the function AND is a T-norm. The u_i can be a single value or a function of the state vector, x. Firing rule strength is developed by each rule and is described as

$$\alpha_i(x) = \text{AND } (\mu_{i,1}(x_1), \mu_{i,2}(x_2), ..., \mu_{i,n}(x_n)) \in [0,1], \forall x \in X, i = 1 \text{ to r.} \tag{9.25}$$

9.3.2   IT2FL AS A COMBINATION OF T1FL

The four blocks of Figure 9.8 are based on the decomposition of T2FMFs into 4 T1FMFs, as shown in Figure 9.9.

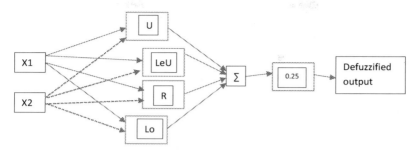

FIGURE 9.8 Simplified T2FL system: the controller output is the average of the four outputs of the embedded upper, left, right, and lower T1FL systems; and x_1 and x_2 are the controller inputs and y is the controller output. (Adapted and modified from [7])

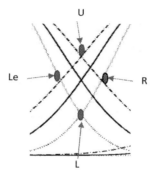

FIGURE 9.9 Decomposition of T2MFs into four 4 T1MFs (Adapted and modified from [7])

The assumption made here is that for any $x \in X$ all the rules exist, among them at least one $\alpha_i(x) \in (0,1]$, $i = 1, \ldots, r$; and the control input u is a function of $\alpha_i(x)$ and u_i. With the help of the weighted sum defuzzification method, the result of the FLC is acquired (based on Figure 9.8) as

$$u = k \frac{\sum_{i=1}^{r} \alpha_i u_i}{\sum_{i=1}^{r} \alpha_i} \qquad (9.26)$$

In eqn. (9.26), k is equal to $\frac{1}{4}$. Certain assumptions used in the stability analysis are [6]: a) If for any input $x_0 \in X$, the firing strength $\alpha_i(x_0)$ corresponding to the fuzzy rule 'i' is zero, then, that fuzzy rule i, for $I = 1, \ldots, r$, is considered as an inactive rule for that input; otherwise, it is considered as an active fuzzy rule; and b) An active region of the fuzzy rule 'I' is defined as a set $X_i^A = \{x \in X \mid \alpha_i(x) \neq 0\}, i = 1,...,r$. With the assumptions a) and b), eqn. (9.26) can be written as

$$u(x(0)) = k \frac{\displaystyle\sum_{i=1,\alpha_i \neq 0}^{r} \alpha_i(x(0))u_i(x(0))}{\displaystyle\sum_{i=1,\alpha_i \neq 0}^{r} \alpha_i(x(0))} \tag{9.27}$$

9.3.3 LYAPUNOV STABILITY ANALYSIS AND NEW INFERENCES

The Lyapunov Energy Function (LEF) considered is $V(x) = x^{T}Px$; it is positive definite, since P is taken as a positive definite; P is also assumed to be independent of time, and is a weighting matrix, and hence, V is a normalized LEF. The LEF, V is regarded as a bounded function of the state trajectories that are governed by eqn. (9.23) to get stable and bounded closed-loop system dynamics/responses. Also, it is assumed that V has continuous partial derivatives, at least of first order. In the Lyapunov stability analysis one obtains the derivative of V with respect to time and establishes that this derivative function is negative definite, based on the constraint of the system dynamics eqn. (9.23); and in the present case eqn. (9.24) also; since FL-based control strategy is used. Thus, one has the following expression for the time derivative of V (for simplicity dependence on x is often not mentioned) [6]:

$$\dot{V}(t) = \dot{x}^T Px + x^T P\dot{x} \tag{9.28}$$

Next, substitute eqn. (9.23) in eqn. (9.28) to obtain

$$\dot{V}(t) = (f(x) + g(x)u)^T Px + x^T P(f(x) + g(x)u) \tag{9.29}$$

Considering, time to be the control input as a scalar quantity without loss of generality, one obtains

$$\dot{V}(t) = f^T(x)Px + g^T(x)u \cdot Px + x^T Pf(x) + x^T Pg(x)u \tag{9.30}$$

$$\dot{V}(t) = f^T(x)Px + x^T Pf(x) + g^T(x)Pxu + x^T Pg(x)u \tag{9.31}$$

$$\dot{V}(t) = [f^T(x)Px + x^T Pf(x)] + [g^T(x)Px + x^T Pg(x)]u \tag{9.32}$$
$$= F(x) + B(x)u$$

From eqn. (9.32), it is seen that, one needs to establish that the time derivative of V, the LHS of eqn. (9.32), is negative definite. To establish this, the following definitions/assumptions on the sets, functions, and input are required to be specified [6]:

i) $B^0 = \{x \in X \,|B(x) = 0\}$; $B^+ = \{x \in X \,|B(x) > 0\}$; and $B^- = \{x \in X \,|B(x) < 0\}$.

ii) The dynamic system described by eqn. (9.23) with $x = 0 \in R^n$ has an equilibrium point.

iii) The LEF $V:R^n \to R$; $V(x) = x^T Px$, $P \in R^{n \times n}$ is positive definite, and assumed bounded as discussed earlier; in order to obtain consistent results with the stability theory of dynamic system (BIBO stability; bounded input, bounded output); in the present case of the nonlinear dynamic system of eqn. (9.23), the BIBO stability theory is considered to be applicable to a good and proper approximation of the nonlinear system or to the linearized nonlinear system. This observation is a different assumption compared to the one in [8]. Also, $V(0) = 0$, $V(x) > 0$, $\forall x \neq 0$.

iv) $F(x) \leq 0$, $\forall x \in B^0$

v) $u_i(x) \leq -kF(x)/B(x)$ for $x \in X_i^A \cap B^+$; and $u_i(x) \geq -kF(x)/B(x)$ for $x \in X_i^A \cap B^-$, $I = 1, \ldots, r$.

vi) The set $\{x \in X \,/\, \dot{V}(x) = 0\}$ contains no state-trajectories except the trivial one, $x(t) = 0$ for $t \geq 0$.

If all these assumptions are valid, then the combined and composite closed loop system with the T-S FLC will be globally asymptotically stable in the sense of Lyapunov at the origin. In [6], only T1FL is considered, however, here the result is extended to IT2FL which can be established as follows:

a)   For $B(x(0))$ strictly positive,

$$u_i(x(0)) \leq -k\frac{F(x(0))}{B(x(0))} \to u(x(0)) = k\frac{\displaystyle\sum_{i=1,\alpha_i \neq 0}^{r} \alpha_i(x(0)u_i(x(0))}{\displaystyle\sum_{i=1,\alpha_i \neq 0}^{r} \alpha_i(x(0))}$$

$$\leq k\frac{-k\dfrac{F(x(0))}{B(x(0))}\displaystyle\sum_{i=1,\alpha_i \neq 0}^{r} \alpha_i(x(0)}{\displaystyle\sum_{i=1,\alpha_i \neq 0}^{r} \alpha_i(x(0))} = -\frac{F(x(0))}{B(x(0))}$$

$$\to \dot{V}(x(0)) = F(x(0)) + B(x(0))u(x(0)) \leq F(x(0)) + B(x(0))\{-\frac{F(x(0))}{B(x(0))}\} = 0.$$

$$(9.33)$$

Hence,

$$u_i(x(0)) \leq -k \frac{F(x(0))}{B(x(0))} \to \dot{V}(x(0)) \leq 0. \tag{9.34}$$

b) For $B(x(0))$ strictly negative,

$$u_i(x(0)) \geq -k \frac{F(x(0))}{B(x(0))} \to u(x(0)) = k \frac{\displaystyle\sum_{i=1,\alpha_i \neq 0}^{r} \alpha_i(x(0)u_i(x(0))}{\displaystyle\sum_{i=1,\alpha_i \neq 0}^{r} \alpha_i(x(0))}$$

$$\geq k \frac{-k \dfrac{F(x(0))}{B(x(0))} \displaystyle\sum_{i=1,\alpha_i \neq 0}^{r} \alpha_i(x(0)}{\displaystyle\sum_{i=1,\alpha_i \neq 0}^{r} \alpha_i(x(0))} = -\frac{F(x(0))}{B(x(0))}$$

$$\to \dot{V}(x(0)) = F(x(0)) + B(x(0))u(x(0)) \leq F(x(0)) + B(x(0))\{-\frac{F(x(0))}{B(x(0))}\} = 0. \tag{9.35}$$

Hence,

$$u_i(x(0)) \geq -k \frac{F(x(0))}{B(x(0))} \to \dot{V}(x(0)) \leq 0. \tag{9.36}$$

c) For $x(0) \in B^0$,

$$\dot{V}(x(0)) = F\big(x(0)\big) + B\big(x(0)\big)u\big(x(0)\big) = F\big(x(0)\big) \leq 0. \tag{9.37}$$

Thus, for all the three cases considered, the time derivative of the LEF is negative definite, and hence, the asymptotic stability result for the combined IT2FL based control and the pilot's situation assessment-cum-aircraft plant dynamics is established.

a) **New Inferences**
The stability result [7] when T1FL is considered can be obtained when $k = 1$, from the results of the Section 9.3.3. Hence, the asymptotic stability result for the combined T1FL based control and the pilot's SA-cum-aircraft plant dynamics is established. It is ascertained here that the pilot's SA was not considered in [7] and

[6]. Further, one can consider the following time derivative of the LEF to satisfy the stability condition

$$\dot{V}(t) = [f^T(x)Px + x^T Pf(x)] + [g^T(x)Px + x^T Pg(x)]u \leq 0. \tag{9.38}$$

From eqn. (9.38), one can obtain for input u the following expression:

$$u \leq -\frac{\|f\|\|P\|\|x\| + \|x\|\|P\|\|f\|}{\|g\|\|P\|\|x\| + \|x\|\|P\|\|g\|} = -\frac{2\|f\|\|P\|\|x\|}{2\|g\|\|P\|\|x\|} = -\frac{\|f\|}{\|g\|} \tag{9.39}$$

$$u \leq -\frac{\|f\|}{\|g\|} \tag{9.40}$$

The condition in eqn. (9.40) is equivalent to assumption (v) of this section:

$$u_i(x(0)) \leq -k\frac{F(x(0))}{B(x(0))} \tag{9.41}$$

It is easily ascertained that the condition in eqn. (9.40) is obtained based on 'no assumption' that the controller is a fuzzy logic-based. However, it is based on the assumptions of the boundedness of the nonlinear functions of eqn. (9.23), and the boundedness of the weighting matrix P. However, even if P is unbounded, the condition in eqn. (9.40) would be still valid [7]. The main aspect is that the control input should be bounded. For a linear dynamic system, the condition eqn. (9.40) yields

$$u \leq -\frac{\|Ax\|}{\|Bx\|} = -\frac{\|A\|\|x\|}{\|B\|\|x\|}$$

$$\leq -\frac{\|A\|}{\|B\|} \tag{9.42}$$

Again, we see that the condition in eqn. (9.41) is equivalent to assumption (v) of this section, and eqn. (9.41). These foregoing conditions and observations can be corroborated based on the following fundamental aspect of the dynamic system. Let a linear dynamic system be considered, for the sake of simplicity,

$$\dot{x} = Ax + Bu \tag{9.43}$$

When the system reaches the steady state, the time derivative of the state is zero, and hence eqn. (9.43) becomes

$$Ax + Bu = 0 \qquad (9.44)$$

From eqn. (9.44), one can obtain the following result

$$u \le -\frac{\|A\|\|x\|}{\|B\|} \qquad (9.45)$$

The condition in eqn. (9.45) is the same as in eqn. (9.42), except for the norm of x since this norm obviously cancels out in eqn. (9.45). Thus, the fundamental condition for the stability, apart from the inherent stability of the dynamic system being controlled, is on the boundedness of the input as specified by all the conditions in eqns. (9.34), (9.36), (9.37), (9.40), (9.41), (9.42), and (9.45), which indicate and signify the same result in some different, but logical and correct ways. Thus, the observations and the inferences made in this section are novel in terms of the interpretation of the Lyapunov stability result in the context of an FL-based control system.

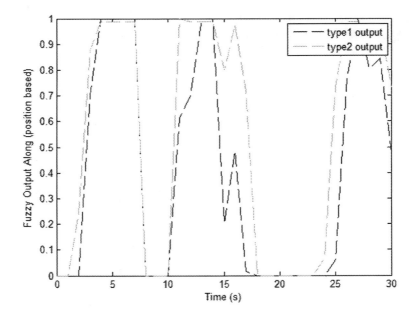

FIGURE 9.10   Final air lane decision output

9.4   AIR LANE MONITORING SYSTEM USING TIFL AND IT2FL

The simulation exercise is carried out to evaluate the performance of the IT2FL Decision System (DS) for air lane monitoring using MATLAB/SIMULINK, and the T2 FL toolbox. Appropriate fuzzy rules, membership functions and FIE are designed to monitor: if an aircraft is flying along the air lane or not. The final decision output for the air lane monitoring system is depicted as shown in Figure 9.9.

Thus, using the LEF, it has been established that the T2 as well as T1 FL-based controllers used in pilot SA in conjunction with nonlinear dynamic plant lead to asymptotic stability results that are further supported by some new intuitive inferences deducted from the theory of control system. The performance of the IT2FL decision system is evaluated by numerical simulations carried out in MATLAB/SIMULINK.

EXERCISES

9.1 What are the two levels of decision architecture in formation flying recognition?

9.2 How are the uncertainties considered in such aviation scenarios?

9.3 Why Lyapunov stability analysis is required in pilot's SA?

9.4 What emerges out of the stability analysis?

9.5 What is the merit of using more rules in a FL based decision fusion system?

REFERENCES

1. Mendel, J. M. General Type-2 Fuzzy Logic Systems Made Simple: A Tutorial, in IEEE Transactions on Fuzzy Systems, vol. 22, no. 5, pp. 1162–1182, Oct. 2014.

2. Klir, G. J. and Yuan, B. Fuzzy Sets and Fuzzy Logic: Theory and Applications. Upper Saddle River, NJ, USA: Prentice–Hall, 1995.

3. Sauvet, F. et al., In-Flight Automatic Detection of Vigilance States Using a Single EEG Channel, in IEEE Transactions on Biomedical Engineering, vol. 61, no. 12, pp. 2840–2847, Dec. 2014.

4. Kayacan, E. and Maslim, R. Type-2 Fuzzy Logic Trajectory Tracking Control of Quadrotor VTOL Aircraft With Elliptic Membership Functions, in IEEE/ASME Transactions on Mechatronics, vol. 22, no. 1, pp. 339–348, Feb. 2017.

5. Raol, J. R. and Kashyap, S. K. Decision fusion using fuzzy logic type 1 in two aviation scenarios, Journal of Aerospace Sciences and Technologies, Vol. 65, No. 3, pp. 273-286, 2013.

6. Precup, R. E., Tomescu, M. L., and Preitl, S. Fuzzy logic control system stability analysis based on Lyapunov's direct method. Int. Journal. of Computers, Communications, & Control, (ISSN 1841-9836, E-ISSN 1842-9844), Vol. IV, No. 4, pp. 415–426, 2009.

7. Ibrahim Abdel Fattah Abdel Hameed Ibrahim. New applications and developments of fuzzy systems. Thesis, Doctor of Philosophy, Korea University, Seoul, South Korea, Feb. 2010.

8. Naidu, V. P. S., and Raol, J. R. Pixel-level Image Fusion using Wavelets and Principal Component Analysis, Defence Science Journal, Vol 58, No 3, May 2008, pp 332–352 © 2008, DESIDOC.

10 Bayesian Mental Models of a Pilot for SA in Air-to-Air Combat

10.1 INTRODUCTION

Decision making in air combat is a complex task accomplished by a team of highly skilled personnel. The region of engagement for air combat is generally categorized into Within-Visual Range (WVR) and Beyond-Visual-Range (BVR). In WVR combat, the pilots visually identify each other and perform maneuvers such as rolls, turns, loops, splits and rolling scissors etc., to attain a superior weapons release position on an opposing aircraft. BVR combat occurs outside the range of the pilot's vision, and therefore, they must rely on information from the aircraft's sensor suite to determine the opposing aircraft's posture. Maneuvering associated with BVR combat is simpler than that of WVR combat. The aircraft in BVR typically performs a sequence of turns to gain a favorable position for weapons launch or to confuse opponent's tracking sensors. Typically, the operators/pilots fuse/combine the information manually to produce a coherent air surveillance picture portraying the tracks of airborne targets and their classification. Then, they analyze the air surveillance picture mentally to determine the behavior of each target with respect to own ship and other targets in the region and assess the intent or threat that they pose or the impact they may have on the mission. This analysis is commonly referred to as Situation Assessment (SA) [1]. As the number of targets in the combat arena grows or the situation becomes more complex, the volume of available data will overload the operators. Therefore, it is desirable to assist the operators by employing an intelligent decision support system. In this chapter, an attempt is made to investigate the possibilities for the design and implementation of such a system.

The crucial problem that decision makers face in air-combat is the problem of uncertainty. Many methods exist in AI and Expert Systems (ES) literature that can handle uncertainty quite adequately, namely, FL, Belief Functions (BNs), and ANNs. However, a probabilistic approach has the advantage that it is based on a rigorous theory with a vast amount of known results. This is a great advantage and has in fact prompted many to claim that the probability is the only sensible description of uncertainty and is adequate for all purposes. But, probability requires a vast amount of storage and computational manipulation making probabilistic methods computationally intensive. To overcome this, Bayesian Networks (BNs) were formulated [2]. The Bayesian approach has many feasible features, but lacks the ability to handle continuous input. If integrated with the FL approach of making the data members of

DOI: 10.1201/9781003370413-10

discrete sets, the hybrid system should be able to handle all the demands of the situation assessment.

This chapter employs a Fuzzy-Bayesian hybrid technique to investigate the possibilities for the design and implementation of a decision support system, called the Intelligent System for Situation Assessment in Air-Combat (ISSAAC) as an aid to pilots engaged in air-combat. Fuzzy logic is used as an event detector to classify the fused information from multiple sensors and sources. BN represents the pilot's mental model and provides a means for constructing and maintaining a hierarchical, probabilistic model linking multiple entities at various levels of the mission. Evidence obtained from the sensors, first undergoes FL classification and is then applied to the appropriate node(s) of the BN. This evidence then automatically propagates throughout the BN resulting in revised probability estimates at hypotheses node(s).

10.2   FUNCTIONAL ARCHITECTURE

The functional architecture of the system, shown in Figure 10.1, consists of five distinct modules: i) an interactive GUI, named the Exercise controller (Execon); ii) the airborne Sensor Model ISM; iii) Data Processor (DP); iv) Fuzzy Event Detector (FED); v) Pilot Mental Model (PMM); and vi) Graphical Display (GD). Arrows in Figure 10.1 indicate the flow of information between the different modules.

10.2.1   EXECON

The Execon consists of platform models of fighters, bombers, missiles, helicopters and transport aircraft. It can be used to create any typical air-to-air combat scenario consisting of a maximum of 6 targets (excluding own ship). It can simulate different weather conditions like rainfall, fog, etc. It has a simple user interface consisting of a display, status, and menu areas. The display area displays the windows, sub-windows and targets during the simulation. The status area displays important simulation related parameters such as speed, course, bearing, coordinates, and RADAR status. Targets are represented by specified shapes and colors to distinguish which platform types they represent. Class and ID of all targets must be specified prior to the simulation. Each target is either controlled via predefined trajectories or via user interaction in real-time.

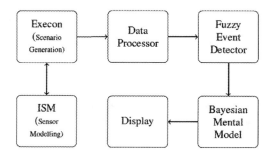

FIGURE 10.1   System Architecture

10.2.2 Integrated Simulink Model

The Integrated Simulink Model (ISM) developed in MATLAB-SIMULINK consists of a functional model of different sensors namely, RADAR (Doppler), Infrared Search and Track (IRST), Radar Warning Receiver (RWR) and Electro-Optical Tracking System (EOTS).

10.2.3 Data Processor

The data processor module combines the data received from multiple sensors. An Extended Kalman Filter (EKF) is used to estimate the states of the targets using fused using measurements from multiple sensors with a provision to handle track loss [3] [4].

10.2.4 Fuzzy Event Detector

The fuzzy event detector classifies the relative kinematics data into qualitative form (events), e.g. Speed is "low", "medium" or "high". A MATLAB-based FL toolbox (FLTB) is used to design appropriate membership functions for data classification.

10.2.5 PMM

The Pilot Mental Model (PMM) emulates the pilot's information processing, situation assessment, and decision-making activities, based on information received from the FED. The MATLAB-based Bayes Net Toolbox (BNT) [5] is used for the construction and propagation of Bayesian networks and it has been validated with commercially available HUGIN [6] software.

10.2.6 GD

The GD provides the updated probabilities of all the targets. More details on the system architecture and its elements are in Ref. [7]. The challenging task in the development of this system is the modeling of Bayesian Networks representing the mental picture of the pilots participating in air combat operations. An in-depth analysis is needed to determine the elements required for SA in fighter aircraft involved in air-to-air combat missions. Endsley [1] formulated a set of requirements by conducting interviews with pilots experienced in air combat and the parameters were classified into: a) not important, b) somewhat important, and c) very important. Some of the very important parameters mentioned in [1] are given in Table 10.1.

In this chapter a new Attack Agent Bayesian Network (AABN, for an old network reference [6]) is developed based on the parameters of Table 10.1, and inputs from the test pilots. The measures of uncertainty, namely, effect of evidence, gain in belief update, and sensor effectiveness for the Bayesian network, are presented along with the results of the simulation.

Section 10.3 describes the architecture of AABN, and section 10.4 provides the results of simulation of an air-to-air combat scenario. Section 10.5 presents the

TABLE 10.1
Important Parameters for classification

ID and Type	Opening/Closing Velocity
Location (Range/Azimuth)	G's/accelerations
Altitude/Elevation	Relative Aircraft Advantage/Disadvantage
Air Speed	Weapons Range
Aspect	Confidence Level of Information
Heading	Weather

measures of uncertainty and its flow in a BN. Appendix 10A contains examples of measures of uncertainty, and Appendix 10B provides the details of the BN-toolbox and its usage.

10.3   NEW ARCHITECTURE OF ATTACK AGENT BAYESIAN NETWORK

The AABN for BVR combat is shown in Figure 10.2. The network consists of 8 information nodes, 5 intermediate nodes and one hypothesis node. All the quantities presented in the network are relative to own ship.

10.3.1   NETWORK NODES

The details of each node of the network are presented below:

VELOCITY (OWN): This node represents the velocity of own ship and has three states: Low, Medium and High. The states are classified as: i) *000–0300 Kmph: Low; ii) 300–0900 Kmph: Medium; and iii) 900–1350 Kmph: High.*
CLOSING VELOCITY: This node represents the closing/opening velocity and has three states: Low, Medium and High. The states are classified as: i) *0000–0400 Kmph: Low; ii) 0400–1000 Kmph: Medium; and iii) 1000–2000 Kmph: High.*
COMBAT GEOMETRY: This node represents the combat geometry of the aircraft based on Deviation Angle (DA) and Aspect Angle (AA). The definitions of deviation and aspect angles are.

Aspect Angle (AA): is defined as the angle between Line of Sight (LOS) vector and opponent's velocity vector [7]. It is represented by α_2 shown in Figure 10.3.
Deviation Angle (DA): is defined as the angle between own ship velocity vector and Line of Sight (LOS) vector [7]. It is represented by α_1 shown in Figure 10.3.

The Aspect Angle (α_2) and the Deviation Angle (α_1) are calculated using the formulas [8]:

$$\alpha_1 = arccos\left(\frac{\left[\left(x_r - x_b\right)cos\left(\gamma_b\right)cos\left(\chi_b\right) + \left(y_r - y_b\right)cos\left(\gamma_b\right)sin\left(\chi_b\right) + \left(h_r - h_b\right)sin\left(\gamma_b\right)\right]}{d}\right)$$

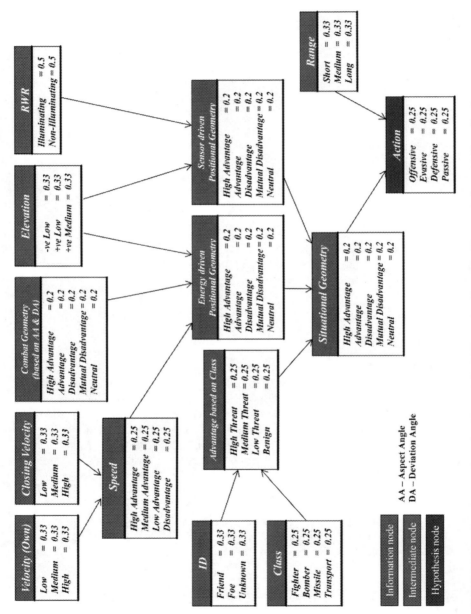

FIGURE 10.2   Attack agent Bayesian Network for BVR combat [Developed in association with Test pilots]

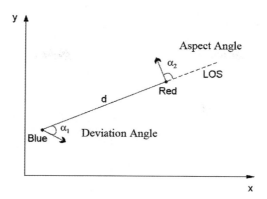

FIGURE 10.3 Representation of Aspect and Deviation angles

$$\alpha_2 = \arccos\left(\frac{\left[(x_r - x_b)\cos(\gamma_r)\cos(\chi_r) + (y_r - y_b)\cos(\gamma_r)\sin(\chi_r) + (h_r - h_b)\sin(\gamma_r)\right]}{d}\right)$$

$$\text{With } d = \left((x_r - x_b)^2 + (y_r - y_b)^2 + (h_r - h_b)^2\right) \tag{10.1}$$

Here x, y and h are the coordinates, γ is the flight path angle, and χ the heading angle. The subscripts r and b indicate red (enemy) and blue (own ship) forces respectively. The Performance Index (PI), which combines Aspect and Deviation angles into a single measure [7] for Combat Geometry, is defined as

$$PI = 50 * (1 - \alpha_1) + 50 * (1 - \alpha_2) \tag{10.2}$$

The Combat Geometry node has five states and are classified as:

PI: *100–083: High Advantage; 083–066: Advantage; 066–033: Mutual Disadvantage /Neutral; 033–000: Disadvantage.*

> **ELEVATION:** This node represents the elevation of own ship with respect to enemy aircraft and has three states: −ve Low, +ve Low and +ve Medium. The states are classified as:
>
> (-15)–000 deg: −ve Low
> 000–015 deg: +ve Low
> 015–045 deg: +ve Medium

RANGE: This node represents the relative distance between own ship and enemy aircraft and has three states: Short, Medium and Long. The states are classified as:

040–080 Km: Short
080–120 Km: Medium
120–200 Km: Long

RWR: This node represents the status of a Radar Warning Receiver (RWR) and has two states: Illuminating and Non-Illuminating.

ID: This node represents the status of IFF (Identification of Friend or Foe) and has three states: Friend, Foe and Unknown.

CLASS: This node represents the class/type of the aircraft and has four states: Fighter, Bomber, Missile and Transport.

SPEED: This node calculates the speed advantage based on own ship velocity and closing velocity and has four states: High Advantage, Medium Advantage, Low Advantage and Disadvantage.

ADVANTAGE BASED ON CLASS: This node calculates the threat posed by a target based on the IFF ID and Class of the aircraft. It has four states: High Threat, Medium Threat, Low Threat and Benign.

ENERGY DRIVEN POSITIONAL GEOMETRY (EDPG): This node calculates the kinetic and potential energy advantages based on the Speed, Combat Geometry, and Elevation. It has five states: High Advantage, Advantage, Disadvantage, Mutual disadvantage and Neutral.

SENSOR DRIVEN POSITIONAL GEOMETRY (SDPG): This node calculates the sensor advantage based on the Elevation, and status of RWR. For example, consider a situation where own ship is at higher elevation compared to the enemy aircraft. In this situation, own ship is at advantage in terms of energy but it is at sensor disadvantage (RADAR is less accurate when looking down). It has five states: High Advantage, Advantage, Disadvantage, Mutual disadvantage and Neutral.

SITUATIONAL GEOMETRY: This node represents the overall situation based on EDPG, SDPG and Advantage based on class. It has five states: High Advantage, Advantage, Disadvantage, Mutual disadvantage and Neutral.

ACTION: This node represents the action to be taken by own ship based on Situational Geometry and Range. It has four states: Offensive, Evasive, Defensive and Passive.

The definition of the position geometry is given in Table 10.2.

10.3.2 CONDITIONAL PROBABILITY TABLES

The Conditional Probability Tables (CPTs) of all the nodes of the attack agent are given in Tables 10.3 to 10.8. The entries of the CPTs have been filled in by the test pilots.

TABLE 10.2
Positional Geometry Definition

Advantage: Own ship behind the enemy   **Disadvantage: Enemy behind own ship**

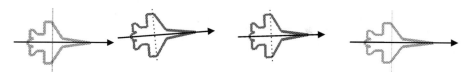

Mutual disadvantage: head on   **Neutral**

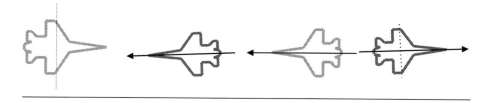

TABLE 10.3
CPT of "Speed" Node of Attack Agent

Velocity (own ship)	Closing Velocity	Speed			
		High Advantage	Medium Advantage	Low Advantage	Disadvantage
Low	Low	0	0	.5	.5
Medium	Low	0	.25	.5	.25
High	Low	0	.5	.25	.25
Low	Medium	0	0	.1	.9
Medium	Medium	0	0	.5	.5
High	Medium	0	.5	.5	0
Low	High	0	0	0	1
Medium	High	0	.25	.25	.5
High	High	.5	.25	.25	0

10.3.3 SIMULATION RESULTS

The Scenario-1 consists of 6 targets and own ship as shown in Figure 10.4. Details of the targets are given in Table 10.9.

Figure 10.4 illustrates target trajectories of the scenario-1 (plotted in a MATLAB graph). It is assumed that all the targets maintain the same altitude during the entire simulation time. It can be seen from Figure 10.4 that targets "1" and "2" form a pair for some time and then target "1" comes towards the own ship. Similarly, targets "3" and "4" converge to form a pair and come towards own ship. Target "5" approaches

TABLE 10.4
CPT of "Advantage Based on Class" Node of Attack Agent

ID	Class	Advantage based on Class			
		High Threat	Medium Threat	Low Threat	Benign
FRIEND	FIGHTER	0	0	0	1
FOE	FIGHTER	1	0	0	0
UNKNOWN	FIGHTER	.9	0	0	.1
FRIEND	BOMBER	0	0	0	1
FOE	BOMBER	.5	.25	.25	0
UNKNOWN	BOMBER	0	.5	.4	.1
FRIEND	MISSILE	0	0	0	1
FOE	MISSILE	1	0	0	0
UNKNOWN	MISSILE	1	0	0	0
FRIEND	TRANSPORT	0	0	0	1
FOE	TRANSPORT	0	.25	.5	.25
UNKNOWN	TRANSPORT	0	0	.5	.5

own ship from behind. Target "6" is flying along the corridor. Using pre-stored points, the commercial corridor is generated.

The updated probabilities of the Action node of the attack agent are shown in Figure 10.5 (follow the color code as in Figure 10.4). The offensive probability with respect to target "2" is increasing because own ship is at an advantage with respect to target "2" (at the end own ship is behind target "2" as shown in Figure 10.4). The evasive probability with respect to target "5" is high as it is a missile and coming towards own ship. The passive probabilities with respect to targets "3" and "6" are high because both aircraft are friends.

The probabilities of offensive, evasive, defensive and passive for each target are shown in Figure 10.6; as shown the pilot has to take offensive action against target "2", evasive action against target "5", passive action against targets "3" & "6". Figure 10.4 shows that targets "1" & "4" are in a mutual disadvantage position with respect to own ship at the end of simulation, so there is an equal probability for offensive, defensive and evasive actions.

10.4   UNCERTAINTY MEASURE PROPAGATION IN A BAYESIAN NETWORK

Bayesian networks are represented by *Directed Acyclic Graphs (DAGs)*, in which the nodes are the random variables of some probabilistic model and *informational* or *causal* dependencies among the variables are represented by direct links. The conditional probabilities represent the strengths of the causal dependencies that are attached to each cluster of parent-child links in the network. In many real-world problems, BNs can be used to model the uncertainties. The uncertainties that exist in various variables taken individually or taken in groups will affect the decision-making

TABLE 10.5
CPT of "Edpg" Node of Attack Agent

Combat Geometry	Speed	Elevation	Energy Driven Positional Geometry				
			High Advantage	Advantage	Disadvantage	Mutual disadvantage	Neutral
HIGH ADVANTAGE	HIGH ADVANTAGE	-VE LOW	.75	.25	0	0	0
ADVANTAGE	HIGH ADVANTAGE	-VE LOW	.5	.5	0	0	0
DISADVANTAGE	HIGH ADVANTAGE	-VE LOW	0	.1	.8	.1	0
MUTUAL DISADVANTAGE	HIGH ADVANTAGE	-VE LOW	0	.25	.25	.5	0
NEUTRAL	HIGH ADVANTAGE	-VE LOW	0	.1	.15	.25	.5
HIGH ADVANTAGE	MEDIUM ADVANTAGE	-VE LOW	.5	.5	0	0	0
ADVANTAGE	MEDIUM ADVANTAGE	-VE LOW	.25	.75	0	0	0
DISADVANTAGE	MEDIUM ADVANTAGE	-VE LOW	0	.1	.75	.15	0
MUTUAL DISADVANTAGE	MEDIUM ADVANTAGE	-VE LOW	0	.25	.25	.5	0
NEUTRAL	MEDIUM ADVANTAGE	-VE LOW	0	.15	.1	.25	.5
HIGH ADVANTAGE	LOW ADVANTAGE	-VE LOW	.6	.4	0	0	0
ADVANTAGE	LOW ADVANTAGE	-VE LOW	.4	.6	0	0	0
DISADVANTAGE	LOW ADVANTAGE	-VE LOW	0	0	.9	.1	0
MUTUAL DISADVANTAGE	LOW ADVANTAGE	-VE LOW	0	.1	.1	.8	0
NEUTRAL	LOW ADVANTAGE	-VE LOW	0	.1	.1	0	.8
HIGH ADVANTAGE	DISADVANTAGE	-VE LOW	.25	.5	.15	.1	0
ADVANTAGE	DISADVANTAGE	-VE LOW	.1	.5	.2	.2	0
DISADVANTAGE	DISADVANTAGE	-VE LOW	0	0	1	0	0
MUTUAL DISADVANTAGE	DISADVANTAGE	-VE LOW	0	0	.5	.5	0
NEUTRAL	DISADVANTAGE	-VE LOW	0	0	.6	0	.4
HIGH ADVANTAGE	HIGH ADVANTAGE	+VE LOW	.9	.1	0	0	0

(continued)

TABLE 10.5 (Continued)
CPT of "Edpg" Node of Attack Agent

Combat Geometry	Speed	Elevation	High Advantage	Advantage	Disadvantage	Mutual disadvantage	Neutral
Advantage	High Advantage	+ve Low	.75	.25	0	0	0
Disadvantage	High Advantage	+ve Low	0	.25	.5	.25	0
Mutual Disadvantage	High Advantage	+ve Low	0	.25	0	.75	0
Neutral	High Advantage	+ve Low	0	.5	0	.1	.4
High Advantage	Medium Advantage	+ve Low	.8	.2	0	0	0
Advantage	Medium Advantage	+ve Low	.5	.5	0	0	0
Disadvantage	Medium Advantage	+ve Low	0	.2	.6	.2	0
Mutual Disadvantage	Medium Advantage	+ve Low	0	.5	.1	.4	0
Neutral	Medium Advantage	+ve Low	0	.5	.1	.1	.3
High Advantage	Low Advantage	+ve Low	.75	.25	0	0	0
Advantage	Low Advantage	+ve Low	.1	.9	0	0	0
Disadvantage	Low Advantage	+ve Low	0	.25	.5	.25	0
Mutual Disadvantage	Low Advantage	+ve Low	0	.5	.25	.25	0
Neutral	Low Advantage	+ve Low	0	.5	0	.1	.4
High Advantage	Disadvantage	+ve Low	.6	.3	0	.1	0
Advantage	Disadvantage	+ve Low	.25	.5	0	.25	0
Disadvantage	Disadvantage	+ve Low	0	0	.75	.25	0
Mutual Disadvantage	Disadvantage	+ve Low	0	0	.5	.5	0
Neutral	Disadvantage	+ve Low	0	0	0	.5	.5
High Advantage	High Advantage	+ve Medium	1	0	0	0	0
Advantage	High Advantage	+ve Medium	.8	.2	0	0	0
Disadvantage	High Advantage	+ve Medium	0	.25	.25	.5	0

Energy Driven Positional Geometry

Mutual Disadvantage	High Advantage	+ve Medium	.1	.6	.1	.2	0
Neutral	High Advantage	+ve Medium	.2	.6	0	.1	.1
High Advantage	Medium Advantage	+ve Medium	.9	.1	0	0	0
Advantage	Medium Advantage	+ve Medium	.75	.25	0	0	0
Disadvantage	Medium Advantage	+ve Medium	0	.2	.3	.5	0
Mutual Disadvantage	Medium Advantage	+ve Medium	0	.6	.1	.3	0
Neutral	Medium Advantage	+ve Medium	0	.7	0	.15	.15
High Advantage	Low Advantage	+ve Medium	.8	.2	0	0	0
Advantage	Low Advantage	+ve Medium	.5	.5	0	0	0
Disadvantage	Low Advantage	+ve Medium	0	.1	.4	.5	0
Mutual Disadvantage	Mutual Disadvantage	+ve Medium	0	.5	.1	.4	0
Neutral	Low Advantage	+ve Medium	0	.6	0	.2	.2
High Advantage	Disadvantage	+ve Medium	.75	.25	0	0	0
Advantage	Disadvantage	+ve Medium	.25	.75	0	0	0
Disadvantage	Disadvantage	+ve Medium	0	0	.75	.25	0
Mutual Disadvantage	Mutual Disadvantage	+ve Medium	0	0	.5	.5	0
Neutral	Neutral	+ve Medium	0	.25	.25	.25	.25

TABLE 10.6
CPT OF "Sdpg" Node of Attack Agent

		Sensor Driven Positional Geometry				
Elevation	RWR	High Advantage	Advantage	Dis-advantage	Mutual dis-advantage	Neutral
-ve Low	Illuminating	0	0	.5	.25	.25
+ve Low	Illuminating	0	.2	.3	.3	.2
+ve Medium	Illuminating	0	.3	.2	.3	.2
-ve Low	Non-Illuminating	0	0	.25	.25	.5
+ve Low	Non-Illuminating	0	.25	.1	.15	.5
+ve Medium	Non-Illuminating	0	.3	.1	.1	.5

exercise. Therefore, it is necessary to handle the measures of uncertainty associated with random variables. This section presents a procedure to compute a few effectiveness measures associated with a BN. The following effectiveness measures are presented in this section [9]: i) Effect of evidence on hypothesis, ii) Effect of belief updating, and iii) Effectiveness of sensor.

10.4.1 A MEASURE OF UNCERTAINTY

A Bayesian network is mainly used to update the probability distribution over the states of a hypothesis variable; a variable which is not directly observable. This probability distribution then assists a decision maker in deciding upon a suitable course of action. The question now arises as to how *effective* such a process can be. It would be helpful to be able to respond to the following questions in particular: a) Every activity that involves acquiring information uses up some resources. Thus, the question of whether a specific step of hypothesis updating was worthwhile can be asked after information gathering for that stage; b) How effective is a given information gathering tool with respect to a specific Bayesian network? and c) Furthermore, a Bayesian network is nothing more than a decision-support tool. How useful is this network as a tool for making decisions given a situation and a related Bayesian network? Does its effectiveness hold up over time as the situation changes?

The main point to keep in mind while attempting to address problems about efficacy is that any decision-making activity will be significantly impacted by the uncertainties that exist in numerous variables evaluated either individually or collectively. Therefore, the first step would be to establish an uncertainty measure for each random variable.

Assume that X IS a discrete random variable that has values $\{x_1, ..., x_n\}$ with probabilities $\{X=x_i\} = P(x_i)$. We have consistently emphasized the idea that the interpretation of probability we are using in this case is subjective or Bayesian. According to

TABLE 10.7
CPT of "Situational Geometry" Node of Attack Agent

Advantage based on Class	Energy driven positional Geometry	Sensor driven positional Geometry	High Advantage	Advantage	Disadvantage	Mutual disadvantage	Neutral
Benign	Advantage	High Advantage	.25	.75	0	0	0
High Threat	Disadvantage	High Advantage	0	0	.75	.25	0
Medium Threat	Disadvantage	High Advantage	0	0	.5	.5	0
Low Threat	Disadvantage	High Advantage	0	.25	.25	.5	0
Benign	Disadvantage	High Advantage	0	.25	0	.25	.5
High Threat	Mutual Disadvantage	High Advantage	0	.25	.25	.5	0
Medium Threat	Mutual Disadvantage	High Advantage	0	.3	.2	.5	0
Low Threat	Mutual Disadvantage	High Advantage	0	.4	.1	.5	0
Benign	Mutual Disadvantage	High Advantage	0	.5	0	.25	.25
High Threat	Neutral	High Advantage	.25	.4	0	.25	.1
Medium Threat	Neutral	High Advantage	.3	.35	0	.25	.1
Low Threat	Neutral	High Advantage	.5	.15	0	.25	.1
Benign	Neutral	High Advantage	.5	0	0	0	.5
High Threat	High Advantage	Advantage	.25	.35	.15	.25	0
Medium Threat	High Advantage	Advantage	.4	.3	.1	.2	0
Low Threat	High Advantage	Advantage	.6	.2	.1	.1	0
Benign	High Advantage	Advantage	1	0	0	0	0
High Threat	Advantage	Advantage	.2	.3	.15	.35	0
Medium Threat	Advantage	Advantage	.35	.25	.1	.3	0
Low Threat	Advantage	Advantage	.55	.15	.1	.2	0
Benign	Advantage	Advantage	1	0	0	0	0
High Threat	Disadvantage	Advantage	0	0	.8	.2	0

(continued)

TABLE 10.7 (Continued)
CPT of "Situational Geometry" Node of Attack Agent

Advantage based on Class	Energy driven positional Geometry	Sensor driven positional Geometry	High Advantage	Advantage	Disadvantage	Mutual disadvantage	Neutral
MEDIUM THREAT	DISADVANTAGE	ADVANTAGE	0	0	.6	.4	0
LOW THREAT	DISADVANTAGE	ADVANTAGE	0	.2	.3	.5	0
BENIGN	DISADVANTAGE	ADVANTAGE	0	.2	0	.3	.5
HIGH THREAT	MUTUAL DISADVANTAGE	ADVANTAGE	0	.2	.3	.5	0
MEDIUM THREAT	MUTUAL DISADVANTAGE	ADVANTAGE	0	.25	.25	.5	0
LOW THREAT	MUTUAL DISADVANTAGE	ADVANTAGE	0	.35	.15	.5	0
BENIGN	MUTUAL DISADVANTAGE	ADVANTAGE	0	.5	0	.25	.25
HIGH THREAT	NEUTRAL	ADVANTAGE	.2	.45	0	.25	.1
MEDIUM THREAT	NEUTRAL	ADVANTAGE	.25	.4	0	.25	.1
LOW THREAT	NEUTRAL	ADVANTAGE	.45	.2	0	.25	.1
BENIGN	NEUTRAL	ADVANTAGE	.4	.1	0	0	.5
HIGH THREAT	HIGH ADVANTAGE	DISADVANTAGE	0	.25	.5	.25	0
MEDIUM THREAT	HIGH ADVANTAGE	DISADVANTAGE	0	.35	.45	.2	0
LOW THREAT	HIGH ADVANTAGE	DISADVANTAGE	.1	.4	.35	.15	0
BENIGN	HIGH ADVANTAGE	DISADVANTAGE	.25	.5	0	0	.25
HIGH THREAT	ADVANTAGE	DISADVANTAGE	0	.2	.6	.2	0
MEDIUM THREAT	ADVANTAGE	DISADVANTAGE	0	.3	.5	.2	0
LOW THREAT	ADVANTAGE	DISADVANTAGE	.1	.3	.35	.25	0
BENIGN	ADVANTAGE	DISADVANTAGE	.25	.45	0	0	.3
HIGH THREAT	DISADVANTAGE	DISADVANTAGE	0	0	.9	.1	0
MEDIUM THREAT	DISADVANTAGE	DISADVANTAGE	0	0	.75	.25	0
LOW THREAT	DISADVANTAGE	DISADVANTAGE	0	.25	.5	.25	0
BENIGN	DISADVANTAGE	DISADVANTAGE	0	.5	0	.25	.25

HIGH THREAT	MUTUAL DISADVANTAGE	DISADVANTAGE	0	0	.5	.5	0
MEDIUM THREAT	MUTUAL DISADVANTAGE	DISADVANTAGE	0	.15	.5	.35	0
LOW THREAT	MUTUAL DISADVANTAGE	DISADVANTAGE	0	.2	.4	.2	0
BENIGN	MUTUAL DISADVANTAGE	DISADVANTAGE	0	.6	0	.25	.15
HIGH THREAT	NEUTRAL	NEUTRAL	0	0	.25	.5	.25
MEDIUM THREAT	NEUTRAL	NEUTRAL	0	.15	.2	.4	.3
LOW THREAT	NEUTRAL	NEUTRAL	0	.2	.15	.35	.3
BENIGN	NEUTRAL	NEUTRAL	0	.4	0	.1	.5
HIGH THREAT	HIGH ADVANTAGE	MUTUAL DISADVANTAGE	0	.25	.25	.5	0
MEDIUM THREAT	HIGH ADVANTAGE	MUTUAL DISADVANTAGE	0	.35	.2	.45	0
LOW THREAT	HIGH ADVANTAGE	MUTUAL DISADVANTAGE	.1	.4	.15	.35	0
BENIGN	HIGH ADVANTAGE	MUTUAL DISADVANTAGE	.25	.5	0	0	.25
HIGH THREAT	ADVANTAGE	ADVANTAGE	0	.15	.25	.6	0
MEDIUM THREAT	ADVANTAGE	ADVANTAGE	0	.25	.2	.55	0
LOW THREAT	ADVANTAGE	ADVANTAGE	.1	.4	.1	.4	0
BENIGN	ADVANTAGE	ADVANTAGE	.2	.55	0	0	.25
HIGH THREAT	DISADVANTAGE	DISADVANTAGE	0	.1	.5	.4	0
MEDIUM THREAT	DISADVANTAGE	DISADVANTAGE	0	.15	.45	.4	0
LOW THREAT	DISADVANTAGE	DISADVANTAGE	0	.25	.4	.35	0
BENIGN	DISADVANTAGE	DISADVANTAGE	.1	.3	.15	.15	.3
HIGH THREAT	MUTUAL DISADVANTAGE	MUTUAL DISADVANTAGE	0	.25	.25	.5	0
MEDIUM THREAT	MUTUAL DISADVANTAGE	MUTUAL DISADVANTAGE	0	.4	.3	.3	0
LOW THREAT	MUTUAL DISADVANTAGE	MUTUAL DISADVANTAGE	0	.5	.25	.25	0
BENIGN	MUTUAL DISADVANTAGE	MUTUAL DISADVANTAGE	.25	.25	.1	.1	.3
HIGH THREAT	NEUTRAL	NEUTRAL	0	.1	.25	.4	.25
MEDIUM THREAT	NEUTRAL	NEUTRAL	0	.15	.15	.4	.3
LOW THREAT	NEUTRAL	NEUTRAL	0	.25	.1	.15	.5
BENIGN	NEUTRAL	NEUTRAL	.1	.3	0	.1	.5
HIGH THREAT	HIGH ADVANTAGE	HIGH ADVANTAGE	.2	.2	.2	.2	.2

(continued)

TABLE 10.7 (Continued)
CPT of "Situational Geometry" Node of Attack Agent

Advantage based on Class	Energy driven positional Geometry	Sensor driven positional Geometry	High Advantage	Advantage	Disadvantage	Mutual disadvantage	Neutral
MEDIUM THREAT	HIGH ADVANTAGE	NEUTRAL	.25	.25	.15	.15	.2
LOW THREAT	HIGH ADVANTAGE	NEUTRAL	.3	.3	.1	.1	.2
BENIGN	HIGH ADVANTAGE	NEUTRAL	.4	.4	0	0	.2
HIGH THREAT	ADVANTAGE	NEUTRAL	.1	.3	.2	.2	.2
MEDIUM THREAT	ADVANTAGE	NEUTRAL	.2	.3	.15	.15	.2
LOW THREAT	ADVANTAGE	NEUTRAL	.25	.35	.1	.1	.2
BENIGN	ADVANTAGE	NEUTRAL	.35	.45	0	0	.2
HIGH THREAT	DISADVANTAGE	NEUTRAL	0	.1	.35	.35	.2
MEDIUM THREAT			0	.25	.25	.3	.2
LOWTHREAT			0	.35	.2	.25	.2
BENIGN			.2	.4	.1	.1	.2
HIGH THREAT			0	.25	.25	.25	.25
MEDIUM THREAT			0	.3	.2	.25	.25
LOW THREAT			0	.4	.1	.25	.25
BENIGN			0	.5	0	.25	.25
HIGH THREAT			0	.2	.2	.2	.4
MEDIUM THREAT			0	.25	.15	.2	.4
LOW THREAT			0	.4	.1	.1	.4
BENIGN			0	.5	0	0	.5

TABLE 10.8
CPT of "Action" Node of Attack Agent

Situational Geometry	Range	Action			
		Offensive	**Evasive**	**Defensive**	**Passive**
HIGH ADVANTAGE	SHORT	1	0	0	0
ADVANTAGE	SHORT	.9	0	.1	0
DISADVANTAGE SITUATIONAL GEOMETRY	SHORT	0	.8	.2	0
MUTUAL DISADVANTAGE	SHORT	.5	0	.5	0
NEUTRAL	SHORT	0	0	.2	.8
HIGH ADVANTAGE	MEDIUM	.7	0	.3	0
ADVANTAGE	MEDIUM	.6	0	.4	0
DISADVANTAGE SITUATIONAL GEOMETRY	MEDIUM	0	.7	.3	0
MUTUAL DISADVANTAGE	MEDIUM	.4	.3	.3	0
NEUTRAL	MEDIUM	0	0	.1	.9
HIGH ADVANTAGE	LONG	.6	0	.4	0
ADVANTAGE	LONG	.5	0	.5	0
DISADVANTAGE SITUATIONAL GEOMETRY	LONG	0	.6	.4	0
MUTUAL DISADVANTAGE	LONG	.25	.25	.25	.25
NEUTRAL	LONG	0	0	0	1

this, a probability measure is a measurement of our belief based on the information we now have. The variable X will assume one of the n alternative values $\{x_1, ..., x_n\}$, if the corresponding experiment is performed. We do not know exactly which alternative will materialise; our knowledge only provides us with a measure that x_i will occur with likelihood $P(x_i)$. In a sense, this probability distribution is a measure of our *current knowledge*, the knowledge that was used to assign the probabilities in the first place. However, this knowledge is not enough to pin down a particular alternative which will materialize when the experiment is performed. This corresponds to our current uncertainty. The amount of information that would be needed in addition to what is already known to identify which specific alternative will occur is a measure of the current level of uncertainty.

A measure of our current uncertainty is equivalently a measure of the amount of knowledge that will be gained once the experiment is conducted and the chosen option is decided. As a result, the quantity of options and the probability distribution $P(\cdot)$ would be used to calculate an uncertainty measure. It can be demonstrated that

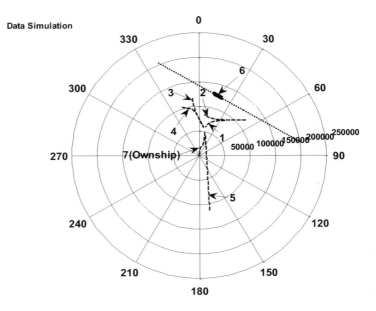

FIGURE 10.4   Target Trajectories of Scenario-1

TABLE 10.9
Scenario 1

TARGET NO	TYPE	IFF
1	Fighter	Foe
2	Fighter	Foe
3	Fighter	Friend
4	Fighter	Unknown
5	Missile	Foe
6	Transport	Friend

---

the average uncertainty associated with the random variable X is given by the logarithmic measure of the number of options if we further require that the measure of uncertainty be given by

$$H(X) = -\sum_{i=1}^{n} P(x_i) log P(x_i)$$ (10.3)

This is merely the Shannon entropy. The unit of entropy is a bit if we use logarithms to base 2. It gauges the typical knowledge needed in addition to the available information to specify a given choice. If our current state of knowledge is complete, i.e.,

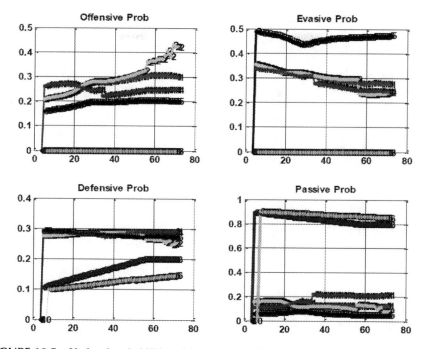

FIGURE 10.5 Updated probabilities of Action node of Attack agent

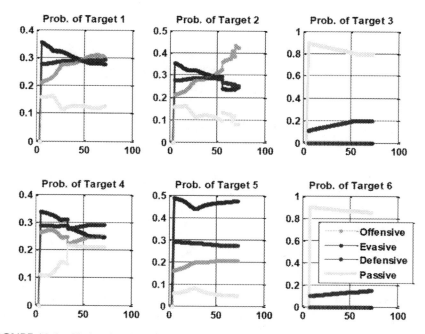

FIGURE 10.6 Updated probabilities of Action node of Attack agent (for individual targets)

if we know that X will assume the value x_j, say, then $P(x_j) = 1$ and it follows that $H(X) = 0$. If our current state of knowledge is *total ignorance* then we will not be able to distinguish between various alternatives, which leads to the uniform probability distribution $P(x_j) = \dfrac{1}{n}$. In this case, the additional information required to pin down an alternative will be maximum. The amount of supplementary information needed in this situation will be at its highest. When we evaluate $H(X)$ with uniform distribution, the value $\log n$ is taken to the utmost extent feasible, and this is exactly what happens. Therefore, in general, $H(X)$ gives an indication of the quantity of knowledge needed to overcome the ignorance represented by the probability distribution $P(x_j)$.

10.4.1.1 Joint Entropy

Let two random variables X and Y be with a joint distribution given by $P(x, y)$. The joint entropy $H(X, Y)$ is given by

$$H(X,\ Y) = -\sum_i \sum_j P\left(x_i, y_j\right) \log P\left(x_i, y_j\right) \tag{10.4}$$

10.4.1.2 Conditional Entropy

The conditional entropy $H(X|y_j)$ of X given that Y has assumed the value y_j is given by

$$H\left(X \mid y_j\right) = -\sum_i P\left(x_i \mid y_j\right) \log P(x_i \mid y_j) \tag{10.5}$$

The conditional entropy $H(X|Y)$ of X with respect to Y is the expected value of the measure of uncertainty in X when it is known that Y has a particular value. Hence, clearly it has the following form:

$$H(X|Y) = \sum_j P\left(y_j\right) H\left(X|y_j\right) = -\sum_j P\left(y_j\right) \sum_i P\left(x_i \mid y_j\right) \log P(x_i \mid y_j) \tag{10.6}$$

$H(X|Y)$ quantifies, on the average, the remaining uncertainty regarding X when it is known that Y has assumed a certain value.

10.4.2 Evidence's Impact on Hypothesis

Consider a Bayesian network and X with values $\{x_1, \ldots, x_n\}$ be a hypothesis variable while $E = \{e_1, \ldots, e_d\}$ is an information variable. If information now arrives that E has been found to be in the state corresponding to e_1, then this propagates through the network and changes the probability distribution of X to $P(x_i|\ e_1)$. The entropy of the hypothesis variable now becomes $H(X|e_1)$. The following two factors determine whether this posterior entropy is greater than, equal to, or less than the previous entropy $H(X)$: i) The prior probabilities $P(xi)$, and ii) The information that is kept in the network's links in terms of conditional probabilities, the network's inference-making process is governed by these conditional probabilities.

We are curious to see how well the network's reasoning system utilizes evidence to lessen uncertainty. To do this, it is necessary to first separate the impacts of the reasoning system from the effects of the prior probability. For this, we employ the basic, yet highly effective technique below. We begin by assuming that we have no prior knowledge of the hypothesis variable, and we then look at how far this total ignorance or maximum uncertainty can be reduced by the evidence.

According to the concept of maximum entropy, if we know nothing about the hypothesis X with values $\{x_1, ..., x_n\}$, $P(x_i) = \dfrac{1}{n}$ for all i, then the prior entropy would be $H(X) = \log n$. This entropy decreases by a certain amount when proof indicating E is in the state e_1 appears.

$$log n - H(X \mid e_1)$$ (10.7)

The aforementioned equation is always positive since log n is the most amount of entropy that X may have. We consequently refer to the aforementioned formulation as the evidence's ability to reduce uncertainty as " *E is in state e_1*". This formalism can be used to determine the set's ability to reduce uncertainty if $\{\varepsilon_1, \varepsilon_2, ..., \varepsilon_s\}$ is a collection of evidence received from diverse sources. This capacity is expressed as $\log n - H(X|\varepsilon_1, \varepsilon_2, ..., \varepsilon_s)$. Additionally, this expression can be used to assess the ability of various collections of data to reduce uncertainty. The challenge of how to use a Bayesian network to determine the ability of some evidence to reduce uncertainty now arises. Three situations occur: i) Assume first that the variable X in the hypothesis is a root node. We give X a probability distribution that makes each of its potential values equally likely, and we do the same for every other root node. We initialize one or more information variables to their matching evidence values once the network has stabilized under these initial conditions. When the network reaches equilibrium once more, the posterior probabilities $P(x_i|\varepsilon_1, \varepsilon_2, ..., \varepsilon_s)$ are generated, and we use these probabilities to determine how well the evidence reduces uncertainty; ii) If the hypothesis variable X is not a root node, we remove X's parents from the network and proceed as outlined in i); and iii) It's also possible that an evidentiary variable affects X by way of one of its parents, let's say Y. In these situations, removing the parents will cause the data and theory to become disjointed. We treat Y as the fundamental hypothesis and fix its prior probabilities rather than X since the evidence has direct influence on Y and only indirect influence on X. Accordingly, if Y is a root node, we treat all of its potential states as equally likely as in i), and if Y is not a root node, we transform it into one using the method described in i), and ii).

Finally, by successively instantiating any evidence variable E to each of its potential values and propagating the effects to X, the average effect of any evidence variable E on a hypothesis variable X may be determined. This will enable us to determine $H(X|E)$, which will result in the average capacity of E to reduce uncertainty, which is $(\log n - H(X|E))$.

10.4.3 EFFECT OF BELIEF UPDATING

Although reduction of uncertainty is the primary motivation for gathering information, there are other subtle features of updated information that play a crucial role when deciding upon a subsequent course of action. Consider again the hypothesis variable X which models various states of a situation. If the probability distribution is such that $P(x_i)$ is very near to 1 for some x_i then we know with reasonable confidence that the state of the situation is given by x_i. This is, however, rarely the case. When the probability distribution is spread out over many states of the hypothesis, it is the nature of the spread, or the form of the probability distribution function P that is very important. The form of P *dictates our belief* regarding the peculiarities of the situation being observed. In a dynamic environment the nature of the situation would change with time. Our observations may never give us an exact description of the situation but the sequence of probability distributions we obtain, as we go on updating information, should inform us how the situation is changing. To formulate these considerations quantitatively, consider the following development. Suppose at time t_1 the probability distribution over the hypothesis X is P_1. A batch of sensor observations arrives at a subsequent time t_2 leading to a new distribution P_2; let us assume that the updated information faithfully captures the change in the situation. Then the increase in uncertainty due to outdated perception is given by

$$-\sum_i P_1\left(x_i\right)logP_1\left(x_i\right)+\sum_i P_2\left(x_i\right)logP_2\left(x_i\right) \qquad (10.8)$$

What we have obtained is the *Kullback distance* between the distributions P_2 and P_1 which is generally denoted by $D(P_2, P_1)$. It can be shown that $D(P_2, P_1)$ is always positive, and this is very interesting; for the amount of uncertainty associated with the updated distribution P_2 may actually be greater than the amount of uncertainty associated with the previous distribution P_1. In other words, obtaining new evidence may not necessarily decrease uncertainty, as we have said before, but not updating information is always inefficient. $D(P_2, P_1)$ therefore correctly measures the worth of the updated information. The amount of resources spent in reconnaissance and surveillance must therefore be weighed against the value of $D(P_2, P_1)$ to determine their effectiveness.

10.4.4 EFFECTIVENESS OF SENSOR

To analyze how the reliability of information gathering devices affects the process of inference making in a Bayesian network, we first define the concept of mutual information.

10.4.4.1 Mutual Information

Given two random variables X and Y, the mutual information $I(X; Y)$ is defined as

$$I(X;Y) = \sum_i \sum_j P(x_i, y_j) log \frac{P(x_i, y_j)}{P(x_i)P(y_j)} \qquad (10.9)$$

It can be shown that

$$I(X;Y) = I(Y;X) \text{ and} \qquad (10.10)$$

$$I(X;Y) = H(X) - H(X|Y) = H(Y) - H(Y|X) \qquad (10.11)$$

The mutual information $I(X;Y)$ is a measure of the amount of information that Y contains about X. In other words $I(X;Y)$ provides the uncertainty reducing capacity, on average, of the random variable Y with respect to the uncertainties in X. Let us now consider the following simple Bayesian network formulation which captures all the essential factors required for an analysis of sensor effectiveness.

Where, X denotes the hypothesis variable (with values $\{x_1, ..., x_n\}$), Y denotes the information, and variable Z represents the sensor for obtaining information for Y; Y and Z *have* similar states as Z gathers information required by Y. Let us represent the values assumed by these variables as follows:

$$Y: \{y1,..., yd\} \qquad (10.12)$$

$$Z: \{z1,..., zd\} \qquad (10.13)$$

If Z were a perfect sensor, then instantiating Z to z_l would imply that the information variable Y is in the corresponding state y_l with probability 1. In general, we have

$$P(z_i|y_j) = \delta_{ij} \quad i, j = 1, ...,d \qquad (10.14)$$

The marginal probabilities $P(y)$ and $P(z)$ are therefore related as:

$$P(z_i) = \sum_{j=1}^{d} \delta_{ij} P(y_j) \qquad (10.15)$$

Hence, for reliable sensors we must have very small values for δ_{ij} if $i \neq j$, and δ_{ii} very near to 1,

$$\delta_{ii} = 1 - \sum_{\substack{i=1 \\ i \neq j}}^{d} \delta_{ij} \tag{10.16}$$

For a perfect sensor we have: $\delta_{ii} = 0$ $if \ i \neq j \ else = 1$.

In other words, we consider the link between Y and Z as a *noisy* information channel. The noise factors are represented by the conditional probabilities $P(z_i|y_j)$. The other link between the variables X and Y quantified by the conditional probabilities $P(y_i|x_j)$ represents the knowledge for inference making about the hypothesis. If X has prior probabilities $P(x_i)$, the initial uncertainty in the hypothesis is given by

$$H(X) = -\sum P(x_i) log P(x_i) \tag{10.17}$$

To calculate the uncertainty reducing potential of the sensor, let us consider the case when the sensor indicates that Z has been found to be z_s. The posterior uncertainty in the hypothesis now becomes

$$H(X \mid z_s) = -\sum_i P(x_i \mid z_s) log P(x_i \mid z_s)$$

$$\text{Here,} \ P(x_i|z_s) = \frac{\sum_k P(x_i, y_k, z_s)}{P(z_s)} = \frac{\sum_k P(z_s \mid y_k) P(y_k \mid x_i) P(x_i)}{P(z_s)}$$

$$= \frac{\sum_k \delta_{sk} P(y_k \mid x_i) P(x_i)}{\sum_k \delta_{sk} P(y_k)} \tag{10.18}$$

For a perfect sensor using the properties we get

$$P(x_i|z_s) = \frac{P(y_s \mid x_i) P(x_i)}{P(y_s)} = P(x_i|y_s) \tag{10.19}$$

Hence, for perfect sensors we have

$$H(X \mid Z) = -\sum_s P(Z_s) \sum_i P(x_i|z_s) log P(x_i|z_s)$$

$$= -\sum_s P(y_s) \sum_i P(x_i|y_s) log P(x_i|y_s) = H(X \mid Y) \tag{10.20}$$

Now the average uncertainty reducing capacity of the sensor Z is given by $I(X; Z)$. Using the independence property of the Bayesian network, i.e., the property that X and Z are independent given Y, it can be easily shown that $I(X; Z) \leq I(X; Y)$. However, for a perfect sensor $I(X; Z) = I(X; Y)$. In other words perfect sensor will on average reduce the uncertainties in X by an amount $I(X; Y)$, as the reliability of the sensor decreases its uncertainty reducing capacity also decreases and the amount by which it decreases is given by $I(X; Y) - I(X; Z)$. We shall use the numerical value of this expression to measure the efficiency of the sensor with regard to its uncertainty reducing capacity–*the less the value is, the more effective is the sensor.*

The foregoing analysis is easily generalized to any Bayesian network. Numerical calculations will proceed along two steps: i) Fix the prior probabilities $P(x_i)$, by making X a root node; and ii) To calculate $I(X; Z)$ start by instantiating Z to its various possible states. The resulting probability distribution of X obtained for each instantiation would allow calculation of the conditional entropy $H(X|Z)$.

10.4.5   SIMULATION RESULTS

Scenario 1: This consists of 6 targets and own ship as shown in Figure 10.7. Details of the targets are given in Table 10.10.

Figure 10.7 illustrates target trajectories of the scenario-1 (plotted in a MATLAB graph). It is assumed that all the targets maintain the same altitude during the entire simulation time. It can be seen from the Figure 10.7 that targets "1" and "2" form a pair for some time and then target "1" comes towards own ship. Similarly, targets "3"

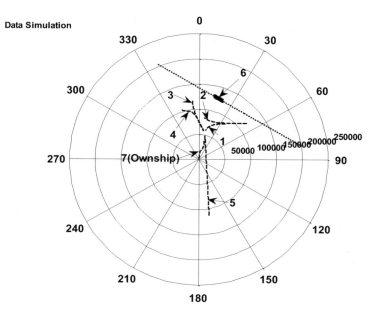

FIGURE 10.7   Targets Trajectories of Scenario-1

TABLE 10.10
Target Scenario

TARGET NO	TYPE	IFF
1	Fighter	Foe
2	Fighter	Foe
3	Fighter	Friend
4	Fighter	Unknown
5	Missile	Foe
6	Transport	Friend

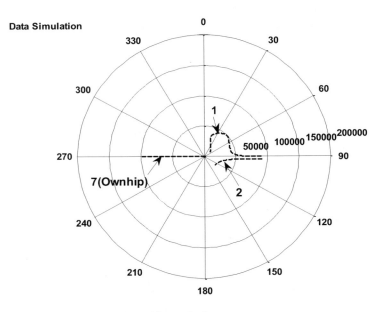

FIGURE 10.8   Targets Trajectories of Scenario-2

and "4" converge to form a pair and come towards own ship. Target "5" approaches own ship from behind. Target "6" is flying along the corridor. Using pre-stored points the commercial corridor is generated.

Scenario 2: This consists of 2 targets and own ship as shown in Figure 10.8. This is a typical beaming by foe (1V2) scenario in which, targets "1" and "2" form a pair for some time and then target "1" comes towards own ship and beams it. Details of the targets are given in Table 10.11.

Effect of evidence on hypothesis: Figure 10.9 shows the effect of newly available evidence on the hypothesis node of the attack agent for scenario-1. It can be seen that the uncertainty reducing capacity of the evidence is higher for targets "3" and "6".

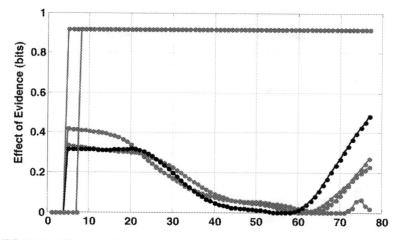

FIGURE 10.9   Effect of evidence for Scenario-1

TABLE 10.11
Target details

Target No	Type	Iff
1	Fighter	Foe
2	Fighter	Unknown

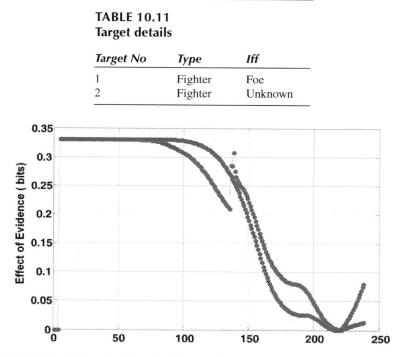

FIGURE 10.10   Effect of evidence for Scenario-2

The effect of evidence for some of the targets becomes zero for small duration (i. e the new evidence has not improved the assessment of the situation compared to the earlier time). Figure 10.10 shows the effect of newly available evidence on hypothesis node of attack agent for scenario-2. There is an increase in effect of evidence of

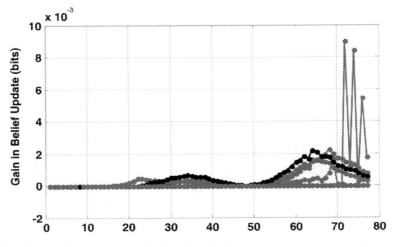

FIGURE 10.11   Gain in belief update for Scenario-1

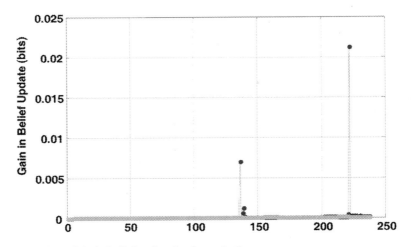

FIGURE 10.12   Gain in belief update for Scenario-2

Target "1" at 130 sec, 180 sec, and 220 sec. This is due to a significant change in the situation (refer to the turnings of target 1 of scenario-2).

Gain in belief updating: The efficiency gained due to updating the information of the attack agent for scenario-1 is presented in Figure 10.11. The gain for all targets is low because there is no significant change in the situation (enemy did not changed his intentions). The efficiency gained due to updating information of attack agent for scenario-2 is presented in the Figure 10.12. The peaks indicate a considerable change in the nature of the situation. The enemy has changed its intentions significantly which is evident from Figure 10.8.

10.5 FINAL ARCHITECTURE OF ATTACK AGENT BAYESIAN NETWORK

The Bayesian network shown in Figure 10.2 is modified after further discussions with the test pilots and it is shown in Figure 10.13. The difference between the two networks is that the node Threat based on Class (Advantage based on Class in Figure 10.2) is connected to the node Action (instead of the node Situational Geometry as in Figure 10.2).

The Conditional Probability Tables (CPTs) for this network are similar to the previous network except for the nodes *Situational Geometry* and *Action*. The pilots advised that it is better to sort the targets based on the threat they pose instead of displaying in the plots. Hence, the display has been modified as shown in Figure 10.14.

Appendix 10A Examples of Measures of Uncertainty
This appendix provides the examples for uncertainty measures presented in section 10.3.1. The examples presented here are [9], [11]:

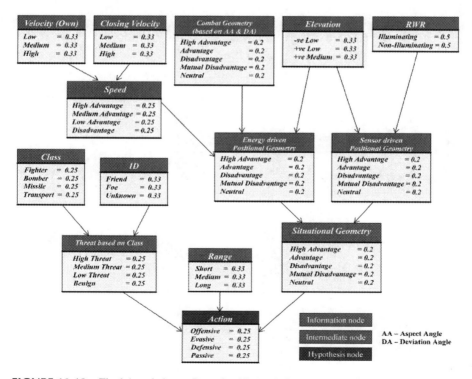

FIGURE 10.13   Final Attack Agent Bayesian Network for BVR Combat

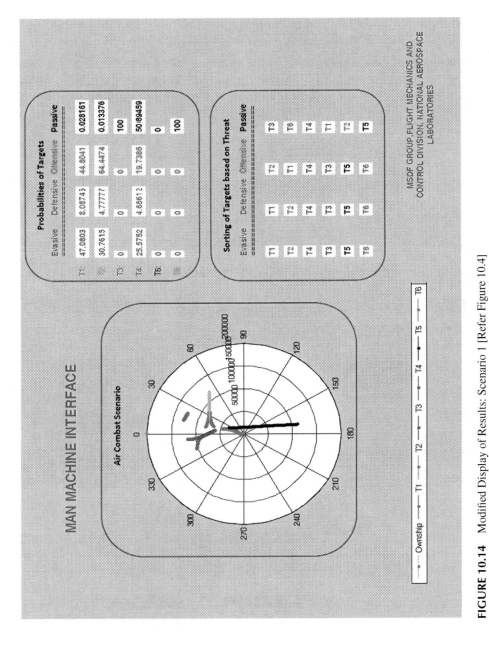

FIGURE 10.14   Modified Display of Results: Scenario 1 [Refer Figure 10.4]

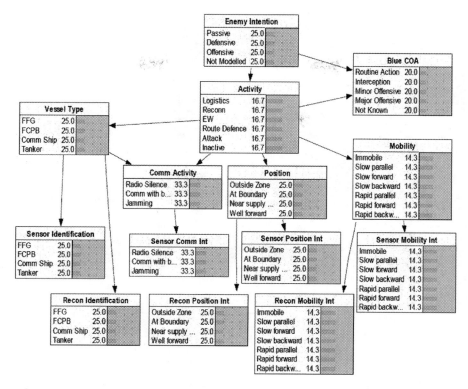

FIGURE 10.15 A Bayesian network for situation assessment

Effect of Evidence on Hypothesis

Consider the Bayesian network for the situation assessment problem as shown in Figure 10.15. Let us choose *Activity* as the target hypothesis variable. We want to calculate the reduction in uncertainty in *Activity* when evidence is obtained regarding the information variables: *Position* and *Mobility*. Since *Activity* is not a root node, we modify the network as shown in Figure 10.16.

Here, the node *Activity* has been disconnected from its parent node *Enemy Intention* and consequently becomes a root node. All the states in *Activity* have the same prior probability giving it the maximum prior uncertainty: $H(Activity) = \log 6 = 2.5849$ bits. Figure 10.17 shows the situation where we have incorporated the evidence: i) *Sensor Position Int (SPI): = Near Supply Route;* and ii) *Sensor Mobility Int (SMI): = Slow Parallel.*

The conditional probabilities can now be read off from the *Activity* node. This immediately leads to the conditional entropy:

$$H(Activity \mid SPI = Near\ supply\ route, SMI = Slow\ parallel)$$

$$= -0.1024 \log 0.102 - 0.276 \log 0.276 - 0.0224 \log 0.0224 - 0.484 \log 0.484$$

DSTO-TR-0918

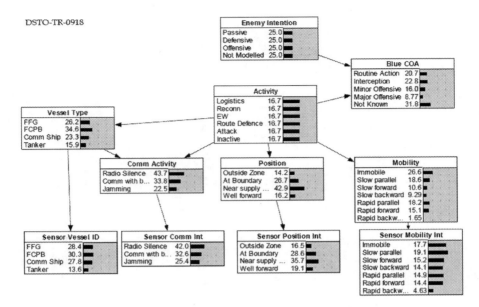

FIGURE 10.16   Modified Bayesian network (Activity as hypothesis node)

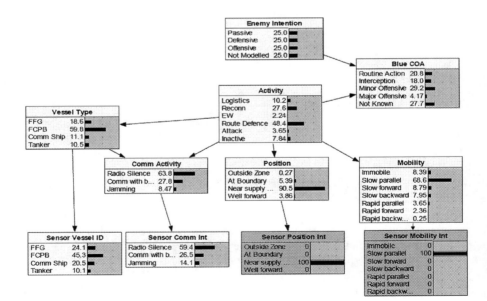

FIGURE 10.17   Updated situation for evidence

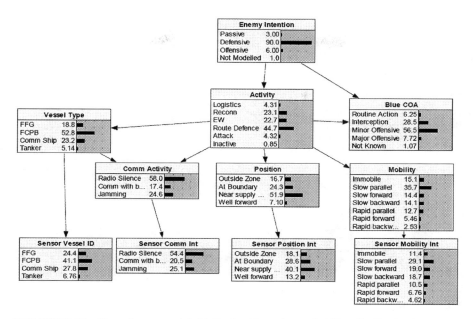

FIGURE 10.18   Bayesian network initialized with a prior probability distribution P1

$$- 0.0365 \log 0.0365 - 0.0784 \log 0.0784$$

$$= 1.9410$$

The uncertainty reducing capacity of the above evidence is $2.5849 - 1.9410 = 0.6439$ bits.

Effect of Belief Updating:

Consider a stage during situation assessment when previous evidence strongly suggests that enemy intention is defensive. This situation is depicted in Figure 10.18 where the Bayesian network is initialized with a prior probability distribution P_1 indicating defensive enemy intentions. Figure 10.19 depicts the updated situation after the latest batches of sensor evidence have been used to update the prior belief. The updated probability distribution over enemy intention is P_2, Table 10.12.

Whereas P_1 was peaked, P_2 is flat. The loss of peak indicates a considerable change in the nature of the situation. The enemy has changed its intentions significantly. It would be unwise to stick to P_1 although that indicated more definitely what the enemy proposed to do. Although P_2 incorporates more uncertainty than P_1 it is a better reflection of the latest observations. The efficiency gained due to updating information is given by $D(P_2, P_1)$ which can be calculated using the formula:

$$D(P_2 \mid\mid P_1) = -\sum_x P_2(x) \log P_1(x) + \sum_x P_2(x) \log P_2(x)$$
$$= 2.41953 - 1.06201 = 1.35752 \, bits$$

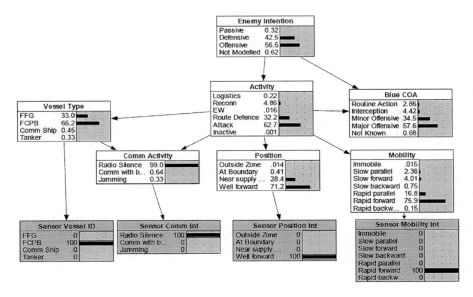

FIGURE 10.19   The updated probability distribution P2

TABLE 10.12
Various updated pdfs.

X	Passive	Defensive	Offensive	Not Modelled
$P_1(x)$	0.03	0.90	0.06	0.01
$P_2(x)$	0.0032	0.425	0.565	0.0062

Sensor Effectiveness:

Consider the situation assessment network again. We denote: i) *X: Enemy Intention;* ii) *Y: Position; and iii) Z: Sensor Position Int.*

The effectiveness of the position detection sensor is then given by $I(X;Y) - I(X;Z)$. To calculate this, we initialize the network with a prior probability which gives maximum entropy to X as shown in Figure 10.20. We get the pdfs as in Table 10.13.

To obtain $P(X|Y)$ and $P(X|Z)$ we successively instantiate Y and Z to their various values and allow the network to calculate the conditional probabilities. Figure 10.21 depicts the case where we have instantiated $Y = Outside$ $Zone$. We get the conditional pdfs as in Table 10.14.

The foregoing data yields:

$H(X) = 2, H(X|Y) = 1.744433, H(X|Z) = 1.897761$ *bits*
Hence, $I(X; Y) = H(X) - H(X|Y) = 0.25567$ *bits* and $I(X; Z) = H(X) - H(X|Z) = 0.102239$ *bits.*

Hence, the uncertainty reducing capacity of the position detection sensor defers from that of an ideal sensor by an amount: $I(X;Y) - I(X;Z) = 0.15343$ *bits.*

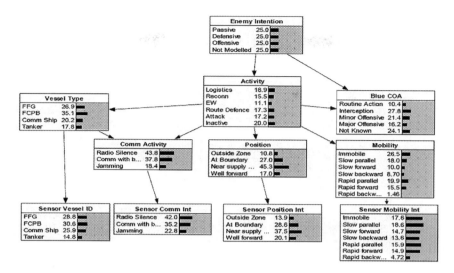

FIGURE 10.20 Prior probability distribution corresponding to maximum entropy

TABLE 10.13
Senser Effectiveness pdfs P(X):

X	Passive	Defensive	Offensive	Not Modelled
P(x)	0.25	0.25	0.25	0.25

P(Y):

Y	Outside Zone	At Boundary	Near Supply Route	Well Forward
P(y)	0.108	0.27	0.453	0.170

P(Z):

Z	Outside Zone	At Boundary	Near Supply Route	Well Forward
P(z)	0.139	0.286	0.375	0.201

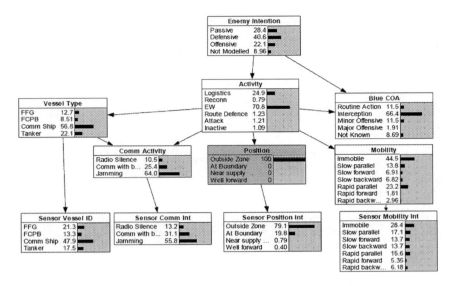

FIGURE 10.21   Posterior probability distribution with Position = Outside Zone

TABLE 10.14
Senser Effectiveness Conditional pdfs P(x | y):

	x = Passive	x = Defensive	x = Offensive	x = Not Modelled
y = Out Zone	0.284	0.406	0.221	0.089
y = At Boundary	0.221	0.232	0.0868	0.47
y = Near Supply	0.355	0.293	0.172	0.180
y = Well Forward	0.0114	0.0648	0.736	0.188

P(x | z):

	x = Passive	x = Defensive	x = Offensive	x = Not Modelled
z = Out Zone	0.258	0.339	0.174	0.229
z = At Boundary	0.248	0.258	0.119	0.375
z = Near Supply	0.316	0.270	0.218	0.196
z = Well Forward	0.124	0.140	0.548	0.188

Appendix 10B Bayes Net Toolbox (BNT)

The Bayes Net Toolbox (BNT) [5] is an open-source MATLAB package for construction and propagation of directed graphical models. BNT supports many kinds of nodes (probability distributions), exact and approximate inference, parameter and structure learning, and static and dynamic models. Various features are briefly stated next:

10B.1   BNT'S CLASS STRUCTURE

- Models–bnet, mnet, DBN, factor graph, influence (decision) diagram (LIMIDs).
- CPDs–Cond. linear Gaussian, tabular, softmax, etc.
- Potentials–discrete, Gaussian, CG.
- Inference engines
- Exact–junction tree, variable elimination, brute-force enumeration
- Approximate–loopy belief propagation, Gibbs sampling, particle filtering (sequential Monte Carlo).
- Learning engines Parameters–EM
- Structure–MCMC over graphs, K2, hill climbing.
- The steps for constructing and propagating the Bayesian network using BNT are below.

10B.2   CREATING A BAYES NET

To define a Bayes net, first specify the graph structure and then the parameters. To specify the Bayesian network shown in Figure 10.2, create an adjacency matrix:

N = 14; dag = zeros(N, N); where N is the number of nodes in the network.

The nodes must always be numbered in topological order, i.e., ancestors before descendants. For the network shown in Figure 10.2 the nodes can be numbered as:

Velocity_Own = 1; Closing_Velocity = 2;

ID = 3; Class = 4; Combat_Geometry = 5; Speed = 6; Elevation = 7; RWR = 8;

Advantage_based_on_Class = 9;

Energy_Driven_Positional_Geometry   =   10;   Sensor_Driven_Positional_ Geometry = 11;

Situational_Geometry = 12; Range = 13;

Action = 14;

Also, the parent-child relationship should be specified as shown below. dag([Velocity_Own Closing_Velocity], Speed)=1; (means 'Velocity_Own' & 'Closing_Velocity' are the parents of 'Speed' node.)

dag([ID Class], Advantage_based_on_Class) = 1;

dag([Speed   Elevation   Combat_Geometry],   Energy_Driven_Positinal_ Geometry) = 1;

dag([Elevation RWR],Sensor_Driven_Positional_Geometry)=1;dag([Advantage_ based_on_Class   Energy_Driven_Positinal_Geometry   Sensor_Driven_ Positional_Geometry],Situational_Geometry)   =   1;   dag([Situational_Geometry Range],Action) = 1;

10B.3   CREATING THE BAYES NET SHELL

In addition to specifying the graph structure, we must specify the size and type of each node. If a node is discrete, its size is the number of possible values (states) each node can take on; if a node is continuous, it can be a vector, and its size is the length of this vector. In this case, all nodes are discrete.

discrete_nodes = 1 : N;

node_sizes = [3 3 3 4 5 4 3 2 4 5 5 5 3 4];

We are now ready to make the Bayes net:

bnet = mk_bnet(dag, node_sizes, 'discrete', discrete_nodes);

By default, all nodes are assumed to be discrete, so we can also just write

bnet = mk_bnet(dag, node_sizes);

You may also specify which nodes will be observed. If you don't know, or if this is not fixed in advance, just use the empty list (the default).

onodes = [];

bnet = mk_bnet(dag, node_sizes, 'discrete', discrete_nodes, 'observed', onodes);

10B.4 PARAMETERS

A model consists of the graph structure and the parameters. The parameters are represented by CPD objects (CPD = Conditional Probability Distribution), which define the probability distribution of a node given its parents. The simplest kind of CPD is a table (multi-dimensional array), which is suitable when all the nodes are discrete-valued. Tabular CPDs, also called CPTs (Conditional Probability Tables), are stored as multidimensional arrays, where the dimensions are arranged in the same order as the nodes. For example, the CPT of the 'Speed' node in Figure 10.2 can be specified as follows:

bnet.CPD{Speed} = tabular_CPD(bnet, Speed, CPT_speed);

where CPT_speed is a vector containing values of Table 10.1, i.e.,

CPT_speed = [(column 1)^T (column 2)^T (column 3)^T (column 4)^T] of Table 10.1.

Similarly for other nodes, CPTs are specified as follows:

bnet.CPD{Advantage_based_on_Class} = tabular_CPD(bnet, Advantage_based_on_Class, CPT_adv_class); bnet.CPD{Energy_Driven_Positional_Geometry} = tabular_CPD(bnet, Energy_Driven_Positional_Geometry, CPT_Energy_driven); bnet.CPD{Sensor_Driven_Positional_Geometry} = tabular_CPD(bnet, Sensor_Driven_Positional_Geometry, CPT_Sensor_driven);

bnet.CPD{Situational_Geometry} = tabular_CPD(bnet, Situational_Geometry, CPT_Situational_Geometry);

bnet.CPD{Action} = tabular_CPD(bnet, Action, CPT_Action);

If a node has no parents, its CPT is a column vector representing its prior probabilities. For example, the node 'Velocity Own' has no parents and its CPT can be specified as

bnet.CPD{Velocity_Own} = tabular_CPD(bnet,Velocity_Own, [Data(7) Data(8) Data(9)]);

Where Data(7), Data(8), Data(9) are outputs of the Fuzzy Event Detector (prior probabilities).

If we do not specify the CPT, random parameters will be created, i.e., each "row" of the CPT will be drawn from the uniform distribution. To ensure repeatable results, use rand('state', seed); randn('state', seed);

To control the degree of randomness (entropy), you can sample each row of the CPT from a Dirichlet(p, p, ...) distribution. If p << 1, this encourages "deterministic" CPTs (one entry near 1, the rest near 0). If p = 1, each entry is drawn from U[0, 1]. If p >> 1, the entries will all be near $\frac{1}{k}$, where k is the arity of this node, i.e., each row will be nearly uniform. You can do this as follows, assuming this node is number i, and ns is the node_sizes.

```
k = ns(i);
ps = parents(dag, i); psz = prod(ns(ps));
CPT = sample_dirichlet(p*ones(1, k), psz); bnet.CPD{i} = tabular_CPD(bnet, i, 'CPT', CPT);
```

10B.5   INFERENCE

Having created the BN, we can now use it for inference. There are many different algorithms for doing inference in Bayes nets that make different tradeoffs between speed, complexity, generality, and accuracy. BNT therefore offers a variety of different inference "engines". For now, we will use the junction tree engine, which is the mother of all exact inference algorithms. This can be created as follows.

```
Engine = jtree_inf_engine(bnet);
```

The joint probability of action (hypothesis) node can be calculated as

```
evidence = cell(1, N);
[engine, loglik] = enter_evidence(engine, evidence); m = marginal_nodes(engine, Action);
```

Here m is a structure. The 'T' field is a multi-dimensional array that contains the joint probability distribution on the specified node/nodes. Therefore m.T gives the probabilities of all states of 'Action' node.

Further details on usage of BNT can be found in [10].

EXERCISES

10.1. When is decision making more critical; in BVR or WVR and why?

10.2. How important is Multi-Sensor Data Fusion in the development of a pilot expert system in air combat?

10.3. What is a Conditional Probability Table (CPT) and what is its role in decision making?

10.4. What are the types of sensors needed in modern warfare and why?

10.5. What are the practical problems in the realization of a pilot expert system in air combat?

REFERENCES

1. Endsley Mica, R. A Survey of Situation Awareness Requirements in Air-to-Air Combat Fighters, International Journal of Aviation Psychology,3:2, 157–168, 1993.
2. Pearl, J. *Probabilistic Reasoning in Intelligent Systems: Networks of Plausible Inference*, Morgan Kaufmann Publishers, Inc. San Francisco, California, 1988.
3. Waltz, E., and Llinas, J. *Multisensor Data Fusion*, Artech House, Boston, 1990.
4. Raol J. R., Girija G., Appavu Raj A., and Kashyap S. K. Tracking Filter and Multi-Sensor Data Fusion, SADHANA, Academy Proceedings in Engineering Sciences, Indian Academy of Sciences, Vol. 25, part 2, pp 159–167, April 2000.
5. Bayes Net Toolbox for MATLAB. http://people.cs.ubc.ca/ ~murphyk/Software/ BNT/ bnt.html, Accessed in July 2010.
6. HUGIN Expert, www.hugin.dk, Accessed in July 2010.
7. Sudesh, K. K., Narayan, R. P., and Girija, G. Bayesian Mental Models of the Pilot for Situation Assessment in Air-to-Air Combat. NAL PD FC 1009, CSIR-NAL, Bangalore, pp. 1–50, October 2010.
8. Burgin, G. H., and Sidor, L. B. Rule-Based Air Combat Simulation, NASA Contractor Report 4160, 1988.
9. Hamalainen, V-P. A Decision Analytic Simulation Approach to A One-On-One Air Combat Game, Independent research projects in applied mathematics, Helsinki University of Technology, 28 August 2002.
10. Das, B. Representing uncertainties using Bayesian networks, Information technology division, Electronics and surveillance research laboratory, Department of defense, Defense science & technology organization (DSTO), Salisbury south Australia, Dec. 1999.
11. How to use the Bayes Net Toolbox, http://people.cs.ubc.ca/~murphyk/ Software/BNT /usage.html, accessed in August 2010.

11 Fuzzy Logic and Bayesian Network-based SA in Air-to-Air Combat

11.1 INTRODUCTION

Important tactical events or situations can occur without the pilot noticing, which can change the outcome of a mission completely. This makes the development of an automated Situation Assessment System (SAS) very important for fighter aircraft. This chapter investigates the possibilities for the design and implementation of an automated SAS for/in a fighter aircraft. A fuzzy logic and Bayesian network-based hybrid technique is used in order to cope with the stochastic environment and making the development of the tactical situations' library as clear and simple as possible. In this chapter, Fuzzy-Bayesian hybrid technique is used to build a situation assessment framework, wherein, i) fuzzy logic (FL) is used as an event detector to classify the incoming data from various sources such as output from Level 1 fusion (kinematics data) or data from sensors itself and ii) a Bayesian network (BN) is used for the inference process by using the classified input data.

Air-to-air combat scenarios are generated using "Air-to-Air Combat Simulation Software" developed in C++. The functional models of air-borne sensors, namely RADAR, RWR, IRST, and EOTS are developed in SIMULINK to generate the realistic sensor data. The HUGIN C++ API software tool [1] is used for the construction and propagation of Bayesian networks to assess the current situation from a given scenario. The complete system is implemented in real time (online) in a C++–MATLAB-SIMULINK environment.

We review here some work done in the area of SA and its applications to battlefield, air combat etc. Ref. [2] describes the software (SW) 'SAMPLE' for pilot-in-loop evaluation, a model-based metric for evaluating subsystems and tactics for enhancing pilot situation awareness in an air combat environment. The SW was developed in C++ on windows 98 platform with a GUI interface using Visual Basic, Visio Technical, and Access. Some important features of SAMPLE are: i) an intuitive graphical facility for specifying basic scenario attributes and key components of the pilot's tactical strategy, ii) the facility to simulate multiple virtual pilots, iii) the provision of replay mode for explicit visualization of platform-related scenario events, as well as implicit events defining each pilot's assessment process and decision-making behavior, and iv) situation awareness metrics and procedural correctness. The overall architecture of SAMPLE is shown in Figure 11.1.

DOI: 10.1201/9781003370413-11

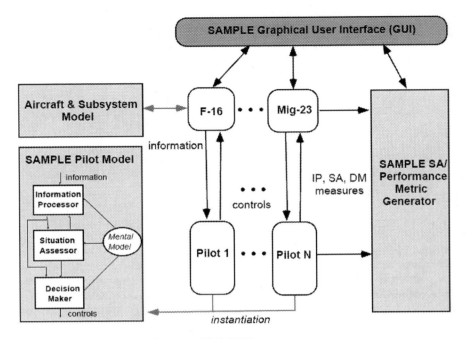

FIGURE 11.1   Overall Architecture of SAMPLE

The four major modules are: i) the aircraft and subsystem model to simulate air-craft dynamics and motion, ii) an SA-centered pilot model to instantiate a virtual multiple pilot mental model for situation assessment and decision making, iii) an interactive graphical interface which provides an interface for setting up simulation, and on-line visualization of simulation results and metrics, and iv) an SA/perform-ance metric generator provides multiple sets of model-based quantitative metrics for quantifying the pilot's Information Processing (IP), Situation Assessment (SA), and Decision making (DM) behavior

The working of SAMPLE was demonstrated using a 2V2 offensive counter air scenario based on an air combat scenario. The SW [2] was shown to have some major advantages over other possible methods e.g. rule-based, handbook, or empirical. SAMPLE assisted in pilot's IP, SA, and DM activities through its trajectory displays, timelines, and especially its on-line visualization of the pilot SA and DM process. SAMPLE also provided model-based performance metrics to measure the pilot's IP, SA, and DM actions.

Other prototype SW for situation assessment available in literature was OLIPSA [3]. This software, for the on-line processing of information and situation assessment, has been developed using C++ and integrated with a flight simulation model on an SGI workstation. OLIPSA performance was demonstrated initially in the defensive reaction portion of an air-to-ground attack mission, in which a pilot must deal with an attack from a threat aircraft. In order to do so, situation awareness models were developed to support the pilot's assessment of the threat posed by the detected air-craft. In general, OLIPSA was used in real-time for these tasks: i) Event detection uses an FL processor and an event rule base to transform fused sensor data into situ-ationally relevant semantic variables, ii) Current situation assessment is performed using a Belief Network (BN) model to combine detected events into a holistic 'pic-ture' of the current situation, for probabilistic reasoning in the presence of uncer-tainty, and iii) Future situation prediction is carried out via case-based reasoning, to project the current situation into the future via experience-based outcome prediction. Figure 11.2 shows the OLIPSA's functional block diagram.

The event detector uses FL for robust event detection. The event detector translates the numerical data obtained from the data fusion processor into symbolic data defining key tactical elements e.g. aircraft speed is 'HIGH' and is 'APPROACHING" etc. The current situation assessor used the output from the event detector and BN (mental model of pilot) to generate a multi-dimensional state vector consisting of a number of possible situations facing the pilot. The future situation predictor used output from the current situation assessor for a limited time window to predict the most likely future situations. The block context processor used output from the event detector, current situation assessor and future situation assessor for threat assessment, decision making and sensor management etc.

Reference [4] discussed the tools and techniques in aid of command, control, communications and intelligence (C3I). The crucial problem that decision makers face in the C3I process is the problem of uncertainty, that can be best solved by using BN (using commercially available software, Netica) and reason about it in both a qualitative (cause & relationship) and a quantitative manner (updating of probability distribution based on fresh reconnaissance and surveillance data). Reference [4] addresses the issues related to: i) probabilistic models, ii) the construction of different types of Bayesian networks and the generation of conditional probabilities, iii) input to network–setting prior probabilities, with the inclusion of evidence to update pos-terior probabilities, iv) scenario generation for Naval anti surface warfare, and v) techniques to analyze the effects of various types of uncertainties and evidence on the Bayesian network.

Reference [5] discusses the implementation of a real-time automated SAS to guide the pilot in tactical decision making. The knowledge and inference part of the system are based on BN. The complete system (for flight missions) is implemented in C++ and connected with TACSI+, a tactical data fusion simulator. The HUGIN Lite 6.6

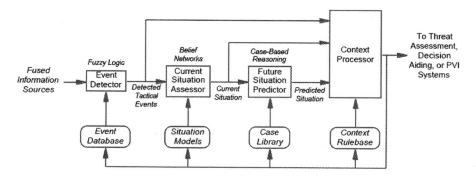

FIGURE 11.2   Function Block Diagram of OLIPSA

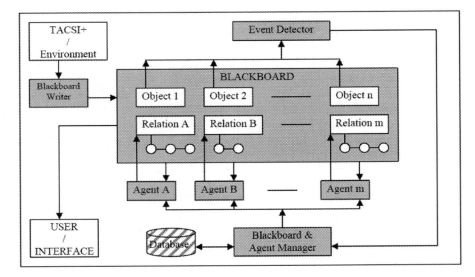

FIGURE 11.3   System Architecture used for Situation Assessment

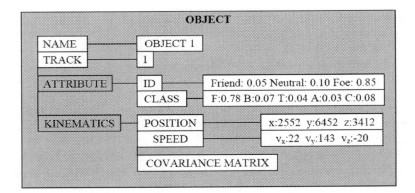

FIGURE 11.4   An Example of an Object Assessment placed on Blackboard

demo version SW with additional C++ API is used to realize the BN. Figure 11.3 illustrates the schematic of system architecture used in situation assessment.

The TACSI simulator in Reference [5] was used for sensor detection in a modeled range of time and space. TACSI was connected to TACSI+ for object assessment through fusion of a detected object's *position, kinematics, class* and *ID*. The object assessment in terms of typical blackboard architecture contained both kinematics and other fused data from the Level 1 data fusion. Figure 11.4 gives a representative picture of what the actual object could look like. The various relations implemented in the situation assessor are Pair, Along, and Attacking. The FL-based event detector is attached as a pre-processor to reduce the workload of the situation assessor. The event detector in Reference [5] was used to compare an object's current data to a stored vector of the previous one. If something significant has happened, the event detector stores the new vector and tells the *Blackboard & Event Manager* to investigate what has happened. Otherwise, nothing is stored and nothing needs to be investigated. The *Blackboard & Event Manager* keeps track of the agent, i.e., the situation assessor in use and knows what the specialty of each agent is, and what kind of event(s) could interest them. When an event is detected, the manager addresses the right agent and tells it for which object(s) the event has happened. It also makes sure that the agent has all the information needed on the blackboard.

11.1.1 SYSTEM ARCHITECTURE

The architecture of the SAS implementation is shown in Figure 11.5. Arrows indicate the flow of information between the different modules. First, a typical air-to-air combat scenario is generated using air combat simulation SW. The data obtained from this SW can be stored in files or can be sent to another PC (through the UDP protocol). The scenario includes targets, labeled T1, T2, …, Tn, which could be

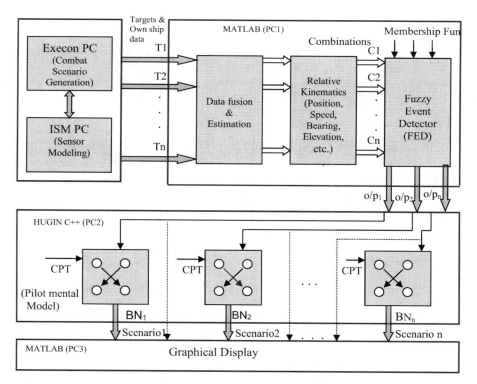

FIGURE 11.5 System Architecture for the Situation Assessor

(T-Target, C-Combination, UDP–communication, CPT-Conditional Probability Table, BN-Bayesian Network, Execon-Exercise Controller, ISM–Integrated Simulink Model)

commercial as well as fighters of own and enemy zone. Then the kinematics data from different sensors are fused to generate tracks using EKF for estimation.

The estimated data (relative kinematics) of different situations (combinations) are passed to the FED block. Then FED fuzzifies the relative kinematics data into quali-tative form (events) e.g. Speed is 'low'. After fuzzification, the fuzzified combination values (o/p$_1$, o/p$_{2,...}$ o/p$_n$) and the particular combination Identity number (Id) are sent to the Hugin C++ program through the UDP protocol. In the Hugin C++ block, for each combination, a BN is constructed and named as an agent [5]. The Conditional Probability Table (CPT) represents the pilot mental model specific to a certain situ-ation that is encountered in air-to-air combat scenario. The entries in the CPT in this chapter are decided based on intuition and in no way reflect an exact pilot mental model. However, further fine-tuning of the CPT can be incorporated by discussion with experienced pilots.

Using the output of FED and CPT, BNs are propagated and the updated probability values, which help in assessing the current situation, are passed to the graphical dis-play block through the UDP protocol. It displays the updated probability values of various nodes of the BNs. The various agents developed to assess the occurrence of different situations are:

- Pair: Two or more targets/aircraft are in formation of a pair.
- Along: Aircraft flying along a corridor. For example a 'transport' aircraft flying along a corridor or air lane.
- Attack: Enemy aircraft attacking own ship.

11.2   SCENARIO GENERATION

Air combat simulation SW is used to generate the different air-to-air combat scenarios. This software can simulate a maximum of 6 targets (excluding own ship) consisting of fighter aircraft, missiles, transport aircraft and helicopters. Three different combat scenarios are presented, in which scenarios 2 and 3 are demo scenarios of air combat simulation software [6]. In all the simulations, an aircraft with ID '7' is treated as own ship.

11.2.1   SCENARIO-1

Scenario-1 consists of 6 targets and own ship as shown in Figure 11.6. Details of the targets are given in Table 11.1.

Figure 11.7 illustrates target trajectories of Scenario-1. It is assumed that all the targets maintain the same altitude during the entire simulation time. It can be seen from Figure 11.7 that targets '1' and '2' form a pair for some time and then target '1' comes towards own ship. Similarly, targets '3' and '4' converge to form a pair and come towards own ship. Target '5' approaches own ship from behind. Target '6' is flying along the corridor. Using pre-stored points, the commercial corridor is generated.

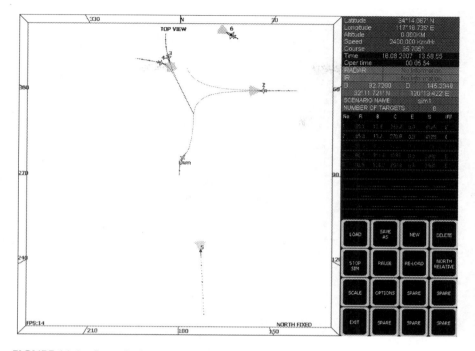

FIGURE 11.6   Scenario-1 generated using simulation software

TABLE 11.1
Scenario-1

TARGET NO	TYPE	IFF
1	Fighter	Foe
2	Fighter	Foe
3	Fighter	Friend
4	Fighter	Unknown
5	Missile	Foe
6	Transport	Friend

11.2.2   SCENARIO 2

Scenario-2 consists of 2 targets and own ship as shown in Figure 11.8. This is a typical beaming by foe (1V2) scenario in which, targets '1' and '2' form a pair for some time and then target '1' comes towards own ship and is beaming it. It is assumed that all the targets maintain the same altitude during the entire simulation time. Details of the targets are given in Table 11.2.

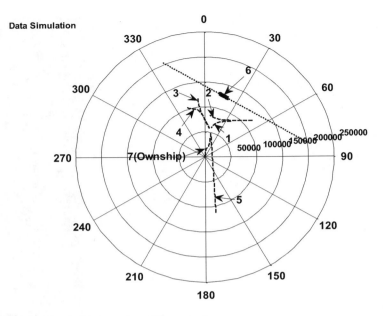

FIGURE 11.7   Targets Trajectories of Scenario-1

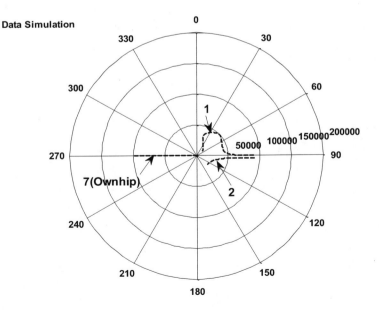

FIGURE 11.8   Targets Trajectories of Scenario-2

TABLE 11.2
Scenario-2

TARGET NO	TYPE	IFF
1	Fighter	Foe
2	Fighter	Unknown

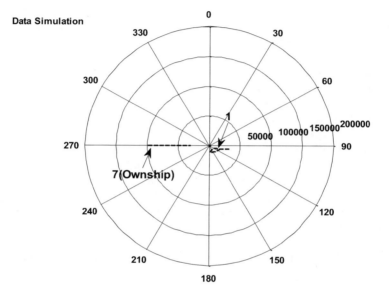

FIGURE 11.9 Targets Trajectories of Scenario-3

TABLE 11.3
Scenario-3

TARGET NO	TYPE	IFF
1	Fighter	Foe

11.2.3 SCENARIO 3

Scenario-3 consists of 1 target and own ship, Figure 11.9. This is a typical foe run away (1V1) scenario. Here, target '1' is coming towards own ship and then takes a 180-degree turn. Details of the target are given in Table 11.3.

11.3   MULTI-SENSOR DATA FUSION AND ESTIMATION

Data fusion is defined as a formal framework in which the means and tools for the special logical alliance of data originating from different sources are expressed. The data fusion problem is not to combine the multiple source information just like that, but to combine the information intelligently. This means fusing the data from multiple sensors to develop a more meaningful perception of the environment than using only one sensor. This is something humans do automatically, using mental reasoning methods and experience. Human perception finds it increasingly difficult to associate and classify the incoming data, due to the increasing complexity and number of sensors. Therefore, there has been an rising interest in making automated systems that combine multiple sensor data and derive a more meaningful picture of the world.

In this example, own ship consists of four sensors: RADAR (Doppler), IRST, RWR and EOTS, which are modeled using ISM (simulink) simulation SW. The RADAR sensor gives the information about range, bearing, elevation, course, Doppler velocity and aspect of the targets. The scanning area of RADAR is ±30 deg from the center point. The RADAR used in this is a Doppler radar, so it detects the target only if there is a difference in velocities between the target and the own ship. Also, the RADAR will not detect the target if the angle off (relative course) between the target and own ship is within 70–110 degrees. The minimum and maximum ranges for RADAR detection are 5 km and 200 km respectively. The IRST (Infra-Red Search and Track) sensor gives the information about range, bearing, elevation, and aspect. The maximum range for IR detection is 90 km. But IR gives the range information, only when targets are 10 km or less from own ship. The RWR sensor gives information about range and bearing only. The EOTS sensor gives information about bearing and elevation only. The maximum range for EOTS detection is 40 km. The decision logic used for data fusion is given in Table 11.4.

EKF is used for estimation and fusion. The results of estimation for each target of all scenarios (scenario-1, 2 and 3) from real time (online) simulation are shown in Figures 11.10–11.18; the '-', '--', ': ', and '-.' lines indicate the measured data from RADAR, IR, RWR and EOTS sensors respectively. The '.-' line indicates the estimated/predicted data. There is loss in data measured from the sensors as seen from the figures. Note that the prediction for long duration is not desirable, especially for the case when the target is executing maneuvers. Even though there is some data loss between the computers in real time simulation, results are very similar to the offline (reading from the log files), the results of which are shown in Appendix 11E.

11.4   RESULTS OF ESTIMATION

Scenario-1: Figures 11.10 to 11.15 show the estimated state of each target of the simulation, Scenario-1.

Scenario-2: Figures 11.16 to 11.17 show the estimated state of each target of the simulation, Scenario 2.

Scenario-3: Figure 11.18 shows the estimated state of each target of the simulation, Scenario 3.

TABLE 11.4
Decision logic for data fusion

Logic no	RADAR	IRST	RWR	EOTS	Estimation & Fusion
1	×	×	×	×	No action
2	×	×	×	√	Use EOTS data (no fusion)
3	×	×	√	×	Use RWR data (no fusion)
4	×	×	√	√	Fuse Bearing only
5	×	√	×	×	Use IRST data (no fusion)
6	×	√	×	√	Fuse Bearing only
7	×	√	√	×	Fuse Range and Bearing
8	×	√	√	√	Fuse Range and Bearing
9	√	×	×	×	Use RADAR data (no fusion)
10	√	×	×	√	Fuse Bearing only
11	√	×	√	×	Fuse Range and Bearing
12	√	×	√	√	Fuse Range and Bearing
13	√	√	×	×	Fuse Range, Bearing, Elevation and Aspect
14	√	√	×	√	Fuse Range, Bearing, Elevation and Aspect
15	√	√	√	×	Fuse Range, Bearing, Elevation and Aspect
16	√	√	√	√	Fuse Range, Bearing, Elevation and Aspect

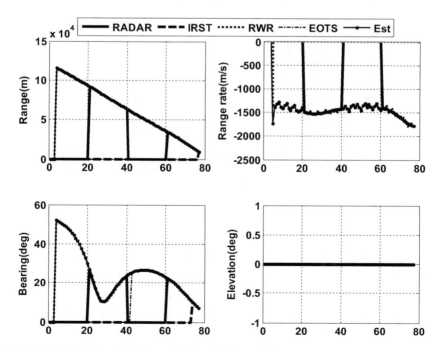

FIGURE 11.10   Estimated values of Target 1 (Aircraft)

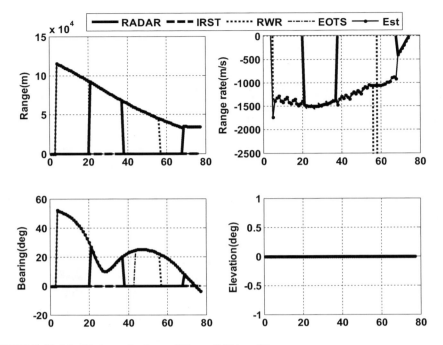

FIGURE 11.11   Estimated values of Target 2 (Aircraft)

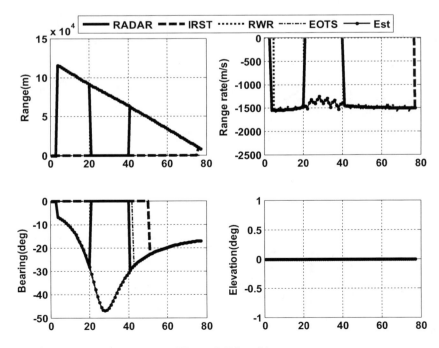

FIGURE 11.12   Estimated values of Target 3 (Aircraft)

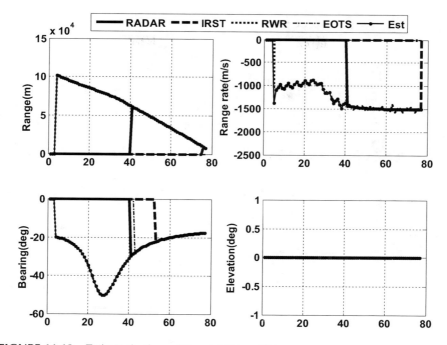

FIGURE 11.13 Estimated values of Target 4 (Aircraft)

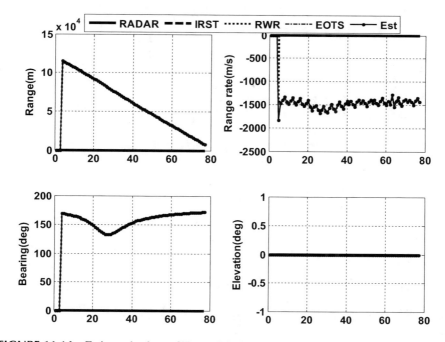

FIGURE 11.14 Estimated values of Target 5 (Missile)

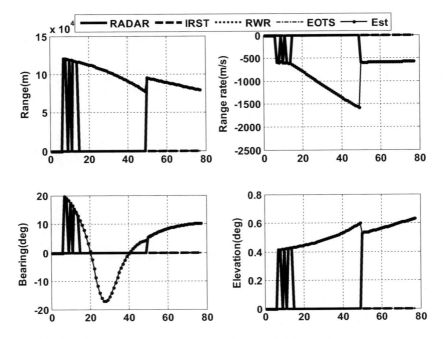

FIGURE 11.15 Estimated values of Target 6 (Commercial Aircraft)

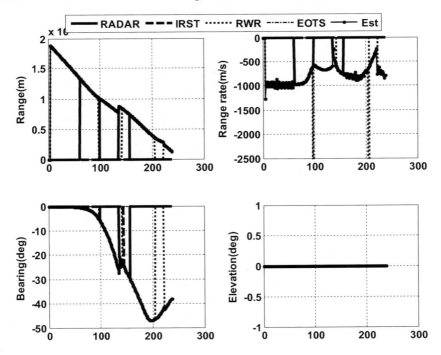

FIGURE 11.16 Estimated values of Target 1 (Aircraft)

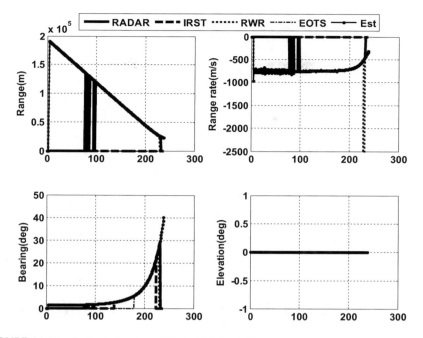

FIGURE 11.17   Estimated values of Target 2 (Aircraft)

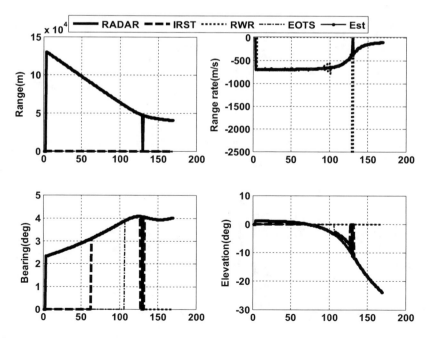

FIGURE 11.18   Estimated values of Target 1 (Aircraft)

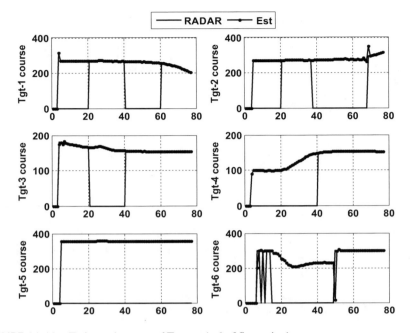

FIGURE 11.19 Estimated course of Targets 1–6 of Scenario-1

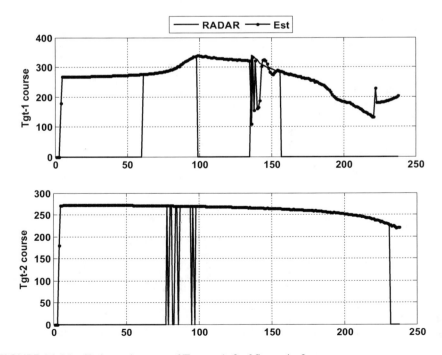

FIGURE 11.20 Estimated course of Targets 1–2 of Scenario-2

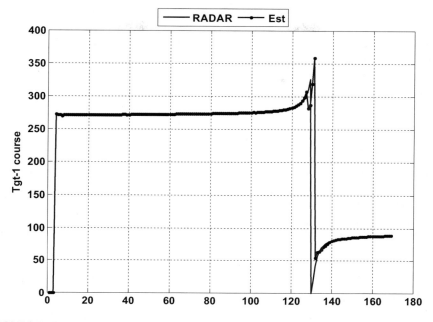

FIGURE 11.21 Estimated course of Targets 1 of Scenario-3

Figures 11.19–11.21 show the measured ('-') and estimated ('.-') values of the 'Course' of targets for Scenarios 1–3. The 'Course' is needed for processing the BN. The 'Course' is estimated from the target co-ordinates using the formula given in Appendix 11B.

11.5 RELATIVE KINEMATICS

Here, the relative kinematics data for all combinations are calculated; the relative values of speed, velocity, course and bearing of one target with respect to all other targets are calculated. The possible combinations for Pair agent (for Scenario-1) are : (T1, T2), (T1, T3), (T1, T4), (T1, T5), (T1, T6), (T2, T3), (T2, T4), (T2, T5), (T2, T6), (T3, T4), (T3, T5), (T3, T6), (T4, T5), (T4, T6), and (T5, T6). The possible combinations for the Along agent (for Scenario-1) are: (T1, Cor), (T2, Cor), (T3, Cor), (T4, Cor), (T5, Cor) and (T6, Cor). Here, 'Cor' stands for corridor (Airliner). Similarly, the possible combinations for Attack agent (for Scenario-1) are: (T7, T1), (T7, T2), (T7, T3), (T7, T4), (T7, T5), and (T7, T6). Similarly, possible combinations for other scenarios can be calculated.

11.6 FUZZY EVENT DETECTOR

A FED uses FL to classify continuous numerical data into fuzzy sets of discrete variables. In this chapter, a MATLAB ® based FL toolbox (FLTB) is used to design appropriate membership functions for data classification. FLTB includes 11 built in MF [4] types such as piecewise linear functions, Gaussian distribution functions, the sigmoid curve, and quadratic and cubic polynomial curves. All MFs have the letters 'mf' at the end of their names; addmf (), evalmf (), plotmf (), etc. The simplest MFs are formed using straight lines. The simplest MF is the triangular MF and it has the function name 'trimf'. The triangular shaped built-in MF is nothing more than a collection of 3 points forming a triangle. The syntax for the triangular membership function is:

$$y = trimf(x, params)$$
$$y = trimf(x, [a\,b\,c])$$

The triangular curve is a function of a vector, x, and depends on three scalar parameters a, b, and c. The parameters 'a' and 'c' locate the 'feet' of the triangle and parameter 'b' locates the peak. The trapezoidal MF, 'trapmf', has a flat top and really is just a truncated triangle curve. The details of other MFs can be found in [4]. Figure 11.22 shows the FMFs of Distance, Bearing, Elevation and Speed nodes for Pair and Along agents.

The ranges of MFs for Distance, Bearing, Elevation and Speed nodes are 0–400 m, 0–12 deg, 0–6 deg, and 0–100 m/s respectively. Similarly, Figure 11.23 shows the FMFs of Distance, Bearing, and Speed nodes for Attack agent. The range of MFs for Distance, Bearing, and Speed nodes are 0–25000 m, 0–120 deg, and 0–300 m/s respectively. For each node, range is divided into 3 parts which are 'Small', 'Medium' and 'Large'. The 'Small' and 'Large' are represented by a 'trapezoidal' MF and 'Medium' by a 'triangular/Gaussian' function. Different line symbols are used to

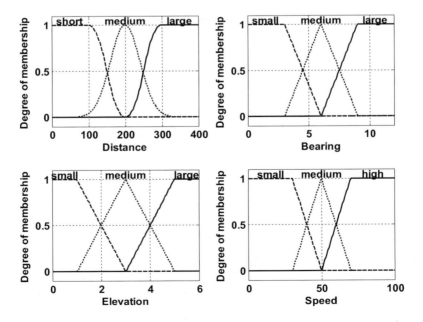

FIGURE 11.22 Fuzzy Membership Values of Pair & Along agents

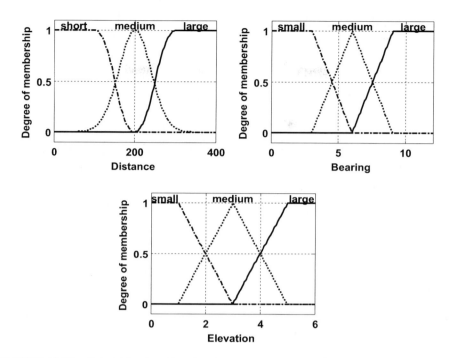

FIGURE 11.23 Fuzzy Membership Values of Attack agent

represent the states of the nodes like: Small ('-.'), Medium (':') and Large ('-'). The following formula is used for membership function evaluation, i.e., o/p of FED:

$$Y = evalmf(X, mfParams, mfType)$$

X is the variable range for the MF evaluation, *mfParams* is the appropriate parameters for the member function and *mfType* is a member function from the toolbox ('*trimf*', '*trapmf*,' etc.). Figure 11.24 shows fuzzified values of the Distance, Bearing, Elevation and Speed for the combination (T1, T2) of the pair agent of Scenario-1.

The fuzzification process converts the relative kinematics data into events, e.g. Speed is 'small' with certain membership degree. The three curves represent the small ('-.'), medium (':') and large ('-') states of BN nodes.

11.7 BAYESIAN NETWORKS

BNs also known as belief networks or Bayesian belief networks, are unidirectional networks with no feedback. In the BN, the connected nodes confer with each other in meaningful ways, and new evidence can be inserted at every single node so that the belief for the rest of the nodes is then updated. BNs have been applied to various applications like: military decisions, heuristic searches, image processing, medical

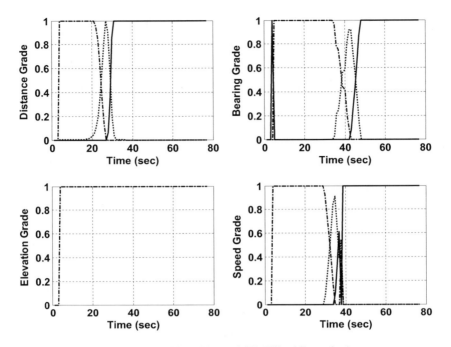

FIGURE 11.24   Pair agent's Fuzzified Values of (T1, T2) of Scenario-1

diagnoses, map learning, text analysis, data fusion and decision support systems, and language understanding. Several commercial software tools such as HUGIN, NETICA, and SMILE are available to realize Bayesian networks.

The BN is a set of probabilistic variables, nodes, and a set of directed links between them. A variable is denoted by an oval and links between the variables as arrows. Each node has a finite set of states that are mutually exclusive and whose likelihood distribution is denoted as a belief value [5]. The directed links represent an associative or inferential relationship between them. Typically, any BN can consist of three types of nodes such as information, intermediate and hypothesis. Information nodes are independent, without any parent and are connected to sensors through an interface e.g. FED. Whereas, hypothesis nodes have no children and are used to determine a posterior probability of some hypothesis, e.g. threat in a war scenario. Intermediate nodes have parents as well as children and they represent events.

Each node of a BN corresponds to some event represented by multiple states with each state defined by its probability. Probabilistic states of each node (except the information node) are updated using the Bayes formula where *posterior* probability is computed using *a priori* probability and likelihood or conditional probability of that node.

Consider two mutually dependent events A and B, i.e., the probability of occurrence of each event depends upon the occurrence of the other event. In such a case, the chance of occurrence of each event is defined by a conditional probability, e.g., given event B, the conditional probability for event A is defined by. The joint probability for event A and B is defined by

$$P(A, B) = P(A|B) P(B) \tag{11.1}$$

Similarly, if we assume that event A has occurred first, followed by B, then the joint probability of A and B is given by

$$P(A, B) = P(B \mid A)P(A) \tag{11.2}$$

Since the Left Hand Sides (LHS) of eqn. (11.1) and eqn. (11.2) are the same, equating the RHS of these equations we get

$$P(A \mid B)P(B) = P(B \mid A)P(A); P(A \mid B) = \frac{P(B \mid A)P(A)}{P(B)} \tag{11.3}$$

In BN terminology: i) $P(A \mid B)$ is known as the posterior probability, or the probability of A after considering the effect of B, ii) $P(A)$ is known as the prior probability of A, iii) $P(B \mid A)$ is known as the likelihood and gives the probability of the evidence, assuming the hypothesis A, and iv) $P(B)$ is independent of A and can be regarded as a normalizing or scaling factor. The Baye's rule, eqn. (11.3) specifies how prior probabilities are updated in the light of new evidence. Now consider three nodes C, D, and E of BN depicted in Figure 11.25; we see that nodes C and D are independent nodes. So, the rule of independence applies here.

$$P(C, D) = P(C)P(D) \tag{11.4}$$

E is the hypothesis node and it depends upon nodes C and D. So, C and D are the parent nodes of E. If there is a route in the directed graph from one node to another, the posterior probability node E (P(E|C,D)) must be calculated using the conditional probability table or likelihood, i.e., P (C,D | E), prior probability of E and joint probability of nodes C and D.

The BNs have many feasible features, but lack the ability to handle continuous input data. However, in order to make it compatible with the BNs inputs, FL can be used to classify the continuous data into events represented through FM values. The

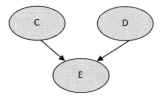

FIGURE 11.25 Typical Bayesian Network Structure

Fuzzy-Bayesian hybrid system handles all the demands of the situation assessor. The HUGIN C++ API software tool [1] is used for the construction and propagation of Bayesian networks to assess the current situation from a given scenario. The HUGIN API (HAPI) is used just like any other library. It does not require any special programming techniques or program structures. The HAPI does not control the application; rather, the application controls the HAPI by telling it which operations to perform. The HAPI is provided in the form of a library that can be linked into applications written using the C, C++, or Java programming languages [2]. The details of HUGIN software, and construction and implementation of BNs using HUGIN are presented in Appendix 11F. The SAS developed for the air combat scenario consists of 'Pair', 'Along' and 'Attack' agents. The scenario under consideration determines the choice of these agents. An expert (in this case a pilot) should be in the loop for developing any SAS since the results produced as a decision-making aid will only be as good as the information used in constructing the various agents in the BN.

11.7.1 PAIR AGENT BAYESIAN NETWORK

Figure 11.26 shows the proposed pair agent BN to compute the updated probabilities. Distance, Id, Class, Course, Elevation and Speed are the independent nodes or Information nodes. It is assumed that the inputs 'Distance', 'Course', 'Elevation' and 'Speed' have three states: Small, Medium and Large. The input 'Id' has three states: Friend, Neutral and Foe. The input 'Class' has four states: Fighter, Bomber, Transport and Civil. The Intermediate node of a Pair BN is Kinematics and it has two states: Yes and No. It depends upon the Course, Elevation and Speed nodes. Finally, the Pair node is the Hypothesis node and it has two states: Yes and No. The Pair node has four dependencies: Distance, Id, Class and Kinematics. The semantic rules of the Pair agent are: i) IF two aircraft have the same bearing, elevation and speed THEN they have the same kinematics, and ii) IF two aircraft have the same kinematics, the same identity, the same class, and are at a short distance from each other THEN they form a pair. According to these rules, the Kinematics and Pair node CPT values are entered. The semantic rule helps to give prior probability values to the Intermediate and Hypothesis node of the BN. For example, the Kinematics node CPT values are entered as follows:

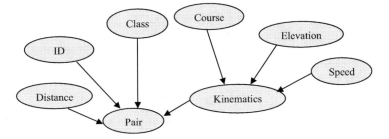

FIGURE 11.26 Proposed Pair Agent Bayesian Network

Size of CPT array = Kinematics node states (Yes, No) × Dependent node states (Course, Elevation, Speed)

$$= 2 \times (3 \times 3 \times 3)$$
$$= 2 \times 27$$

The size of array should be 2 × 27. Refer Appendix 11D for CPT of Kinematics (Table 11D.1) and Pair (Table 11D.2) node.

11.7.2 ALONG AGENT BAYESIAN NETWORK

Figure 11.27 shows the proposed Along agent BN to compute the relationship between the air lane and the aircraft. Class, Distance and Course are the Along agent input nodes. These input nodes have three states: Small, Medium and Large. The Along node is the Hypothesis node and it depends upon all the input nodes. It has two states: Yes and No. The semantic rules of the Along agent are: i) IF an aircraft has the same course as an air lane, and if it is close to the air lane THEN the aircraft is flying along the air lane, and ii) IF an aircraft is civil there is a higher possibility that the aircraft is flying along the air lane. The Along node CPT values are entered as per the semantic rules. Refer to Appendix 11D for CPT values of Along node (Table 11D.3).

11.7.3 ATTACK AGENT BAYESIAN NETWORK

Figure 11.28 shows the proposed Attack agent BN to compute the attacking probabilities of all the aircraft. The Id, Class, Distance, Bearing and Speed nodes are the input nodes. These input node states are the same as given in the Pair agent. The Intermediate node of the attack agent is the Closing node. It has two states: Yes and No. It depends upon the Distance, Bearing and Speed nodes. Finally the Attack node is the Hypothesis node. It has two states: Yes and No. It depends upon the Id, Class and Closing nodes. The semantic rules of Attack agent are: i) IF an aircraft has high Speed, has a close distance to another aircraft and has a bearing towards it THEN the aircraft are flying close to one another, and ii) IF an aircraft is closing in on another, and has a different id and is a fighter aircraft THEN the aircraft is attacking the other. According to the semantic rules, the Closing and Attack node CPT values are entered. Refer to Appendix 11D for the CPT of the Closing (Table 11D.4) and the Attack

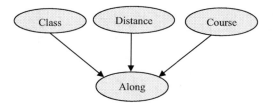

FIGURE 11.27 Proposed Along Agent Bayesian Network

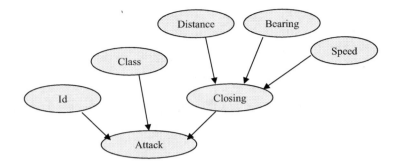

FIGURE 11.28   Proposed Attack Agent Bayesian Network

(Table 11D.5) node. The values entered in the CPTs are based on intuition and could be altered based on feedback from experienced pilots.

11.8   SIMULATION RESULTS

The results of all three scenarios are presented here. In all the figures, numbers represent different combinations of targets and '0' indicates the prediction (sensors data not available).

11.8.1   SCENARIO-1

Figure 11.29 shows the updated probability values of various nodes of the Pair agent BN. In the beginning, the combination '1' and '2' forms a pair with a probability of approximately 0.72 and then gradually diverges. Combination '3' and '4' forms a pair after some time and stays there for the rest of the simulation. It is noticed from the figure that other combinations have a very low probability of making a pair.

Figure 11.30 shows the updated probability values of various nodes of the Along agent Bayesian network. The Along agent found only one active relation between aircraft 6 and the corridor, i.e., aircraft 6 is moving along the corridor. Here '0' indicates that no sensor detected the target, so a prediction is performed. From the figure, we can see that the prediction for a long time is not good.

Figure 11.31 shows the updated probability values of various nodes of the Attack agent Bayesian network. Here, the probability values of targets '1' and '5' are high compared to others because both the targets are foe and coming towards own ship (refer to Scenario-1). Target '4' (also coming towards own ship) probability is less than targets '1' and '5' because it is unknown (IFF). The probability of target '3' (also coming towards own ship) is very much less because it is a friend.

11.8.2   SCENARIO-2

Figure 11.32 shows the updated probability values of various nodes of the Pair agent Bayesian network. In the beginning, the combination '1' and '2' forms a pair with a

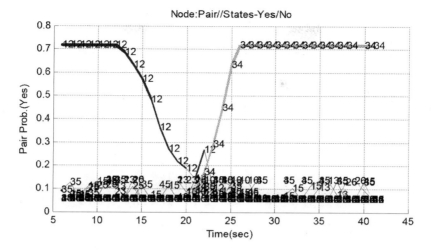

FIGURE 11.29 Updated Pair Agent Probability of different combinations

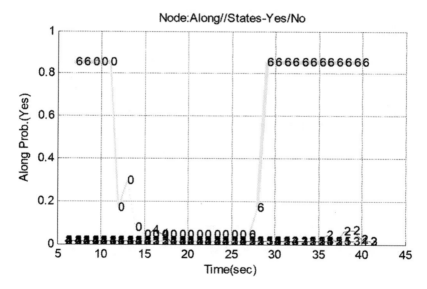

FIGURE 11.30 Updated Probability of Along Agent

probability of approximately 0.14 and then gradually diverges. Figure 11.33 shows the updated probability values of various nodes of the Attack agent Bayesian network.

11.8.3 SCENARIO-A3

Figure 11.34 shows the updated probability values of various nodes of the Attack agent Bayesian network.

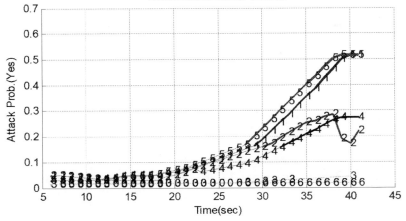

FIGURE 11.31   Updated Probability of Attack Agent

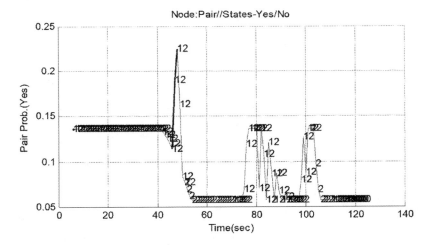

FIGURE 11.32   Updated Probability of Pair Agent

Summary: SAS is implemented using FL and a Bayesian network hybrid technique to find out the exact situation in an air-to-air combat scenario, which helps the pilot to take a correct and quick decision. The capability of SAS has been demonstrated by simulating a typical air-to-air combat scenario. It is observed that the BNs based on several agents were able to accomplish the job assigned with a fairly good amount of precision. However, further improvement of SAS performance is envisaged by the fine-tuning of entries of CPTs corresponding to different agents with the help of experienced pilots for typical combat scenarios.

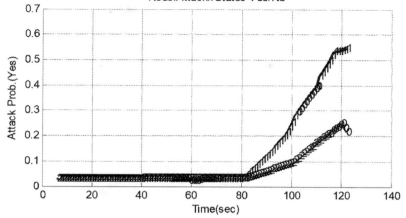

FIGURE 11.33   Updated Probability of Attack Agent

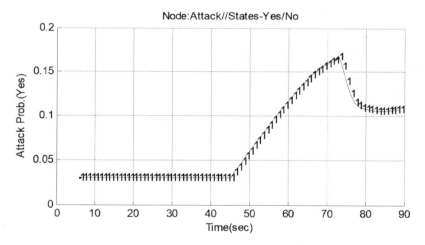

FIGURE 11.34   Updated Probability of Attack Agent

APPENDIX 11A

Configuration Specifications for Communication between PCs

Communication between PCs is done through UDP (User Data gram Protocol). The process is shown in Figure 11A.1. Before sending the input data from the Execon PC, PC1, PC2 and PC3 should be in receiving mode to read that data, i.e., the receiving program should be executed first. In the PC1, MATLAB based 'udp' objects are first created using the statements:

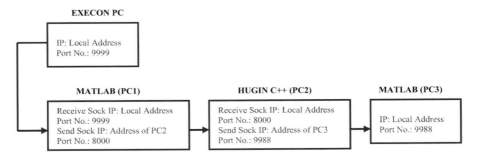

FIGURE 11A.1   Communication diagram

$$u = udp('PC1', 'Localport', 9999); \quad (for\ receiving)$$

$$u = udp ('PC2\ IP\ Address', 8000); \quad (for\ sending)$$

In receiving mode, the first parameter is the Logical Name of PC1 and the second parameter is the port number. In sending mode, the first parameter is the IP address of PC2 and the second parameter is the port number. The '*fwrite (u, data)*' function is used to send the input data to PC2. The same port number should be used in the receiving program, i.e., HUGIN C++. The data transmission from PC1 to PC2 continues until the end of the simulation and after that '*fclose ()*' and '*delete ()*' functions are used to close and delete the created object, respectively.

Bayesian networks are constructed before reading the input data from MATLAB through UDP. The input values are read and used by the Bayesian network for propagating the newly formed events and it computes the probability of occurrence of a particular situation. After propagation, the updated probability values are displayed on the MS DOS screen of PC2 and sent through the UDP socket to the MATLAB program running on PC3 for plotting purposes. Also, the UDP object should be created to read the output data: $u = udp ('PC3', 'Localport', 9988);$

Here '*PC3*' is the logical name of the PC3 system. The 'Localport' specifies the local host port for connection and the last parameter specifies the port number. The '*fread (u)*' function is used to receive the output data from PC2. The updated probabilities of various nodes of the Bayesian network are plotted using the '*plot ()*' function. After plotting the graph, the object is closed, deleted and cleared by using '*fclose ()*', '*delete ()*' and '*clear ()*' functions.

APPENDIX 11B: FORMULAE USED

$$Range = \sqrt{x^2 + y^2 + z^2} \tag{11B.1}$$

$$Bearing(relative) = (\tan^{-1}(y,x) - Course) * R2D; \tag{11B.2}$$

$$Elevation(relative) = (\tan^{-1}(z, HorizontalRange) - Pitch) * R2D \qquad (11B.3)$$

$$Course(relative) = (\tan^{-1}(dy, dx)) * R2D; \qquad (11B.4)$$

Using the equation $y = mx + c$ a commercial corridor is generated, where m is the slope. The perpendicular (shortest) distance between the line $y = mx + c$ (corridor) and a point (x_1, y_1) (aircraft co-ordinates) is given by $\dfrac{|y_1 - mx_1 - c|}{\sqrt{m^2 + 1}}$

APPENDIX 11C: EXTENDED KALMAN FILTER

The conventional Kalman filter is a recursive-minimum variance estimator, which is often used in target tracking to provide an optimal performance in terms of estimated states of that target. In the case of non-linear systems, an Extended KF filter (EKF) is used wherein non-linear models are linearized with respect to predicted/estimated filter states with the assumption that local linearity is not violated within a given sampling interval. The states of the EKF are updated by processing the measurements originating from different sensors in a sequential manner. The advantage of having a sequential update is due to the fact that it may happen that sometimes a target will not be in the field of view of some of the sensors, for example, RADAR but in the field of view of EOT that provides only angle information. In such a case EKF with batch processing of measurements will not work. The equations needed to implement EKF with sequential updates are:

STATE AND COVARIANCE PROPAGATION

$$\tilde{X}(k+1/k) = F\,\hat{X}\,(k/k) \qquad (11C.1)$$

$$\tilde{P}(k+1/k) = F\,\hat{P}\,(k/k)F^T + GQG^T \qquad (11C.2)$$

STATE AND COVARIANCE UPDATE

For j = 1: m

$$H = \left.\frac{\partial h}{\partial x}\right|_{x=\tilde{x}(k+1/k)} \qquad (11C.3)$$

$$\left.\begin{aligned} K &= \tilde{P}(k+1/k)H(j,:)^T S^{-1} \\ S &= H(j,:)\tilde{P}(k+1/k)H(j,:)^T + R(j,j) \end{aligned}\right\} \qquad (11C.4)$$

$$\left.\begin{aligned} \tilde{X}(k+1/k) &= \tilde{X}(k+1/k) + Ke(k+1) \\ e(k+1) &= Z_m(k+1,j) - H(j,:)\,\tilde{X}(k+1/k) \end{aligned}\right\} \qquad (11C.5)$$

$$\tilde{P}(k+1/k) = \left[\text{I-}KH\right]\tilde{P}(k+1/k) \tag{11C.6}$$

end

$$\hat{X}(k+1/k+1) = \tilde{X}(k+1/k) \tag{11C.7}$$

$$\hat{P}(k+1/k+1) = \tilde{P}(k+1/k) \tag{11C.8}$$

Where, F is the state transition matrix, G is the process noise gain matrix, Q is the process noise covariance matrix, $\tilde{X} = \begin{bmatrix} x & \dot{x} & \ddot{x} & y & \dot{y} & \ddot{y} & z & \dot{z} & \ddot{z} \end{bmatrix}$ is the predicted state vector, $\tilde{P}$ is the predicted state covariance matrix, Z_m is the measurement vector consisting of range (r), range rate ($\dot{r}$), bearing (ϕ) and elevation (θ) from the sensors, H is a Jacobean matrix computed by linearizing the measurement model given below:

$$Range(r) = \sqrt{x^2 + y^2 + z^2} \tag{11C.9}$$

$$Range\ rate(\dot{r}) = \frac{(x\dot{x} + y\dot{y} + z\dot{z})}{\sqrt{x^2 + y^2 + z^2}} \tag{11C.10}$$

$$Bearing(\phi) = (\tan^{-1}(y,x) - Course\_ownship) * R2D; \tag{11C.11}$$

$$Elevation(\theta) = (\tan^{-1}(z,\sqrt{x^2 + y^2}) - Pitch\_ownship) * R2D \tag{11C.12}$$

R is the measurement noise covariance matrix, K is the Kalman gain, S is the innovation covariance matrix, e is the innovation sequence vector, $\hat{X}$ is the estimated state vector and $\hat{P}$ is the estimated state covariance matrix. It is assumed that course and pitch information of own ship are available from an appropriate source.

APPENDIX 11D: CONDITIONAL PROBABILITY TABLES

TABLE 11D.1
CPT for Kinematics Node

	Spe Elev Bear	Small			Small Medium			Large		
		S	M	L	S	M	L	S	M	L
Kin	Yes	0.99	0.6	0.4	0.6	0.3	0.25	0.4	0.25	0.15
	No	0.1	0.4	0.6	0.4	0.7	0.75	0.6	0.75	0.85
	Speed Elev Bear	Medium Small			Medium			Large		
		S	M	L	S	M	L	S	M	L
Kin	Yes	0.6	0.3	0.25	0.3	0.10	0.05	0.25	0.05	0.04
	No	0.4	0.7	0.75	0.7	0.90	0.95	0.75	0.95	0.96

TABLE 11D.1 (Continued)
CPT for Kinematics Node

	Speed	Large								
	Elev	Small			Medium			Large		
	Bear	S	M	L	S	M	L	S	M	L
Kin	Yes	0.4	0.25	0.15	0.25	0.05	0.04	0.15	0.04	0.01
	No	0.6	0.75	0.85	0.75	0.95	0.96	0.85	0.96	0.99

[Kin-Kinematics, Spe-Speed, Elev-Elevation, Bear-Bearing, S-Small, M-Medium, L-Large]

TABLE 11D.2
CPT for Pair node

	Kin	Yes								
	Cla	Fighter								
	ID	Friend			Neutral			Foe		
	Dist	S	M	L	S	M	L	S	M	L
Pair	Yes	0.99	0.79	0.59	0.8	0.6	0.4	0.7	0.5	0.3
	No	0.01	0.21	0.41	0.2	0.4	0.6	0.3	0.5	0.7

	Kin	Yes								
	Cla	Bomber								
	ID	Friend			Neutral			Foe		
	Dist	S	M	L	S	M	L	S	M	L
Pair	Yes	0.99	0.79	0.59	0.8	0.6	0.4	0.7	0.5	0.3
	No	0.01	0.21	0.41	0.2	0.4	0.6	0.3	0.5	0.7

	Kin	Yes								
	Cla	Transport								
	ID	Friend			Neutral			Foe		
	Dist	S	M	L	S	M	L	S	M	L
Pair	Yes	0.99	0.79	0.59	0.8	0.6	0.4	0.7	0.5	0.3
	No	0.01	0.21	0.41	0.2	0.4	0.6	0.3	0.5	0.7

	Kin	Yes								
	Cla	Civil								
	ID	Friend			Neutral			Foe		
	Dist	S	M	L	S	M	L	S	M	L
Pair	Yes	0.99	0.79	0.59	0.8	0.6	0.4	0.7	0.5	0.3
	No	0.01	0.21	0.41	0.2	0.4	0.6	0.3	0.5	0.7

	Kin	No								
	Cla	Fighter								
	ID	Friend			Neutral			Foe		
	Dist	S	M	L	S	M	L	S	M	L
Pair	Yes	0.01	0.01	0.01	0.01	0.01	0.01	0.01	0.01	0.01
	No	0.99	0.99	0.99	0.99	0.99	0.99	0.99	0.99	0.99

(*continued*)

TABLE 11D.2 (Continued)
CPT for Pair node

	Kin	No								
	Cla	Bomber								
	ID	Friend			Neutral			Foe		
	Dist	S	M	L	S	M	L	S	M	L
Pair	Yes	0.01	0.01	0.01	0.01	0.01	0.01	0.01	0.01	0.01
	No	0.99	0.99	0.99	0.99	0.99	0.99	0.99	0.99	0.99

	Kin	No								
	Cla	Transport								
	ID	Friend			Neutral			Foe		
	Dist	S	M	L	S	M	L	S	M	L
Pair	Yes	0.01	0.01	0.01	0.01	0.01	0.01	0.01	0.01	0.01
	No	0.99	0.99	0.99	0.99	0.99	0.99	0.99	0.99	0.99

	Kin	No								
	Cla	Civil								
	ID	Friend			Neutral			Foe		
	Dist	S	M	L	S	M	L	S	M	L
Pair	Yes	0.01	0.01	0.01	0.01	0.01	0.01	0.01	0.01	0.01
	No	0.99	0.99	0.99	0.99	0.99	0.99	0.99	0.99	0.99

[Kin-Kinematics, Cla-Class, Dist-Distance, S-Small, M-Medium, L-Large]

TABLE 11D.3
CPT for Along node

	Bear	Small											
	Cla	Fighter			Bomber			Transport			Civil		
	Dist	S	M	L	S	M	L	S	M	L	S	M	L
Along	Yes	0.1	0.05	0.05	0.4	0.1	0.05	0.8	0.2	0.1	0.99	0.4	0.2
	No	0.9	0.95	0.95	0.6	0.9	0.95	0.2	0.8	0.9	0.01	0.6	0.8

	Bear	Medium											
	Cla	Fighter			Bomber			Transport			Civil		
	Dist	S	M	L	S	M	L	S	M	L	S	M	L
Along	Yes	0.05	0.05	0.01	0.1	0.05	0.03	0.2	0.1	0.05	0.4	0.3	0.1
	No	0.95	0.95	0.99	0.9	0.95	0.97	0.8	0.9	0.95	0.6	0.7	0.9

	Bear	Large											
	Cla	Fighter			Bomber			Transport			Civil		
	Dist	S	M	L	S	M	L	S	M	L	S	M	L
Along	Yes	0.05	0.01	0.01	0.05	0.03	0.02	0.1	0.05	0.03	0.2	0.1	0.05
	No	0.95	0.99	0.99	0.95	0.97	0.98	0.9	0.95	0.97	0.8	0.9	0.95

[Cla-Class, Dist-Distance, Bear-Bearing, S-Small, M-Medium, L-Large]

TABLE 11D.4
CPT for Closing node

	Dist	Short								
	Br	Small			Medium			Large		
	Spe	S	M	L	S	M	L	S	M	L
Clo	Yes	0.5	0.6	0.7	0.6	0.7	0.8	0.7	0.8	0.99
	No	0.5	0.4	0.3	0.4	0.3	0.2	0.3	0.2	0.01

	Dist	Medium								
	Br	Small			Medium			Large		
	Spe	S	M	L	S	M	L	S	M	L
Clo	Yes	0.05	0.1	0.2	0.1	0.2	0.3	0.2	0.3	0.4
	No	0.95	0.9	0.8	0.9	0.8	0.7	0.8	0.7	0.6

	Dist	Large								
	Br	Small			Medium			Large		
	Spe	S	M	L	S	M	L	S	M	L
Clo	Yes	0.0005	0.005	0.01	0.005	0.01	0.05	0.01	0.05	0.1
	No	0.9995	0.995	0.99	0.995	0.99	0.95	0.99	0.95	0.9

[Clo-Closing, Spe-Speed, Dist-Distance, Bear-Bearing, S-Small, M-Medium, L-Large]

TABLE 11D.5
CPT for Attack node

	Cla	Fighter						Bomber					
	Id	Friend		Neutral		Foe		Friend		Neutral		Foe	
	Clo	Yes	No	Yes	No	Yes	No	Yes	No	Yes	No	Yes	No
Attack	Yes	0.01	0.01	0.05	0.05	0.99	0.01	0.01	0.01	0.05	0.05	0.9	0.1
	No	0.99	0.99	0.95	0.95	0.01	0.99	0.99	0.99	0.95	0.95	0.1	0.9

	Cla	Transport						Civil					
	Id	Friend		Neutral		Foe		Friend		Neutral		Foe	
	Clo	Yes	No	Yes	No	Yes	No	Yes	No	Yes	No	Yes	No
Attack	Yes	0.01	0.01	0.05	0.05	0.1	0.1	0.01	0.01	0.01	0.01	0.01	0.01
	No	0.99	0.99	0.95	0.95	0.9	0.9	0.99	0.99	0.99	0.99	0.99	0.99

[Cla-Class, Clo-Closing, S-Small, M-Medium, L-Large]

APPENDIX 11E: OFF-LINE RESULTS

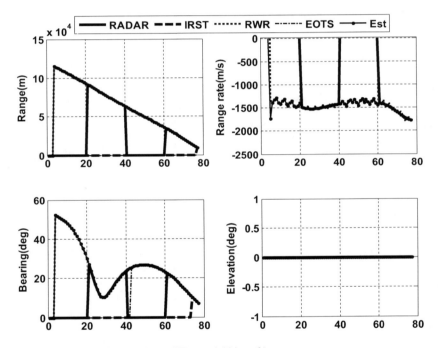

FIGURE 11E.1   Estimated values of Target 1 (Aircraft)

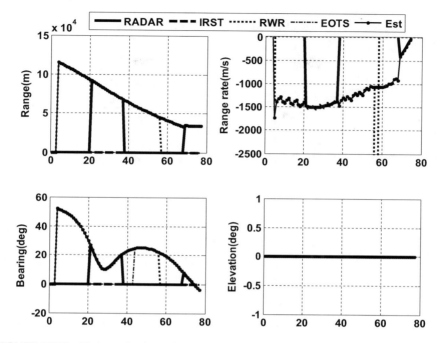

FIGURE 11E.2   Estimated values of Target 2 (Aircraft)

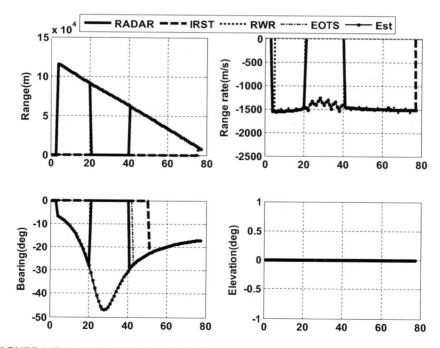

FIGURE 11E.3   Estimated values of Target 3 (Aircraft)

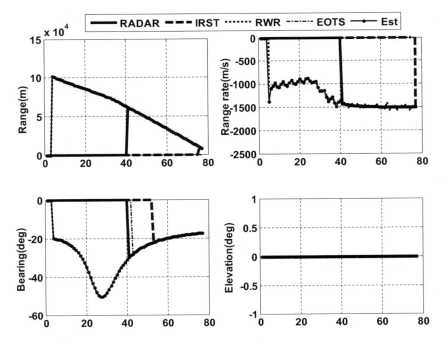

FIGURE 11E.4   Estimated values of Target 4 (Aircraft)

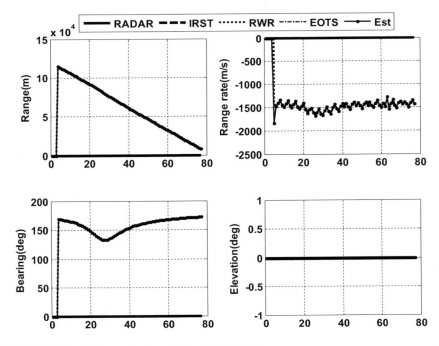

FIGURE 11E.5   Estimated values of Target 5 (Missile)

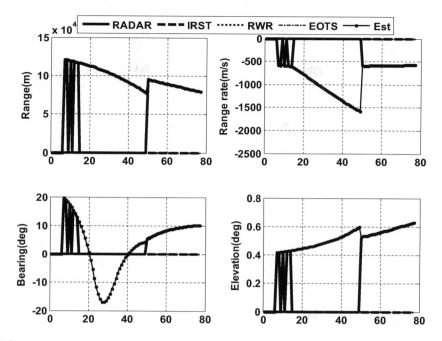

FIGURE 11E.6 Estimated values of Target 6 (Commercial Aircraft)

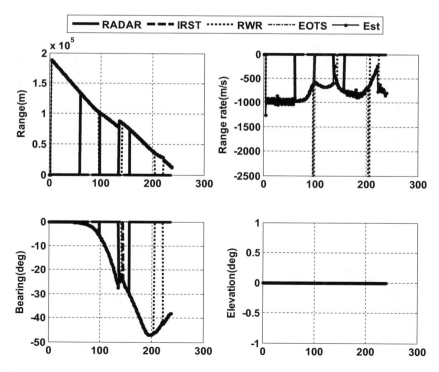

FIGURE 11E.7 Estimated values of Target 1 (Aircraft)

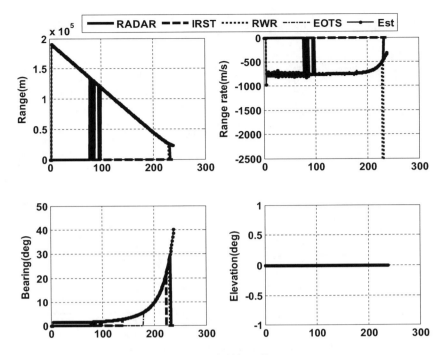

FIGURE 11E.8   Estimated values of Target 2 (Aircraft)

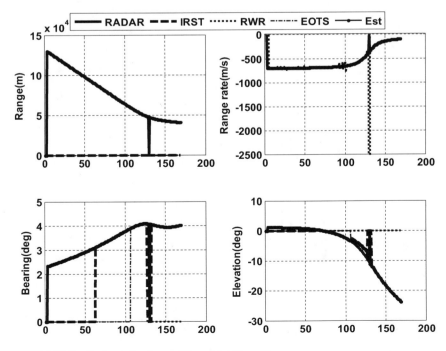

FIGURE 11E.9   Estimated values of Target 1 (Aircraft)

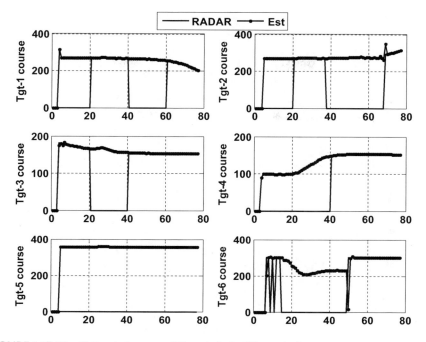

FIGURE 11E.10 Estimated course of Targets 1–6 of Scenario-1

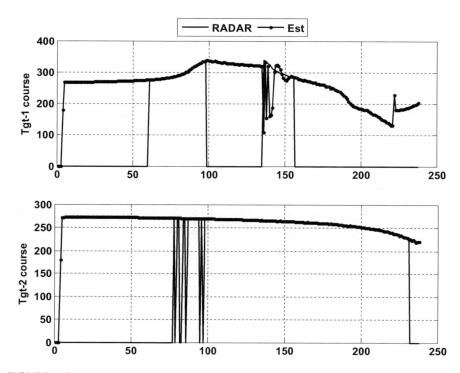

FIGURE 11E.11 Estimated course of Targets 1–2 of Scenario-2

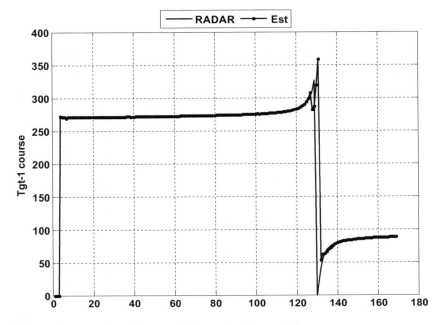

FIGURE 11E.12   Estimated course of Targets 1 of Scenario-3

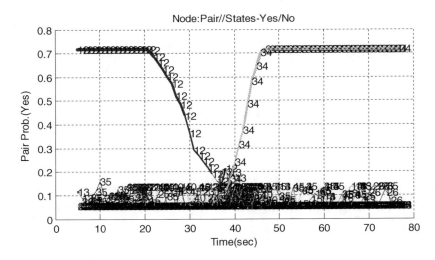

FIGURE 11E.13   Updated Pair Agent Probability of different combinations

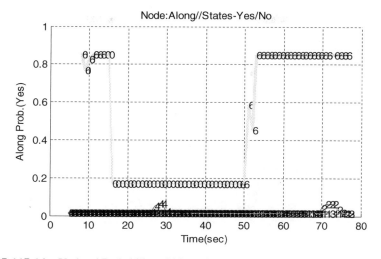

FIGURE 11E.14   Updated Probability of Along Agent

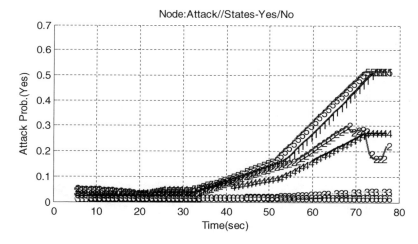

FIGURE 11E.15   Updated Probability of Attack Agent

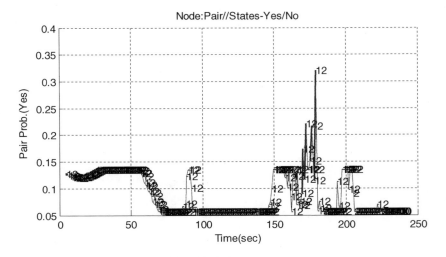

FIGURE 11E.16   Updated Probability of Pair Agent

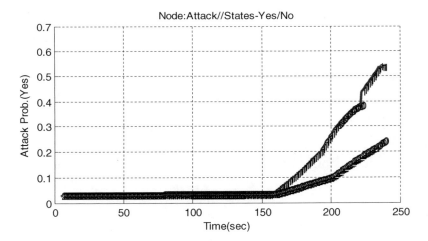

FIGURE 11E.17   Updated Probability of Attack Agent

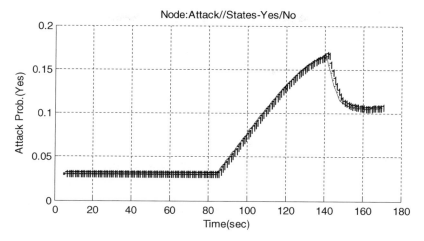

FIGURE 11E.18   Updated Probability of Attack Agent

APPENDIX 11F: HUGIN

HUGIN Developer 6.6 consists of C, C++, Java, and Active-X 6.4 API. These APIs are provided in the form of a library which can be interfaced or linked to an application program written using C, C++ or Java. Version C provides a function-oriented interface, whereas, C++ and Java provide object-oriented interfaces. The directory structure of HUGIN Developer 6.6 is shown in Figure 11F.1. From the figure, we can find out the directories of HUGIN C/C++/Java/Active-X 6.4 APIs. For example, HDE6.4CPP is for HUGIN C++ API. Similarly, HDE6.4C, HDE6.4J, and HDE6.4X are for C, Java, and Active-X APIs respectively. In this chapter, HUGIN C++ API 6.4 has been used for constructing and propagating the Bayesian network. The configurations required to realize the Bayesian network using the HUGIN developer are given in Table 11F.1.

HUGIN C++ API 6.4 consists of three directories: *Doc, Include* and *Lib*. The *Doc* directory is for API-manual; The *Include* directory contains the *"hugin"* header file, where the declaration/definition of HUGIN C++ APIs are provided. To use the C++ HUGIN API definitions in the user code, we must include the *"hugin"* header file (no suffix for that). The *Lib* directory has two directories *VC6* and *VC7* consisting of different versions of the library. Again, the *VC6* and *VC7* directories have two directories *Debug* and *Release* to represent which version of the C++ run time DLL is to be used. For example, when we select the *Debug* DLL configuration, a special debug version of the C++ run-time DLL will be linked to our application. Similarly, if we select the *Release* DLL configuration, a "release" version of the C++ runtime DLL will be used. Some of the HUGIN classes and their member functions are given in the Table 11F.2

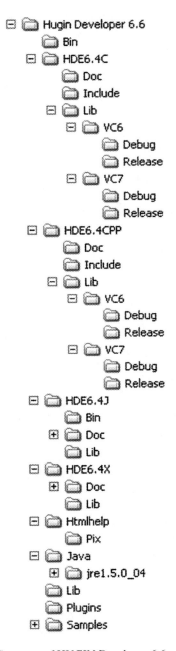

FIGURE 11F.1   Directory Structure of HUGIN Developer 6.6

TABLE 11F.1
Configurations

Processor	Intel Pentium Processor IV
Speed	100.0 Mbps
RAM	256 MB
Operating System	Windows XP
Environment	Visual Studio 6.0
Language	C++
Tools	HUGIN C++ API 6.4 and HUGIN GUI

TABLE 11F.2
Classes and member functions of Hugin

Classes	Member Functions
Domain	Domain (), compile (), propagate (), saveAsNet ()
Class	Class (), setName (), getName (), getNodes ()
Node	setName (), getName (), setLabel (), getLabel (), setPosition ()
NumberedDCNode	NumberedDCNode (), setNumberOfState (), setStateValue (), getStateValue ()
Table	setData (), getData ()
JunctionTree	hasTableToPropagate (), isLikelihoodPropagated (), getRoot (), getCliques ()
Cliques	getJunctionTree (), getMembers (), getNeughbour ()

11F.1 FUNCTIONALITIES OF THE CLASSES

Domain: A domain is the HUGIN representation of a Bayesian network. It is one of the principal structures in the HUGIN. The objects of the domain are used in the construction of a Bayesian network and influence diagram models in HUGIN. It must be constructed before any nodes belonging to the network. A new empty object is created by using the Domain class. We can also delete the created object by using the *delete* keyword. If creation fails, NULL is returned. When a domain is no longer needed, the internal memory used by the object can be reclaimed and made available for other purposes.

Class: The Class is one of the principal structures in HUGIN used for constructing the object-oriented Bayesian network and the influence diagram models. Like a Domain, Class has an associated set of nodes connected by links. A Class may also contain special nodes representing instances of other classes. Object-oriented models cannot be used directly for inference i.e. it should be instantiated into a Domain.

Node: Nodes are one of the fundamental objects used in the construction of Bayesian and influence diagrams. All nodes need a Domain* as arguments, that is, the Domain must exist before nodes can be created into it. The links between the nodes represents the relationships between the nodes. If a node doesn't have any parents (i.e. no links pointing towards it), the node will contain a marginal probability table. If a node does have parents (i.e. one or more links pointing towards it), the node will contain a conditional probability table (CPT).

Table: HUGIN uses Table for representing the marginal/conditional probability and utility potential of individual nodes. A potential is a function from the state space of a set of variables into the set of real numbers. A Table (CPT) is a representation of a potential.

JunctionTree: JunctionTree class represents the junction trees in the compiled Domain. We can access the junction tree of a compiled Domain using HUGIN API functions.

Cliques: It represents the cliques in the Junction tree. The cliques (maximal complete sets) of the triangulated graph are identified, and the collection of cliques is organized as a tree (with the cliques forming the nodes of the tree). Such a tree is called a Junction Tree. If the original network is disconnected there will be a tree for each connected component.
   'Type definitions' of HUGIN software are given below:

NumberList: NumberList definition is a standard C++ library vector of floating-point numbers for holding Table data.
NodeList: It is a standard C++ library container for holding nodes.
CliqueList: It is a standard C++ library container for holding cliques.
JunctionTreeList: It is a standard C++ library container for holding junction trees.
ClassList: It is a standard C++ library container for holding classes.
ExpressionList: It is a standard C++ library container for holding expressions.
AttributeList: It is a standard C++ library container for holding attributes.

11F.2 HUGIN DEVELOPER SETTINGS FOR WINDOWS PLATFORM

The Single-precision version of the Hugin API uses single-precision floating–point numbers to represent probabilities, whereas the double-precision version of the HAPI uses double-precision floating-point numbers to represent probabilities. The double-precision version will use twice as much space (RAM) as the single-precision version, but the computations will be more accurate. HUGIN developer settings for the single-precision version of the HUGIN API are as follows:

- For setting, we should know the HUGIN installation path (C:\Program Files\ Hugin Expert\Hugin Developer 6.6) and the active Configuration (either Debug or Release).
- Click "Settings" on the "Project" menu bar, click the "C/C++" tab and select "Preprocessor" in the "Category" box.
- Under "Preprocessor" category, add <installation path>\HDE6.4CPP\Include to the "Additional include directories" box. The *Include* directory contains *hugin* header file. (Refer Figure 11F.2).
- Click "Settings" on the "project" menu bar, click the "Link" tab, and select the "Input" in the "Category" box:
   a) Add <installation path>\HDE6.4CPP\LibVC6\(Configuration) to the "Additional library path" box.
   b) Add hugincpp.lib to the "Object\library modules" list. (Figure 11F.3).

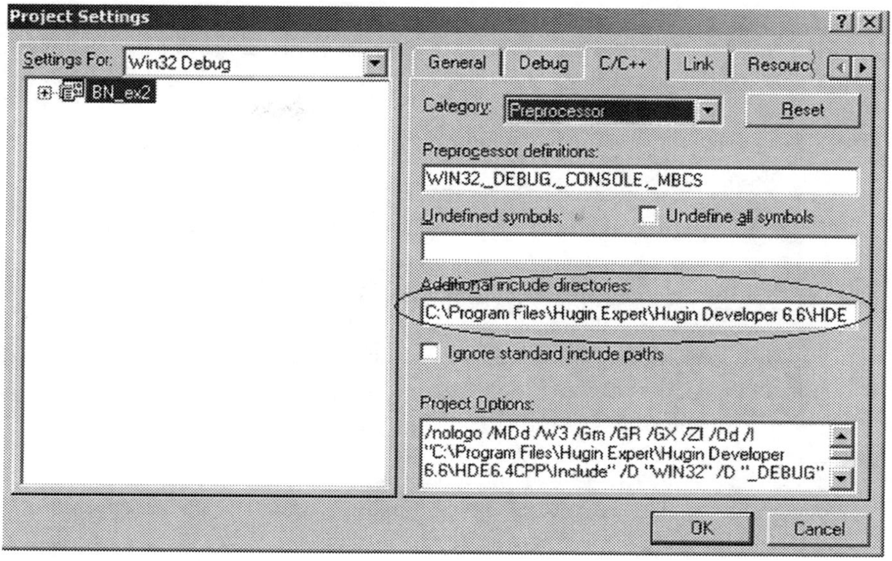

FIGURE 11F.2 Preprocessor Setting

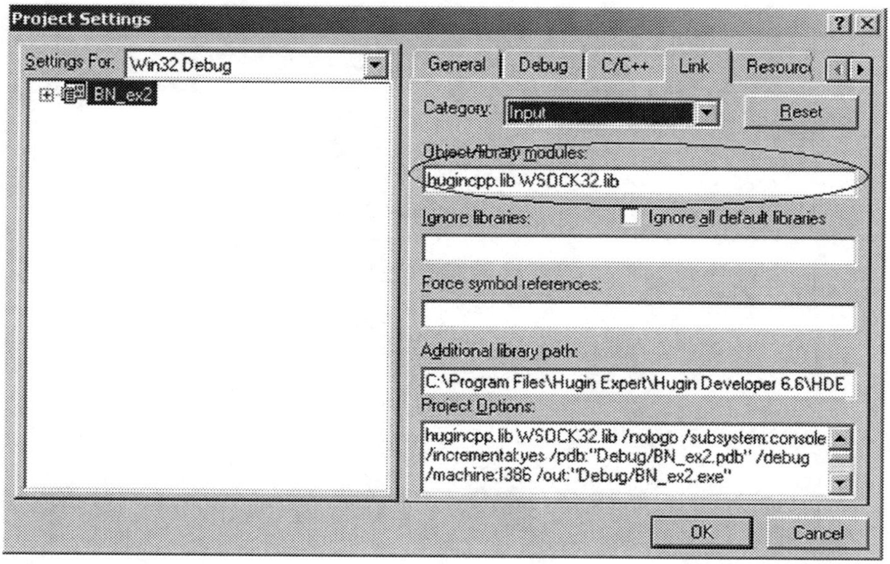

FIGURE 11F.3 Input Setting

Note 1: to use the double-precision version of the HUGIN C++ API, we must specify the preprocessor symbol H_DOUBLE during compilation (this is usually done by giving the option-DH_DOUBLE to the compiler). On the Windows platform, each library consists of two files: an import library and a DLL. For the single-precision library, the import library is named hugincpp.lib and the DLL is named hugincpp.dll. Similarly for the double-precision library, the import library is named hugincpp2.lib and the DLL is hugincpp2.dll.

Note 2: To use network facility of Windows Socket, we must add 'WSOCK32.lib" file to the "object\library modules" list.

- Click "Settings" on the "Project" menu. Click the "C/C++ "tab, and select "Code Generation" in the "Category " box.
    c) If (Configuration) is Debug, make sure "Debug Multithreaded DLL" is selected in the "Use run-time library" box (Figure 11F.4).
    d) If (Configuration) is Release, make sure "Multithreaded DLL" is selected in the "Use run-time library" box.
- Click "Settings" on the "Project" menu, Click the "C/C++ "tab, and select "C++ Language "in the "Category" box (Figure 11F.5).
    e) Make sure "Enable exception handling" is selected.
    f) Make sure "Enable Run-Time Type Information (RTTI)" is selected.
- HUGIN C++ API identifiers are defined within the HAPI namespace [1]. In order to access these entities, either we have to use HAPI::<API identifiers> or we have to place the *<using namespace HAPI>* declaration before the first use of C++ API entities.

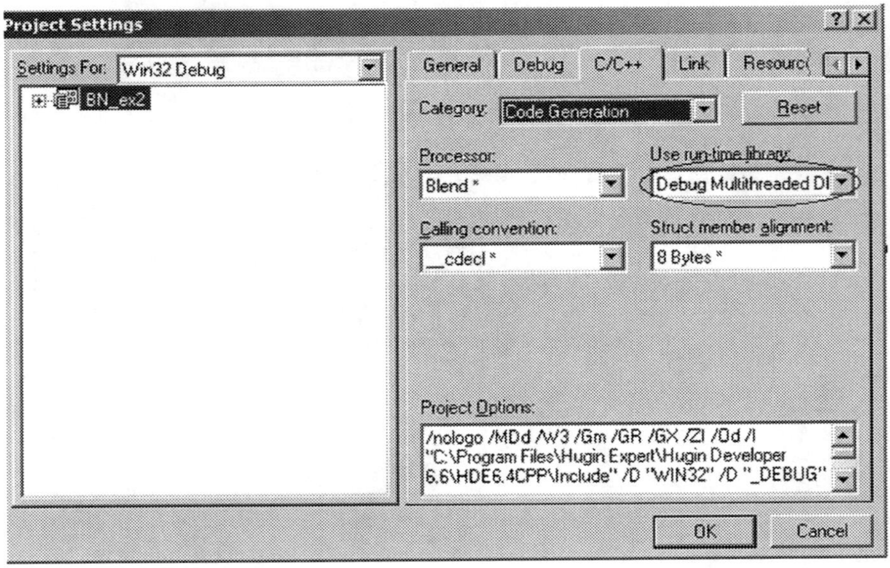

FIGURE 11F.4 Code Generation Setting

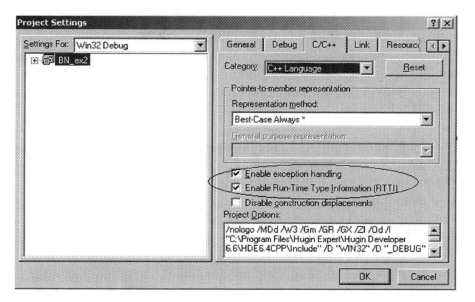

FIGURE 11F.5   C++ Language Setting

11F.3 REALIZATION OF BAYESIAN NETWORK USING HUGIN GUI

HUGIN GUI is a graphics-based utility to create and propagate the Bayesian network models. It can be operated in two different configurations, namely, Edit mode and Run mode [1]. In Edit Mode, nodes can be created and linked, states or actions through new evidence can be specified and finally conditional probability/utility tables can be entered using a window, menu and mouse driven interfaces. In order to propagate the constructed network, HUGIN GUI should be in Run mode, where, HDE is executed to propagate the new evidence from information nodes to the hypothesis node. Figure 11F.6 shows a typical threat assessment BN to compute the threat probability.

SPEED and ACTION are the Independent nodes or Information (input) nodes. It is assumed that input SPEED has two states *High* and *Low* with probability values of 0.2 and 0.8 respectively. Similarly, the input ACTION has two states *Away* and *Towards* with values of 0.1 and 0.9 respectively. The intermediate node of a BN is TYPE that has two states: *Fighter* and *Transport*. It depends upon the SPEED node. It is assumed that, if an aircraft speed is *High* then the chance of it being a *Fighter* plane is more; if the speed of the aircraft is *Low*, then there is a chance of it being a *Transport* plane. At the TYPE node, we can see that there is reasoning involved. According to Bayesian terminology it is represented by the CPT. Finally, the THREAT node is also known as the Hypothesis node. It has 2 dependencies, TYPE and ACTION. It has two states, *Yes* and *No*. The conditional probability values for a THREAT node are given in Table 11F.3; these values are based on intuition and could be altered based on the feedback from experienced pilots for typical combat situations.

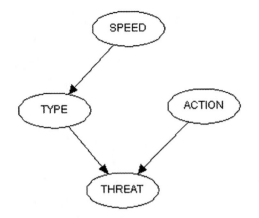

FIGURE 11F6   Typical Threat Assessment Bayesian Network

TABLE 11F.3
Conditional probability values

	ACTION			
	Away		Towards	
THREAT	**Fighter**	**Transport**	**Fighter**	**Transport**
Yes	0.75	0.02	0.9	0.6
No	0.25	0.98	0.1	0.4

11F.4 CONSTRUCTION OF BAYESIAN NETWORK BY USING HUGIN GUI

The steps used to construct a BN using the HUGIN GUI are described next.

STEP 1: OPEN A NETWORK WINDOW

The execution of the HUGIN GUI opens the main window containing an empty network, named "unnamed.net" which provides an environment for construction and propagation of the BN. Figure 11F.7 shows the 'unnamed' empty network with the provision of a *Toolbar* that constrains various tools such as: *'network properties', 'node properties', 'select tool', 'discrete chance tool', 'link tool', 'show node tables'*, and many more.

STEP 2: ADDING NODES TO THE NETWORK WINDOW

In this step, the network is formed by adding nodes into the opened empty network window. The procedure to add nodes to the network is:

- Select the *"Discrete chance tool"* in the *Tool Bar* of the *"unnamed.net"* network window.
- Click somewhere in the empty network.

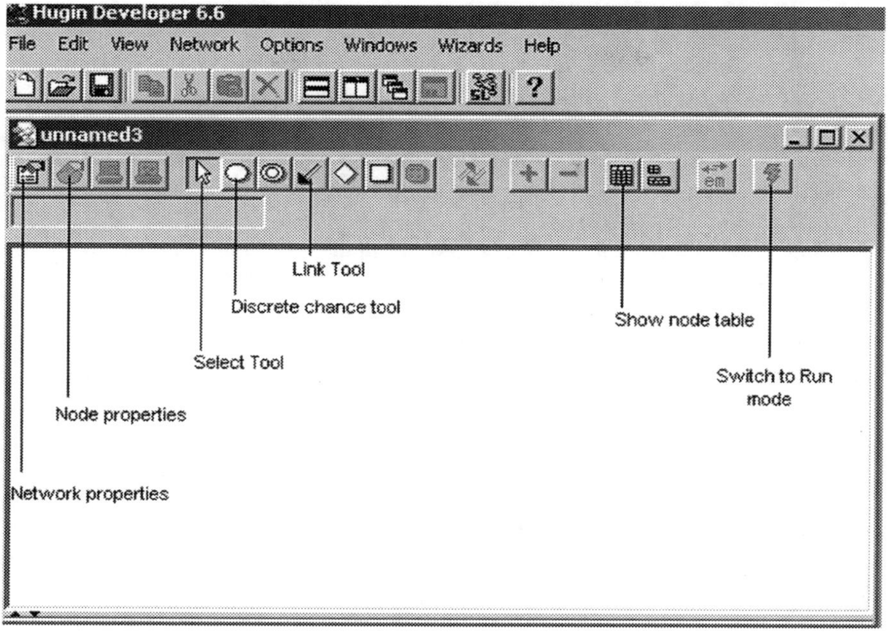

FIGURE 11F.7   Empty Network Window Containing a Tool Bar

A node labeled "C1" appears when we click in the empty network, which is re-named as "SPEED" using the steps:

- Select the node with the mouse cursor.
- Enter "Node Properties" by pressing the node properties tool.
- Change both the "Name" and "Label" fields to "SPEED".
- Press the "OK" button.

The same procedure is used for ACTION, TYPE and THREAT nodes.

STEP 3: ADDING LINKS TO NODES

So far we have created a network containing the required nodes. In this step, the links between the appropriate nodes are provided using the steps:

- Press the "*link tool*".
- Drag a link from "SPEED" to "TYPE" with the left mouse button while holding down the "Shift" key. The "Shift" key ensures that we can add more links without having to press the "*link tool*" again.
- Similarly drag a link from "TYPE" to "THREAT" and "ACTION" to "THREAT".

STEP 4: ADDING STATES TO NODES

This step is for setting the state labels for each node. *Table pane* is opened by clicking the *"Show node tables"* tool. "SPEED" node states are specified using the steps:

- Select the node "SPEED" by holding "ctrl" key and press the left mouse button while the cursor is inside the node. As a result, the CPT for "SPEED" gets displayed in the *Tables Pane*.
- Click the field containing the text "State1" in the CPT in the *Tables Pane*.
- Type the text "High" in the field to give the state this name.
- Click the field containing the text "State2" in the CPT.
- Type the text "Low" in the field.
- Similarly, the ACTION, TYPE and THREAT node state labels are added.

STEP 5: ENTERING CPT VALUES TO NODES

The individual nodes CPT table is selected by holding "Ctrl+" key and pressing the particular node. The CPT values are entered into the table which is displayed in the *Table Pane*. For example, the THREAT node CPT values are entered as specified in Table 11F.3. Click the field representing "THREAT = Yes"

- Enter the values.
- Click the field representing "THREAT = No".
- Enter the values.

Figure 11F.8 shows the CPT of the THREAT node. Similarly, SPEED (0.2, 0.8), ACTION (0.1, 0.9) and TYPE CPT values are entered. After entering CPT values, the constructed network is saved using user specified filename.

STEP 6: COMPILATION AND EXECUTION OF THE NETWORK

In the *Run mode*, the *network window* is divided into two sub-windows portioned by a vertical bar. The left window corresponds to *Node List Pane* and right window to *Network Pane*. We can view the updated probabilities of a node by expanding the node in the *Node List Pane*. We can expand or collapse a node by clicking its *expand* or *collapse* icon in the *Node List Pane*, by double clicking its node symbol in the *Node List Pane*, or by selecting (deselecting) it in the *Network Pane*. We can also expand or collapse all the nodes at once by pressing the *"Expand node list"* or *"Collapse node list"* tool in the *Tool bar* just to the right of the *node properties* tool. It is observed from Figure 11F.8 that SPEED and ACTION node values are not changed since they belong to information nodes. After the propagation of BN the states of TYPE (intermediate node) and THREAT (hypothesis node) nodes are changed.

Example 11F.1 demonstrates the BN construction using HUGIN API. The HUGIN settings are a must for all the examples given below.

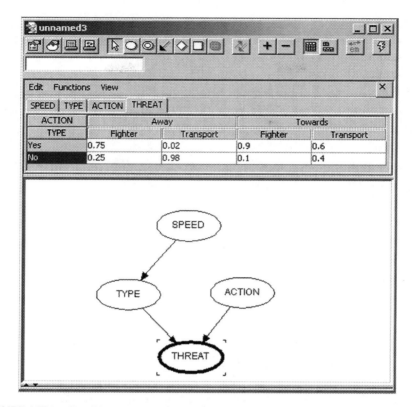

ACTION	Away		Towards	
TYPE	Fighter	Transport	Fighter	Transport
Yes	0.75	0.02	0.9	0.6
No	0.25	0.98	0.1	0.4

FIGURE 11F.8 Conditional Probability Table of Threat Node

Example 11F.1: Construction of BN Model for Threat Assessment

The following steps are used to construct the BN using HUGIN C++ API.

STEP 1: Construction of Nodes

The object named "domain" of class "Domain" is constructed using the syntax:

Domain *domain;
Domain = new domain ();

Thereafter individual nodes are constructed by using the class named "NumberedDCNode". For example, the SPEED node is constructed using the definition:

NumberedDCNode *speed = new NumberedDCNode (domain);

A similar procedure is followed to construct TYPE, ACTION, and THREAT nodes.

STEP 2: Settings

The following functions, for the SPEED node, are used to set the name, label, number of states, position, state values and state labels of the node:

setName ();	*: speed->setName ("SPEED");*
setLabel ();	*: speed->setLabel ("SPEED");*
setNumberOfState ();	*: speed->setNumberOfStates (2);*
setPosition ();	*: speed->setPosition (150, 200);*
setStateValue ();	*: speed->setStateValue (i, i);*
setStateLabel ();	*: speed->setStateLabel (0,"High");*

Similar procedure is used for TYPE, ACTION, and THREAT nodes.

STEP 3: Connectivity

The *addParent ()* function is used to provide connectivity between the nodes. For TYPE node, SPEED is the parent node and for the THREAT node, TYPE and ACTION are the parents:

type->addParent (speed);
threat->addParent (type);
threat->addParent (action);

STEP 4: Input to Information Nodes

The information nodes are connected to sensors by an interface known as a Fuzzy Event Detector (FED). In this example, it is assumed that the states value of information nodes SPEED and ACTION are provided by FED. The class *Table* is used to set the table's data of each input node. For example, the High and Low values of SPEED input node are set as follows:

Table *table = *speed->getTable ();*
NumberList data = table->*getData ();*
data [0] = 0.2;
data [1] = 0.8;
table->*setData ();*

Similarly, the ACTION node values are assigned with the values of 0.1 (away) and 0.9 (towards).

STEP 5: Entering CPT Values to Nodes (Intermediate and Hypotheses)

This step is used to enter the CPT values for intermediate and hypotheses nodes. For example, THREAT is the hypotheses node having 2 states: *Yes* and *No*. It has 2 parents: TYPE and ACTION.

CPT = THREAT node states * dependent node states (TYPE and ACTION)
        = THREAT node states * 2 * 2
        = 2 * 4.

So, the size of array should be 2 × 4.

```
Table *table = threat->getTable ();
NumberList data = table->getData ();
        double arr1 [2][4] = {    {0.75, 0.02, 0.9, 0.6}, (values are from Table 2)
                                  {0.25, 0.98, 0.1, 0.4}
                              };
int m1 = 0;
for (int c1 = 0; c1<4; c1++)
  {
        for (int r1 = 0; r1<2; r1++)
        {
                data [m1] = arr1 [r1][c1];
                m1 = m1 + 1;
        }
  }
table->setData (data);
```

Similarly TYPE node conditional probability values are entered.

STEP 6: Compilation

The constructed Bayesian network is compiled by using the compile () function.

$$d omain->compile ();$$

STEP 7: Propagation

After the compilation process the BN is propagated using the propagate () function:

$$domain->propagate ();$$

The propagated BN is saved in ".net" format using the saveAsNet () function:

$$domain->saveAsNet ("BNNet.net");$$

After the propagation of BN, SPEED and ACTION node state values are not changed since they belong to information nodes. Only the TYPE (intermediate node) and THREAT (hypothesis node) node state values are changed. The updated probability values are displayed on the MS DOS screen by using *getLabel (), getName (), and getBelief ()* functions. We can compare the output of the BN using HUGIN API with the output of the BN using HUGIN GUI. Also, we can see the saved constructed Bayesian network by opening the 'BNNet.net' file. It looks exactly the same as the constructed Bayesian network by HUGIN GUI. Refer to Figure 11F.9 for the textual display of HUGIN output.

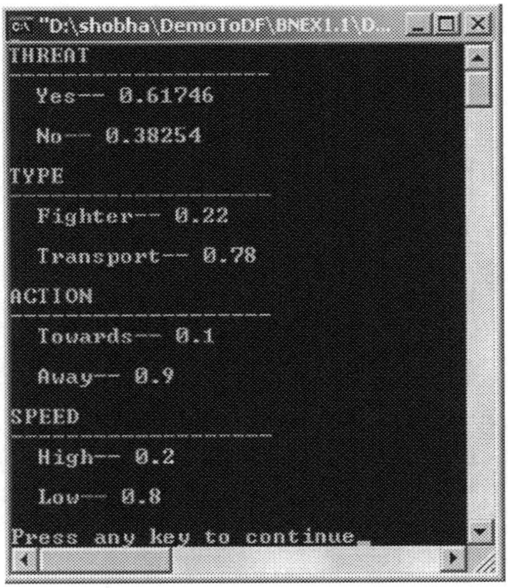

FIGURE 11F.9   Textual Display of HUGIN Output

APPENDIX 11G: FLOW-CHART

The flow chart of the HUGIN for the construction of a Bayesian Network is given in Figure 11G.1.

EXERCISES

    11.1. How can the Situation Assessment System (SAS) reduce the pilot work load?

    11.2. What is decision logic for data fusion and what are the parameters to construct the decision logic?

    11.3. What is difference in the working principles of Radar and IR? Which is preferred for use in close combat?

    11.4. What is RWR and why does it play an important role in modern warfare?

    11.5. What are the various sub-systems of SAS?

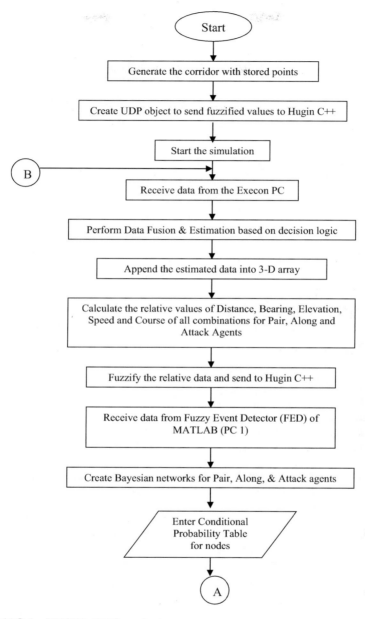

FIGURE 11G.1 HUGIN : BN flow chart

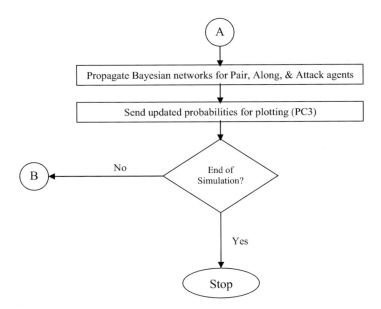

FIGURE 11G.1   (Continued)

REFERENCES

1. HUGIN Expert A\S www.HUGIN.dk. Accessed in Sept 2007
2. Zacharias, G. L., Miao, A. X., Illgen, C. and Yara, J. M. "Sample: Situation awareness model for pilot in-the-loop evaluation"
3. Mulgund, S., Rinkus, G., and Friskie, J. "Olipsa: On-line intelligent processor for situation assessment, Annual symposium and exhibition on situation awareness in the tactical air environment, June 3–4 1997, Patuxent River, MD.
4. Das, B. "Representing uncertainties using Bayesian networks", Information technology division, Electronics and surveillance research laboratory, Department of defense, Defense science & technology organization (DSTO), Salisbury south Australia, Dec. 1999.
5. Ivanson, J. Master's thesis entitled "Situation assessment in a stochastic environment using Bayesian networks", Division of Automatic control, Department of electrical engineering, Linkoping University, March 2002.
6. Kashyap, S. K., NarayanaRao, P., and Gopalaratnam, G. Fuzzy Logic and Bayesian Networks Based SAS in Air-to-Air Combat Scenarios, Project Document FC 0706, CSIR-NAL, Bangalore, November 2007.

12 Approaches of Artificial Intelligence-based Situation Awareness and Assessment

12.1 PHYSIOLOGICAL CUES FOR ASSESSMENT AND SITUATION AWARENESS

Situation AWareness (SAW) has three levels which operate sequentially [1]: i) Level 1: **perception**, several elements in the environment must be perceived or seen correctly; ii) Level 2: **cognition**, once perceived, these elements must be interpreted and understood correctly, i.e., they must be recognized and validated; and iii) Level 3: **application** or **prediction**, once the elements are interpreted and understood correctly, they can be applied to events or they can be used to predict future events.

12.1.1 REASONS FOR ERRORS IN SITUATION AWARENESS

A SAW error taxonomy is described as follows:

a) Loss of Level 1 SAW (~76.3%): i) Information is not available (11.6%): due to system and design failures, failure of communication, failure of crew to perform the required task; ii) Information is difficult to detect (11.6%): poor runway markings, poor lighting, noise in the cockpit; iii) Information is not observed (37.2%): omission from scan attention narrowing, task related distractions, workload and other distractions; iv) Misperception of information (8.7%): prior expectations; and v) Memory error (11.1%): due to the distractions and higher work load.

b) Loss of Level 2 SAW (~20.3%): i) Lack of (or incomplete) mental model (3.5%): automated systems, unfamiliar airspace; ii) Incorrect mental model (6.4%): mismatching information to expectations of model or model of usual system; and iii) Over reliance on default values in the mental model (4.7%): general expectations of system behaviour; and

c) Loss of Level 3 SAW (~3.4%): i) Lack of/incomplete mental model (0.4%); ii) Over projection of current trends (1.1%); and iii) Other (1.9%).

DOI: 10.1201/9781003370413-12

12.1.2 PHYSIOLOGICAL CUES

Physical measures in SAW are: aircraft speed, altitude, attitude, heading angle/direction and other parameters related to aircraft performance. Physiological measures are: body temperature, heart rate, eye movement, and facial expression. Sudden fluctuations in these physiological parameters may indicate changes in a person's/pilot's psychological state and would suggest that a pilot is losing situational awareness.

One can investigate the use of physiological parameters like: i) brain waves, ii) heart waves, iii) heart rate, iv) body temperature, v) eye movement, and vi) blink rate, etc., to determine loss of situational awareness. However, most of these techniques to monitor such parameters are somewhat invasive for a pilot in the cockpit and require measuring devices to be attached to the pilot's body. This has the potential to cause significant interference to the pilot during flight operations and would introduce further forms of human error. Other physiological factors that may be monitored with a somewhat less invasive technique are eye movement, pupil dilation, blink rate, heart rate and facial expression.

Initially, one can focus on eye movement, in particular saccades, fixations, and pupil dilation. Saccades are quick and jerky movements with rapid shifting from point to point. Fixations are events where gaze becomes steady or fixed for a short period of time. Pupil dilation is indicated by a change in pupil intensity, shape and size. Fixations with a longer duration than the standard fixation or pupil dilation, can indicate instability in the psycho-physiological state of the pilot [1]. The sequence of fixation, fixation duration and locus are closely related to the cognitive process during a cognitive task.

It has been found from the literature (and maybe conversations with pilots) that two potential precursors to the loss of SAW are attention focusing and attention blurring. When a crew member begins to lose SAW, they tend to either i) concentrate (fixate) on one instrument or problem and exclude all other information including communication between other flight crew, or ii) they tend to try and scan many more instruments than necessary, including attempting to access as much information as possible.

The physiological parameters including eye fixation duration, fixation loci and pupil dilation can be used to determine the state of the SAW trainee. A flight simulator and eye tracking device can be used to record sample gaze patterns from trainee pilots.

12.1.3 A PROBABLE DESIGN FOR AN INTELLIGENT SOFTWARE AGENT

A commercially available eye tracker can be used in the project to provide gaze positions. Eye tracker data can be translated into gaze fixation patterns using fixation identification algorithms.

The three algorithms that can be investigated are: i) A dispersion based algorithm that uses a spatial constraint on pilot gaze positions, such that different gaze positions within a prescribed area become part of the same single fixation if the gaze duration is greater than a set time interval (100–200 ms); ii) A velocity based algorithm that considers the speed at which fixation loci change and where the velocity is computed by taking the distance between a locus and its neighbor divided by the time difference. Fixations are grouped together based on velocity profile; and iii) A Hidden Markov Model (HMM) that uses a statistical model to determine the most likely hidden sequence of states or features, from the observable data or signal. The features are defined based on specific classification parameters, for example, using the velocity feature, eye gaze events, that have a small velocity, have a higher probability of being a fixation event and a lower probability of being a saccade event.

Then, such a SAW agent will learn to identify pilot eye movement patterns that are consistent with a student losing SAW from the comparison of simulator data and knowledge of domain experts. The two basic learning methods for an agent are: a) unsupervised learning, and b) supervised learning. The SAW training/teaching agent will utilize supervised learning and will use a database of eye gaze patterns, established in consultation with domain experts, to recognise patterns in the input data so as to classify pilot's gaze behaviour as examples of good or poor SAW. This will be passed in real time to the trainee pilot to indicate their level of SAW. The simulator sessions can also be recorded and the feedback can be used as an enhanced learning or revision tool.

In case of an emergency the pilots will tend to scan many more instruments than necessary failing to register the information on critical instruments; or they will fixate on a particular instrument and fail to look at other situation critical instruments. This visual behaviour can be picked up by the eye tracker and processed by the SAW agent. The agent will, then, classify the behaviour as safe or unsafe and alert the trainee pilot so that they may increase their ability to learn from the situation. The whole process is intended to occur in real time, on-line and be non-intrusive and provide a SAW learning tool that may be widely accepted by trainee pilots.

12.2 SITUATION ASSESSMENT IN SEARCH AND RESCUE OPERATIONS

The coordination of a Search And Rescue (SAR) operation is a highly knowledge intensive task [2]. Once, information is received about a possible air incident, for example, a plane crash in a hazardous area, a Rescue Coordination Center (RCC) controller sets out a search operation to determine the cause of the incident. This involves checking on various information sources from: i) air traffic controllers, ii) satellite data, iii) Emergency Locator Transmitter (ELT) signals, and iv) the relatives of the pilot involved. If the controller has to deal with more than one case at a time, then it requires continual re-prioritization of tasks and resources. In such situations, it is likely that some important tasks might be overlooked by even an experienced SAR controller. Here, we describe a problem-solving model for building an intelligent multi-agent system to assist the air SAR controller in situation assessment.

In the agent-based SAR, the agents continuously monitor the coordinator and the information sources as a situation unfolds, and provide user-friendly messages to the human controller when he/she misses some critical actions in solving the problem. The agent model is based on a combination of analogical reasoning based on similarities, and Hierarchical Task Network (HTN) planning techniques: analogical reasoning is advantageous in approximate reasoning from the current situations in real time, and is good in dealing with loosely structured descriptions of domain knowledge; and the HTN provides a formalism for organizing tasks and their relations in a hierarchical and temporal framework. The combination of these two techniques provides an underlying model for solving the SA problem. Here, one uses cases to describe hypotheses and to encapsulate information-gathering queries for identifying the correct hypothesis. The information gathering task is known as 'Communications Search' (COMSEARCH) in the SAR domain. Once a hypothesis is identified as a candidate, a task network model for the information gathering queries encapsulated within the case is retrieved. The agent is goal-directed, autonomous and capable of learning new knowledge to adapt itself.

12.2.1   SA IN SAR OPERATION FUNCTIONALITY

The role of the RCC is to coordinate, control and conduct search and rescue operations in Canada's area of responsibility: i) When a call is received (first time), the operation enters an uncertainty phase, the air SAR controller will collect the information about the details of the flight plan and people involved, a request may be sent out to different agencies, airports and vessels in response to an ELT signal for more information to verify the exact location and cause of the signal, the air SAR controller conducts what is known as the communication search using telecommunication channels such as the telephone or satellite information to obtain more detail; ii) If the information is not enough, the operation will progress into the alert phase whereby the operators will expand the search area and means and alert various search and rescue agencies; iii) If a certain amount of time has passed after the uncertainty phase without obtaining more information about the plane, the operation enters the distress phase, in this phase the air SAR controller should develop a search plan and task any additional resources to assist in the plan, finally, when the details of the incident are known, a rescue plan must be developed and monitored by the air SAR controller.

A case report will be filed in the end, and news dispatches will be sent out to various media agencies before the case is closed. A first indication of trouble can be signaled by a phone call reporting on overdue personnel, an ELT report received by a high-flying aircraft, a satellite or an airport tower operator. In addition, a search and rescue satellite may report the reception of an ELT signal when it passes over the area in question.

Over 90% of the cases are false alarms. If the controller becomes convinced that the missing plane is in distress, then he/she may initiate the tasks associated with the distress phase which consists of planning, coordinating, and monitoring search missions. Once the cause of the incident and the location of the aircraft are determined, an air SAR controller mobilizes and monitors the rescue process. Tasks are to notify various agencies involved, including hospitals and police, the relatives and dispatching planes or helicopters to the crash site. An Air SAR case often requires extensive investigation and complex hypothesis generation. The controller keeps constant contact with the search crew. This case is more complicated because the information requested by the controller went out on several channels. Additional information from the air traffic control tower indicated the possibility of a stroke, which prompted further actions by the controller. In this example, the SA aspects are: i) the hypotheses formation and elimination for the cause of the incident (stroke), and ii) the communications search plan developed for the retained hypothesis (crash due to stroke).

An intelligent agent system to monitor and assist the air SAR controllers in their SA work will be an autonomous agent running in the background performing tasks such as monitoring the COMSEARCH activities of the controller and various information sources, and providing assistance in the form of reminders and checklists for critical information gathering tasks that might have been overlooked. The agent can make the current candidate hypothesis list explicit for the controller who is often overloaded with a vast amount of information.

The agent-based system will benefit the SAR controller in several ways: i) Because the agent is constantly monitoring a variety of information sources, it can help filter out a large quantity of irrelevant information, and help the air SAR controller concentrate on the critical information only; ii) Given the overwhelming workload during the high season for air incidents, the agent system can help improve the accuracy and shorten the time required for assessing a case; and iii) For junior air SAR controllers, the agent-based system can become a handy decision support system and a tutoring system. It is expected that the learning speed of the new (RCC-) controllers will be improved with the help of this agent system.

12.2.2 AGENT MODEL

The main aim of the agent system is to plan the information queries. The action and query model in the proposal bears similarity to a system designed for fighting forest fires, with a major difference being that the present system is mainly aimed at SA as opposed to resource and strategic planning.

12.2.2.1 A Process Model

The agent system functions as follows: i) Upon receiving an initial indication of a problem, the available relevant information is input into the system. The system retrieves a collection of similar hypothesis objects (corresponding to different scenarios describing the situation) constructed from previous situations having similar initial information. These consist of the hypotheses H1, H2, ..., Hn which can be used to characterize the current situation, where each Hi provides a plausible cause for the current case such as "plane crashed"; and ii) then, the system enters a cycle in which: a) it identifies (from the case base) the communications search tasks described by the task network, associated with each hypothesis object, b) performs these tasks (or recommends to the user the execution of some of these tasks), and c) then uses the results to rank and retrieve the current and new hypotheses.

A hypothesis object is like an object in Object-Oriented Technology (OOT). It consists of both the problem attributes used to describe the context of a situation and the associated hypothesis-evaluation and task-suggestion methods to operate on them. In particular, a hypothesis object consists of: i) a hypothesis for the cause of the incident, b) a Hierarchical Task Network (HTN) for the communications search used to confirm the hypothesis and assess the situation, c) a record of executed communications search steps for the current hypothesis object, and the communications search steps yet to be executed for further confirming the hypothesis, d) an evaluation function of priorities for not-yet executed communications search tasks, and e) indices with weights attached to the expected values of the answers to the queries that can be used to provide a similarity based ranking for the hypothesis object.

12.2.2.2   Hypotheses

A hypothesis is a plausible cause and outcome for the case. The space of hypotheses naturally forms a hierarchy. In the air SAR domain, some of the hypotheses are:

    i)   Overdue aircraft triggered hypotheses: a) refueling midway, b) landed somewhere else, c) never took off, and d) crashed; and

    ii) ELT signal triggered hypotheses: a) ELT left on by the pilot, b) crashed, and c) ELT malfunctioning.

The SA phase of the SAR operation involves finding out which of the hypotheses holds for the current situation, as well as the context, such as the number of people on board and the seriousness of the problem, in which such a hypothesis holds. Initially none of the hypotheses relevant to the current case can be ruled out. More information will be requested by the RCC controller in order to narrow down the hypothesis space. For example, an air SAR controller may check the weather condition to see whether the likelihood of a crash is high given an overdue report. At the same time, a request will be sent out to get the flight plan of the pilot in order to find all airports where the pilot might have landed, and so on.

12.2.2.3   Hierarchical Task Networks

The basic structure of the SA part of the RCC controller's tasks can be broken down into a hierarchically structured set of tasks. At a very high level, the tasks correspond directly to the steps defined in the standard operation procedures such as the National SAR Manual. At the next level down, the tasks are broken into several detailed sub-steps. An example of the top two levels of the hierarchy associated with SA is given next.

    Manage and collect case information:

    i)   receive and analyse the initial notification: a) detect new case, and b) manage general occurrences; and

    ii) collect and evaluate information: a) situation refinement, b) determine POW, c) communication search, and d) update the case.

Although SA for all cases follow the same pattern of tasks as presented above, the lower levels of the task networks associated with the communications search efforts differ depending on the hypothesis of the incident involved. For example, the communications search task hierarchy triggered by an overdue aircraft report has a different, although overlapping, set of tasks from those involved with an ELT signal case.

These two task networks are separately associated with different hypothesis objects. For example, the ELT task network is associated with an ELT related hypothesis such as ELT-malfunction and crashing-aircraft. Similarly, the task network for overdue aircrafts is associated with overdue hypotheses, including overdue-due-to-crash and overdue-landing-elsewhere hypotheses. Take, for example, the task "verify parked airplanes". This task can be accomplished in several ways, including either checking with the airport security authority or checking directly with the air traffic control tower. Which method to use for accomplishing a particular task depends on the cost of using the method, the reliability of the information source, and potential delays and the availability of the resources. Therefore, a particular function of the agent is to plan the method in which to expand a task in order to maximize the information gain in a minimal time frame under the circumstances.

12.2.2.4   Indexes and Their Weighted Connections

For the RCC controller to assess the current situation, rank the remaining hypotheses, and weigh the next steps, a channel must exist between the known facts and knowledge, and the system stored HTN's and hypotheses. This channel is provided by a layer of indexes. The index structure is very similar to that of a case-based reasoning system. Its main purpose is to enable a system to perform approximate and similarity-based reasoning, a key part of CBR. A key issue here is real-time performance.

In a hypothesis retrieval and ranking cycle, the indexes located on the first level have connection weights that can directly affect the result of matching and ranking the hypotheses on the second level. The process of retrieval is very similar to that in a case-based reasoning process, in which a CBR retrieval process scans a case base for the most similar cases to a new problem, ranks the high-ranking hypotheses in response to the input index values. For each candidate hypothesis object, an evaluation of its similarity with the current situation will be conducted. This evaluation will consider the weights of the matching indexes. The highest ranked cases will then be presented to a task manager for selecting the next tasks to perform. In the SAR domain, the indexes for a similarity-based evaluation can be performed based on past cases and the current problem instance which is a SAR case with all its known facts and unknown facts. We consider all the tasks in a task network to be potential indexes to any hypothesis object in the HTN library. An information gathering task can be seen as having the structure: "Get info on TOPIC from SOURCE". In this regard, a task to be performed (combination of TOPIC and SOURCE) and an index are interchangeable. The outcome of a task corresponds to the different values of an index (answer to the TOPIC from the SOURCE). Each time the execution of a task (query) obtains a value (answer), the score for the related hypothesis is correspondingly re-evaluated. As an example, consider the task of checking SARSAT for an overdue aircraft information. The task "check SARSAT for overdue aircraft" is an index to the case that can take on the values: received signal once; continuous signal; no signal; no continuous signal. Each value will provide a different weight for the case. For example, if the value "received continuous signal" is obtained for the index, then the index should contribute to a "plane crashed" hypothesis with a weight higher than that for "received signal once", and so on.

12.2.3   AGENT DESIGN AND INFORMATION FLOW

Here, we discuss how these indexes and their weights are integrated to compute an overall ranking for the case.

12.2.3.1   An Architecture

The overall objective of the agent system is to assist the controllers at the RCC in dealing with complex tasks. As an assistance system, the goal is the same as that of the overall intelligent agents research-to design assistance systems that act autonomously, to be goal oriented, and to have the ability to learn from its own experiences and from the interaction with the user. The design goal is for the system to be incrementally more competent by integrating a variety of intelligent techniques including case-based reasoning, rule-based reasoning, HTN planning, process monitoring, active databases and machine learning. Each agent will have its own set of goals, implemented based on active database technology.

12.2.3.2   Task Monitoring

What is envisioned is a monitoring agent for each source of information. We can attach one agent for the SARSAT database to provide a layer of translation between the SARSAT signal and the task network-based indexes. Similarly, another agent is designed to be in charge of monitoring the telephone information source, keeping a tap on calls made to different agencies and resources, and calls received from other telephones. At the Canadian Rescue Coordination Centers, a case tracking system known as the CaseMaster has already been developed. The aim of this system is to replace the handwritten logs that the controllers use for recording all the major steps and tasks they perform. The CaseMaster thus provides an ideal channel for interaction with our agent system. Moreover, certain information can be obtained directly from the databases using the active database technology, by assigning triggers to various data sources which can provide information based on an event-based system. Where automatic means are not available for obtaining the current value of a particular index, we can prompt the users through the CaseMaster system to obtain the answers. This data is then useful for both statistical case tracking and for real time evaluation of the case score.

12.2.4   SIMILARITY BASED RETRIEVAL OF HYPOTHESES OBJECTS

When, the first evidence of an incident (first notice) is received, a process of hypotheses evaluation would begin. The initial evidence, or the evidence set would be translated to a set of index values for various tasks and sub-tasks in the task networks associated with different cases in a case base. Using these networks, a ranking process would determine the most promising cases, in terms of similarity to the current situation, given the current problem–solving context, such as weather conditions and time of day. The ranking would continue, making some cases more likely than others at any given time, until a final hypothesis or collection of hypotheses is confirmed. Several strategies have been proposed in the CBR literature for case-retrieval algorithms. Some of them are serial, while others are parallel; some use flat-indexed structures, but others use hierarchical-indexed structures. Some use indices to construct structures that distinguish cases from each other at a very small granularity while others discriminate cases at a coarser level. For a flat case base the best case will be retrieved, but if the case base is very large, the search would be very time consuming. If a case base is organized into a tree structure, the search cost is relatively small, but there is no guarantee that the most similar cases will be retrieved. One of the most popular methods is the Nearest Neighbor Algorithm (NNA). It assumes that each case in a case base is defined or indexed by a set of 'n' (numeric or symbolic) features. Given an input query Q, k-NN retrieves a set of k cases most like Q from the case base. These k cases have the least distance from Q. For a case C and a query Q. The following formula is used to compute a similarity measure between a case C and an input query Q, in terms of the similarity between two indexes or features:

$$\text{Sim}(C, Q) = \text{norm} * \left(\sum (W_i * sim(f_i^c, f_i^Q)^2) \right)^{1/2}$$

Here, f_i is the i-th feature or index for case C or Q, respectively, norm is a normalization factor, and W_i is a weight attached to the i-th feature. In some implementations of the formula, all features use the same weights. This will allow redundant, irrelevant, and other imperfect features to skew the similarity computation. Hence, many variants have been proposed to assign higher weights to more relevant features in a case base. After the similarity to the input query is computed for each case, a set of highly relevant candidate cases in a case base are scored. Cases with high similarity scores are presented to the user.

12.2.5 HTN Guided Task Prioritization

A task network provides a precedence constraint on the tasks. Horizontally in a task network, some tasks must be executed before others, while other tasks can be executed in parallel. Vertically in a task network, every task has a parent (except the root task), so there is a task and subtask relation. This relation allows the non-primitive tasks to be expanded, exposing the sub-tasks in a top-down manner.

In selecting a task, there are several heuristics that one can follow: i) a task should be selected only when its predecessors are satisfied; ii) if there are several tasks in the same hierarchy that can be executed, a priority ordering can be imposed on the tasks such that a top priority task is able to affect the ranking of the case more than other tasks; and iii) if a task is non-primitive, there may be several ways to achieve it according to a number of task reduction schemata. Thus, there is a process of selecting an appropriate information source to answer a query, based on knowledge of the availability of the information source, the quality of the potential information and the reliability of the source, and the cost and duration of performing such a task.

12.2.6 AN EXAMPLE

Consider a scenario where a pilot flying a small airplane goes missing. A report comes in from the designation airport where the pilot was supposed to land indicating that the pilot has still not landed 2 hours after his expected arrival time. Our SA agent starts by accumulating information which will serve as a basis for hypotheses formation. The agent, based on the reported information about an overdue aircraft, will find all standard information such as time of day when the report was received, the weather report and so on. This information together with the knowledge that the plane is overdue is used to perform the hypothesis retrieval task from the case base.

Next, suppose that two hypotheses are retrieved. These hypotheses are "H1: plane crashed somewhere with serious damage" and "H2: plane landed somewhere to refuel." Both are possible hypotheses at this moment so these both have to be evaluated.

The SA is guided by the HTN's that are attached to the two hypotheses to be evaluated. According to the suggestions given by these task networks, there are four sub-tasks that can be immediately executed: check ELT signals, check SARSAT satellite reports, check airports along the flight path of the missing plane, and contact the pilot's wife for additional information. Of these four sub-tasks, the "check ELT" and "check SARSAT" sub-tasks can be carried out automatically by the agent, using monitoring agents attached to the ELT signal and SARSAT report databases. Suppose that at this point, both reports come back negative. The agent, based on similarity-based ranking of the hypothesis's objects, will decrease the likelihood of the plane crashed hypothesis.

The RCC controller, based on the information accumulated so far by the SA agent may proceed to phone the airports along the plane's flight path to get more information. Now, suppose that in the thick of things, the controller had forgotten to phone the pilot's wife. The agent would have sensed this not-yet performed task, and printed a friendly message to remind the controller to do that. Suppose now that when talking to the pilot's wife, she reports that the pilot had called home. It now turns out that the hypothesis "H2: plane landed somewhere to refuel" is a correct one in that the pilot did indeed decide to land in an intermediate airport in order to refuel, and while refueling, phoned home to tell his wife about the change of his plan. The case is now closed with a report.

12.3 AN ARTIFICIAL INTELLIGENCE ARCHITECTURE FOR BATTLEFIELD INFORMATION FUSION

Here, we describe a hybrid Artificial Intelligence (AI) architecture that provides an integrated framework for analysis of information in support of enhanced tactical awareness and need-based sensor asset management to assist in battlefield intelligence processing [3]. The architecture combines two AI techniques for model-based approximate reasoning: i) fuzzy logic, and ii) Bayesian belief networks. The hybrid AI battlefield Information Fusion (IF) system applies a coordinated application of FL and BNs to the problem of tactical fusion. Fuzzy logic provides a means of converting low-level imprecise information in non-numerical format into mid-level knowledge units about individual battlespace entities. Belief networks provide a means for constructing and maintaining a hierarchical, probabilistic model linking multiple entities, at various levels, in the context of the overall mission goals, rules of engagement, etc. Evidence gathered incrementally and in real-time first undergoes FL filtering and is then applied to the appropriate node(s) of the BN. This evidence then automatically propagates throughout the BN resulting in revised probability estimates concerning the higher-level tactical situational hypotheses. Experiences from prior research efforts have shown that this approach provides an effective solution to the problem and offers a natural framework for encoding complex tactical knowledge.

12.3.1 DESCRIPTION OF THE SYSTEM

Information concerning the various entities present in the battlespace are collected by a variety of sensors or collection assets (JSTARS, AWACS, etc.) and then fused (Level 1) within the architecture to generate individual target tracks and to classify and characterize targets. The SA module of the architecture uses this fused track data to generate a probabilistic situational state hypothesis from detected events. The overall scope of the hybrid architecture for battlefield IF falls within the various levels of fusion and other key components of tactical C4I (command, control, communication, and computer-C4I, intelligent) systems: i) from the external environment, ii) to the collection assets; and then iii) to the system scope, which then consists of the two aspects: a) object assessment→asset management (AM), and asset coordination (AC); and b) situation assessment. This finally flows to the decision-making system; and the feedback from the OA and SA goes to collection assets via AM and AC. This SA information is then forwarded to Level 3 impact or threat assessment and decision-aiding modules. Finally, the SA information is used by the architecture's sensor or collection management module to assign, prioritize and communicate intelligence requests. The overall architecture, incorporating all modules necessary to support management and control of Level 1 fusion processing, SA, and enhanced collection management functionality can be found in Figure 2 of Ref. [3].

The system incorporates three specific and distinct modules: i) a FL-based Level 1 fusion module responsible for the management and control of observation-to-track gating and assignment, state estimation, and track database management; ii) a combination FL-based event detection and BN based Level 2 SA modules responsible for generating probabilistic hypotheses for high-level situational state descriptors; and iii) a FL-based Level 4 collection management expert system responsible for mapping informational requirements and current state information into asset resource requests. The architecture encompasses all aspects of Level 1 OA fusion processing including data association, state estimation, identification, and track management. The FL manager for Level 1 has direct responsibility for management and oversight of these Level 1 functions. Specifically, data association management provides gating technique selection, gating parameter modification (gating constant for rectangular gate), and use of multi-level gating schemes. For correlation, the FL Manager also specifies algorithm selection and threshold levels with final oversight of assignment. For filtering/prediction management, the manager specifies algorithm type, filter parameters and model choice. For example, the FL Manager may inspect residuals from a bank of Kalman filters to determine the most appropriate model or for target maneuver detection. It may also update measurement noise models based on target range (i.e., increased angular measurement accuracy with decreasing range for a radar sensor) or based on sensor confidence levels. The FL Manager also monitors and controls the track identification process. Here, again algorithm selection and output monitoring are its key functions. The final element of the Level 1 FL Manager is track management; track initialization and confirmation (based on data association results), as well as track deletion. Specific items addressed in track management include: i) track initiation criteria, ii) track confirmation logic including required number of assignments and time window, and iii) specification of last update time threshold for track deletion.

Level 2 processing has two primary functions: detection of key events and assessment of the current situation. Event detection is performed using FL reasoning in conjunction with a pre-defined library of domain-relevant events. This event library is of a broad enough nature to encompass typical tactical engagements. Event detection automatically translates information gleaned from incoming Level 1 information into domain-relevant events (presence of specific enemy units at a specific location), along with an associated measure of certainty of the event. Key events are then sent to the BN that determines the current situation.

At the heart of Level 2 processing is a BN which is a probabilistic model of the battlefield tactical situation. The BN allows uncertain evidence concerning any of the represented battlefield and unit features to be incorporated to consistently update any other contingent features of the model. The BN can be interpreted as representing causal relationships between the variables. A particular enemy mission (E.Miss) combined with enemy knowledge about where friendly forces are located (F.Loc) causes a rational enemy to choose a specific objective (E.Obj) which will maximize its utility. Similarly, the choice of a specific objective causes a rational enemy to choose a specific route or Course Of Action (COA), denoted by the node E.COA, that maximizes its utility in prosecuting that objective. The bottom-most nodes (MC-1, MC-2, ...), represent the belief that the enemy is present within the specific regions of the battlefield termed Mobility Corridors (MC). While we interpret these relationships as causal, we represent the inherent uncertainty of the battlefield environment by encoding them probabilistically. Specifically, each link between nodes has a corresponding Conditional Probability Table (CPT) which encodes the probability of the child variable given the parent variable. In the more general case in which a node may have more than one parent, the node's CPT encodes its probability given all its parents. At Level 4, a FL collection manager maps the current SA State, and enemy track information, into sensor (intelligence assets gathered by some small devices including Humint, the human intelligence) requests. The mapping is performed using a repository knowledge of sensor/asset capabilities and enemy tactical doctrine. High-level event notifications and observations relating to asset requests are also relayed to the user. The mapping from situational state and track information to asset request is based on several appropriateness metrics: i) timeliness, ii) desired classification level, iii) availability, and iv) geographic coverage. Timeliness refers to an asset's turnaround time to meet a given request. Classification level refers to the asset's classification capabilities, i.e., detection (find enemy units), classification (discriminate enemy units, tanks v/s APCs), and identification (type or model of tank). Availability refers to the time period in which the asset is accessible.

12.3.2 FUNCTIONALITY OF A PROTOTYPE

To assess the feasibility of this hybrid architecture, a battlefield scenario can be developed by subject matter experts covering a 24-hour period in which friendly ground forces, a mechanized infantry brigade, defend against an adversary consisting of a Motorized Rifle Division (MRD). A terrain analysis stage results in a constrained set of possible enemy objectives, courses of action, and mobility corridors. Friendly intelligence-gathering assets include: i) ground-based reconnaissance units, ii) Electronic Support Measures (ESM) equipment, iii) reconnaissance aircraft, and iv) the Multi-Mode Radar (MMR) capabilities of the airborne J-STARS platform. The Level 1 fusion simulation would consist of: a) a main window that displays the evolution of the battle, and b) a track database window that displays the current associations of individual sensor reports to tracks. The overall qualitative results could be: a) FL provides a natural human-like reasoning mechanism for handling uncertainty, and b) the Level 1 FL manager would be able to: i) discriminate multi-level unit types, ii) perform track generation and maintenance, and iii) aggregate lower echelon units into higher echelons.

The fusion manager would be able to discriminate between battalion and regimental units. Gating and assignment control would ensure reasonable track maintenance. Finally, the fusion manager could aggregate lower units into higher echelon units, e.g., battalion units into regiments. The Level 2 demonstration entailed the sequential posting of sensor evidence to the BN model. In most cases the model would be able to maintain correct hypotheses regarding the higher-level (hidden) variables, e.g., enemy objective, for the range of scenarios, and would demonstrate the feasibility of the BN framework for modelling causal battlefield relationships. A single, integrated model combines variables of differing scales and allows probabilistic inferencing of higher-level, hidden variables, e.g., enemy objective, intent, based on evidence concerning lower-level variables, e.g., enemy unit locations, types, movements, etc. The BN formalism simultaneously allows a consistent means for combining prior information, e.g., derived from terrain analysis, weather reports, and enemy doctrine and order of battle information, with evidence gathered in real-time from sensor assets and units deployed in the battlespace.

The Level 4 demonstration would test the fuzzy rule base for collection or sensor management. The system would display basic capabilities for combining hypothesized unit locations and intents with friendly intelligence requirements and asset capabilities to produce asset requests sufficient to acquire the needed intelligence. The fuzzy expert system rule base contains over 100 rules and assumes an asset suite consisting of the JSTARS platform, including both Moving Target Indicator (MTI) radar and imaging Synthetic Aperture Radar (SAR), and a generic Electronic Support Measures (ESM) platform. The rule base uses several fuzzy variables including sensor resolution, timeliness, availability, area coverage, and a user-specified information criticality level.

The main interface window for the FL Collection Manager prototype: the Graphical User Interface (GUI) has two sets of edit boxes, a list box, a textbox, and two buttons. The two sets of edit boxes would provide the means to directly input BN node values from Level 2 processing. These values correspond to the presence of enemy units at the eleven mobility corridors or segments and to the belief in the three possible enemy objectives (A, B, or C referring to NAI 1, 2, or 3, respectively). The informational requirements would specify the request priority level, the coverage area, and type of coverage required.

Further efforts on extending the hybrid AI architecture could focus on: a) integration of the three major modules (for Levels, 1, 2 and 4) to produce a full-scope system for enhanced battlefield information processing and situation assessment; b) incorporation of temporal/spatial aspects of battlefield information processing to enhance current situation assessment and to facilitate prediction of future enemy evolutions; c) evaluation of a full-scope prototype in an empirical study employing multiple tactical scenarios; d) system enhancement based on the evaluation findings; and e) specification of H/W and S/W requirements for follow-on development within fielded C4I-related information processing systems to enhance overall information fusion, situation assessment, and collection management. Additionally, a parallel effort could be to develop a Level 3 (impact assessment) component with the functionality to infer enemy intent, capabilities, and vulnerabilities, and how that component could be integrated within the hybrid AI architecture.

12.4 PILOT'S SA BY NEUROADAPTIVE COGNITIVE MODELLING

It is essential for flight safety that pilots understand the criticality of flight deck alerts, and do not accidentally miss alerts, e.g., due to high workload and cognitive tunnelling. Human-Machine Interfaces (HMI) on the flight deck therefore need to ensure that the messages are processed correctly to reduce the risk of Out-Of-the-Loop problems (OOL). The failed, delayed, or inadequate response to flight deck alerts has been associated with several fatal accidents in the past. Automation has transformed pilots' role from hands-on flying to monitoring system displays which is ill-matched to human cognitive capabilities. Furthermore, reduced-crew (single-pilot) operations can increase demands on pilots in commercial aircraft through elevated workload of the remaining crew and higher complexity imposed by additional automation. More complex automation can impede the detection of divergence in the situation assessment by the human operator and the automated system, neither of which may adequately reflect reality. It is believed that neuro-technologies can be used for cognitive enhancement and support for pilots in the face of increased demands. One way to achieve this is by monitoring the pilots' cognitive states and performance during flight deck operations in order to detect the onset of such divergence e.g., cognitive phenomena that may lead to OOL situations. Being able to detect such cognitive states, corrective measures may be initiated to prevent or reduce the risk of OOL situations and to maintain a high level of safety in aviation.

This study presents the integration of a Passive Brain-Computer Interface (pBCI) and cognitive modelling as a method of tracing pilots' perceptions and processing of auditory alerts and messages during operations [4]. Missing alerts on the flight deck can result in OOL problems that can lead to accidents. By tracing pilots' perceptions and responses to alerts, cognitive assistance can be provided based on individual needs to ensure that they maintain adequate situation awareness. Data from 24 participating aircrew in a simulated flight study that included multiple alerts and air traffic control messages in single pilot setup are presented. A classifier was trained to identify pilots' neurophysiological reactions to alerts and messages from participants' ElectroEncephaloGram (EEG). A neuroadaptive ACT-R model using EEG data was compared to a conventional normative model regarding accuracy in representing individual pilots. Findings show that passive BCI can distinguish between alerts that are processed by the pilot as task-relevant or irrelevant in the cockpit based on the recorded EEG. The neuroadaptive model's integration of this data resulted in significantly higher performance of 87% overall accuracy in representing individual pilots' responses to alerts and messages compared to 72% accuracy of a basic model that did not consider EEG data. It was concluded that neuroadaptive technology allows for implicit measurement and tracing of pilots' perceptions and processing of alerts on the flight deck [4]. Careful handling of uncertainties inherent to passive BCI and cognitive modelling showed how the representation of pilot cognitive states could be improved iteratively to provide assistance.

12.4.1 OOL AND THE SITUATION AWARENESS

Out-of-the-loop problems arise when pilots lack SAW, that is progressively developed through the levels of perception (1), comprehension (2), and projection (3) of a situation's elements. Missing critical alerts impair situation perception and inhibit the development of higher SAW levels. In a study on pilot errors, most errors could be accounted to incorrect perception (70.3%) and comprehension (20.3%) of situations. SAW is commonly measured by sampling with the help of probing questions. Probes can give insights into pilots' deeper understanding of a situation as well as whether a probed piece of information can be retrieved from memory. However, probing methods either require flight scenarios to be frozen or incur extra workload when assessing pilots' SA. Physiological and performance-based metrics are less direct measures of memory contents, but they can be used unobtrusively in operations. As an example, eye tracking can serve as an indicator of pilots' perceptual and attentional processes. The abundance of visual information in the cockpit, however, makes tracing visual attention very challenging and susceptible to selective ignoring and inattentional blindness. Alerts in the cockpit are presented both visually and acoustically, while acoustic stimuli have been shown to be more effective in attracting attention. Physiological responses to alert stimuli may reveal whether alerts have been perceived and processed. For example, Event-Related Potentials (ERPs) in operators' EEGs were proposed as indicators of attended and unattended stimuli in the assessment of SAW. It was demonstrated that ERP components indeed allow differentiation between missed and processed auditory stimuli in the cockpit, even in single trials. It was noted that these differences are primarily reflected in early perceptual and late attentional stages of auditory processing. Failure to adequately perceive or process an alert is likely due to excessive demand on cognitive resources in terms of attention and memory at a central executive level. In addition, deterministic modelling of individual processed or missed alerts requires lots of data about the situation and the pilot's state and neurophysiological measures can help reduce uncertainty. Thus, by monitoring what stimuli are provided when and checking for ERPs at stimulus onset, perception of a situation could be tracked in real-time. After that, performance metrics in terms of comparing pilots' actual behaviour to normative procedures can provide information on later SA stages.

12.4.2 Requirements for Cognitive State Assessment

As cognitive states underlying SA are not directly observable, their detection and prediction are done by neurophysiological measures and cognitive modelling. Tracing perceptual and cognitive processing can best be done implicitly by interpreting psycho-physiological measures so as not to increase the pilots' load or otherwise interfere with operations. As we are interested in event-related cognitive processing, i.e., the processing of specific visual or auditory alerts, one requirement is that the onset of these alerts is captured accurately. This allows the timing of each alert to be synchronized with a measurement of the pilots' neuroelectric activity, which is sensitive to even slight temporal misalignments. This activity can then be analysed relative to each alert's exact onset, allowing alert-specific cognitive states to be decoded. Such automated, non-intrusive detection of cognitive processing can be done using pBCI, based on a continuous measurement of brain activity. If unprocessed alerts are detected, cognitive assistance can be offered depending on the alert's significance for the course of the operation. This way, critical drops in pilot performance can be anticipated and assistance can be provided to prevent the pilot from getting out of the loop. This simulation can be performed using cognitive models that capture the characteristics of the human cognitive system such as resource limitations.

12.4.3 Cognitive Pilot Models

ACT-R (Adaptive Control of Thought—Rational") is the most comprehensive and widely used architecture to build models that can simulate, predict, and keep track of cognitive dynamics. It is based on accumulated research about the human brain's modular architecture, where each module maps onto a different functional area of the brain. In its current 7.14 version, the ACT-R architecture comprises separate modules for: i) declarative and procedural memory, ii) temporal, and intentional ("goal") processing, and iii) visual, aural, motor, and speech modules for limited perceptual-motor capabilities. While highly interconnected within themselves, exchange of symbolic information between modules is constrained by a small number of interfaces that are modelled as buffers. These intermodular connections meet in the procedural memory module (representing the caudate of the basal ganglia), where condition-action statements ("productions") are triggered depending on buffer contents. Actions can be defined for example in terms of memory retrieval, directing attention or manipulating the outside world through speech or motor actions. Based on sub-symbolic mechanisms such as i) utility learning, ii) spreading activation, iii) memory decay, and iv) random noise, the ACT-R models can adapt to dynamic environments and represent average human behaviour in a non-deterministic fashion; and it allows for the creation of cognitive models according to specific task descriptions, e.g., a goal-directed Hierarchical Task Analysis (HTA). When this task description focuses on maintaining good SA, a normative cognitive model can be developed that acts in order to optimize SA. Normative models can be compared to individual pilot behaviour to detect deviations and to make inferences about individual pilots' SA.

The uncertainty in tracing can be reduced by using physiological data alongside system inputs to build richer models of individual performance. An ACT-R model allows us to modulate the interface complexity according to operator workload measured by the EEG. A synthetic teammate able to pilot unmanned aerial vehicles and communicate with human teammates based on an extensive model of SA has been developed [4]. Both these models demonstrate how selected human capabilities such as piloting and communicating or being empathic to operators' cognitive states can be allocated to an ACT-R model in human autonomy teaming.

12.4.4 NEUROADAPTIVE TECHNOLOGY

Neuroadaptive Technology (NT) refers to technology that uses cognitive state assessments as implicit input in order to enable intelligent forms of adaptation. One way to achieve this is to maintain a model that is continuously updated using measures of situational parameters as well as the corresponding cognitive states of the user. Adaptive actions can then be initiated based on the information provided by the model. Generally, certain cognitive states result, on average, in specific patterns of brain activity, and can be inferred if the corresponding pattern distributions are known. As patterns differ to some extent between individuals and even between sessions, it is usually necessary to record multiple samples of related brain activity in order to describe the pattern distribution of cognitive responses in an individual. Given a sufficient number of samples of a sufficiently distinct pattern, a so-called classifier can be calibrated which is capable of detecting these patterns in real time, with typical single-trial accuracies between 65 and 95%. Importantly, since these cognitive states occur as a natural consequence of the ongoing interaction, no additional effort is required, nor task load induced, for them to be made detectable. It is thus possible to use a measure of a user's cognitive state as implicit input, referring to input that was acquired without this being deliberately communicated by the operator. Without the pilots explicitly communicating anything, a measure of their brain activity revealed indices of engagement or workload, allowing the automation to be increased or decreased accordingly [4]. In the cockpit, each alert can be expected to elicit specific cortical activity, e.g., an ERP. If this activity can be decoded to reveal whether the alert has been perceived, and potentially whether and how it was processed, it can be used as implicit input. By interpreting this information alongside historic pilot responses and further operational parameters, an informed decision can be made about the current cognitive state of the pilots and recommended adaptive steps.

12.4.5 THE CASE STUDY

In contrast to conventional measures of SAW, the present method is designed for application in operations that require unobtrusive tracing of cognitive states. The method is applied to explore how to anticipate pilot behaviour and when to help according to their cognitive state [4]: i) the feasibility of distinguishing between processed and missed alerts based on pilots' brain activity, ii) whether individual pilot behaviour can be anticipated using cognitive models, and iii) how the methods of pBCI and cognitive modelling can be integrated. Results are based on the implications for cognitive assistance on the flight deck and potential benefits for single pilot operations.

12.4.5.1 Material and Methods

This research complied with the American Psychological Association Code of Ethics and was approved by the Institutional Review Board at TU (Technical University) Berlin. Informed consent was obtained from each participant.

Participants: twenty-four (24) aircrew (one female) with a mean age of 49.08 years (SD = 6.08) participated in the flight simulator study [4]. Participants were predominantly military pilots with an average experience of 3230 hrs. of flight (SD = 2330.71), of which on average 51.21 hrs. (SD = 90.76) were performed in the previous year. All participating aircrew had normal or corrected to normal vision, all but two were right-handed.

Procedure: These aircrew were asked for information on their flight experience and physical health relevant for physiological data assessment in the simulator. After application of EEG sensors, participants performed a desktop-based auditory oddball training paradigm. Participants performed 10 blocks during each of which a sequence of 60 auditory tones was presented. Each tone could be either a standard tone of 350 Hz occurring 70–80% of the time, a target deviant tone of 650 Hz (10–15%), or non-target deviant (2000 Hz, 10–15%). There was a variable interval between stimulus onsets of 1.5 ± 0.2 s, and a self-paced break after each block. Each tone lasted 339 msec. The participants were instructed to count the target tones in each block with eyes open, and to verbally report their count after each block to ensure they stayed attentive during the task. Thus, the standard tones represent frequent but task-irrelevant events, target tones represent rare task-relevant events, and the deviants were rare but task-irrelevant. For the flight scenario, participants were instructed to avoid communicating with the experimenter during the scenario but were allowed to think aloud and to perform readbacks of Air Traffic Control (ATC) messages just as they would during a normal flight. After the scenario, a debriefing session was conducted in order to collect feedback from participants.

Simulator and Scenario: The participants flew a mission in the fixed-base simulator of a mission aircraft similar to current-generation business jets certified according to EASA CS-23, which may be operated by a single pilot. The mission was simulated using the open-source flight simulation SW "FlightGear 3.4". The participants' task was to perform a fictitious routine VIP passenger transport from Ingolstadt-Manching (ETSI) to Kassel (EDVK) airport. To keep workload levels associated with basic flying low, the scenario started with the aircraft already airborne at cruise flight level (FL 250) with autopilot (altitude and NAV4 mode) engaged. According to the Flight Management System (FMS) flight plan presented; the remaining flight time was approximately 40 min in fair weather conditions. To maintain speed, thrust had to be adjusted manually, since the aircraft was-like most business jets today-not equipped with auto-thrust. To simulate interactions with ATC and to ensure a consistent flow of the scenario for all participants, pilots were presented with pre-recorded routine ATC instructions relating to flight level and heading changes at fixed time intervals after the start of the scenario. Also, at pre-defined times, pilots would encounter a series of flight deck alerts of varying, but generally increasing severity: i) first, 4 min into the scenario, the main fuel pump in the right-wing tank failed, resulting in a caution level flight deck alert and, subsequently, the display of a simple recovery procedure, which was automatically presented as electronic checklist; ii) after 6 min, a small fuel leak appeared in the right fuel tank, which had initially no salient flight deck effects and would therefore go mostly unnoticed; and iii) contributing to this was a TCAS traffic advisory (caution level alert) after approximately 7 min, which would coincide with an ATC instruction to descend due to traffic (e.g., "F-UO, due to traffic, descend and maintain FL 280" or "F-UO, direct TUSOS and descend FL 200").

Moreover, to simulate the effects of an intermittent spurious alert, and to divert pilot attention from the FUEL format to decrease the chance of the pilot noticing the leak, an identical caution-level alert of an electrical bus system failure was triggered four times throughout the scenario. This alert would automatically be removed after 5 s without any pilot action, and before pilots were able to access the associated recovery procedure. When the fuel leak had caused a fuel imbalance exceeding a certain threshold, a caution-level alert relating to the imbalance would be raised. The associated procedure would then guide pilots through several steps intended to find the root cause of the fuel imbalance. The scenario ended once an in-flight fire of the left engine initiated after 16:40 min, resulting in a warning level alert, had successfully been extinguished by the pilot. To make sure that all participants encountered all events of the scenario, speed warnings were issued dynamically by the simulated ATC whenever airspeed did not remain within a predefined range.

Normative responses to the simulated events would result in the following respective parameter changes: i) ATC 1: Altitude-Select 280 and Speed-Select 220, ii) ATC 2: Altitude-Select 300, iii) Fuel Pump Failure: Right-Main-Pump Off, iv) Electrical Systems Alert 1: No parameter change, v) ATC 3: Altitude-Select 280, vi) TCAS TA-Alert: No parameter change, vii) ATC 4: Altitude-Select 300, viii) Electrical Systems Alert 2: No parameter change, ix) ATC 5: Altitude-Select 320, x) ATC 6: Heading-Select 325, xi) Electrical Systems Alert 3: No parameter change, xii) Fuel Imbalance: Fuel-X-Feed True (not included in data analysis), xiii) ATC 7: Heading-Select 350, and xiv) Electrical Systems Alert 4: No parameter change.

12.4.5.2   EEG

EEG was recorded continuously at 500 Hz using a mobile, wireless LiveAmp amplifier (Brain Products, Gilching, Germany) using 32 active Ag/AgCl electrodes arranged on actiCAP caps according to the international 10–20 system and referenced to FCz. EEG was synchronized with both the desktop stimuli and the flight events using the Lab Streaming Layer software framework to ensure that EEG data could be related to the respective simulator events with adequate temporal resolution. FlightGear was configured to log the status of each of the alarms and send it at 100 Hz to a UDP port, where a custom Python script listened for incoming data and immediately forwarded each packet through LSL. A change in alert status could then be interpreted as the on/ or offset of the alert.

12.4.5.3 ERP Classification

A windowed-means classifier was calibrated on the EEG data to distinguish between the subjects' neurophysiological responses to two different categories of tones: i) the mean amplitudes of eight consecutive non-overlapping time windows of 50 msec., each starting at 150 msec., and ii) onset of the auditory tone, after band-pass filtering the signal between 0.3 and 20 Hz. Shrinkage-regularized linear discriminant was used for classification. A five-fold cross-validation with margins of five was used to obtain estimates of the classifier's coefficients.

The classification algorithm was implemented using BCILAB. The trained classifier was capable of distinguishing between the two categories of tones based solely on the participant's brain activity. Having trained the classifier on detecting differences between these events, the classifier was applied to the data recorded during that same participant's simulation trial. This allowed us to investigate to what extent flight deck alerts could be reliably identified as the comparable equivalent of "standard" (task-irrelevant, unimportant) or "target" (etc.) tones, based solely on the pilots' EEG data (less than 1 second after onset of each event). For each simulated experiment, the classifier returned a number between 1 and 2, signifying that the neurophysiological response was closest to the activity following standard (1) or target (2) tones in the oddball paradigm, respectively.

12.4.5.4 Cognitive Model

A normative and a neuroadaptive cognitive model were created following a HTA (performed with a subject matter expert) for the scenario using ACT-R. For the HTA and the cognitive model, good SA Level 1 was defined as perceiving and paying attention to all auditory stimuli provided in the scenario. While adequacy of responses depended on the type of alert or contents of ATC messages, the time limit for initiating a first reaction to an alert was set to 25 sec. for all events. The interface between the models and the simulator/Flight Gear was implemented as an extended version of ACT-CV, where log files of cockpit system states recorded with a sampling rate of 20 Hz served as ACT-R task environment. Both normative and neuroadaptive models were based on a routine loop consisting of monitoring flight parameters and managing thrust accordingly in order to have comparable workload as participants in the simulator.

In order to illustrate the model's flow of information from one module to another with respect to ACT-R's neuroanatomical assumptions, associated brain areas would be given in parentheses behind each module. In the fuel pump failure alert mode, the model would go through the steps: i) a chunk representing a sound activates the aural module (mapped to the superior temporal gyrus) by being put in the model's aural-location buffer; ii) this allows the procedural module (basal ganglia) to fire a production that starts counting seconds passed since the alert with the temporal module and that decodes the sound as an alert sound using the aural buffer; iii) this latter information would trigger productions that make the model shift its visual attention to the warning display by calling on the visual module's (fusiform gyrus) visual-location buffer; iv) read the written fuel pump failure message using the visual buffer; v) the following production would result in calling up the corresponding pump failure checklist, memorizing its first item (pressing the right main fuel pump push-button) in the imaginal buffer (intraparietal sulcus), representing the model's short-term memory problem state; vi) then, using its motor module (precentral gyrus), the model acts as if pressing the pump pushbutton (without changing any of the flight parameters); vii) reading and carrying out of the remaining checklist items in the same fashion while it keeps counting; and viii) finally when the count in the temporal module has reached 25 sec., the module checks the flight parameters for the state of the right main fuel pump's pushbutton to verify whether the pilot has carried out the action required by the first checklist item as memorized in the model's imaginal buffer.

Adequacy and timeliness of responses were scored according to criteria assessed in the HTA. For example, if an ATC message requested a flight level change to 300, entering an altitude-select of 300 in the flight control unit within a time window of 25 sec. was scored as good performance; all other responses such as entering an altitude-select of 280 or entering the correct altitude-select after 25 sec. were classified as a missed ATC message. The fraction of incorrect classifications was treated as epistemic uncertainty ($\mu_{Epistemic}$) as the model had no information about why the pilot did not respond as expected.

The pBCI data were provided to the model along with the cockpit systems data. After each acoustic alert and message was decoded, the neuroadaptive model checked if the sound was processed as task-relevant by the participant according to pBCI data before shifting its visual attention to read the actual contents of alerts or messages. If pBCI data showed that a message was processed as irrelevant (classifier output <1.5), the model scored 'lacking or inadequate' responses as correct behaviour classification. If the message was processed as relevant but no adequate response can be found, the model scored its classification as incorrect and treats these cases as epistemic uncertainty. Responses were assessed for 10 events for each of the 21 pilots were of eight ATC messages, one amber, and one red alert. The normative and neuroadaptive models were compared by a paired samples t-test. Effect size is reported as Cohen's d_{av}. Aleatory uncertainty ($\mu_{Aleatory}$) was defined as one minus EEG classifier accuracy. Though aleatory uncertainty affects correct and incorrect classifications, an accuracy corrected for aleatory uncertainty was computed for the neuroadaptive model. The distribution of lacking and inadequate responses was tested for a relationship with EEG classifications by a Chi-square test.

12.4.5.5   Results

12.4.5.5.1   ERP Classification

It was previously estimated that stimulus presentation pipeline to contain a lag of approximately 150 msec. The classifier was trained to detect the differences between single-trial ERPs using all 32 channels and had a cross-validated averaged accuracy of 86%. Given the class imbalance between the standard deviant tones, the chance level was not at 50% for this binary classifier. Instead, significant classification accuracy ($p < 0.05$) is reached at 78%. The classes could be separated with significant accuracy for all but three participants. This was in part due to technical issues with the EEG recording. These three participants were excluded from further analysis. The classifier trained on data from the oddball paradigm was subsequently applied to data following four flight events: ATC messages, the spurious electrical bus system failure alert, the fuel imbalance alert, and the fire alert. These classification results provided information to be used in the neuroadaptive cognitive model.

12.4.5.5.2 Cognitive Model

The normative model correctly described participants' behaviour for 162 of the total 210 observed events (MNormative = 0.72, SD = 0.09), indicating that participants missed to respond to 48 events. The neuroadaptive model was able to simulate 182 of participant's responses correctly (MNeuroadaptive = 0.87, SD = 0.13), resulting in a significant added value of including pBCI data compared to the normative model [$t(20) = 5.62$, $p < 0.01$, dav = 1.3]. Epistemic uncertainties for the models are $\mu_{Epistemic} = 0.28$ for the normative and $\mu_{Epistemic} = 0.13$ for the neuroadaptive model. The added value of the neuroadaptive over the normative model is 0.15, so the neuroadaptive model's accuracy corrected for EEG-classifier accuracy of 0.88 is 0.85 with $\mu_{Epistemic} = 0.15$ and $\mu_{Aleatory} = 0.02$. Of the 58 events left unexplained by the normative model, 22 events did not show a response to the respective alert or message and 36 showed an incorrect response by the participant. Chi-square tests yielded no significant relationship between EEG classifier output (standard/target) and the event having missing or incorrect responses [$\chi 2$ (1, N = 58) = 1.04, $p = 0.31$), i.e., pBCI-data do not predict whether a participant will respond incorrectly or not at all to missed alerts.

12.4.5.6 Discussion

The results have demonstrated the feasibility of implicitly detecting and handling of emerging divergence in SA with the help of a neuroadaptive cognitive model. Using a pBCI for real-time assessment of cognitive responses provides insight into subjective situational interpretations.

In general, it can be concluded that the combination of pBCI approaches with advanced methods of cognitive modelling, leads to an increase in the reliability and capability of the resulting cognitive model; leading to the idea of neuroadaptive cognitive modelling. Specifically, the ERP produced by the oddball paradigm shows clear differences between the different categories of tones. In particular, a P300 at Pz clearly distinguishes between target (task-relevant) and standard (task-irrelevant) tones. The classifier was capable of distinguishing between target and standard tones with single-trial accuracies significantly higher than chance in the training session. The improvement in the cognitive model indicates that it is possible to obtain informative cognitive state information based on a pilot's brain activity immediately following an auditory event. The normative model results suggest that individual pilot behaviour can be traced and anticipated by a cognitive model. By comparing individual pilots' actions to the normative model behaviour, deviations could be detected and inferences about SA could be made without intruding the task. Twenty-eight percent of epistemic uncertainty, with lacking and incorrect responses evenly distributed, indicate that additional diagnostic information is required for meaningful analysis and support in cases of deviating behaviour.

A top-down modelling of human cognition in a task can be complemented by bottom-up integration of (neuro-) behavioral data (for example to account for behavioral moderators), and the process can also provide contextual information required for situation-dependent interpretation of EEG data. The different types of uncertainties inherent to model tracing and pBCI determined the model's systematic design: pBCI data could only be used to reduce the fraction of the normative model's unexplained behaviour to deal with aleatory uncertainty.

For a true neuroadaptive solution, a subject-independent classifier would be required. This requires the need for additional behavioral measures (neurophysiological activity, speech, or gaze) to provide individual assistance. Pilots can anticipate complex system behaviour but reports of automation surprises and OOL situations emphasize the importance of a shared understanding of situations by pilot and cockpit automation.

REFERENCES

1. Thatcher, S. J. The use of artificial intelligence in the learning of flight crew situation awareness in an undergraduate aviation programme. World Transactions on Engineering and Technology Education 2014 WIETE, Vol.12, No.4, pp. 1–5, 2014.
2. Yang, Q., Abi-Zeid, I., and Lamontagne, L. An Agent System for Intelligent Situation Assessment; In the International Conference on Artificial Intelligence: Methodology, Systems, and Applications, AIMSA 1998, pp.466–474, www.researchgate. net/publication/225331273; accessed March 2023.
3. Gonsalves, P. G., Rinkus, G. J., Das, S. K., and Ton, N. T. A Hybrid Artificial Intelligence Architecture for Battlefield Information Fusion. https://citeseerx.ist.psu. edu/ document?repid=rep1&type=pdf&doi=61b08bf07d0e06910d0a16f3f9918554ac 0dcfe5; accessed Jan 2023.
4. Klaproth, O. W., Vernaleken, C., Krol, L. R., Halbruegge, M., Zander, T. O., and Russwinkel, N. Tracing Pilots' Situation Assessment by Neuroadaptive Cognitive Modelling. In Frontiers in Neuroscience, Vol. 14, no. 795, pp. 1–2, August 2020 www. frontiersin.org. Accessed October 2022.

Appendix A: Aviation Safety and Security

Usually the words 'safety' and 'security' signify associations of freedom from harm and threats. Despite being treated as synonymous, the two concepts also have different meanings: i) frequently, the concept of safety is utilized to distinguish between the management of hazards from non-malicious intent, and ii) security as the management of threats received from rational humans with a malicious intent, such as sabotage, hacking, or terrorism [1]. Accidents are neither arbitrary nor random but rather a result of insufficient resources, organization, and planning. Human intent sometimes plays a role in causing accidents, and organizations should design robust measures that consider the fact that workers sometimes intentionally diverge from standard procedures. Neither intentionality nor crime is sufficient to distinguish safety from security. The difference then should be the malicious intent of the actor who plans to cause harm. Security is often jeopardized by external threats that are most often beyond the capability of organizations to fully know and handle. Such risks are not linked as directly to the economic profit and production system as safety risks. This means that, even though a company may have an optimal security culture, it can still be the target of a terrorist attack and experience major damage.

A.1 SAFETY AND SECURITY IN AVIATION

Traditionally, the two aspects safety and security are kept separate in aviation industry. While the safety treats risks associated with aviation activities, the security safeguards civil aviation against unlawful interference. An appropriate application of established quantitative and qualitative assessment techniques is crucial to both regimes. The empirical example and data stem from safety risk assessments in HEMS (Helicopter Emergency Medical Service) flight operations. These flight operations use advanced instrument flight procedures in obstacle-rich situations under low visibility conditions and are therefore a safety concern. One analyses security, whenever HEMS flights are operated in adverse weather conditions, having as a sole navigation source signals from a GPS. Under these circumstances, a traditional safety risk assessment considers only factors of human performance under technical failure conditions. A security analysis should treat all forms of jamming, meaconing, and spoofing of the satellite signals and the adverse impact on the performance of the receiver to calculate a valid position.

Over the last few years based on certain experience with light helicopter operations for disaster relief, search and rescue, and HEMS, the necessity of an ever-widening operational scenario with all-weather capability has become apparent [1]. The use of Global Navigation Satellite Systems (GNSS) as a primary navigation source under low visibility conditions has been obvious.

The concerned signals containing navigational data, allowing the receiver to estimate position, are transmitted over an openly accessible RF channel. Also, such a channel is prone to noise and interference stemming from different radio sources. If such transmissions are intentional, then one can classify it as an unlawful interference. So, while the former aspects are safety-related, the latter is a security-related issue. In the literature security is defined as 'Safeguarding civil aviation against acts of unlawful interference,' and safety is 'The state in which risks associated with aviation activities, related to, or in direct support of the operation of aircraft, are reduced and controlled to an acceptable level.' The security is handled by entities like law enforcement agencies and airports, the safety is said to depend on personnel, procedures, and equipment, which is foremost for the field of air operators and air navigation service providers. The Systems Engineering (SE) philosophy is quite in line with that 'hazards lead to safety incidents in the same way that vulnerabilities lead to security incidents.'

A.2   USE OF THE SATELLITE NAVIGATIONAL SIGNALS

An RF channel used for communications in aviation operations, the practical example chosen is at the same time relevant and valid, since, satellite navigation signals are extensively used for all sorts of critical infrastructure and hazardous operations. Such a channel can be characterized by simple metrics, the BandWidth (BW) and the Signal-to-Noise Ratio (SNR). For this example, we would extend this ratio to also include any interfering signal power. The metric would then be signal-to-(noise + interference, SNIR). We consider a situation where only machines or one operator are present $N = \{0, 1\}$. The system BW is largely given by the base-band signal, and any interference being natural or human-caused is, to the first order, only relevant within this channel BW, because the receiver (RX) will band-pass all signals and suppress the others.

The only free variables for the interferer are the duration and the radiated power. Jamming is the emission of RF signals of sufficient power and with such characteristics to prevent the receivers from working properly. Meaconing is the reception, delay, and rebroadcast of a signal with a larger power than it was received at; and at the receiving antenna, wanted and unwanted signals are added to confuse the system. Ground–and space-based augmentation radio links could also be prone to meaconing, especially if the correct differential signal is suppressed with a stronger one containing false corrections. In the case of spoofing, a receiver is caused to lock onto legitimate-appearing false signals; here any attack will inject misleading information and thereby eventually even control the flight.

An air navigation service provider, supporting hazardous flight operations, must inform the user of three probabilities: i) Reliability: using the service and not losing it, ii) Availability: requesting the service and getting it, and iii) Integrity: correctness of the information supplied.

The constant presence of interference from natural sources is an important aspect; in the absence of human-caused interference, the receiver must cope with noise from intra–or extra-system sources. Another aspect indicated by the SNIR is the diminishing of the signal power due to an increase in radio path attenuation. These two factors are relevant when discussing game-theoretic approaches, namely in the absence of an attacker $N = \{0, 1\}$.

A.3   USE OF A GAME-THEORETIC APPROACH

In this analytical approach the situations considered are games with different parties having common/different interests. The situations include true games as well as real-world problems in politics, economics, or warfare; players may strategize, decide, and act. A game consists of players (individuals/organizations), strategies (a plan, objectives, decisions, and actions), situations, and a gain from participating (utility function). A theory of mathematical models is applied to formalize interdependent players with their decisions and actions under a condition of conflict or cooperation.

What are the provisions of such an approach to safety and security and what are the elements necessary to model the chosen real-life situation?' The elements are discrete and can, therefore, be described in a set-theoretic way. If an attacker intends to maximize impact while minimizing the probability of being detected, then the radiated power is bounded; and accessible to set theory. So, with the radiated power $P = \{0, Pmax\}$; the two values are then equivalent to abstaining from or executing an attack.

A.3.1   THE PLAYERS

The whole setup consists of three players with different coalition aspects. Even though a coalition of interest exists between the user and the service provider, it may not be strong enough to have the service provider actively taking part in the game. The reason lies in important investments like upgrading or replacing space-based assets. Such actions would have a negative impact on a service provider's utility, which is cost versus the number of users. Thus, the service provider is excluded.

A.3.2   AVAILABLE STRATEGIES

The possible strategies form finite sets (SA and SU): the setup of the game has one Attacker (A) and one victim, the GNS User (U) in a flight under low visibility conditions (LVC, IMC), under Instrument Flight Rules (IFR) with no redundancy in navigation. The attacker intends to deny the use of only this system. This situation asks for an offensive strategy on the side of the attacker and a defensive one on the side of the user. The attacker has three distinctive but feasible strategies, and they constitute a finite set: SA = {Jamming, Meaconing, Spoofing}. The location of the jammer could be on a fixed, ground-mobile, or airborne platform (here it is limited to the fixed option). An airborne jammer would offer a number of attacking advantages, but operating costs would be considerable, to be effective. Moreover, detecting and locating the attacker would be simple. The set of strategies of the attacked U (the user), on the contrary, is a purely defensive set: SU = {spectrum/signal monitoring, reducing the coupling between receiving antenna and attacker's transmission, minimizing the exposure time}.

A.3.3 THE SITUATIONS

The situations are the Phase of Flight (FP) and its need for a precise aircraft position. The user counts on the three probabilities indicated by the service provider; and these are estimated from empirical failure rates or reliability calculations. Together with corresponding exposure times, it results in failure probabilities. A FP is ended and another started as decided from the flight deck (decision instance, say player A). Possible scenarios are determined and finite. The set is consequently reduced to FP = {Take-off, Departure, Enroute, Approach, Landing}.

Various parameters and the results of the present case study can be found in Tables 4.3 to 4.8 of reference [1].

The exposure time changes by an order of a magnitude along the flight trajectory. The distance and the radio path attenuation for a potential interfering source toward the victim's receiving antenna also change. There is a relation between exposure time and the height of the victim above the antenna of a potential interferer. If the signal is in use, then the loss of the signal leads to a hazardous situation and the risk of an accident. If the signal is to be acquired, yet not available, then the mission will be aborted and economic loss results. The attacker 'A' may of course choose the interfering power at his/her discretion; radiating too much power increases the Probability of Intercept (POI). Increasing the possibility of being detected by some monitoring processes.

If the Quality of Service (QoS) is repeatedly degraded, and if detected, the victim will initiate an evasive action rendering futile the attempted attack. Detection could lead to being located by an authority in charge, so the attacker has to make a trade-off. The maximum radiated power of the interferer is bounded for tactical reasons and for technological ones.

A.3.4 THE OUTCOMES OF THE GAME

The outcomes should illustrate potential gains in the areas of cost, risk, and utility. The risk R for the attacker may be determined as: $R = (I + K) \cdot POI$, where I is the investment for the equipment, K is the knowledge, POI is the detection of a monitoring instance within the interfered region. In this example, the gain of attacker A is the loss of the attacked U. The gain matrix could suggest a strategic advantage to attack. The likelihood of being detected is nearly two orders of a magnitude smaller for meaconing and spoofing compared to jamming due to the difference in signal formats.

A.3.5   GAME-THEORETIC CLASSIFICATION

Games are classified according to the different sets discussed in the foregoing. The most obvious is the number of players; a game can have one, two, or more players. The players might be a group of persons with common interests being part of some organization.

An empty and the unit set of players could be included to propose a possible unified approach in the game-theory. The empty set (no players) would be a purely machine-to-machine interaction, unless AI is actively involved. The unit set (1 player) is also called a one-person game. If there are no rivals, the player only needs to list available strategies to choose an optimum outcome. When probabilities are involved, the game may turn out to be more complicated. Another aspect of the classification is whether the objectives of the players coincide or conflict. The constant-sum games show an entirely conflicting situation (pure competition), with no communication between the adversaries. Whether a game is called finite depends on finite sets specified in the previous section. The game cannot have an indefinite duration and there exists a window to act. A finite non-cooperative game between two players is called a bi-matrix game. It is specified by two matrices $A = \|a_{ij}\|$ and $U = \|u_{ij}\|$ of the same dimension of $m \times n$; and these represent the payoff matrices (gain matrices) of the players. The strategy of player 'A' is the selection of a row, that of player 'U' the selection of a column. Let player 'A' choose i $(1 < i < m)$, while player 'U' chooses j $(1 < j < n)$. Then their respective payoffs or gains will be a_{ij} and u_{ij}. If $a_{ij} + u_{ij} = 0$ for all i, j, then the bi-matrix becomes a matrix game. The two candidates reflecting this example are either a bi-matrix or a matrix game; and the latter matched the situation.

REFERENCE

1. Bieder, C., and Pettersen Gould, K. (Editors). *The Coupling of Safety and Security Exploring Interrelations in Theory and Practice.* Springer Briefs in Applied Sciences and Technology-Safety Management. Springer Open. Gewerbestrasse 11, 6330 Cham, Switzerland, August 2020.

Appendix B: Aviation Sustainability

B.1 AVIATION SUSTAINABILITY

The aviation industrial-network needs operational policies and managerial directives to improve efficiency, new technologies that aim at incrementing existing capacity, and infrastructure investment in the form of new airports to cope with air traffic trends [1]. Effective Air Traffic Management (ATM) is needed to avoid airspace congestion, especially in Terminal Maneuvering Areas (TMA) around busy airports; using remaining underutilized infrastructure would ease pressure off the most congested airports, but the geographical location of served markets, business models in aviation, interests and regulations deem this option to be unsuitable. These aspects need an approach that ensures sustainability of aviation operations to cope with demand growth. Sustainability is simplified to just focusing on the evaluation of environmental costs, but it has multiple dimensions as briefly discussed next.

B.1.1 SUSTAINABLE GROWTH

It is important to determine current capacity, its limiting factors, and match it to forecast demand. A mismatch between demand and supply may lead to congestion issues. Better management of existing capacity can extend assets' life with limited investment. Capacity studies may aid at directing infrastructure investments in the most efficient way.

B.1.2 ENVIRONMENTAL SUSTAINABILITY

Aviation operations have a significant impact in terms of green-house gas emissions and noise. Technology advances, and optimisation of current operations play a big role in reducing emissions: reduced fuel consumption due to uninterrupted taxis, less gate blockages, point-to-point optimized trajectories, and reduced TMA holding stacks.

B.1.3 SOCIO-POLITICAL SUSTAINABILITY

Aviation and airports are main drivers of local and regional economies; this comes at a cost: residents need to deal with high levels of noise, pollution, and traffic congestion;

thus local authorities need to balance economic growth with regional developments, knowing that expansion of aviation activities has a major impact on urban planning, ground transportation and quality of living. Carefully analyzing expansion needs by means of simulation may help determine the most efficient way of managing infrastructure; e.g., London multi-airport system.

B.1.4 OPERATIONAL SUSTAINABILITY

The nature of aviation implies the existence of inherent variability and uncertainty, mainly due to operational practices, congestion, weather conditions, and legacy rights: i) the proposed schedules and plans should be developed to allow revenues in a market where margins are generally quite low; and ii) these plans should also be reliable, and able to absorb most disturbances without causing a knock-on effect.

To limit the high costs, disruption management policies should focus on efficiently using existing and available resources rather than introducing new ones (e.g., ferrying an empty aircraft), or outsourcing services only when strictly necessary (e.g., rebooking passengers with a different airline).

B.2   AIRSPACE CAPACITY

Airspace capacity is signified as the number of aircraft that can fit into Air Traffic Control (ATC) sectors in a specific time frame, given separation and safety standards. When traffic exceeds the arrival/departure capacity, or that of the different air sectors the flight needs to traverse, congestion-caused delays start to arise throughout the network.

Airport capacity may be broadly defined as the volume of operations an airport can handle in each time frame. If an imbalance is predicted between traffic demand and available capacity at airports or the airspace, the ATM authorities may issue a regulation to maximise the flow in these sectors. When such delays are imposed on departing flights, they are green delays, due to savings on fuel consumption, gas emissions, and noise reduction when compared to airborne delays. However, as most aircraft are used for consecutive flights, these delays may still have an impact on the airline's network, their operations, and crew availability.

B.3   RUNWAY/TAXIWAY CAPACITY

Defining the capacity of an airport is a key element for carrying out daily operations. It is used for tactical decisions such as the number of slots offered at the airport (available time periods for landing/take-off operations) and controlling daily operations.

B.3.1 DECLARED CAPACITY

This is the stated limiting capacity of the airport in aircraft movements per hour. It controls the number of slots available for allocation per unit of time and these translate into additional costs due to delays, fuel consumption, and increased noise and emissions. The close interdependency of slot scheduling and declared capacity levels turns estimation of airport capacity into a key procedure to ensure sustainability of operations for all the involved stakeholders

B.3.2   SUSTAINED CAPACITY

This is the maximum runway throughput that can be achieved over a sustained period of time when aircraft operate under instrument flight rules (IFR), under a specific traffic mix, in good weather conditions, with good air traffic and runway management. Acceptable delays are those airlines can accept, due to their compatibility with their schedules and aircraft utilization policies. The tolerance for longer delays may increase the airport capacity, but at the cost of increasing congestion and making it less attractive for airlines.

B.3.3   UNCONSTRAINED CAPACITY

This is the maximum runway throughput which can be achieved under ideal conditions, considering only safety requirements. An airport's runway capacity is normally expressed as the hourly rate of aircraft operations which may be reasonably accommodated by the runway system. This capacity is mainly dependent on the runway occupancy times and separation standards applied to successive aircraft in the traffic mix. Other elements affecting runway capacity are: i) availability of exit taxiways, ii) aircraft types operating at the airport, iii) sequencing of aircraft, iv) ATC policies, v) weather conditions, vi) runway configuration and spacing between parallel runways, and vii) mode of operation (segregated or mixed).

Runway capacity may be determined by means of analytical and simulation models. Analytical models are over-simplified mathematical representations of airport and airspace characteristics, and are mainly used for policy analysis, strategy development and cost-benefit evaluation. The simulation models permit the obtaining of more realistic estimates of capacity and have been widely used to study different airports and their corresponding expansion projects. Discrete-event simulation models replicate more accurately traffic flows and aircraft movements within the airport. This allows representing actual constraints, uncertainties, and interactions. Techno-technical and operational innovations (time-based approach) permit the increase of runway capacity in the medium-term, while infrastructure investment (building new additional runways) and operational changes (multi-airport systems) represent a long-term approach to capacity increase.

B.4   AIRCRAFT GROUND OPERATIONS

Ground operations at the airport are aimed at providing efficient services that facilitate aircraft turnarounds. Here, the ground handling agents try to maintain the integrity of their ground staff and equipment rosters, even with the disruptions from flight operations, while airlines are busy maintaining the on-time departure and arrival performance of follow-up flights for the rest of the day. Technology and efficient process design provide a means to increase infrastructure capacity.

B.5   FLIGHT OPERATIONS

The increased time aircraft spend at the gate due to airport ground congestion consumes more energy than expected. This congestion also causes aircraft to spend more time taxiing in and out between runway ends and airport terminal gates, burning more fuel than normal flight operations and aggravating the environmental impact.

With advances in robotic technology and scheduling methodologies, one can use conflict-resolution algorithms which are designed to schedule autonomous taxi-bots for towing aircraft without burning fuel by running aircraft engines during the taxi phase of flight operations. Past efforts in flight operations on the ground focused more on the taxi phase of operations because of delays due to taxiway congestion, taxiing conflicts and long take-off queues at runway ends. Various optimisation models were developed to improve taxi operations and hence reduce the time spent running engines for taxiing.

B.6   STAND AND GATE ALLOCATION

Gate blockage occurs when an inbound aircraft arrives at a gate, but the gate is still occupied by an outbound aircraft. By considering inherent delays in the system, the expected impact of gate blockage could be reduced and this contributes to fewer and shorter connection delays to passengers, crew, and less aircraft idle time on the taxiway (reducing fuel consumption).

Allocation of other ground service equipment and staff is a less considered aspect of resource allocation.

B.7   TERMINAL OPERATIONS

Two value chains take place in any airport, whose related activities mostly unfold within the physical boundaries of airport terminals: i) the passenger, and ii) baggage/cargo value chains. Operations like passenger check-in, security check, passport control and boarding highly contribute to the so-called passenger experience. Each airline targets this differently. Also, inbound and outbound baggage operations contribute to the formation and realization of the intended passenger experience. Technologies have been developed in the last few decades to help improve the way departing passengers make their way to the aircraft: i) self-service kiosks, ii) facilities for automated check-in, iii) common use passenger processing systems, iv) biometrics, v) passenger tracking, vi) video surveillance, vii) risk-based security, viii) access control, and ix) queue management.

B.8   AIRLINE OPERATIONS

Robust and dynamic OR methodologies have gained popularity among companies and researchers for scheduling airline operations. The main benefit lies in having a responsive approach towards possible perturbations, as the model itself contemplates these disruptions and constructs a solution that makes it possible to absorb them. There are two main areas of robust and dynamic applications in the airline industry.

These are aircraft and crew scheduling. In most studies in the literature, optimisation and simulation techniques are used sequentially: first, the optimisation procedure is used to find an optimal solution and the result is later tested by using simulation.

Crew scheduling is a process that presents serious challenges. The aim of airlines is to distribute the workload evenly between crew members to ensure equity between workers. A higher number of crews with more balanced workloads may also increase planning robustness, as more resources and additional flexibility are introduced in the system to respond to disrupted scenarios. An approach to model robustness in crew scheduling is by maximizing the number of move-up crews, which are the crews that can be potentially swapped at a specific airport to provide for more flexibility in response to disruptions.

B.9   DISRUPTION MANAGEMENT

Airline operation is the most complex transportation system and is commonly introduced as a network. This network is composed of/by the entities: i) Airports are referred as system nodes, which are linked between them using arcs considered to be flights or legs. These airports can be inter-connected either by point-to-point (commonly seen in low-cost airlines; ii) Aircraft are the main resource of the system, which provide the transportation method between nodes; iii) Crew is assigned to a specific flight and aircraft family. The crew scheduling process is also a complex problem in the system as it must tackle a vast number of constraints, such as those imposed by safety regulations or restrictive union agreements; and iv) Passengers define the demand between nodes. In case of disruption, passengers have to be re-allocated to new flights minimizing the impact on their journey. Due to its complexity, a disruption in one of the system's processes might have a massive impact on the overall network performance. A disruption is a perturbation which interrupts a process, activity or event. A disruption in one of the network's flights will implicate a cascading effect of delays and cancellations in future flights. This is a common case in hub-and-spoke configurations, as flights are highly interconnected at the hub airport(s). Hence, disruption management techniques need to be applied.

Two approaches are: i) creating a more robust schedule for flights, aircraft and crews, which can absorb more perturbations or even work with different scenarios; and ii) once the disruption has occurred, the goal is minimizing the time required to get back to normal operations, which in turn reduces the total of the disruption.

B.10   THE AIRCRAFT RECOVERY PROBLEM (ARP)

The aim is to reduce the disruption from the aircraft perspective, by swapping, delaying, or cancelling flights assigned to the aircraft: i) The Crew Recovery Problem (CRP) re-arranges the crews of each flight after a perturbation occurs, a typical issue is that the crews are not being able to fly as scheduled due to labour-related restrictions; and ii) The Passenger Recovery Problem (PRP) looks at minimizing the cost of reassigning all affected passengers until they reach their destination, and is normally formulated in combination with the ARP. Due to its complexity, recovery of the entire system is generally solved hierarchically, with decisions made for one resource defining constraints for subsequent recovery problems.

B.10.1 AIRCRAFT RECOVERY

The ARP is the most studied of the three sub-problems, because its constraints are less complex than those to be considered in the CRP. The procedures are: i) minimise passenger delay by retiming and swapping aircrafts; use a network flow model and branch-and-bound to solve the problem; ii) a more complex model allows swapping aircraft from different fleets by using a local search-based heuristic; and iii) use a model to solve the multi-fleet ARP with the temporary closure of a specific airport.

B.10.1 CREW RECOVERY

The CRP aims at reassigning as quickly as possible all the crew personnel affected by any perturbation. It is regarded as the most complex recovery problem, as there are many constraints attached to it (flight hours, resting periods). If the problem is tackled individually, the main assumption is that it is solved after knowing the aircraft schedule. Crew scheduling is split into two sub-problems: i) the crew pairing (combination of tasks within a working period, which may extend over several days) aims at optimizing the number of crews for a given flight schedule; and ii) the crew rostering assigns pairings to specific crew members.

B.10.3 INTEGRATION OF PASSENGER RECOVERY

Passenger recovery seems to be the least complex operation in a disrupted scenario, due to available options to reallocate passengers in different flights, or even rebook them with a different airline; yet, it may become a challenging process due to the limitation of seats if airlines do not agree to cooperate.

Some units utilize an approach to solve a combination of fleet assignment, aircraft routing, and passenger reallocation problems by adopting heuristic alternates between construction, repair, and improvement phases.

REFERENCE

1. Guimarans, D., Arias, P., Tomasella, M., and Wu, A review of sustainability in aviation: a multi-dimensional perspective. Sustainable Transportation and Smart Logistics Decision-Making Models and Solutions, 2019, pp. 91–121, 2019, Available online 16 November 2018, Version of Record 16 November 2018. Accessed December 2022.

Appendix C: Situation Assessment Case Study-1

C.1 HUMAN SITUATION ASSESSMENT (SA) AND A CASE STUDY OF AIR COMBAT

Premise: The present study examined if SA by experienced military pilots could be modelled by using BNs [1]: i) are the SA causes supported by the knowledge structures?, ii) how does knowledge help the information search?, and iii) how is the new information integrated with the available knowledge/information to revise the beliefs?

This study examines the most fundamental of inferences made by military personnel: the identification (ID) of entities as either friendly, neutral, or hostile.

C.2 METHODS

C.2.1 DOMAIN ELICITATION FROM SUBJECT-MATTER EXPERTS

Two experienced F/A-18 pilots (of the Royal Australian Air Force, RAAF) participated in structured interviews to elicit the variables related to the task of identifying airborne entities, context variables, and evidences available from cockpit-systems. The feasible states of each variable that were meaningful to the pilots in the context of the task and the presence of causal relationships between these variables were elicited. The pilots would estimate the probability of observing each state of any variable/s that were directly causal to it. The declarative model was defined by the elicited structure and conditional probabilities. Preliminary validation of the declarative model was conducted in many informal scenario-walk-throughs with the two pilots from whom the model was elicited and the other experienced F/A-18 pilot. These experiments were conducted by setting node states of hypothetical scenarios and evaluating the model's inference of ID for sensibility. Minor adjustments were made to the parameters (conditional probabilities) of the model so that inferences of ID by the model were as expected.

C.2.2 SIMULATION EXPERIMENT

It was investigated to see if the skilled behaviour of the pilots was consistent with the declarative model elicited during the interviews. Twenty scenarios were generated

393

by random sampling from the declarative model. These scenarios were expected to approximate a sample of real-world circumstances and also 19 additional scenarios were generated for selection of node states other than ID; one of which was selected to be highly ambiguous between hostile and neutral ID. This information was presented in the form of a simulated cockpit display. The pilots did not know the structure, conditional probabilities, or inferences of the model. Their task was to identify unclassified airborne entities from the available information in a pre-flight brief and from evidence from their cockpit.

The pilots were instructed to search each of seven available sources in order of perceived utility for inferring ID; they selected a source of information, and then indicated their revised belief about ID by moving a mouse cursor within a triangle in the top centre of the display. Their degree of belief in a particular state of ID (friendly, hostile, or neutral; civil or military) was indicated by positioning the cursor in relative proximity to the vertices of the triangle. This sequential search and response allowed the development of pilots' beliefs about ID to be tracked. There were 2,960 judgments of target identity, where each judgment required pilots to state the degrees to which they believed the target to be friendly, hostile, and neutral.

C.2.3 Model Selection

The goodness of fit of the declarative model to the responses of the pilot was assessed by calculating the Kullback–Leibler (KL) divergence criterion, that varies from zero for perfect agreement to infinity. The conditional probabilities were estimated from the pilots' responses using the expectation maximization method of estimation. Each model was trained on 80% of the data and tested on the remaining 20%.

C.3 RESULTS

C.3.1 The Declarative Model

The context variables studied were: i) commercial corridor nearby, ii) lodged flight plan, iii) stage in war, and iv) current threat level. These have a causal influence on the type of aircraft likely to be flying. The actual ID of the target has a bearing on the evidence that would be obtained from: i) cockpit systems (identification friend or foe, IFF; radar warning receiver, RWR; noncooperative target recognition, NCTR), and ii) the behaviour of the entity (radio challenges, group posture, group origin). The utility of each BN-node for inferring ID is given by its mutual information (MI) with ID; which is the expected reduction in the entropy of ID resulting from evidence for that node and is also dependent on the state of evidence for other nodes. The declarative model generated evidence in 20 of the scenarios for the simulation experiment.

C.3.2 Pilot Responses in Simulation

At step 0 (after the contextual information only), the pilot did not revise his belief from the uniform prior (equal probabilities of friendly, hostile, and neutral). As evidence became available during his search, the pilot revised his belief to be more certain of neutral. For the 53% trials, pilot/s did not revise their belief from the uniform prior probabilities in response to context. A strong trend was observed: i) first for group posture, ii) second for IFF, iii) third for group origin, iv) the last for NCTR. The pilot/s' beliefs were revised on 76% of occasions, when data were pooled across pilots, scenarios, and search steps.

A few major inferences are: i) Nine pilots reached certainty in their beliefs during the course of some (on average 2.4) scenarios and did not revise their beliefs further; ii) In most searches, ID was classified friendly if IFF was Mode 4; according to the declarative model, there is a probability of 0.99 of friendly ID if IFF is Mode 4 in the absence of other information; iii) A non-compensatory search was also occasionally observed for hostile identifications; ID was classified as hostile if IFF was unresponsive, group origin was hostile airspace, and group posture was aggressive; according to the declarative model, these states result in a probability of 0.96 of hostile ID in the absence of other information; iv) Pilot beliefs were highly consistent for scenarios 15 and 20, but differed greatly for others; v) Variation in pilot/s' belief was mainly along the friendly, neutral, or hostile-neutral axis; vi) Of particular interest for understanding friendly fire incidents, there were two scenarios (36 and 38) where there was substantial variation in pilot response across the friendly hostile axis; and vii) For each scenario, the context and evidence were consistent with a high probability of friendly, as indicated by the declarative model.

C.3.3   Modelling SA

It was found that the revisions of the belief by pilot/s do not necessarily conform to Bayes' rule. Modelling of pilot inference with a BN has certain merits: i) the 2,960 observed judgments of ID (each with 2 DOF) can be reduced to a small number of model parameters; ii) the ability of pilots to discriminate between their cognitive categories of friendly, hostile, and neutral entities may be determined from the model; and iii) information search, pilot beliefs, and the revision of the beliefs may be evaluated against those of the model.

One can use the behavioural model to investigate a more general aspect: the pilot/s' discrimination of their cognitive categories of friendly, hostile, and neutral across the range of possible scenarios. In an experiment, 100,000 friendly, hostile, and neutral entities in the behavioural model to generate evidence (IFF, group origin, and group posture) were simulated. The recovery of ID by the same model was examined: the majority (56.9% of friendly, 50.8% of neutral, and 70.5% of hostile cases) of inferred IDs were correct, but, there were a substantial number of incorrect inferences.

C.3.4   Revision of Beliefs

Bayes' rule specifies how beliefs should be revised in the light of evidence. This rule is expressed as Revised odds = prior odds × LR of evidence, here, LR is the likelihood ratio, the ratio of probabilities of observing the evidence under each hypothesis. In the present study the pilots demonstrated a large range of beliefs and large revisions of those beliefs. The behavioural model fits the beliefs better than the revisions of beliefs; and this is consistent with maximizing the likelihood of the model, given the data (beliefs) during the learning of the model conditional probabilities.

C.4   DISCUSSION

Finally, the following observations and inferences have been made in this case study of Air Combat [1]:

i)   The declarative models were moderately successful in predicting the behaviour of subject-pilots during a low-fidelity simulation; wherein their behavioural data were needed to develop more robust models of pilot behaviour in simulation. The predictive (-accuracy) ability of the declarative model was improved when conditional probabilities were determined from pilot performance rather than from elicitation in interview.

ii)   The pilots were kept ignorant of the structure, conditional probabilities, and inferences of the declarative model.

iii)   The behavioural model differed greatly in structure from the declarative model, signifying that sampling scenarios from the declarative model did not largely constrain pilot inferences in the experiment.

iv)   A pilot's behaviour was best predicted by a much simpler model in the situation where the ID was inferred from only three attributes: IFF, group posture, and group origin. This suggested that the variables that were identified during elicitation to be important in the inference of ID might be different to that which influenced skilled behaviour.

v)   The pilots revised their beliefs when they were presented with evidences from other sources, however, their revision was not consistent.

vi)   In an interview-session, the pilots would take time to consider all the relevant variables. They can use a pen and a paper to reduce working-memory load. However, in an experiment and even in a flight, pilots should keep information related to a task in their working-memory, and this would impose a limit to the number of variables that might be considered.

vii)   The behavioural model included four variables (including ID), and this was found to be consistent with other similar research wherein they used only four variables in the information processing of complex tasks.

viii)The best model of the pilot inference was that of three attributes: IFF, group origin, and group posture. In actual practice, the military personnel perform ID of entities using legally binding decision trees, like rules of engagement (ROE).

ix)   If the sufficient data are available to generate normative models of real-world processes, then, BNs would also prove to be useful in refining ROE, in addition to the modelling of pilot behaviour,

x)   The causal models were found to be successful in predicting pilot inference of ID but it was not clear that their mental models for this task were causal.

xi)   It cannot be said that the inference about ID was based on causal reasoning.

xii) It is not asserted that the pilots were Bayesian reasoners, however, pilot beliefs were well described by the Bayesian behavioural model.

xiii) In the present experiment, the pilots searched information sources in order of decreasing utility and the search by pilots resulted in a near-optimal rate of reduction in the uncertainty of ID.

xiv) The BNs may provide aids to human inference where good real-world data are available.

The Bayesian models of expert behaviour would prove to be useful in training for good inference. It would be feasible to represent the domain knowledge of experts in a BN and to train that BN on their behavioural inferences; this trained model could be used to train less-experienced people.

xv) The present experiment establishes that the Bayesian networks have the potential to provide a unified and coherent framework for the study of expert knowledge, information search, and inference in complex environments. It could lend itself to the study of prediction and decision making in complex environments, a possible futuristic research study.

REFERENCE

1. McAnally, K., Davey, C., White, D., Stimson, M., Mascaro, S., and Korb, K. Inference in the Wild: A Framework for Human Situation Assessment and a Case Study of Air Combat. Cognitive Science, A multidisciplinary journal, Vol. 42, pp. 2181–2204, Cognitive Science Society, Inc. ISSN: 1551-6709; online.

Appendix D: Situation Assessment Case Study-2

D.1 TEAM SITUATION ASSESSMENT AND INFORMATION DISTRIBUTION IN COMMAND AND CONTROL–C2 UNIT

Premise: This study describes the cooperative work of constructing team situation awareness within two teams of a military command and control (C2) unit: how the distributed cognitive and cooperative work of decision-making of the two teams is structured [1]. One team chose concurrent information transfer, and the other team serial information transfer. The interaction patterns that emerge in the respective teams are discussed.

D.2 INTRODUCTION

The C2 unit is a military staff unit at battalion level. Its tasks are to [1]: i) ensure that its company units can control the enemy forces; ii) plan and transmit orders to its subordinates and artillery units; iii) construct an overall picture of the situation at the front, to be able to direct and coordinate action between troops and companies; iv) forecast what the enemy will do next and how to best utilize its own forces both now and in the near future; v) assess the emerging situation; vi) produce an appropriate SAW of the front, and ensure that its own forces may be able to hinder unwanted developments; vii) gather information from several units in order to understand and predict the situation; and finally viii) produce SAW of the whole battle front which includes both their own forces and the enemy forces.

The team is considered to be the primary cognitive information-processing unit. It was found that the hierarchical condition managed to control the system better, although marginally. In the present case: i) one person is responsible for handling the companies and their information; for coordinating the actions, that must be performed in conjunction with several units; and for keeping track of where the forces are; and ii) another person is assigned to fight enemies and to control the enemy by using the artillery forces which the battalion and the brigade have at hand. This bifurcation of simple tasks calls for distribution and coordination of information at the local level of the team in order to construe appropriate SAW.

D.3   TEAM SITUATION ASSESSMENT

In a team, one member may focus on gathering information, and the other one on analyzing the information. They do not have to communicate about the actual decision, because it is the responsibility of a third person. The teams that work together learn to know each other's needs, knowledge, and tasks. Cognitive empathy means that someone with a shared understanding of how to coordinate does so in an appropriate way.

D.4   TECHNOLOGY AND INFORMATION DISTRIBUTION

The idea is to discuss information distribution and technology assisted communication: i) How are the teams structured in terms of information flow and means of coordination?, and ii) What difference do different information flows imply for the team SA and SAW?

This case study is intended to be hypothesis generating. We look at two organizations that emerge in two military command teams; the organizations emerged spontaneously, during training in a simulator, and originate from a very small change in the technology.

D.5   THE CONTROL ROOM

The battalion-team must coordinate its forces and the brigade artillery to delay and prevent the enemy from invading its territory. Battalion personnel constitute two teams working in shifts. The staff is housed in a small, tracked vehicle identical to the one used in an actual combat situation; 6×2.5 square meters, with a big table in the center where the staff keep all their equipment. The staff consists of four people, two signallers and two officers.

D.5.1   STAFF AND RESPONSIBILITIES

The signallers S1 and S2 each have a small computer. They write and receive messages from hierarchically subordinated units. Each one has a small printer on which they print out the messages and distribute them to the officers within the team: i) Coordinator (C) responsible for coordination and communication with the distributed forces, as well as for accurate updating of the map, and for gathering and analyzing information and then updating the map and distributing relevant information (situation reports, orders) to appropriate units; and ii) Artillery leader (A) to decide how the artillery resources are to be used and which unit should use them, he has to analyse, prioritize, issue orders and inform the units about when and how much artillery they can use, as well as to order the artillery units when and where to fire. He must inform the supervisory battalion major, situated in an another tracked vehicle, about the actions. To decide 'A' uses the information that 'C' has gathered and organized.

D.5.2   ARTEFACTS

'C' and 'A' use a map, and a voice-radio system to keep in contact with outside units. The map is the main tool combined with verbal communication. C is responsible for updating the map with symbols relating to the movement of his own forces and the enemy forces. The map has two purposes: i) it is used as an overview of the battalion and the enemy forces about which they have information, and ii) it is used as a tool for discussing and hypothesizing about what the enemy is up to and what they themselves can do with their forces to hinder them. Thus, the map is a physical representation of the team's situation awareness. The team receives all new information by a voice-radio or by e-mail, and occasionally directly via other members of the battalion. The voice-radio console includes two radiophones to contact distributed units. One phone has loudspeakers and the other phone is a "private phone" and is connected to a tracked vehicle where the supervisory battalion major is located.

Before collecting the data, Swedish Army C2 units had been equipped with a new, complementary, tool for communicating with distributed units, called DAta Reporting Terminal (DART). This is a notebook computer designed for handling electronic mail. Each C2 unit has two DARTs. Each DART has a printer and a memory unit. The DART can be programmed with certain formats to ease and standardize message writing. The printed messages are given to the officers who take care of the written messages and then put them on pins for incoming or outgoing messages, which are time-logged.

D.5.3 PROCEDURES THAT MUST BE ACCOMPLISHED

The CC2 unit receives a message from their subordinates, either via the radio or the e-mail system: i) if the message is received by e-mail it is confirmed by one of the signallers; ii) the message is printed out and given to C; iii) C evaluates the message and transcribes the information onto the map; iv) if the message is of importance for the artillery (for example if a company or troop calls for artillery fire) C gives A the message, else he sticks it on the incoming pin; v) when A has received the message, he reads it and evaluates what the artillery can do; vi) when he has decided on artillery fire, he must send a message to the artillery (either subordinate, supervisor, or both); vii) he tells one of the signallers to prepare for such a message and then dictates it to the signaller, who transmits it to the originator of the request and to the supervisor major; and viii) every now and then A and C have to confer about what the enemy is doing and how they can plan in order to be one step ahead and delay or stop him.

D.6 TECHNOLOGY ARCHITECTURES

The two DART notebook computers can be connected to other units in two different configurations: i) one architecture lets one DART computer be connected to subordinates (hierarchically below); and ii) the other to the supervisor units, where the battalion major is located or to battalion commanded fire units (hierarchically above); iii) the other architecture lets both computers be connected to the subordinates and only one to the supervisors; iv) the point of having the two structures is that if the S1-DART breaks down, then all the messages can still be received by the team, making communication more robust; v) in both structures the signaller (S2) operating S2-DART must transmit information to the subordinate as well as to the supervisor;

vi) the direct communication mode makes all the information from subordinate units reach directly to the S2-DART; and vi) these different communication structures have an effect on how SAW is shared within the team.

D.7 METHOD

In the present study, the main data collection resources are: i) video-audio recordings; ii) computer logging; iii) a full battalion staff training session is video-recorded.

The procedure was: i) The training was divided into two parts, the first lasting from 0830 to 1930 hours, and the second from 0800 to 1100 hours (total fourteen hours); ii) One of the teams used nine hours of the training session; iii) The two teams took over each other's combat situations every 2–3 hours, signifying some differences in workload; iv) The sessions were observed from a monitor connected to the video; v) Four hours of sampled chunks of the video recording were transcribed and also, eight messages were sampled out of 71 for a specific type of message; and vi) 28 (39.4%) of the 71 messages were covered, one team processed 20 of this type of message and the other sent eight messages. It was inferred that the teams used the technology differently. This is detailed in the excerpts (of Tables 2–4, Ref.[1]).

D.8 INTERACTION PATTERNS

The connections of the DARTs in different configurations (serial and parallel) gives rise to different demands on the team and different forms of information distribution. The interaction patterns follow a mild form of Schmidt's distinction between the collective (overt and conscious) and the distributed cooperation, divided and semi-autonomous. Using the serial technology architecture enables more collective cooperation than the parallel architecture.

D.8.1 SERIAL WORK ORGANIZATION-TEAM 1

This team works calmly and methodologically through all incoming information; and seems socially oriented.

The serial organization works as: i) S1 monitors his DART to see when an incoming message is received; ii) When the DART tells him that a new message is received, he prints this message on a small printer; iii) S1 lays it in front of C, who then can deal with it as soon as he has time; iv) S1 is repeatedly directed to tell C when the message is an urgent one, and he also sends an acknowledgement to the originator of the message; v) C then picks up the paper and evaluates it; vi) C transforms the message to symbols and colours on the map, this is accessible to all members and constitutes a second-order time-scale; vii) From the map, the team members can read out possible ways of reacting to the situation; viii) The coordination between C and A, who have different aims with the same information, is mediated both verbally and by paper strip and by map; and ix) A is dependent upon information that C distributes, hence A is constantly monitoring C's work and information, this helps at all times to update A's mental situation awareness in concert with C's.

C is central in respect of information gathering, but A is central for getting the information through. In this serial procedure, A becomes central as he relies on information from C and S1 on his left, and must also tell S1 to re-send the message going back to the originator. A has to monitor outgoing messages to ensure they are forwarded. C will always update the map before A gets this information. In that way this organization is dependent upon C's interpretations.

D.8.2   PARALLEL WORK ORGANIZATION-TEAM 2

This team is working hastily, processing the information as quickly as they can and using the technology as efficiently as possible. This team re-uses the information in the electronic message they received, thus saving time. The information processing procedure started as it did in the other team, but when A had decided, he told S1 to send the message received via the local link to S2, A switches over to the parallel architecture enabling them to send the message directly to the originator, without sending it via S1. For this cycle to continue, the team must switch between the two architectures every time a message is sent.

D.9   ASSESSING THE SITUATION

These two types of work organizations have implications on how the teams coordinate and construct a situation awareness model of the front. The members of Team 1 continuously talk more with one another, while Team 2 work steadily with individually assigned tasks and choose the technology that supports such an organization. This may show differences in the participants' shared representations of the battle situation. The information distribution (by either serial or parallel connected DARTs) may explain the dramatic differences in hypotheses about future development generated by the two teams briefly discussed next.

D.9.1   EXAMPLE 1

C, A and S1 are discussing ideas about the future state of the situation, that is a rare occasion in the other team. They form a hypothesis about what could happen and what the enemy might do next, by using the map. They actively try to construct the development by forming a hypothesis and anchoring these on the map; and try collectively to assess the situation.

D.9.2   EXAMPLE 2

Here, A asks C questions but does not (as A in the other team) give his interpretation about the current situation. The link is developed by C in order to inform A about the status of the map. They have constructed different models of the situation, and must resolve this difference; C communicates the most developed model; 'A' mainly questions C to get a situation report; A does not know exactly what to do; he does not have, mentally, the information from which he could start to assess the situation properly; but does not contribute to the collective situational model himself.

D.10   INFERENCES

The two teams share operative information by three means: artefacts, attentive monitoring, and negotiation. The arrangement and use of the technology makes the means of information sharing weighted differently. Each arrangement poses different valuable trade-offs.

   a) **Serial information processing as Team 1 did**: i) C will always receive any information before A; ii) A will always be dependent upon the fact that C is passing information to him; iii) The tasks and information flow are sequentially constrained; iv) This dependence allows A to continuously monitor C; v) When A receives information, he has already seen the changes in the context and the decision environment has been documented; and vi) attentive monitoring is at the heart of the cooperation.
   b) **Concurrent information processing as Team 2 did**: i) The cooperation is more discontinuous; ii) C is working by updating the map; iii) A is fully occupied in filtering information from his parallel-connected DART in order to find the information that is relevant to him; iv) There is a little time for A to attend and monitor C's work; v) When A runs into a problem that must be resolved by earlier information, A could either try to interpret the map, directly ask C about the problem and start a negotiation phase instead; and vi) they do not share an understanding of the current state because they process the information themselves and consequently may develop individual situation awareness.

The study suggests that the serial Team 1 generates a hypothesis of the future state of the enemy versus their units for every message, and the parallel Team 2 only generate 1 hypothesis of the 20 messages that were analysed. This dramatic difference is the result of how these two teams share their information. A parallel organisation may create more breakdowns between team members, due to different degrees of SAW. It is important for any artillery leader to have an authorized and well-informed decision ground to not fire on its own forces or civilians; hence a sequentially constrained arrangement may be the best solution. In this study it has been shown that one team uses the technology in an innovative way that makes it possible to speed up the decision process.

The two hypotheses emerge: i) Serial processing/Team 1 is better for high reliability when workload is low due to the availability of physical representation of collective and physical situation awareness; and ii) Parallel processing/Team 2 is better when workload is high and quicker decisions are called for. Although, the presented field study generated some hypotheses, the issue of trade-offs remains to be solved, the members: i) must trade off shared situation assessment/SA against decisions (this may lead to slowness); and ii) have to trade-off between the filtered information intake and the nonfiltered information (this may lead to information overload).

REFERENCE

1. Artman, H. Team Situation Assessment and Information Distribution. Ergonomics, www.researchgate.net/publication/12347389, pp. 1–25, September 2000; accessed December 20022.

Index

Printed in the United States
by Baker & Taylor Publisher Services